Educating in the Spirit

Educating in the Spirit

Evidence-Based and Theological Foundations
for High Impact Educational Systems

ERIC J. KYLE

WIPF & STOCK · Eugene, Oregon

EDUCATING IN THE SPIRIT
Evidence-Based and Theological Foundations for High Impact Educational Systems

Copyright © 2019 Eric J. Kyle. All rights reserved. Except for brief quotations in critical publications or reviews, no part of this book may be reproduced in any manner without prior written permission from the publisher. Write: Permissions, Wipf and Stock Publishers, 199 W. 8th Ave., Suite 3, Eugene, OR 97401.

Wipf & Stock
An Imprint of Wipf and Stock Publishers
199 W. 8th Ave., Suite 3
Eugene, OR 97401

www.wipfandstock.com

PAPERBACK ISBN: 978-1-5326-7319-1
HARDCOVER ISBN: 978-1-5326-7320-7
EBOOK ISBN: 978-1-5326-7321-4

Manufactured in the U.S.A.   APRIL 8, 2019

Contents

Acknowledgements | vii

    Introduction | 1
1   Stimulating the Students: The Learner Tier | 11
2   Teaching the Teachers: The Instructor Tier | 89
3   Admonishing the Administrators: The Organizational Tier | 89
4   Discerning Direction: Applying the Guidelines | 276
5   Educating in the Spirit for Global Change | 291

Appendix A: Foundations for Theistic Educational Research | 295

Appendix B: Guidelines' Statistics Table | 310

Appendix C: Broad Overview of the Guidelines | 313

Appendix D: Case Study—Organization Tier | 314

Appendix E: Case Study—Instructor Tier | 331

Appendix F: Case Study—Learner Tier | 349

Bibliography | 361

Acknowledgements

THIS BOOK WOULD NOT be possible without the holy inspired desires of many educators to tirelessly and continually strive for excellence in their classes and school systems. To the many mentors and colleagues that have and continue to empower and challenge me to improve in this sacred vocational craft, I give a humble and heartfelt thank you. In particular, my co-workers at Nebraska Methodist College have provided key intellectual and rigorous insights and models of educational excellence that are inspiring beyond measure. In addition, my colleagues in the Midwest Consortium of Faculty Development Directors have provided much needed guidance and innovative ideas that have helped refine this project. Finally, to my family who have patiently listened to my various ramblings and insights about this work. In particular, to our son Alex who laboriously and methodically reviewed specific chapters and provided editorial feedback as well as philosophical revisions. Throughout this project that lasted over three years, God has (and I pray will continue to do so) guided the development and application of these theoretical formulations for the betterment of our education and formation systems and the communities that they impact.

Introduction

ONE TEACHER, TWO STRUGGLES

Samartha is a novice instructor who is excited for her new position and wants her students to do well. Having transitioned into education from another field, however, she is not quite sure how to change her classes so that learners excel. Turning to the internet, Samartha looks for guidelines, resources, and checklists that help her know where and how to focus her efforts. Being a newer faculty member with numerous classes to prepare and committees to support, Samartha doesn't have extra time to explore the ins-and-outs of educational theory and practice, or how these may or may not apply to her classes.

What she finds, however, is perplexing. Numerous organizations have guidelines and checklists that instructors might use to help them develop their classes: Quality Matters, the Interstate New Teacher Assessment and Support Consortium (INTASC), Teachstone's Classroom Assessment Scoring System (CLASS), and the Association of College and University Educators (ACUE) all reportedly have evidence-based guidelines to help Samartha. At first glance, this seems to be a veritable goldmine of support. As she explores these resources and compile these guidelines together, however, she begins to realize her dilemma. Collectively, these and many other similar checklists of teaching excellence cover a wide range of considerations. These include everything from how to facilitate a class discussion to making sure that the links on her online course site work. Among these hundreds of potential guidelines, Samartha wonders, which ones are likely to have the highest impact on student achievement? Would fixing the links on her course site significantly improve students' knowledge, skills, and/or attitudes (KSAs)? In addition, how would she ever manage to address every one of these guidelines?

What Samartha longs for is a set of comprehensive, yet manageable, guidelines that she can turn to throughout the course of her educational career so that she can continually improve teaching and learning in her classes. As she thinks about and continues to work with her students, she also realizes that they may also benefit from guidance on how they can become better students. Education research studies have shown, for instance, that students who learn metacognitive and study skills significantly outperform their peers who are not taught these skills, making it one of the most impactful teaching and learning strategies that there is.[1] As she steps back and looks at her school as a whole, Samartha also realizes that while she is receiving close mentoring and support from others, there is likely more that her administration could be doing to support and guide all teachers and students. Looking back at the guidelines that she has compiled, Samartha notices that there are very few sets of guidelines for students and school administrators to turn to.

However, Samartha has another struggle. She is deeply religious and strives to approach her life from a theological worldview. As a "theist," or someone who believes in God and strives to live their life with God, Samartha is also searching for resources that can help her to engage her educational calling in these theistic ways. Doing so is especially important for her because she works at a secular school, where religion is not openly discussed, and she teaches classes in a science department which is commonly approached from a secular worldview. While she is able to find numerous resources on religious education and spiritual formation, Samartha has been unable to find many resources that can help her prayerfully think about and engage her secular classes from a theistic perspective. She believes that God is dynamically active and fully present in her classes, but she yearns for more guidance on how to recognize God's movements and invitations in them. In short, Samartha is a "theistic educator" who would like further guidance on how to facilitate high impact classes by discerningly partnering with God's life in her courses, even though she may openly discuss religion or theology in her classes.

THREE EVIDENCE-BASED SOURCES

This book is therefore an attempt to respond to both of these struggles for Samartha and others. For the first struggle, as stated above, there are numerous guidelines that can be compiled. However, the resulting checklists can contain more than one hundred criteria to consider when attempting to significantly impact teaching and learning. So, how might we sift through these numerous criteria and discern which ones are likely to have the greatest impact on student achievement? At least three sets of sources exist that can help us distill these checklists.

First, we can look through individual books and articles that have documented a significant and positive impact on student achievement. As we continue to look through resource after resource, we can begin identifying those educational theories, methods, and strategies that are repeatedly being found to positively impact teaching and learning. This can be tedious and very time-consuming work but doing so provides us with a broader understanding of the many factors that can and do influence education. For this text, as may be seen by the references, we have focused specifically

---

1. Hattie, *Visible Learning*, 188–92.

on healthcare education resources as a case example. Various disciplines in education (from religion to languages, chemistry to engineering) have volumes of literature that have been generated to date. By choosing just one of these fields of study and showing how the literature in this focused field aligns with the guidelines, we are further demonstrating their validity.

Second, we can look to evidence-based course assessment rubrics and guidelines. The Quality Matters rubric, INTASC Standards, CLASS, and ACUE's Effective Practice Framework are all examples of these types of resources. They are "evidenced-based" because they have identified specific educational research studies that have demonstrated the significant impact of each of their criteria. In essence, they have already engaged the first approach: looking to individual resources and identifying criteria that appear in the educational research literature again-and-again. So, by looking for criteria that are common across all of these evidence-based resources, we can identify guidelines that are more likely to be impactful because they have been repeatedly found by others to have a positive impact on student learning and development.

Finally, we look to metanalysis studies of educational research. Metanalyses typically focus on a very specific educational theory or practice and then provide an integrated review of the evidence-based findings for this specific focus. John Hattie's book, *Visible Learning*, is an example of a text that has compiled numerous educational metanalyses.[2] As Hattie's book illustrates, such metanalyses can be useful because they can help identify those practices that have been documented to have a significant impact on a larger scale. Using something known as the "effect size" or "impact factor," Hattie is able to rank different factors that influence teaching and learning. Hattie's ideal effect size, which he refers to as the "hinge point," is 0.40, something which he asserts is large enough of an impact to be valid across classrooms and school systems.

As with all research results, however, we do need to be cautious of large-scale educational findings because they only document the impact for the majority of students. Such large-scale approaches can sometimes overlook the impact that these educational practices do or do not have on subgroups (e.g., based on race, class, gender, etc.) within the larger population. Nevertheless, these metanalyses can help us identify those guidelines and criteria that are likely to have an impact on teaching and learning.

SIX CATEGORIES, TWENTY GUIDELINES

Appendix B provides a list of twenty evidence-based guidelines that were identified using each of these three approaches. As this appendix shows, these specific guidelines were chosen because they meet the search criteria noted above. First, as the numerous citations used throughout this book demonstrate, many of these guidelines

2. Hattie, *Visible Learning*.

were found to be repeating themes across individual educational research studies, and healthcare education more specifically. Second, as the table in Appendix B documents, these guidelines were also found to be repeated across other evidence-based guidelines and assessments, particularly Quality Matters, INTASC, and CLASS. Third, according to Hattie's metaanalyses, most of these guidelines were also found to have a significant impact on many thousands, and in some cases millions, of students. Most of the guidelines, as may be seen in Appendix B, are also near or well above Hattie's recommended 0.40 hinge point for the effect size, or impact factor.

Finally, looking back at Samartha's needs, having twenty high impact guidelines to continually look to across one's teaching career is much more manageable than trying to look to more than a hundred different criteria across several different sets of educational guidelines. We therefore assert, based on these extensive compilations, that this set of twenty guidelines has the highest likelihood of having a significant and positive impact on teaching and learning. In other words, if we as educators first focus our time and energy on these twenty areas, then our students and school systems should be able to measurably document improvements in student achievement. Of course, as they are formulated and presented herein, these guidelines still need to be validated via additional educational research studies.

So, what are these high impact evidence-based guidelines? To begin, it might be helpful to first think about the broad categories that these twenty guidelines fall within. The figure below shows these categories and how one might relate them to each other:

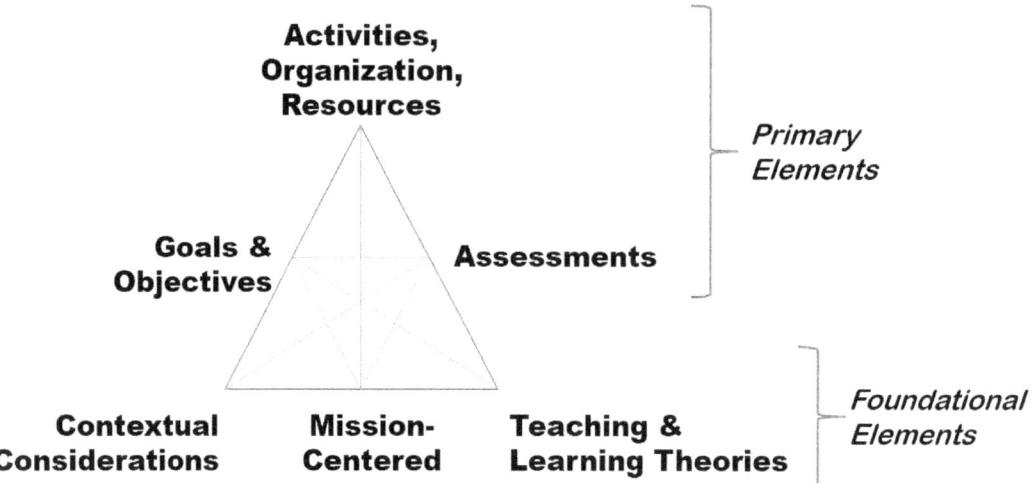

Figure 1—Broad Categories for the Guidelines

When we think about our classes, the first obvious category is the activities that we engage our students in, the resources we share with them, and how we organize the unfolding of our class. This first category, which is the proverbial tip of the educational iceberg, is what actually transpires in our courses. Parents do not usually send their children to school, nor do adults usually attend university, merely for the sake of engaging in randomly selected activities and resources. Turn the cover on any introductory educational textbook, and you will find an equal emphasis being given to the development of clear objectives or outcomes, which is another broad category. As numerous governmental and accreditation bodies around the globe have increasingly asserted, our school systems need to be able to clearly document, via assessments, the extent to which students are achieving these identified learning outcomes. These three broad categories, the activities-organization-resources, objectives, and assessments, comprise the primary elements that are commonly acknowledged to be a necessary part of education.

There are, however, additional foundation elements that are, in many cases, more important for developing high impact educational systems. As may be seen in Appendix B, Guideline #3 in the Teaching and Learning Theories category is the most significant criteria that we can address in terms of impacting student achievement. With an effect size, or impact factor, of 0.69, using course development methods and ensuring close alignment among objectives, activities, and assessments may be considered as essential to education as the other primary elements described above. The foundational elements shown in the figure above are therefore considered by these guidelines to be a necessary part of high impact educational systems.

So, what are these additional and foundational categories? The first are learner-background considerations. As we shall see in the coming chapters, high impact approaches integrate students' current capabilities, knowledge, interests, cultural heritages, etc. Doing so is particularly important for students from under-resourced and marginalized backgrounds. Another important category, as we just learned, is the teaching and learning theories that inform and guide how instructors and learners engage with teaching and learning.

A final broad category is related not so much to the teaching and learning activities themselves, but rather to how students and teachers prepare for, institutionally support, and learn from these activities. According to this final category, professional development in educational theory and practice is essential. Being actively engaged in one's school as a leader who is committed to helping continually improve the educational system is also important. In addition, we need to be continually assessing the extent to which our educational improvement efforts are impacting student achievement. Evidence-based and scholarly projects are therefore another essential part of this final broad category. Collectively, these six broad categories comprise the primary and foundational elements of high impact educational systems.

So, what are these guidelines? Appendix C shows the brief "user-friendly" version of these six broad categories and their twenty guidelines. In the coming chapters, we will be exploring each one of these guidelines in greater detail. The following are the twenty guidelines in their brief form:

- Objectives:
  - Objectives are SMART (Specific, Measurable, Achievable, Relevant, and Timely)
- Assessments:
  - Draws on multiple and varied assessments
  - Uses effective feedback
  - Follows evidence-based practices
  - Integrates self- and peer-assessments
- Activities, Organization, and Resources:
  - Fosters learner-learner interactions
  - Supports higher-order thinking
  - Integrates relevant and interactive technologies
  - Addresses real-world problems
  - Scaffolds progress
  - Safe, inclusive, and caring environments
- Teaching and Learning Theories:
  - Employs holistic learning theories
  - Utilizes active teaching/learning strategies
  - Follows course development methods
- Learner-Background Considerations:
  - Adapted to learner knowledge, skills, and interests
  - Follows culturally responsive methods
  - Engages with marginalized and under-resourced communities
- Professional Development, Leadership, and Scholarship:
  - Engages in ongoing professional development
  - Active in leadership roles
  - Conducts evidence-based and scholarly projects

THREE LEVELS, THREE TIERS

Reading the list above, one might be struck by the apparent simplicity of these guidelines. In addition, for anyone who has been exposed in an introductory way to educational theory and practice, none of these are really groundbreaking. This should come as no surprise because they were selected and developed based on numerous educational resources that addressed these areas again-and-again. Returning to Samartha's yearnings for a set of guidelines that can help her continually grow across the course of her entire career, we might wonder if these are sufficient to fulfill this need.

As we shall see in the coming chapters, each guideline has three scaffolded levels that we can work with ourselves and one another to continually develop. The figure below captures some of the significant differences between each of these levels:

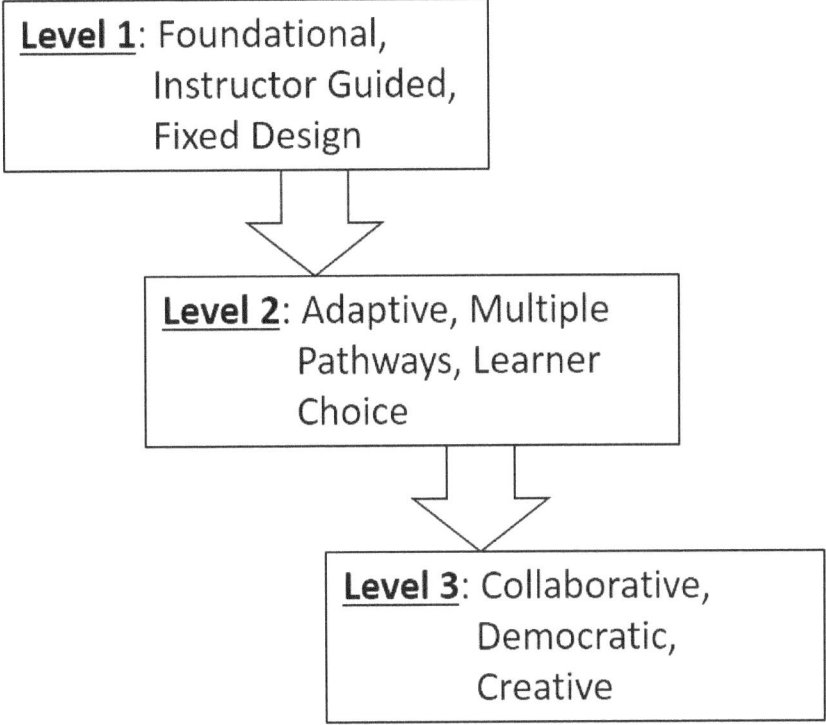

Figure 2—Three Levels of the Guidelines

For most guidelines, Level 1 is often found in our classes. These courses are well-designed with clear outcomes, well-aligned assessments, and actively engaged students. Here, the instructor and students move through a pre-designed class together, with the instructor guiding students each step of the way. At Level 2, which builds directly on Level 1, the class' complexity would increase with students being offered multiple activities, resources, and assessments that they could choose from. With some versions of Universal Design for Learning being examples of these kinds of classes, these multiple pathways are specifically developed for current students, and the instructor continually works to adapt the class to each student's varying competencies. Finally, at Level 3, the class achieves creative emergence as students take a more central role in helping develop the course. In their better forms, Level 3 classes build directly upon Level 2 as students use the already existing multiple pathways as foundational resources from which to democratically derive the new class. As we will see, achieving these higher levels requires not only a significant amount of work, but also knowledge, skills, and attitudes (KSAs) that students, teachers, and administrators need to continually cultivate over many years.

As we also saw with Samartha, we know that instructors and the classes that we teach are not the only significant factors that influence teaching and learning. Obviously, the students themselves are also an integral part of learning processes. Less obvious, however, are the roles that school staff and administrators play in providing the necessary training, resources, and support that learners and teachers need to engage in high impact teaching and learning processes. The figure below shows the relationship between three tiers of educational systems:

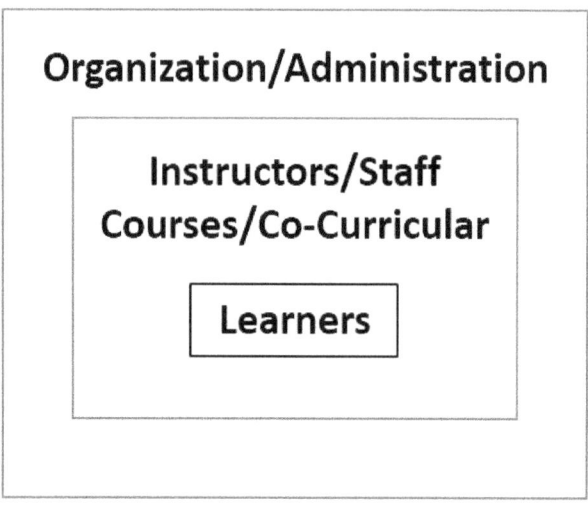

Figure 3—Three Tiers of Educational Systems

Each one of these tiers contributes significantly to educational processes. As a result, we should be developing guidelines for each one of these tiers. In doing so, we would be providing guidance to students, faculty, and administration on how they might prioritize and focus their efforts. In addition, if these guidelines for each tier were similar then, theoretically, learners, instructors, and staff could work closely together to achieve these criteria. In doing so, we would be able to cultivate a well-coordinated culture where excellence in teaching and learning would be realized.

This is what has been done in this text. We started with a set of guidelines that was developed for instructors to help improve their courses and then expanded them to the learner and administrative tiers. In other words, each broad category and each of the twenty guidelines can be applied each one of these three tiers. "How?" you might ask. We answer this question with a chapter that is dedicated to exploring the guidelines for each one of these three tiers.

ONE RELIGIOUS TRADITION

With these twenty guidelines in place, and their three levels and tiers, we have addressed the first of Samartha's struggles. So, what about the second struggle for theistic educators? In Appendix A, we will be exploring and asserting theological foundations for educational research. In doing so, we will be developing a set of theistic lenses through which to view the guidelines. In essence, we will be making the following claims: first, we will be asserting that God works with and through the repeating patterns that educational research has documented through the use of scientific methods. Knowing that God strives to have the most significant impact on teaching and learning that is possible, then we can also assert that these high impact guidelines are manifesting of God's educational life in our schools.

Based on these claims, we can then develop a more fully theistic view of God's work in our educational systems using the guidelines. As we shall see in the coming chapters, such a bottom-up approach to developing a theology of education is not foreign to the theological claims found in some theistic religious traditions such as Western Christianity. As a result, and because Western Christianity is the tradition that I practice, I will be highlighting where in this religious tradition each guideline aligns—particularly for the course/instructor tier. Our purpose here, however, is not to argue for the validity of each guideline based on Western Christian resources. Rather, it is to help develop a theology of education based on these guidelines and further refine these theological claims in dialogue with this particular religious tradition. Readers from other faith traditions are encouraged to review the beliefs and practices of their own traditions for convergences or divergences with these guidelines. Ideally, these guidelines and the theological claims that we will be making based upon them will be of relevance, resonance, and validity for all educators who strive to engage in their vocational calling via a theological lens. Overall, the goal is to provide a strong evidence-based and theological foundation for all theistic educators.

THREE ROADS, ONE HORIZON

We hope that this text will more than adequately support God's ongoing work with and through on-ground and online educational systems around the world. Teachers like Samartha struggle in every school to provide the best quality education that they can. In the coming chapters, we will be exploring in great detail the foundational guidelines that can help to support students, instructors, and administrators. Appendix A offers a beginning theistic foundation for the theological claims that will be made in relation to each guideline. The reader is encouraged to begin with this brief, though theoretically complex appendix. After reading this theistic framework for understanding educational research findings, you are then encouraged to move onto the next chapter where we will begin to cover each one of the three tiers. In essence, each tier represents a different road that members of our schools are on. Students have learning journeys that they are actively working to traverse. Instructors should labor continuously across their careers to increase their competencies and impact in their classes. Finally, staff and administrators can ideally provide the training, support, and resources that learners and faculty need.

Each of these three roads (or tiers) of educational excellence are intimately intertwined and tend toward one bright horizon. After exploring each of the tiers, a real-world case example that applies all three sets of guidelines to an educational system will be presented. From this case example, we can see how these closely aligned guidelines may be used to identify and prioritize the most significant areas for a school to focus on. By discerning the current assets and needs of students, faculty, and staff, we can—as theistic educational developers—more closely harmonize with what God has been and continues to do in our schools. Step-by-step, year-by-year, we joyfully labor with God to ever more fully realize the kin-dom of God in our high impact educational systems.[3]

---

3. The term "kin-dom" here is used throughout this book in place of the more common Christian term, "kingdom." In vernacular English, "kin" means family while "dom" is taken from the root of the Latin word "dominus," which means "master," and in the Christian tradition refers to Jesus and/or God. Together, then, "kin-dom" is intended to equitably and lovingly mean "family of God" as opposed to the more traditional image of a kingdom, which is historically hierarchical and patriarchal.

1

Stimulating the Students
The Learner Tier

A GREAT DEAL OF educational literature focuses on what happens with classes. However, we also know that students bring significant factors to learning processes.[1] More and more texts are becoming available to help guide learners on how to more effectively engage with their own study processes.[2] Using the evidence-based guidelines detailed in the next chapter, we have developed this set of guidelines to help students better help themselves. They are intended as a guide for how learners can more effectively engage in self-regulated learning. By directly aligning these with the guidelines at the course-instructor tier, we will be in a better position to articulate how school administrators can support both groups in that chapter. Such alignment is also intended to help instructors and students work more closely together on the educational aims and methods. Theologically, the following guidelines outline how God strives to work with each student to help them every step of the way on their educational journey.

OBJECTIVE GUIDELINES

Just as each class needs to have clear objectives to pursue, students should also have clear outcomes that they are striving towards. These objectives should be personally tailored in ways that are meaningful and relevant for their lives. Spiritually speaking, students should discern where God is striving to lead them so that they can more closely follow the Spirit's guidance. In doing so, students will be better enabled to focus their time and energies in these directions and thereby achieve these goals more effectively.

---

1. Hattie, *Visible Learning*, ch. 4.
2. Brown, Roediger III, and McDaniel, *Make It Stick*; Mach and Lash-Rabick, *Effective Study Strategies*; McGuire, *Teach Students How to Learn*.

Guideline #1—SMART Objectives

Learner is able to integrate learning objectives into their professional, civic, and/or personal life (Core Guideline).

Setting clear learning objectives is generally considered to be essential for educational processes. Learners should therefore have clear goals in mind when they are studying and working to learn more deeply. As a result, this guideline highlights the importance of having learning objectives that relate to their personal, professional, and/or civic life. Moving from Level 1 to Level 3, there is a growing emphasis on the learner being able to articulate learning objectives in ways that are more meaningful and relevant to them personally, as well as being able to see the relationship between these personal learning objectives and the classes that they are taking. Theologically, learners should be continually discerning the directions that God is inviting them toward via these learning objectives. They, ideally, should be able to see where God is inviting them to learn and develop in every part of their life and how their schooling relates to these sacred goals.

Level 1

The learner is able to state general learning goals for their own educational journey. The learner is also aware of course/program objectives and knows where to find them.

At this level, learners should be able to describe general goals for their own educational journey. They should also be able to state where to find course objectives, but they may not be able to name what these objectives are. At this level, then, learners will have a vague notion why their education is important and will be able to articulate these understandings in very broad and general ways. Examples of this might include "to get a degree," "to get a good paying job," "to learn more," etc.

From a theistic perspective, learners at this level may struggle to understand where God is seeking to guide them toward via their current educational path. They may not yet see the value of their schooling and/or their classes may not seem fully relevant or meaningful for their lifelong journey with God. Such possibilities are not necessarily a negative, as discerning God's goals for us is often a process that only unfolds with ongoing experiences, mentoring, and reflection. Being at this level, then, is not a judgment but rather an acknowledgement of where the learner is in relation to both their unfolding educational journey with God as well as the school system itself.

Specific examples of evidence at of this level might include:

- Student articulates their learning goals in broad and general ways.
- Student course work shows evidence of a vague understanding of the importance of their classes for their own educational goals.

- Student is observed questioning the relevance of specific classes for their learning journey.
- Student is able to state where learning objectives for a specific course may be found.

Level 2

Learner is able to articulate the relevancy of learning objectives for their professional, civic, and/or personal life.

At this level, the learner will be able to articulate their own learning goals with much greater detail and complexity. Learners at this level will be able to state how their education directly relates to goals that they have for their personal, professional, and/or civic life. They should also be able to relate these goals to specific courses that they are taking and the learning objectives in these classes. Overall, Level 2 learners have a much clearer sense of their own learning goals in relation to their education.

Spiritually speaking, learners at the level are ideally much clearer on where God is leading them via their educational journeys. While clarity of goals does not necessarily equate with accuracy of theistic discernment, it is still a possible indicator of this. Nevertheless, learners should take care to ensure careful spiritual discernment when clarifying their personal, professional, and civic goals as well as how their current courses relate to these.

Examples of this might include:

- Learner is able to state what their personal learning goals are and can clearly relate these goals to their personal, professional, and/or civic life.
- Learner is able to state what the course/module objectives are for the course(s) they are taking.
- Learner is able to state the relevance of course/module objectives for their personal, professional, and/or civic life.
- Student assessment data demonstrates that they are aware of course/module objectives and/or understand the relevance of these objectives for their personal, professional, and/or civic life.

Level 3

The learner collaborates with others in adapting learning objectives in ways that will help them reach long term goals for their professional, civic, and/or personal life. The learner is able to articulate learning objectives in their own words and can describe how the activities in their course(s)/program(s) relate to these objectives.

At this level, learners will collaboratively work with others to further adapt their own learning objectives. These adaptations should more closely align with their long-term professional, personal, and/or civic aspirations. This level is therefore focused on the learner taking more ownership and responsibility for their lifelong learning trajectories. Such ownership should therefore be reflected in the learner's ongoing revisions to their learning goals in light of their long-term plans.

As a part of these processes, the learner should additionally turn to community resources (such as instructors, mentors, family members, or experts in the field) to help shape these lifelong learning objectives in ways that still align with the accreditation, institutional, program, and/or course outcomes of the educational institution that they are currently a part of. For example, learners should be able to articulate course/module objectives of the classes they are currently taking in ways that are personally meaningful and relevant to them. Overall, the emphasis here is on learners having internalized and made sense of learning objectives in their own ways, ways that directly align with their lifelong plans and goals.

Building upon the previous level, the learner will work with others to help them continually adapt and integrate personal and course-related goals to one another in accordance with how they believe that God is guiding them. As stated above, a learner at this level will take greater initiative in adapting learning goals, and the motivations that prompt such initiative should be discerned to be God-centered. Theologically, we can see God seeking to work more proactively within the learner as well as through those with whom the learner is collaborating with to make these adaptations.

Examples of this might include:

- Learner can state how they have collaboratively worked with others to develop learning objectives for themselves and ensure that these align with: 1) their own lifelong personal, professional, and/or civic goals, and 2) accreditation, institutional, and/or program-specific outcomes of the school they are attending.

- Learner and their instructor(s) are observed collaboratively working to adapt given course/module objectives to align with learners' personal, professional, and/or civic goals.

- In consultation with others, the learner should also be able to state why they are engaging in given course activities and how these relate to the course/module objectives.

- Learner assessment data demonstrates that the learner worked with others to understand course/module objectives and how these relate to their personal, professional, and/or civic life.

ASSESSMENT GUIDELINES

In order to guide students towards these aims, God works through assessments to help them know how they are doing and where they can improve. These guidelines are therefore intended to help learners better know how to develop and/or use assessment information in more detailed ways. Overall, the goal is for students to learn how to make use of this information as the backbone of their spiritual discernment processes. When they do, the result should be the cultivation of more effective learning strategies and processes.

Guideline #1—Varied Assessments

The learner utilizes assessment information to support their own development towards their learning goals (Core Guideline).

Using assessments is central to education and learning processes. For learners following this guideline, these assessments should play a central role in at least two ways. First, the learner should use assessments to help ensure that their proficiencies are being more accurately measured. Each type of assessment (e.g., exams, research papers, portfolios, etc.) is inherently limited in the kinds of information that it can give; using multiple types of assessments therefore helps to provide a more robust picture of the learners' actual capabilities. Secondly, assessment data should be used by the learner to continually modify their study strategies to better meet their own unique needs. Overall, the trend for this guideline is from more individualistic to more collaborative analyses.

Holistic spiritual discernment encourages the use of a wide variety of sources to help inform one's decision-making processes.[3] For the learner, this means drawing from multiple assessment sources to help provide a more well-rounded picture of what God is wanting them to notice about their learning journey and how they are progressing. Theologically, each assessment can be viewed and approached as another way that God is seeking to guide each student. While many western cultures often use assessments in negatively deconstructive and punitive ways, theistic education must not follow in this contemporary tradition. At their heart, learners should view assessments as the love and "voice" of God striving to lead them in more positive and constructive directions that he is personally inviting them toward. As part of this, and because assessment information is potentially distorted due to human imperfections, learners must learn to filter out the more God-centered invitations from these assessments and discern what to take away from assessments individually and collectively. To help with such discernment, a variety of different kinds of assessments should be utilized by the learner in spiritually discerning ways.

---

3. Isenhower and Todd, *Living into Answers*.

Level 1

The learner uses assessments to draw conclusions about their own progress toward their learning goals.

At this most basic level, the learner will work individually to gather and analyze assessment data. The learner should be able identify the multiple types of assessment that they are gathering, whether these assessments are formal (e.g., how they performed on exams and papers) or informal (e.g., self-observations, passing conversations with classmates, and emails/correspondence with the instructor). Learner might also use information from previous experiences to inform their ongoing reflections (e.g., "Have I had a class like this before? If so, how did I do? What contributed to my success/failure in that class?"). At this level, the learner is essentially in a continual listening mode for what God is seeking to communicate to them about their learning progress. It is therefore a foundational level of the educational spiritual discernment process and must be well-practiced before moving onto higher levels of this guideline.

Examples of this might include:

- Learner is observed using assessments (formal and/or informal) to assess their competencies in relation to specific KSAs.

- Learner can state assessments (formal and/or informal) that they use to assess their competencies in relation to specific KSAs.

- Learner is able to talk about their performance on assessments in ways that can be used to improve their progress in the future (e.g., "I didn't study very hard for this exam, but I am planning on working harder before the next one").

- Learner is able to critically reflect on their assessment performance (e.g., being able to identify which parts were more/less difficult for them, able to state which parts they should have received more help on, etc.).

Level 2

The learner uses assessment information to modify their study strategies to better support their own learning progress.

At this level, a similar kind of process is present as with Level 1: gathering and analyzing data by utilizing multiple types of assessment. However, at this level, the learner will additionally be observed working to further improve the quality and effectiveness of their study strategies based upon the assessment data that they have gathered. The emphasis here is on continually modifying these strategies in real-time in response to their performance on assessments. In other words, the learner actively works to adjust these in an effort to further maximize their learning.

From a religious perspective, at this level the learner is progressing in their spiritual discernment processes from deep listening towards using assessment information to make tangible changes to their study strategies. Theologically, it is a shift towards responding to the God-centered invitations that they are discerning. Here, the learner is developing the realization that God is seeking to guide them through assessment information for the purpose of helping them continually improve in the KSAs that God is inviting them to develop proficiencies in. In order to respond to these invitations, the learner will therefore be observed at this level making tangible changes to their study strategies so that they perform better on future assessments.

Examples of this might include:

- Learner is observed using assessment data to modify their study strategies.
- Learner is able to state how they are using assessment data to modify their study strategies.
- Learner can identify specific assessments that they have used to help them improve how they study and learn.
- Learner is able to articulate why they are using their current study strategies and can provide examples of assessments that support the effectiveness of these strategies.
- Learner can state how they have changed their study strategies in response to how they did on specific assessment(s).

Level 3

The learner collaborates with others to analyze their performance on a variety of formative and summative assessments to help them better understand what is influencing their learning. The learner then uses this information to help scaffold their own development towards their learning goals.

Level 3 continues with the work of Levels 1 and 2, only now the learner is observed to be working with others on many of these tasks. Though, in addition to the previous levels, the learner continually works to expand upon the range of assessments that they are using to provide insights into their learning progress. The learner is also observed working together with others to decide how they can continue to improve in relation to relevant KSAs based upon assessment data. Being more collaborative, Level 3 for this guideline is characteristically different from the previous levels as the learner works directly with others to identify and analyze assessments as well as modify their own study strategies in light of this assessment data.

As mentioned above, at its best, spiritual discernment processes are more holistic in nature. These processes should therefore include not just our own interpretations of information that we have gathered from multiple sources, but also insights from trusted peers and mentors as God speaks to us through our community as much as

God does to us personally. At this level, then, the learner will have developed an active understanding of this and apply it to their uses of assessment data. They will be observed working with others to continually discern where God is inviting them towards based on their assessments. In addition to increasing the chances of clarity and accuracy of such collaborative spiritual discernment, the learner will also automatically have a sympathetic communal support system that can then help them pursue these God-centered invitations. At this highest level, the learner will therefore not only have achieved a more robust discernment process in relation to assessment data, but also cultivated the community that will be needed to help them follow in the footsteps that God is laying out before them.

Examples of this might include:

- Learner is observed working with others to reflect on their performance on assessments and to then decide how they might modify their study strategies.
- The learner is able to state how they have worked with others to develop a study plan that is based on how they have done on assessments.
- Learner can name specific and multiple assessments that they have used to modify their study strategies in consultation with instructors, peers, student achievement staff, etc.
- Instructors, staff, peers, etc. are able to state how they have worked with the learner to develop a study plan that is based on how this learner has done on specific assessments.

Guideline #2—Intentional & Focused Feedback

The learner uses feedback from assessments to continually improve their competencies in their courses as well as to build their own self-regulated learning capabilities (Core Guideline).

Numerous studies continue to show that learners benefit from detailed feedback that aids them in better knowing where and how they can continue to improve in their learning.[4] This feedback should therefore be used by the learner to help clarify where they are doing well in addition to where they will likely need to focus forward in order to continue to improve in their course KSAs. As a part of this process, the learner should seek out opportunities that more directly help them continue to improve in their areas of strength as well as addressing their noted areas for improvement. At the highest level, the learner will be observed taking initiative to then use this feedback to develop more effective learning strategies in collaboration with others. Overall, the trend for this guideline is from the learner simply using feedback to identify their

---

4. See the resources listed for this guideline in the next chapter.

strengths/weaknesses to their working with others to help them identify strategies that will improve their performance going forward.

For the previous assessment guideline, the learner was encouraged to use multiple sources and types of assessments to inform their spiritual discernment processes and thereby more clearly identify God's invitations for their learning journey. This guideline is focused more directly on how the learner uses this information to direct their educational processes. Here, the learner should be interested in what God is seeking to tell them through their assessments in terms of what they are doing well with as well as what they still need to improve upon. Theologically, it is an assertion that God not only seeks to provide learners with evaluative results, but to also provide detailed guidance on where and how to continually improve.

Level 1

The learner uses feedback from assessments to identify their own strengths and weaknesses in performance as well as strategies for how they might improve their progress towards learning goals.

At Level 1, there will be evidence of the learner intentionally using feedback from instructors, peers, mentors, and assessments to help them identify their own areas of strength in additional to areas that need improvement. They will also be open to and looking for strategies that might help them improve, though they may not use these strategies in an intentional or ongoing way. The learner, at this level, will therefore likely have more of a positive view of feedback that is provided, recognizing that these bring ideas and opportunities for continual learning and development.

Developmentally, a learner at this level will therefore know that God is seeking to provide them with guidance via the feedback that they have received on their assessments. Following holistic and sound spiritual discernment processes and principles, they should be able to identify strengths and weaknesses in their performance that God is striving to draw their attention to. While there may be fears and resistances to facing such feedback, the learner will still have the courage to recognize these well-discerned invitations at this level.

Examples of this might include:

- Learner is able to state when and how they have received timely, detailed, and constructive feedback from others as well as the areas of strength/improvement that this feedback identified.
- Learner is observed reviewing feedback on papers and exams and can highlight the areas that they are doing well on as well as what they need to revisit and improve upon.

- An instructor/staff is able to share conversations (face-to-face or via technology) that they have had with the learner where they discussed feedback and the areas of strength/improvement that were identified.
- Learner is able to state how they have used feedback from others to improve in one or more of their courses, being able to highlight the areas of strength/improvement that were identified by the feedback that was provided.

Level 2

In addition to meeting Level 1, the learner engages in additional/supplemental learning experiences that will help them apply feedback from assessments and thereby improve their competencies in their courses.

Building upon the previous level, at Level 2 the learner will be observed engaging in activities that directly help them act on the feedback they have been provided with, and thereby improve their competencies in relation to relevant KSAs. These learning activities may be ones that are a part of their courses or they may be external ones that the learner seeks out on their own initiative. Regardless of where these activities are engaged, the key purpose of them should be to help the learner improve in the areas of strength/improvement that the feedback has identified. If the learner is unable to state how these activities are directly related to feedback that they have received, then they have not achieved this level according to this guideline.

Though contemporary secular education (as well as many religious communities) tends to focus on weaknesses, more positive theological formulations depict God as also empowering already existing strengths and assets as discussed in this book. At this level, having already identified both strengths as well as the areas of improvement that God is wanting them to focus on (Level 1), the learner will then set out to discern how God is inviting them to improve in these areas. This means that the learner will strive to identify and engage with effective learning strategies that are most likely to directly impact the already identified areas. Following this, the learner will be found utilizing the resources, training, and support that are needed to actively engage with these spiritually discerned strategies that God has been proactively working to lead the learner into.

Examples of this might include:

- Learner is observed completing an activity that has them apply feedback that they received previously.
- Assessments data (formal and/or informal) shows evidence of the learner being required to complete an assignment where they had to apply instructor feedback.
- Learner can state how they have applied feedback that they have been provided on previous assignments to subsequent assignments.

- Learner is observed seeking out activities that directly help them improve on areas of strength/improvement that specific feedback has identified.

Level 3

In addition to Level 2, the learner takes initiative and collaborates with others to use feedback to reflect on their own performance and to then develop and apply their own concrete strategies for how they will continue to improve their progress towards learning goals.

Further building upon Level 2, at this level the learner will work with others to identify and utilize strategies that will help them improve their learning and development based upon the feedback that they have been provided. This level is more collaborative as well as self-directed as the learner reflects on their performance in relation to the feedback that has been provided as well as in determining the steps that they might take to improve.

While this level uses the same processes as the two previous levels (i.e., using feedback to identify areas of strength/improvement and then engaging with activities as a result), there are two significant difference. First, a Level 3 learner will be observed working with others to engage in these Level 1 and 2 processes. Second, the learner will work to identify and/or develop their own learning strategies/activities as a result of the feedback that they have been provided. At Level 2, these activities/strategies may be part of a class, but at Level 3 the learner will collaboratively work to find/create their own additional/supplemental activities. This level therefore represents a higher level of self-regulated learning, where the learner takes more ownership (in collaboration with others) of their learning journey based upon the feedback that they continually receive.

Theologically, Level 3 essentially describes a learner who has connected with God-centered movements within themselves that are strongly and intrinsically motivating them to want to improve in relation to the given set of KSAs that they have been receiving feedback on. While manifestations of these inner movements will vary depending on the specific KSAs, the learners' capabilities, and contextual dynamics, the inner drive to act on the feedback should be readily apparent via the initiative that the learner takes as a result of the feedback as described above. Here, there is also the spiritual understanding that the actions that result from feedback are best discerned collaboratively with others who know the learner well. It is a theological realization on the learners' part that God's guidance is not only most clearly discerned but also more effectively enacted via communities that are more purely responsive to God's ever guiding Spirit. Educationally, then, a learner at Level 3 will work closely with well-informed spiritual mentors who can effectively help them both analyze and act on the recommendations and invitations that have come from the feedback.

Examples of this might include:

- Learner is able to state how they have used feedback that has been provided by one of their instructors to modify their study strategies in consultation with others to continue to improve in their classes.

- Learner is observed working with others to reflect on feedback that they have received and then identify and/or develop activities that will help them continue improving in one or more of their classes.

- Instructors, staff, and peers are able to state how they have worked with the learner to reflect on feedback that they have received, and then identify and/or develop activities that will help them continue to improve in one or more of their classes.

- Learner is observed completing an activity where they have collaboratively reviewed feedback that has been provided by one of their instructors and then developed a concrete plan for how they will use this feedback to continue to improve in their classes.

Guideline #3—Evidence-Based Assessments

Assessments are utilized by the learner to improve their learning in ways that are in accordance with best practices.

For learners who are committed to improving their competencies, as we have learned, assessments are an integral part of the learning processes. However, it is equally important that the learner understand what their performance on quizzes and exams means and how they might more effectively use them to improve their study strategies. Following this guideline, then, the learner will be observed adhering to best practices when interpreting and applying the results of formal and informal assessments to improve their learning. At higher levels, the learner will do this in collaboration with others and they will be an integral part of helping to ensure that these assessments are both valid (e.g., the information gleaned from them accurately represents the learner's capabilities) and reliable (e.g., there is consistency for the assessments across students and graders). Overall, the learner will therefore work to use assessments in accordance with best practices.

If we theologically lived in a spiritually perfect world, we might expect the assessments and feedback that we receive from one another to be an accurate, reliable, and completely unbiased depiction of what God wants us to learn and focus on. However, the current human condition is such that God's life and work within and to the world is often distorted. As this relates to assessments, then, it means that some work must be done to help ensure that the assessments themselves as well as the conclusions that are being drawn from them are as valid and reliable as possible. For the learner, ideally, they should be an integral part of the process to continually critically reflect on and spiritually discern to what extent each assessment more precisely captures their competencies. These validity and reliability checks should also help clarify the overall picture that is emerging from the multiple assessments that they are engaging with. The goal for this guideline is to utilize current best practices for ensuring assessment validity and reliability so that the most accurate representation of God's guidance through the assessments is realized.

Level 1

The learner follows best practices in engaging, interpreting, and applying insights from specific assessments to help improve their learning.

At this level, learners should be able to identify and/or be observed using specific recommendations and/or best practices to help guide their understanding and use of assessments. These resources (e.g., mentors, web sites, handouts from instructors/staff) should help the learner better understand what their assessment results mean. These resources should also help the learner think about how they might use assessment results to improve their study strategies. As a result, learners at this level should be able to articulate how they are interpreting and applying assessment results as well as how these interpretations and applications align with the recommendations and/or best practices that they are drawing from.

Following the core theological assertion of this book, we can trust that God has been working within and through educational processes since before the dawn of time to help prepare for and improve the quality of education for each learner. As this applies to assessments, we can have faith that best practices that have been developed for using, interpreting, and applying assessments and their results embody God's educational life and work in central ways. As a result, the learner at this level should look to existing resources that provide guidance on how best to interpret and use assessment results to improve their own learning and development. In doing so, the learner will be increasing their likelihood of more accurately distilling the invitations that God is seeking to make them aware of through their assessment results and feedback.

Examples of this might include:

- Learner is observed using specific recommendations that provide insights into how to interpret and/or apply assessment results to improve their study strategies.
- The learner is able to state which best practices they are using to help them interpret and/or apply the information that they are learning from their assessment results.
- The student's coursework shows evidence that they are using specific recommendations to guide how they are interpreting and/or applying the information that they are learning from their assessment results and feedback.

- An instructor/staff confirms that the learner attended a workshop on how to use specific recommendations to provide insights into how students can interpret and/or apply assessment results to improve study strategies.

Level 2

The learner works to help ensure that their use of specific assessments is valid and reliable in helping them improve in their learning and development.

Level 2 extends the work of the previous levels by ensuring that the learner's interpretations and uses of assessment results/feedback are valid and reliable. In other words, learners at this level will be observed working to verify that the changes they are making to their study strategies (based upon assessment results) really are improving their achievement (i.e., establishing validity). There should also be evidence at this level of the learner working to help confirm that such positive changes are being made in consistent ways (i.e., reliably). At this level, then, there will be clear evidence of the learner working to establish processes that continually result in improvements to their learning strategies based upon best practices for interpreting assessment results and feedback.

At Level 1, the learner is found to be merely following prescribed best practices for interpreting and applying assessment results. At this level, the learner will additionally work to confirm that these interpretations and applications really are providing insights that are resulting in improvements to their study strategies and competencies. While these improvements, obviously, include the effectiveness of their study strategies, they are also inherently based upon how they are interpreting and using assessment results and feedback, which is what this level focuses on. Spiritually, this level represents the learner's ability to more closely partner with God's efforts to teach them how to more effectively and reliably use assessment results. It is also an invitation for the learner to help ensure that the assessments that are being used by the school system are valid, reliable, and unbiased. If the learner is finding, for instance, that their assessment does not accurately capture their competencies, then they should let their instructors and school staff know so that changes can be made. From an organizational perspective, then, this level is an invitation to the learner to be a more integral part of God's positive systemic change movements as much as it is an invitation to more effectively utilize assessment results and feedback to improve their learning strategies.

Examples of this might include:

- The learner can describe how they have worked to verify that the improvements they have made to their study strategies (in response to their performance on quizzes, papers, etc.) are leading to positive improvements in their achievement.

- There is evidence that the learner is consistently making effective improvements to their learning strategies as a direct result of assessment results.
- The learner is observed regularly reflecting on their assessment results and then continually making positive improvements to their study strategies.
- Learner can show evidence of working to establish the validity and/or reliability of their efforts to improve their learning strategies in response to their performance on quizzes, papers, etc.

Level 3

The learner collaborates with instructors, staff, and/or peers to engage in Level 1 and 2 activities.

Building upon the previous levels, at Level 3 the learner will be observed proactively working with others in ways that helps them better utilize best practices to guide their understanding and use of assessment results. Such collaboration should focus on helping them analyze their performance on assessments as well as adapting their study strategies in reliable and valid ways that lead to improved achievement. The learner will therefore be observed working closely with their instructors, organizational staff, outside mentors, and classmates to engage in these kinds of activities.

As with many other guidelines, this level theologically asserts that God works most fully and effectively via close collaborations. As it relates to this guideline, the learner will seek to work with others to collectively discern the validity of assessment results and feedback as well as how these might be used to more reliably improve the learner's study strategies. As with the previous level, the learner should also work with others to help ensure the general reliability and validity of the assessments when it is appropriate to do so. Overall, such communal efforts are intended to help ensure that God's educational life is able to work most effectively through the assessment results and feedback for both the individual learner as well as the community-at-large. As a result, the learner at this level is invited to be an integral part of these collective spiritual discernment processes as they relate to the validity and reliability of assessments.

Examples of this might include:

- The learner is observed working with their instructors, classmates, and staff to help them reflect on their assessment results in light of specific best practices.
- The learner can state who they have worked with to collaboratively decide how to use assessment results to help improve their achievement in a course, following evidence-based recommendations.

- An instructor, staff member, and peer can describe how they worked with the learner to reflect on and use the results of the learner's assessments to help them continue to improve in reliable and/or valid ways.

- The learner can articulate how they have worked with others to modify their study strategies based upon specific assessment results and following best practices.

Guideline #4—Self- and Peer-Assessments

Learner utilizes self- and/or peer-assessments and reflections to improve their own and/or their peers' learning and development.

Social-cultural learning theories and its associated research has shown that students learn a great deal when working with their peers.[5] Peer tutoring, for example, has been found to be one of the more effective means to foster learning.[6] As it relates to assessments, evaluating their own and one another's work can be a powerful strategy that learners can use to improve their competencies. Doing this requires them to better understand the criteria that they are using to self- and/or peer-assess as well as to be able to apply these criteria to actual examples of work. Another primary purpose of these kinds of assessments are to help learners not only to continue to progress in relation to their learning goals, but also to take more responsibility for their own and one another's learning and development. As a result, having learners adopt this strategy is considered to be a best practice for the learner's development of collaborative self-regulated learning skills.

As we shall learn more in the next chapter, Western Christianity places a primary emphasis on community and God's life being active within and to these interactions. Peer-assessments are therefore another way that God's seeks to help the student continue to grow along their unfolding learning journey through such relationships. Both peer- and self-assessments are fundamentally intended to help the learner more intimately understand what God is expecting of them, as well as how they are currently doing in relation to these expected outcomes. In addition to the instructor spiritually helping to guide them through their learning, the student is empowered via self- and peer-assessments to take a more central role in better understanding and evaluating their own and one another's work. Theologically, it is an invitation for the learner to more intimately understand and more directly partner with God in their own and another's educational journeys.

---

5. See the references for this guideline in the next chapter.
6. Hattie, *Visible Learning*, 186–87.

Level 1

The learner uses criteria provided for an assignment to guide their performance. Using these criteria, the learner examines her/his and/or classmates' work in relation to the criteria.

Learners at this level will use criteria from course assignments, or other sources, as the basis for guiding how they will study, prepare, and ultimately assess their own and their peer's work. These criteria might be detailed criteria (e.g., course rubrics, information sheets, guidelines, etc.) or they may be general expectations that the learner is familiar with in relation to the assignment. Here, the learner will be observed proactively using these criteria to better gauge how well they are grasping concepts, skills, and/or expected attitudes. They will also work with their peers to help one another to continually improve in relation to their learning goals.

Guidelines, expectations, and outcomes, as we have learned, are ideally the levels of achievement that God is working with the learner to journey towards. As a result, following this guideline, the learner should therefore take the initiative to use these criteria to assess their own and/or their classmates' work as they are working on them. Is essence, it is a more direct and dynamic partnership with God to continually assess one's efforts in order to improve them. At each step of the way, as the learner writes a paper, prepares for a test, or compiles material into a portfolio, the learner and their peers can be using the God-centered criteria to formatively assess their work and competencies. Peer- and self-assessments are therefore an invitation for the learner to take a more direct and proactive part in their own and one another's educational journey with God.

Examples of this might include:

- Learner will be observed using rubrics or guidelines that have been provided by one or more of their classes to assess their own and/or their classmates' competencies.
- Learner can state how they have engaged in self- and/or peer-assessments in relation to course concepts/skills.
- Learner participates in course activities where they are guided in evaluating their own and/or one another's work using a set of guidelines that the instructor has provided.
- The learner's discussion board posts and/or other course materials show evidence of the learner critically reflecting on their own and/or their peer's work in relation to a set of standards that they have learned about in class.
- Instructors/staff can state how they have seen or worked with the learner to utilize self- and/or peer-assessments.

Level 2

Building on Level 1, the learner works with instructors, staff, and/or peers to apply the results of self- and/or peer-assessments in order to strengthen their own and/or their peers' competencies.

Level 2 is similar to the previous level in that the learner will still utilize criteria to complete self- and peer-assessments to improve and deepen their learning and development. At this level, however, the learner will then collaboratively use the results of these assessments to improve their study strategies and engage in additional activities that will help them strengthen their competencies. An example might include working with a staff member to revise the draft of a paper that has been self-assessed or improving their discussion board posts based on replies they have received from their peers. This level is therefore distinguished by activities that explicitly empower the learner to act on the suggestions that have been gathered from self-/peer-assessments. There should also be evidence that these changes and/or additional activities were chosen in consultation with instructors, staff, and/or peers.

A life with God often involves an increased awareness of God's actions and invitations. However, consciousness-raising is usually not enough as greater understanding is often an invitation towards new or modified actions. Following these theological assertions, self-/peer-assessment results should therefore be used as part of holistic spiritual discernment processes that guide the learner to further improve their study strategies. For this guideline at this level, such discernment will be collaborative as the learner works with others to determine how best to respond to the godly invitations that have come from the self-/peer-assessments.

Examples of this might include:

- Learners are observed completing activities that guide them in applying the results of self-/peer-assessments, such as revising a draft of a paper.
- Instructor is able to articulate how they helped to guide the learner in a step-by-step manner to use self-/peer-assessment data to revise assignments, modify their study strategies, etc.
- Learner has attended organizational events where they worked to alter their learning strategies, conduct and/or reflect on self- and/or peer-assessments, etc.
- Peers/classmates are able to state how they worked with the learner to complete peer-assessments and subsequently improve their study strategies.

Level 3

The learner works with instructors and/or peers to collaboratively generate assessment criteria. The learner then utilizes self-regulated learning skills by analyzing and applying the results of self- and/or peer-assessment data to improve their own and/or their peers' competencies.

A learner at Level 3 for this guideline will still engage in Level 1 and 2 kinds of activities. At this level, however, the learner will participate in these activities in more proactive and collaborative ways. For instance, there will be evidence of the learner working with their instructors and/or peers to generate self-/peer-assessment criteria. Doing so requires a deeper level of understanding of course concepts, skills, and/or attitudes as well as self-motivation to set higher standards for their own learning. In addition, the learner will be observed taking more self-initiative to collaboratively reflect on and respond to the results of these kinds of assessments. At Level 2, such analyses and applications could have been a required part of the courses that they are they are taking. At Level 3, however, the learner will be observed engaging in these kinds of activities on their own initiative, whether their courses require them or not.

This highest level represents a more sophisticated and integral understanding on the part of the learner of what God is inviting them towards in relation to specific course KSAs. Such in-depth understandings are necessary in order to help develop the assessment criteria that can become the basis of self-/peer-assessments. At this level, the learner will therefore not only seek to proactively discern what these criteria are, but also to apply them to their own and/or their classmates' work. They will also be found working with others to determine how God is then inviting them to respond to the results of these assessments. Overall, this level depicts a learner who is more fully and directly immersed in the work that God is trying to achieve via self-/peer-assessments, from the development of these assessments to the application of their results. It is therefore a learner who is more genuinely a spiritual self-regulated learner.

Examples of this might include:

- Learners are observed working in study groups outside of class to create their own self-/peer-assessment criteria.
- The learner is observed using self-/peer-assessments as part of their self-regulated learning processes (e.g., goal setting, developing learning strategies, evaluating progress, revising strategies).
- Peers, instructors, and/or staff are able to describe how the learner has taken the initiative to create, implement, and then use the results of self-/peer-assessments to improve their learning strategies.
- The learner can provide evidence (e.g., study notes) of self-/peer-assessments that they have helped to create and utilize.

ACTIVITIES, ORGANIZATION, AND RESOURCE GUIDELINES

Without action, there is no change. This is especially true for students who want to excel in their learning. Rather than merely showing up at school and obediently going through their classes, these guidelines depict learning approaches that are much more proactive. Not only should students strive to follow the guidance of their instructors, they should also be laboring to develop strategies that are ever more effective and appropriate for themselves. In doing so, according to the theological foundations for this text, they will be responding more fully to God's educational initiatives in their life. Each of these guidelines therefore provide guidance on some of the more effective ways that God has been documented by educational research studies to work with students both within and outside of the class.

Guideline #1—Learner-Learner Interactions

The learner intentionally seeks to engage in learner-learner interactions to support learning and development (Core Guideline).

Evidence-based studies and assessment tools have confirmed the substantial impact that learner-learner interactions have on student achievement.[7] In their simpler forms, these kinds of learning interactions are generally shorter and engage in course KSAs in more superficial ways. As learner-learner interactions become more substantial, however, the learner will be observed to critically reflect on their own and their peers' perspectives in greater detail, perhaps questioning not only what each other thinks about course related materials, but also how they came to hold these views. At higher levels, these types of interactions are usually more long-term and are more focused on collaboratively engaging with more complex decision-making and innovative processes. As a result, learner-learner interactions are deeper and more intentional at higher levels and require more complex collaboration and group work skills as well as higher order thinking. Overall, this guideline is intended to encourage these kinds of in-depth engagement on the part of the learner with their peers.

Throughout these guidelines, there is an emphasis on collaborative engagement at higher levels. This guideline, however, emphasizes the importance of learners engaging with one another even in simplistic ways based upon the theological assertion that God's educational life acts more effectively in community. This is particularly important for novices in a subject matter because they can help one another better understand core concepts and learn the required skills at their current levels of competency. In essence, this is God working through peer support and tutoring processes wherein learners aid and guide one another along their learning journeys. With God being within and through all that is, and working towards more integrated harmonies

---

7. See references for this guideline in the next chapter.

of every part of creation, such learner-learner interactions are an intrinsic part of God's synthesizing endeavors as they ever manifest in our educational systems.

Level 1

The learner intentionally engages in simple interactions with other learners to support their learning and development.

At this level, the learner will seek out interactions that are shorter and more superficial. If restricted only to these kinds of interactions, learners would not come to know one another in more detailed ways, especially in terms of their academic competencies or learning strategies. In addition, these kinds of interactions typically engage with content/skills in simpler ways. For instance, students might meet to memorize definitions, quiz one another on key terms, or share notes with each another. Following Bloom's Taxonomy, these kinds of learner-learner interactions would be at the remembering or understanding levels.[8] As these types of peer engagement are beneficial to learning and development, there should be evidence of the learner seeking these out.

While such simple interactions are limited in their contributions to learning processes, they are a necessary foundation for building the kinds of relationships that are needed for the higher levels of this guideline. Theologically, God can work through these kinds of interactions to develop these necessary relational foundations. In addition, even in these simpler and shorter interactions, much beneficial learning can and does happen as God works within and through them to help students grow. These kinds of interactions are therefore a foundational strategy that the learner can find and partner more fully with God to learn through.

Examples of this might include:

- Learner is observed working in short-term groups on simpler activities and problems related to key course concepts and skills.
- Course assessments have evidence of the learner completing assignments where they were required to collaborate on short-term projects.
- The learner participates in peer tutoring activities for short periods of time and they focus mostly on simply reviewing common terms and definitions from their classes.
- The learner is able to describe group-work activities that they have engaged in that were of shorter duration focused mostly on reviewing key concepts or practicing skills that they are expected to memorize.

---

8. Krathwohl, "A Revision."

Level 2

The student proactively learns about other students' diverse perspectives, critically reflects on these, and/or helps others to engage with relevant KSAs in improved ways.

At this level, there will be evidence of the learner engaging with their classmates in deeper and more intentional ways. Again, following Bloom's Taxonomy, the learner will work with their peers to apply, analyze, and/or evaluate course concepts and skills. As an integral part of these processes, the learner will be observed critically reflecting on their own and their classmates' views of course content. Here, the goal is not just to understand what each other believes but also how each person came to these positions. In addition, learners at this level will also be more supportive of one another's educational journey by intentionally helping each other to engage with course KSAs in deeper ways.

At this level, we can find God working towards greater complexity in at least two ways. First, the holy invitation is for the learner to interact with peers in ways that help them develop more sophisticated understandings and advanced competencies for key KSAs. As has been asserted in Appendix A, a core evolutionary-based theological assertion is that God is ever laboring towards greater complexity and these efforts apply to learner-learner interactions as students help one another to develop in these directions. Second, God may be found to work towards greater relational intimacy and maturity among student groups. Not only are these relationship skills essential for a healthy life, they also empower more authentic and extensive learning processes to emerge as students engage more critically and constructively with each other. Here, then, we find the Spirit to be inviting and guiding students through these deeper and more substantive relationships with each other as they learn together in more open, honest, and intimate ways.

Examples of this might include:

- The learner is observed engaging with course content in more critically reflective and long-term ways with their peers, either as part of course assignments or on their own initiative.

- Learners are observed questioning their own and one another's assumptions, exploring how/why they understand course content in the ways that they do, and providing constructive feedback and support to one another.

- There is evidence of the learner working in long-term groups where they are required to engage with course content and one another in increasingly complex ways (e.g., applying, evaluating, analyzing).

- The learner can describe semester-long study groups that they are a part of where they work together to question one another's assumptions, exploring how/why they understand course content in the ways that they do, and providing constructive feedback to each other.

Level 3

Building on Level 2, the learner participates in long-term group activities where they are required to collaborate in substantive ways (e.g., decision-making, problem solving, exploration, invention) in relation to relevant KSAs.

In addition to engaging with others in mutually supportive and critically reflective ways, learners at this level will be observed to be a part of long-term groups that are working on more complex projects. These kinds of projects, which may or may not be a part of course or program requirements, involve learners collaboratively engaging in long-term decision-making, problem solving, and real-world projects. Following Bloom's Taxonomy, these projects will have the higher cognitive tiers of creativity, synthesis, and innovation. As a part of these groups, the learner should be observed transitioning through normal group development processes (e.g., forming, norming, storming, performing, adjourning). Overall, these in-depth group projects should have the primary purpose of helping the learner to continue to progress towards their learning goals.

At this level, God's work of increasing complexity continues as learners support one another in more in-depth ways, as well as use key KSAs to complete these projects. As it relates to the complexity of their relationships, learners at this level will have developed beyond getting to know and critically reflecting on one another's views and competencies. Such relational development is essential if learners are going to work on complex projects that require substantial commitments from each group member. We can therefore find God to be working with student as well as the group as a whole to progress towards these more harmonious, well integrated, and synchronous group dynamics. As it relates to the complexities of the core KSAs, well-discerned projects will challenge the group of students to move beyond simplistic understandings and applications towards more innovative and genuinely creative uses of these KSAs. Partly overlapping with the real-world applications guideline below, the holy invitation here is for students to more fully respond to God's movements as their group carefully and collaboratively selects and engages with projects that stretch each of their individual as well as collective abilities. Learner-learner interactions at this level are therefore following God's educational life as it strives to help students learn and develop through these increasingly complex group interactions and activities.

Examples of this might include:

- Student is able to articulate and present evidence of how the long-term groups that they have been working with have required them to collaborate on activities such as service-learning projects, design projects for ill-defined problems, and long-term peer-assessment partnerships.

- As part of a long-term group project, the learner and their peers are observed transitioning through typical group development processes (e.g., forming, norming, storming, performing, adjourning).

- A faculty or staff member is able to describe a long-term project that they have been working with the learner on that has required the team (including the learner) to critically collaborate on decision-making and problem solving.

- Course assessments show clear evidence of the learner completing activities that have required them to demonstrate their abilities to critically collaborate with others on long-term problem-solving, research, and service-learning projects.

Guideline #2—Higher Order Thinking

The learner strives to engage in higher order thinking in order to support their learning and development (Core Guideline).

When learners simply work to memorize concepts and skills from class, their long-term retention is limited. When, however, they engage with KSAs in critically reflective ways, their understanding and capabilities deepen. As a result, following this guideline, learners should be observed using higher order thinking skills to strengthen their competencies. At lower levels, this will involve applying, analyzing, and/or evaluating the concepts/skills that they are learning. At higher levels, the complexity of their critical engagement will increase as will the initiative that they take to find/develop these kinds of activities. Overall, learners should be observed utilizing these critical thinking skills to help pursue their learning goals.

In addition to the theological complexity discussions from the previous guideline, here we find God working to help the learner integrate what they are learning more deeply into their existing neuro-cognitive-affective processes. Critical, or higher order, thinking skills are one of many different ways that educational research has shown God to utilize towards these ends.[9] In essence, as learners dissect, evaluate, innovatively and apply the concepts/skills that they are learning, they are responding to God's integrative life as it works within and through their internal critical learning processes. New insights emerge, new connections are made with existing knowledge, more nuanced and critical understandings develop and God's educational movements progress for the learner. Higher order thinking strategies are one of the more impactful ways that God works, and the student should therefore endeavor to partner with God in these ways via the study strategies that they use.

---

9. See the references for this guideline in the next chapter.

Level 1

The learner intentionally engages with simpler critical thinking skills (e.g., apply, analyze, and evaluate) for course KSAs.

At this level, there is evidence of the learner using basic critical thinking skills to deepen their learning. For instance, the learner might use criteria/guidelines from one of their classes to reflect on and/or evaluate a real-world situation, they might be observed comparing and contrasting course concepts, or they might be found using inductive/deductive reasoning skills. Overall, the learner should be observed applying, evaluating, and analyzing the KSAs that they are learning about in an effort to further develop in these KSAs.

At this level, the student will partner with God's higher order thinking strategies in more accessible ways. For instance, the ability to apply a concept or skill to a given scenario, while it can be challenging, is a strategy that students can actively work on when learning course materials. Here, God may be asserted to be inviting the student beyond mere memorization towards more advanced adaptations of core KSAs so that they can understand and integrate these KSAs into their lives more fully. Doing so will not only require more of an active investment on the part of the student, it will stretch them towards more in-depth and detailed understandings. Keeping their spiritually discerned learning goals in mind, the learner should know that working with key KSAs in these dynamic and challenging ways is intended to better prepare them for the work that God has for them both now and later on in their lives. At this level, then, we find God inviting the learner into these easier and more accessible, though still very challenging, higher order thinking skills in an effort to better prepare them not only for the higher levels below but also for their future.

Examples of this might include:

- The learner is able to state how they have applied specific skills they are learning to a real-world situation.
- Study groups are observed comparing and contrasting course concepts in an effort to better understand them.
- A course that the learner is taking requires the learner to analyze a case study using concepts from the class.
- Staff and/or instructors are able to state how they have worked with the learner to analyze, evaluate, and apply specific concepts/skills.

Level 2

The learner uses more complex higher order thinking skills (e.g., synthesizing, creating, innovating) for course KSAs and/or challenges assumptions inherent in course concepts, materials, theories, methods, and activities.

For this level, the learner would be expected to engage with higher order thinking skills that are more synthesizing, integrative, and multi-dimensional in nature. Here, the learner will be observed seeking out ways to engage the concepts/skills they are learning about in these kinds of ways. These activities may be a part of a course they are taking, co-curricular activities that they participate in, or they may be self-initiated. The learner will also be found to continually and critically question the limitations, inherent biases, and underlying assumptions of the course materials that they are required to engage with. Participating in these kinds of higher order thinking skills has the intention of deepening the learner's understandings and insights into the concepts and skills that they are learning.

Building upon and moving beyond the previous level, God may be found working to further stretch the learner even further. To be able to use core KSAs in more creative, innovative, and synthesizing ways requires a more extensive, nuanced, and advanced level of comprehension, skill, and experience. In a world that is ever-changing and therefore needs such creative innovations, this level depicts the work of God in trying to better prepare the learner for these challenges. While such higher order engagement with KSAs does result in deeper learning, it may be asserted that God's purposes for and work through them go well-beyond the student's achievement on assessments. Much more important is the work that God is seeking to do as he helps the student to develop these world-changing skills. As a result, the learner should work to respond to these invitations and movements of God by engaging in higher order thinking study strategies and learning experiences that help them to grow in these ways.

Examples of this might include:

- As part of a class, the learner completes a semester-long project where they have to propose novel solutions to real-world problems.
- The learner is observed participating in a small group activity that requires them to use concepts/skills to create, innovate, and design.
- The learner can identify what they believe to be some of the limitations, inherent biases, and underlying assumptions of the course materials that they are using.
- Instructor/staff can describe how they have worked with the learner to complete quality improvement projects that required the learner to use knowledge/skills in more integrative ways.

Level 3

The learner seeks to design and implement higher order thinking experiences that will help them better learn course KSAs, are aligned with course objectives, and that build on their own interests and background.

Learners at this level will intentionally work to help design and implement activities that engage with higher order thinking skills. These activities may occur as part of curricular or co-curricular projects or the learner might seek out or create these on their own initiative. Learners, for example, might adapt discipline-specific methods (e.g., scientific methods, engineering design processes, philosophical analyses) for a specific application that was developed by the learner, they might identify and address ill-defined problems in the community, or they might choose and assess specific critically reflective study strategies to use in one or more of their courses. As a result of engaging with these activities, the learner is not only using higher order thinking skills in the activities they are helping to develop but they are also using these skills as part of the activity development process itself.

While there are numerous higher order thinking activities that the learner can simply select and engage, there will always be a need for more to be created that are more meaningful, relevant, and impactful for ever-changing local realities. This level therefore captures the work that God labors to do by working through the student to help create and facilitate these kinds of contextualized activities. With God being the master of efficiency, as stated above, the learner will not only be using higher order thinking skills when they engage in these activities, but they will also be using them when they help to develop the activities. As a result, the learner at this level should endeavor to look for and respond to God's invitations to help develop such higher order thinking experiences and projects.

Examples of this might include:

- Learner helps to develop a rubric to assess a course paper and then make revisions based upon self-/peer-assessments using this rubric.
- The learner can describe study groups where they have worked to identify and address an ill-defined problem in their local community using concepts/skills from one or more of their courses.
- Learner states how they have continually assessed higher order thinking study strategies and can identify specific changes they have made to these that have resulted in higher achievements in one or more of their courses.
- The learner is observed collaborating with faculty and/or staff to develop a research project that is directly related to concepts/skills from one or more of their courses.

Guideline #3—Use of Technologies

Learner intentionally uses relevant and interactive technologies to improve their learning and development.

Obviously, technologies are becoming a pervasive presence in schools across our globe. One of the primary questions in educational research is whether and how students are effectively utilizing these to increase their achievement. This guideline is therefore focused on attempting to assess and guide such usage both in and out of their classes. At lower levels, the learner will be found using technologies in more simplistic ways (e.g., using a word processing software to write papers) that do not require more advanced technical skills. At higher levels, the learner will be observed using more sophisticated and possibly even discipline-specific software packages and skill sets (e.g., SPSS, augmented/virtual reality, coding in HTML/CSS) to help them complete assignments and/or improve their competencies. Overall, one of the primary aims of this technology usage is for the learner to gain the competencies they will need in order to more effectively utilize relevant technologies in their personal, civic, and/or professional lives, in addition to helping to improve their learning and development.

As discussed in the next chapter for this guideline, God uses technologies of all sorts to help achieve his aims. For the learner, the invitation is therefore to discern which technologies that God is inviting them to utilize so that he can more effectively help them to grow educationally in the ways that he is leading them towards. In addition, as asserted in Appendix A, from an incarnational theological perspective, God's life is also active within and through the technologies themselves. Following this, the learner must discern where and how God is likely working through the technologies that they are called to use so that they can more clearly discern how best to partner with his technological life. Overall, the goal is for the learner to discern where and how God is calling them to engage with technology so that their educational aims are realized in ways that harmonize with God's life within and through the technologies themselves.

Level 1

The learner makes use of relevant technologies in simpler ways to support their learning. Their technology engagement might support but does not fundamentally alter their learning strategies and only very basic technology skills are used by the learner.

At this level, the learners will be observed using technology to support their educational journey in ways that are more of a convenient "means-to-an-end" rather than being integral to their own learning processes. In addition, their technology use will only require basic technical competencies. Here, the learner will therefore be observed actively using technology to support their learning, but in shorter and more simplistic ways.

At this level, God's work with the learner through the technology is one that is more for the sake of convenience and efficiency. For instance, in writing a paper using word processing software can make editing, formatting, citations, and revisions much easier. Engagement with God's technological life is therefore more focused on using the tool quickly and easily to accomplish a specific task that is part of the learning activity. As a result, spiritual discernment of which technology to use may be driven mostly by practicality and usefulness.

Examples of this might include:

- The learner is observed using their device (e.g., computer, tablet, smartphone) to take notes.
- Learner participates in online discussion boards.
- The learner can state how they have used online resources (e.g., videos, blogs, articles) to help them better understand course concepts.
- Learner is observed using software to manage and format citations for a course paper.

Level 2

The learner expands the options for their own responsible use of relevant and more interactive technologies to improve their learning. The technologies are integral to their engagement with learning experiences and intermediate technical skills may be required.

Moving beyond Level 1, learners at this level will be observed proactively engaging with more sophisticated technologies to improve their knowledge/skills. Such usage will involve technology that is integral to the learning process by requiring more direct engagement with these concepts/skills via the technology. This level might also require the learner to have and/or develop more sophisticated technological skills in order to be able to effectively use these kinds of technologies. Overall, there will therefore be evidence of the learner using such technologies (as part of their courses and/or on their own) to achieve their learning goals.

At this level, the integration of God's educational and technological life begins to become more apparent. The technologies that the learner is utilizing will require them to progress in their learning journey more directly by having them engage with and practice the KSAs via the technologies themselves. Here, we can see God's life within and through the specific technology working to help the student learn and develop as a direct result of their interactions with the technology. In other words, just as God works through instructors, peers, and mentors to help the student to learn, we can start to see how God can also work through technology to help achieve God's educational aims for the student.

At this level, another part of this work is to help the learner continue to develop their technical competencies in an increasingly technological world. One can see these changes through a negative lens, but we can also see it as another arena through which God is manifesting his multitudinous and infinite life that we are called to partner with. Such theological claims become clearer at this level as the God of education and technology harmonize more fully to help the learner to grow. The student is therefore invited to discerningly partner with God's educational technologies on their path of lifelong learning.

Examples of this might include:

- The learner is observed creating a digital image collage in order to help them better understand course concepts.
- Learners are observed submitting digital storytelling projects in place of written papers for an assignment.
- The learner can describe online interactive sites and/or apps that they are using to help them better understand concepts and/or practice skills.
- The instructor can show interactive e-learning modules that the learner has been required to complete.

Level 3

The learner collaborates with others in identifying relevant interactive technologies that redefine their learning strategies in significant ways. The technologies are essential in order to engage in the learning experiences and advanced technical skills may also be required.

At this highest level, the learner will be found engaging with more sophisticated technologies, ones that have activities that would be very difficult to complete without the use of technology as the technology itself redefines the nature of the activity. These technologies should be observed facilitating the learner's direct engagement with course concepts/skills and they may require more advanced technical skills in order to be effectively utilized. In addition, there should be some evidence of the learner collaborating with others in choosing and implementing these technologies.

The theological assertions of the previous level continue with this one, but to a much greater extent. In some cases, such as with intelligent tutoring systems, the technologies themselves are directly guiding the student through specific learning processes and activities. It is here that one can see God's educational life fully at work within and through the technologies themselves. At this level, as stated above, the technology is the primary medium for the learning experience and the student is therefore invited to discerningly partner with God's life as it works through the technology to help them achieve their educational aims. Such spiritual discernment should be done communally, and the engagement with the technologies should help the learner continue to develop more advanced technical competencies. In doing so, the learner will therefore be better equipped to respond to and partner with God's educational technology life for the advancement of themselves, their communities, and ultimately our world.

Examples of this might include:

- Working with others, the learner is observed collaborating via online technologies with a community from another part of the world to complete a real-world project together.
- The learner works with their classmates to use an intelligent tutoring system or virtual simulation software to help them to better understand concepts and/or practice relevant skills.
- As part of one of their courses, the learner works with their group to create an e-learning module that other groups will complete.
- The learner works with their study group to develop a website so that they can communicate and collaborate together more effectively.

Guideline #4—Real-world Applications

The learner seeks to adapt relevant KSAs to address real-world issues in authentic contexts

Following this guideline, the learner will recognize the importance of being able to apply the KSAs that they are learning in real-world situations. Doing so will not only help them with transference of these KSAs to authentic situations but it will also aid in helping these KSAs to be more relevant and meaning to them, which is an important part of fostering deeper learning. As the learner moves from Level 1 to Level 3, they will be observed moving from simply engaging KSAs within authentic settings/scenarios towards more actively identifying and directly addressing specific real-world problems in close collaboration with others. Overall, the learner should to be able to utilize KSAs in ways that are directly related to the authentic settings of their personal, professional, and/or civic lives.

It can be asserted that while learning is full of truth, beauty, and goodness in and of itself, it should often, if not always, also have particular aims in mind. It might further be argued that one of these aims is to better empower the learner to more fully partner with God's transforming life in the world. To help achieve this aim, the learner must begin relating and applying what they are learning as soon as they are able to in the real-world situations that God is calling them into. As stated above, doing so will not only help them attune to the kinds of learning that God is actively working with on with them, it will also help them continually practice partnering with God to have the kinds of impact on the real-world situations that God is readily working with them towards.

Level 1

The learner seeks to apply course KSAs in authentic contexts/scenarios in direct and unmodified ways.

Here, the learner will be found working to take the concepts/skills that they are working to develop their competencies in and apply these in real-world situations. At this level, such KSA applications will be will be direct and unmodified. This means that the learner will only seek to apply the KSAs in the exactly the same way as they have been introduced to them, without any kind of adaptations or modifications (KSA adaptations and modifications are a Level 2 competency according to this guideline.) In addition, such applications will have the primary purpose of helping the learner better acquire the concepts/skills rather than attempting to address a specific real-world problem/issue (again, this is a Level 2 competency.) By participating in these kinds of activities, the learner will therefore have the added benefit of engaging with KSAs in similar contexts/scenarios as they will need to apply them in their professional, civic, and/or personal lives.

At this level, we might assert that God is working to help the learner begin the process of using the concepts/skills that they are learning in real-world situations. Concept/skill adaptations require a strong foundational understanding, and this level is intended to help the learner strengthen these foundations. This level can also be seen God working with the student in simpler ways to help them learn the necessary basics of partnering with God in real-world situations. Being mindful of the very real possibilities of cognitive overload that can come with attempting to apply course concepts/skills, along with the complex dynamics of real-world contexts, it might be claimed that God is attempting to scaffold the student's growth. As a result, the learner is encouraged to seek to partner with God as they move from the classroom to these real-world situations.

Examples of this might include:

- The learner is observed engaging in role-playing activities that mimic real-world situations.

- The learner is observed practicing a skill in a real-world setting (e.g., taking blood pressures at a community center, learning how to collect water samples from a local creek, etc.).

- The learner can describe immersion trips that they have participated in that have had the primary purpose of exposing them to specific contexts to learn about course concepts, but not addressing specific issues/problems in the community.

- The learner has taken classes that met in real-world settings (e.g., hospitals, public schools, community centers).

Level 2

The learner works to adapt relevant KSAs for authentic contexts/scenarios in order to address a given real-world problem or issue.

Extending beyond Level 1, at this level the learner will work to address a given problem, or they will engage with a real-world issue that they might be expected to find in an authentic context. As part of this work, the learner will be observed adapting key KSAs in significant ways. This requires a higher level of competency on the part of the learner compared with Level 1, where they merely had to apply what they have learned in direct and unmodified ways. This level is therefore distinguished from the previous level by: 1) the learner addressing a real-world issue that has been provided by instructors/staff and/or community partner(s), and 2) these activities requiring them to modify relevant KSAs in significant ways in order to address these problems/issues.

From a theological perspective, we might claim that God is helping the student learn how to partner with God more fully in the world. Here, the learner seeks to engage with real-world problems in ways that require them to adapt what they are learning in order to more appropriately address these issues. It is a task that compels their spiritual discernment to progress beyond direct and unmodified application of concepts/skills by inviting them to see how the actual situation or issue demands a slightly altered version of these concepts/skills. Such refined insights represent a more advanced level of both discernment and understanding of the concepts/skills. God may therefore be seen as working with the learner to progress towards these more refined insights, and the learner is therefore invited to seek out such opportunities in spiritually discerning ways.

Examples of this might include:

- The learner is observed adapting course skills (such as healthcare skills, conflict mediation, strategic planning, and web development) to help an organization.
- The learner can describe work that they have completed for a community organization where they have adapted the concepts/skills they are learning in their classes to these community settings.
- The learner is observed working with peers to adapt problem solving strategies for real-world case studies.
- Staff can state how they have worked with the learner to complete a service-learning project in the community where the learner had to adapt relevant concepts/skills as part of their analyses and planning.

Level 3

Working with others, the learner identifies real-world problems or issues in authentic contexts/scenarios that require KSA adaptations and they develop and implement plans to directly address these issues.

Level 3, as with many other guidelines, is more collaborative in nature in that the learner will be found working with others to identify real-world problems or issues and then engage with these within authentic contexts/scenarios. This therefore differs from Level 2 where the learner was provided with a real-world issue by their instructor, a staff member, or an organization. However, this level also builds upon Level 2 by still requiring significant adaptations to be made to relevant KSAs. Overall, the focus for this level is therefore on learners having more collaborative responsibility and leadership with peers, staff, instructors, and/or community partners in identifying real-world issues and then working to find effective ways to address these issues by adapting relevant KSAs in relation to their authentic contexts.

At this highest level, the learner has achieved significant milestones in partner with God in their personal, professional, and/or civic lives. In its more theologically ideal form, the learner will have learned how to partner with others in this work. They will also have developed the skills needed to discerningly assess which community issues are more important as well as how to adapt key concepts/skills in ways that more directly and effectively address these issues. In some ways, this level represents one of the core theological aims of education: a learner who is able to use their KSAs to better partner with God in addressing specific community issues in transformative ways. The learner is therefore admonished to actively seek these kinds of experiences with the help of mentors and peers.

Examples of this might include:

- There is evidence of the learner working with a community partner to conduct an asset/needs assessment and create a plan to address identified assets/needs via adapting relevant course KSAs.

- The learner is observed partnering with an organization to complete a Continuous Quality Improvement (CQI) project that aligns with their own learning objectives and results in recommendations being made to the organization.

- The learner can describe specific volunteer experiences where they completed an advocacy project that they were passionate about that included working with an organization to strategize and/or work towards making change. They should also be able to state how this project has helped them to further develop their competencies as a student.

- As part of one of their courses and/or a study group, the learner is observed working with their classmates to generate case studies that require their peers to use modified versions of course KSAs.

Guideline #5—Scaffolding Guidance

The learner engages in activities in ways that consistently scaffolds their increasing competencies for key KSAs.

While the other guidelines in this area are more focused on specific activities that the learner might engage with, this one centers more on how the learner organizes and manages their engagement with these activities. The learner, according to this guideline, should minimally move through their learning and development in a step-by-step manner. This means that the concepts and skills that they are learning should build upon previous ones. The learner should also work to ensure that they are generally competent in core KSAs before moving on to subsequent ones. At higher levels, the learner will partner with others in developing and selecting varied pathways that support their own growth in core course KSAs. These pathways should be tailored to better match their own unique backgrounds and capabilities. Such pathways should also support scaffolding wherein the learner's progress towards advanced KSAs is dependent upon the achievement of given levels of competency for the more basic KSAs that these advanced topics/skills are founded upon. Overall, this guideline is therefore focused on how the learner engages in their learning experiences.

Lifespan developmental (as well as education research) studies document the progressive nature of human learning and growth.[10] A student doesn't understand the finer technical nuances of calculus without first learning basic arithmetic. Following the incarnational and non-dualistic theology of this book, based upon these studies we can assert that God seeks to guide each student through their learning journey in ways that build upon previous capabilities and concepts. As a result, the learner is therefore encouraged to continually discern where and how the Spirit is leading them next as they move through course content and learning experiences. While this learning journey can be nonlinear, with spontaneous breakthroughs and/or spiral learning trajectories, this journey can still be expected to continually and gradually build upon prior competencies. The student should therefore seek to partner with and respond to God's educational life as God works to scaffold their learning development in a step-by-step manner. Overall, this guideline should help the learner to discern where they are on the learning journey and how God is inviting them to progress next.

---

10. See the references for this guideline in the next chapter.

Level 1

The learner seeks out activities that repeatedly engage key KSAs and scaffolds their growing competencies in these areas (i.e., ensures achievement before moving on to new KSAs).

Numerous educational research studies have and continue to show that repeated and distributed engagement with core KSAs is better than engaging with these KSAs in a very intense and shorter period of time. As a result, there should be clear evidence that the learner is continually engaging with key concepts/skills as they work to attain competencies in these areas. In pursuit of these competencies, the learner will be observed moving through core KSAs in scaffolding ways. This means that the learner will proactively work to ensure that they adequately grasp foundational KSAs in deeper ways before moving on to newer and more complex ones. Overall, then, a learner at this level will show evidence of working to master key KSAs in scaffolded ways.

Life with God can be viewed as a marathon, especially when viewed through the eyes of eternity. Cultivating a similar view of learning, the student is invited at this level to realize more fully that their spiritually guided learning will come one step at a time (though quick sprints in learning are also common). This foundational level can therefore help the learner to be very intentional about discerning which core KSAs they are strong in and where they need more work so that they can better ensure that they are well-prepared before moving onto more advanced KSAs. A central part of this level, then, also includes discerning which learning activities to engage with in order to help them to address their weaker areas. Overall, the student's faith in God's ever guiding hand should continue to deepen as they progressively move throughout their lifelong learning journey.

Examples of this might include:

- The learner makes use of learning modules that help them master foundational concepts before moving onto more advanced ones.
- The learner is observed using self-check/assessment activities to ensure that they understand core topics.
- The learner can show evidence of studying key concepts/skills repeatedly over an extended period of time.
- The learner is observed seeking out additional resources (e.g., tutoring, online videos) to help them better understand topics that will be foundational for subsequent ones.

Level 2

The learner engages with a variety of sequenced resources and learning experiences that scaffolds their competencies for key KSAs and are matched to their own experiences, needs, and interests.

Level 2 builds upon the activities of Level 1 but does so in more varied ways. Here, the learner will be found scaffolding their learning by seeking out multiple and varied activities. At Level 1, the learner may simply participate in class or meet with a tutor and follow the single learning path that has been set by the instructor/tutor. At Level 2, however, there will be strong evidence of the learner taking initiative to seek out multiple and diverse learning activities to scaffold their progress. There should also be strong evidence of the learner choosing multiple and varied learning activities that are better matched to their own unique background, learning preferences, and interests. At Level 1, the learner may simply utilize resources and support systems that are most convenient and readily available. At Level 2, however, the learner will be more discerning in choosing the ones that are a better match for themselves personally.

This level also represents a more sophisticated understanding of God's action in their learning journey. Rather than viewing God as providing a "one-size-fits-all" approach to education, a student at this level will implicitly know that God ever seeks to tailor their learning to the infinitely unique gifts, passions, and experiences of each individual. As a result, the student will strive to engage with multiple and varied study strategies and aides that collectively catalyze their rate of learning. Such spiritual discernment will therefore include ongoing evaluation and modifications of these strategies and support systems so that the learner continues to progress.

Examples of this might include:

- The learner is observed seeking multiple ways of learning about core concepts/skills (e.g., lecture, demonstration, videos, etc.).
- The learner can describe multiple learning activities that they have used to help them to better understand/demonstrate key concepts/skills.
- The instructor is observed helping the learner to choose an assignment to complete that better matches the student's background and interests from among a wide range of possibilities.
- The learner can demonstrate how they are using supplemental apps or other software to help them learn course concepts or practice key skills.

Level 3

The learner collaborates with others in identifying sustained and varied pathways to the development of key KSAs using a range of resources, learning experiences, and ways of demonstrating scaffolded progress towards these relevant KSAs.

Similar to Level 2, a learner at Level 3 for this guideline will still seek out multiple and varied pathways to engaging with core concepts and skills. At this level, however, the learner will collaboratively work with others to help them develop these varied and scaffolded pathways. Here, there is a much greater emphasis on working directly with others to help them develop their self-regulated learning skills as they collaboratively create these varied and scaffolded learning paths.

Similar to many other guidelines, the emphasis at this most sophisticated level is on collaboration. Here, the learner will seek out competent and trusted peers and mentors to help them engage in their spiritual discernment processes related to scaffolded learning. The student will be found proactively seeking out ideas, advice, and feedback that helps them: 1) more clearly asses their current competencies, and 2) identify and develop strategies and activities that will help strengthen these current competencies before moving onto more advanced ones. Theologically, we can assert that God is working at this level within and among all who are involved in these communal discernment processes to help the learner to continue to grow in a step-by-step manner. Throughout these processes, we should therefore see God helping the student to further develop their collaborative self-regulated learning skills.

Examples of this might include:

- The learner works with their instructor and classmates to create a rubric that outlines the scaffolded progress (i.e., different levels of competency) that learners in the class will need to demonstrate across the course.
- The learner is part of a study group that uses supplemental textbooks and articles to help them study for exams.
- The learner is observed working with a tutor to help them map out a scaffolded study plan that will enable them to be more successful in one of their courses.
- The learner is taking a class where they are required to work with other students as well as with the instructor(s) to identify the articles, videos, and books that each learner will use to develop their course competencies.

Guideline #6—Caring Learning Environment

Mission-Centered Focus: The learner helps to nurture a learning environment that is safe, inclusive, and caring.

Some cognitive science studies have shown that we learn and retain more when we are less stressed, so learning in these kinds of environments is particularly important for education.[11] Learning, as may be seen by these Educational System Guidelines, is an iterative process of trial-and-error, continuous feedback, and ongoing efforts to continually improve. As a result, the learner should seek to help their schools be safe spaces that allow for risk-taking without fear of failure, encourage free and positively supported exploration of ideas and diverse perspectives, and ones in which participants support and challenge one another in affirming and constructive ways. In order to help facilitate such learning environments, there needs to be clear expectations that the learner not only adheres to but also takes an active part in developing. Overall, then, the trend across these levels is from the learner more simply following the behavioral expectations that have been set by the institution towards their collaborating with others to set these expectations. When assessing a learner for this guideline, we can therefore look at the extent to which the learner is involved in both setting these expectations as well as proactively working to nurture these kinds of learning environments.

A fuller version of God's kin-dom is one in which not just individuals manifest and respond to God's life, but whole communities, organizations, and systems as well. As this relates to our school systems, it might be asserted that the learner is therefore invited to discern where and how God has been and continues to work to manifest his communal compassion, constructive critiques, and positive coaching. With such spiritual awareness, the learner can then more clearly determine how they can be a more proactive part of participating in and responding to God's life in these ways. The learner's goal, according to this guideline, is to therefore partner with God to further foster a positive, safe, and inclusive learning environment in which all students can spiritually thrive.

Level 1

The learner adheres to explicit expectations for a safe and positive learning environment and their behavior demonstrates respect and caring for others.

At Level 1, the learner will be observed following given expectations for a safe, inclusive, and caring learning environment. Such adherence should not only occur when instructors and staff are present, but at all times. At this level, there will therefore be clear evidence of the learner interacting with others in ways that are congruent with the school's behavioral expectations as well as the learner positively and proactively working to ensure that they are adhered to.

At this foundational level, theologically speaking, the learner will recognize that behavioral expectations are essentially the school's attempt to codify God's enduring movements of love in the community. In other words, these policies and expectations should outline what the school has spiritually discerned are necessary foundations for safe and healthy learning environments (i.e., learning environments that are more

---

11. See references for this guideline in the next chapter.

manifesting of God's educational life and love). Recognizing this, the learner will be found at this level embodying these guidelines. Ideally, for a learner who is more genuinely seeking to live a more spiritual life, they will do so without much effort or cognitive consideration as the work that God is doing within them will naturally align with the work that God is doing in the communities to which the learner is called.

However, as a cautionary note, school faculty, staff, and administration must also remember at least two possibilities for existing policies: 1) the school's behavioral expectations may not fully reflect the work that God is doing in their community, and/or 2) God is seeking to continually improve upon what he has been able to do in the school in the past. As a result, when a learner violates one of these rules, great care and discernment must be taken to recognize if the rule itself is what needs to be changed rather than or in addition to the student. 2,000 years of Western Christian history have clearly shown that God's life is fully organic and ever-adapts with each new generation,[12] so we can expect that God is striving to help this planet and our educational systems to continually progress towards greater embodiments of his life. At this level, then, the learner is invited to be aware of the school's expectations and discern how they might live in accordance with them, thereby helping God's life and kin-dom thrive more fully.

Examples of this might include:

- The learner is observed affirming others' efforts (e.g., saying "Good job," thanking others for their help, etc.).
- The learner is observed correcting others when they act in ways contrary to given expectations (e.g., asking a classmate to put their phone away, redirecting a peer who is off-task).
- The learner is observed affirming others when they share their diverse beliefs, viewpoints, and answers.
- The learner intervenes when one of their peers acts negatively towards another classmate.

Level 2

In addition to Level 1, the learner proactively engages in activities that help to foster a learning environment of respectful interactions, mutual support, and individual/group responsibility for the learning environment.

Level 2 includes the previous level's recommendations where the learner adheres to clear behavioral expectations for the learning contexts that they are a part of. However, the student then goes beyond Level 1 when they actively seek out and participate in activities that intentionally facilitate safe, inclusive, and caring interactions.

12. Kyle, *Sacred Systems*.

Overall, the goal here is for the learner to actively seek out opportunities where they can intentionally practice these expectations. It is one thing to have clear expectations that the learner minimally complies with (Level 1), but quite another for them to proactively participate in projects and activities where they are required to utilize these expectations (Level 2).

At this level, God's invitations for the learner entail greater responsibility and leadership. Here, the learner will be found spiritually discerning and actively engaging with opportunities that further challenge themselves and others to help nurture more of God's safe, inclusive, and caring life as outlined by the school's behavioral expectations. Moving beyond responding to God's life within their own zone of activity, the learner at this level becomes a more active participant and leader in helping the wider community embody such care and inclusivity. Such efforts can be well-planned and pre-arranged, but they can also be a natural part of how the learner engages with those around them.

Examples of this might include:

- The learner is observed participating in a class debate where they are led by their instructor in positive and constructive ways, engaging with viewpoints and opinions that are different from their own.
- The learner is involved in a curricular or co-curricular leadership position where they are expected to model specific behavioral expectations for the community (e.g., demonstrating academic excellence, supporting anti-hate initiatives, etc.).
- There is evidence of the learner selecting projects where they have to interact with people/communities that are different from themselves in ways that are safe, caring, and inclusive.
- As a team leader, the learner is observed coaching their peers in relation to behavioral expectations as they work on a small group activity.

Level 3

The learner collaborates with others in developing and applying expectations for a learning climate that includes openness, mutual respect, and positive peer relationships.

This level includes the previous levels' recommendations for having clear behavioral expectations that the learner is committed to. However, at this level, the learner will also be found working with others to develop and implement these expectations. A learner at this level is therefore someone who is more collaboratively involved in developing expectations that are more meaningful for themselves and others.

As asserted above, God's organic life ever-adapts to each new cohort of students. In line with Level 3 of other guidelines, this level embodies collaborative approaches to fostering safe, caring, and inclusive learning environments. The learner will therefore be found participating in communal spiritual discernment processes that clarify the kinds of behaviors and interactions that God can be more fully manifested through. Such engagement will not only help the learner to be more aware of where and how God is actively seeking to nurture positive learning environments, but God's life should be more tangibly present within and among the discerning group. At this highest level, then, the learner will be a more intimate part of God's organizational development life as God continually works to build safe, inclusive, and caring learning environments in which all students, faculty, and staff can thrive.

Examples of this might include:

- The learner participates in a small group that has worked to set their own ground rules for how they will interact and resolve conflicts together.
- The learner is an active participant in a course where the instructor has led students through a brainstorming process to generate behavioral expectations for the class.
- The learner is observed modeling expectations that have been developed collaboratively with others.
- The learner is observed correcting others when they act in ways contrary to expectations that have been established cooperatively.

TEACHING/LEARNING THEORY GUIDELINES

Without a map, it is difficult to know where to go. Such an analogy applies to learning processes. By better understanding the theories, strategies, and methods of learning, students will be in a much better position to help themselves and one another to learn more effectively. This collection of guidelines therefore has the goal of encouraging students learn more about these theories, strategies, and methods. In doing so, they should be better enabled to develop the knowledge and skills to more closely partner with God in their learning processes.

Guideline #1—Holistic Teaching and Learning Theories

Learner is able to articulate: a) specific holistic learning theories that they might utilize, and b) when and how these theories might apply to their own learning.

What a learner believes about learning and development and can greatly influence the learning strategies that they utilize. For instance, a learner who believes that they learn best via rote memorization will likely approach their studying differently from someone who thinks that learning happens by building on their own prior knowledge via applying, analyzing, and/or evaluating using the concepts/skills they are learning about. As a result of this claim, this guideline is intended to help learners to reflect upon their understanding of learning processes. Overall, the trend is from simply being more explicit about these theories to drawing from multiple ones to help guide how they study.

Like having a map that helps one to get to where they are going, the better that one understands where and how God is active within and to them the better they will be able to partner with his work. This guideline therefore captures and encourages the learner to more fully understand how God has worked within and through learning processes. By understanding and applying learning theories, the learner will be empowered to more clearly discern how God might be laboring to work within them to continue to advance in their studies. As the levels below outline, such awareness can be quite complex. The learner is therefore invited to join with others in their ongoing spiritual discernment that is related to their ever-growing understandings and applications of learning theories.

Level 1

The learner is able to articulate their own holistic understanding of learning and development and seeks to adjust their study strategies in light of these understandings.

At this level, the learner will be able to explicitly state what their own views of holistic learning and development are and how they are using these models to inform and guide their study strategies. The learner does not necessarily need to be able to label these learning theories (e.g., "constructivism," "information processing"). Rather, it is more important they are able to clearly articulate: 1) the processes by which they believe they holistically learn/develop, 2) strategies they can use to help themselves grow along these paths (i.e., strategies that align with their understandings of learning processes), and 3) how they have chosen study habits that support such learning and development (i.e., habits that align with their learning theories). Overall, inconsistencies between these theories and how they are studying should be pointed out at this level.

At this foundational level, the learner is invited to reflect on and discern where and how they believe that God has and continues to work to help them learn more deeply. Here, there should be some level of clarity on how they have learned past concepts and skills. This clarity is itself a work of God within the learner, and the learner is invited to seek such understanding of learning processes in spiritual discerning ways. As part of these efforts, the learner might turn to resources on learning theories, using these as a tool to provide further insights on how their own learning happens. Overall, the learner at this level will be able to articulate a basic understanding of how God works via their learning processes, and identify specific ways they seek to partner with God's educational life within them via their study strategies.

Examples of this might include:

- The learner is able to state the general processes by which they believe learning happens.
- The learner articulates how their study strategies help them learn more effectively.
- The learner is observed using study strategies that directly align with their stated understanding of learning processes (e.g., they believe that learning happens best via real-world scenarios and they are observed using case studies to help them prepare for an exam).
- Study groups are observed discussing what strategies they should use to prepare for a test and how these relate to their understanding of learning.

Level 2

The learner uses observations of their own and others' progress as well as evidence-based resources to inform their own holistic learning theories. Based upon this information, they adjust their study strategies.

Level 2 extends beyond Level 1 when the learner reflects upon their own and others' experiences and how they seem to be holistically learning and developing. These reflections can be based upon assessment data and/or conversations with others about this topic. The learner should then be able to compare this information with their own views of holistic learning and development and note similarities and differences. Finally, by additionally drawing from evidence-based holistic learning theories, the learner should then be able to articulate how they are using this synthesized knowledge to modify and improve their study strategies.

Level 1 reflections will be primarily based upon personal ideas and experiences with learning. At this level, however, the learner will look to assessment-based data to support their assertions of how learning happens for them but also the successfulness of the study strategies they are using. In essence, they will be looking for confirmations of their Level 1 spiritual discernment processes about their theories of learning. In further support of their discernment, the learner will also turn to evidence-based educational resources. These resources, as argued in other parts of this book, can help the learner better understand how God has and continues to successfully work via others' learning processes. Given the similarities of the human species' neuro-psychic-social functioning, such insights might therefore help the learner to more clearly discern God's work in their own educational journey. This level therefore expands upon the learner's understandings of and partnership with God's life within and through their learning processes.

Examples of this might include:

- The learner can state how they have used their performance on exams and papers to understand how they learn best in their classes.

- The learner can identify specific evidence-based learning theories to inform their understanding of learning processes.

- The learner is a part of a study group that is observed using a specific evidence-based study strategy (e.g., distributed practice, mnemonic devices, concept mapping) and can state how these strategies relate to their views of learning.

- The learner can articulate how their understanding of learning processes is based upon both evidence-based theories and their self-observations of how they seem to learn best.

Level 3

Recognizing that they might learn and develop in diverse ways for different situations, and building on Level 2, the learner collaborates with others to develop and utilize multiple evidence-based holistic learning theories to help guide their learning. They are also able to articulate when and how each theory is being utilized.

This more complex level further builds upon the previous level when the learner is able to articulate how a diversity of learning theories is needed to support their own holistic learning and development. In other words, a student at this level will recognize that different kinds of KSAs require different theories in order to maximize their learning for each KSA. For instance, if they are studying for an exam that will have many terms and definitions, then they might look to cognitive psychology theories of memory to help them choose study strategies that will better help them to memorize these terms. Alternatively, if they their exam is a demonstration of specific skills, then they might look to skill development learning theories to help them prepare. This level therefore represents an intellectual advancement for learners in relation to these theories/strategies when they come to realize that one holistic learning theory is usually not sufficient to provide the kinds of nuanced and more complex insights and guidance that are needed when working with diverse KSAs. The learner should therefore be able to clearly articulate why and how multiple holistic theories are needed to direct their learning strategies. Finally, and related to other guidelines, Level 3 here is intended to support more collaborative engagement with others as the learner works to develop and use these multiple theories to support their learning.

Given the complexity of neurophysiological, psychological, and social-cultural learning processes, the learner at this level should be able to articulate a more sophisticated understanding of how they learn. In essence, the learner will realize that God necessarily works with them in different ways for different situations. In response, there will therefore be evidence of the learner looking to multiple learning theories to help guide their study strategies. Following Level 2 competencies, they will continue to look to assessment-based evidence to validate their selection and use of these different learning theories. Clearly, this is a complicated level of engagement with God's educational life. As a result, the learner should work closely with others to help them in these spiritual discernment processes. Overall, at this level, we might assert that God is seeking to help the learner develop a more sophisticated understanding of how God works via their learning processes so that the learner can better partner with God in these ways.

Examples of this might include:

- The learner is able to identify two or more evidence-based learning theories that have worked with others to help guide their study strategies.
- The learner can state how they have worked with others and used their performance on exams, papers, etc. in addition to two or more evidence-based learning theories to better understand how they learn best in their classes.
- The learner is part of a study group that is observed using multiple study strategies to prepare for an exam and can identify two or more learning theories to support the use of these strategies.
- Staff/instructor(s) can state how they have worked with the learner to improve their study strategies using two or more evidence-based learning theories.

Guideline #2—Active Teaching and Learning Strategies

Learner utilizes active learning strategies to support their learning and development.

Increasingly over the past few decades, educational literature has given a central emphasis on the use of active teaching and learning strategies. For learners, this means using study strategies that empower them to engage with KSAs in more active ways. In particular, the following active learning strategies are repeatedly highlighted in the literature as being high impact practices: elaboration and self-reflections; self-regulated learning and study strategies; direct instruction or modeling followed by learner practice; peer teaching/tutoring; concept mapping; class discussions, debate; problem solving, problem-based learning; real-world and clinical simulations; inquiry-based pedagogies; real-world projects, service-learning; workplace experiences, internships; role-playing; and game-based strategies.

As this list suggests, there are numerous strategies that the learner can draw from to support their learning. The challenge to using these strategies are twofold: 1) choosing which learning strategy(ies) to use, and 2) how to adapt them for the learner's purposes. Overall, the trend for this guideline is from using these strategies in basic ways towards the learner developing multiple evidence-based strategies in collaboration with others. In addition, as the learner moves to higher levels, the strategies should more closely match their background, interests, and capabilities while simultaneously ensuring that these active learning strategies foster genuine progress towards their learning goals.

As the previous guideline alluded to, learning and development is a complex set of processes that requires a myriad of theories to even begin to understand. Even more holistic views of human nature are quite complex in the frameworks they depict.[13] As this relates to study strategies, one can assert that God is actively striving to engage with the learner via all of these learning avenues. In other words, a theistic view of active learning strategies is that God labors to dynamically and holistically work with the learner in a myriad of ways, ways that have them engage as fully as possible. It is a great tragedy when learners (and school systems) rely almost solely on lecture-based and cognitive-only strategies. Educational and psychological research is finally verifying a reality that has been long known by many religious and spiritual traditions: growth and development happens most effectively when the whole person (e.g., mind, body, heart, relationships, society, etc.) is involved in these processes. God may therefore be asserted to be working to help the student learn and develop simultaneously via all of these channels, and the learner is therefore invited through this guideline to identify and utilize study strategies that are more active and holistic.

Level 1

Drawing on specific active learning strategies, the learner seeks to apply these to help improve their learning and development.

Level 1 is achieved by the learner with the acknowledgement of their use of active learning strategies. The learner should be able to articulate/demonstrate what strategy(ies) they have chosen and how these are being used to help them to progress towards their learning goals. These strategies should be more than merely reading, highlighting, or copying notes. Rather, these learning approaches should have the learner engage with the concepts/skills in ways that require them to manipulate, create with, apply, and critique these KSAs. These strategies can be engaged on their own, with peers and study groups, or as a part of one or more of their classes. Overall, these learning strategies should clearly help the learner actively engage with relevant KSAs.

At this foundational level, from the theistic view being developed in this text, the learner will recognize that God is seeking to work with them in more dynamic and holistic ways. They will therefore work to utilize study strategies that are more actively engaging for them. Through these strategies, the learner has the opportunity to recognize God's more energetic educational life working with them. A part of this shift for the learner can be the image of God moving from being a more authoritarian "sage-on-the-stage," telling them what they need to know, towards more of a "guide-by-side" (as well as within them), where the Spirit is viewed as an incarnational companion helping them learn through these active learning strategies. In this way, the learner's theological views of learning can move from passive to more active ways of engaging with God in their educational journey.

13. For examples of such models, see: Kyle, *Spiritual Being & Becoming*.

Examples of this might include:

- The learner is able to articulate which study strategies they are using and how these strategies require active engagement.
- The learner can state how they have reflected on their own progress in one or more of their classes and then developed a plan for improving their achievement through active study strategies.
- The learner is observed participating in class discussions/debates or other active teaching strategies.
- The learner is observed working with their study group to assess each other's work and offer suggestions of how to improve through active study strategies.

Level 2

The learner utilizes one or more evidence-based active learning strategies and is able to articulate how they have adapted these strategies to fit with the classes they are currently taking.

This level further extends upon the previous one when the learner is able to articulate/demonstrate how they are using specific evidence-based active learning strategies (see a beginning list of such strategies above). Ideally, they should be able to identify specific evidence-based source(s) (e.g., articles, workshops they have attended, their instructors, etc.) that they are relying on, as well as how they are currently using these strategies. Finally, the learner should be able to state/demonstrate what adaptations they have made to these active strategies based upon the classes they are currently taking. These strategies, as with the previous level, can be engaged either as a part of one of their classes and/or on their own initiative.

From a spiritual discernment perspective, this level represents an advancement in sophistication. Here, the learner will additionally look to how God has and continues to successfully work with others to improve learning processes via active study strategies (i.e., evidence-based educational resources). The student will also then seek to discern how these evidence-based strategies need to be modified so they are equally impactful for themselves and the classes/KSAs that God is currently working with them to develop in. Overall, the learner at this level strives to partner with God in more impactful and evidence-based ways that are discerningly tailored for their current courses.

Examples of this might include:

- The learner actively participates in evidence-based class activities.

- The learner can state which active evidence-based study strategies they are using and can name which source(s) support the use of these strategies as well as how they are adapting these in light of the classes they are currently taking.
- The learner is observed participating in a study group that uses evidence-based learning strategies.
- The learner attends a workshop where they learn about and then use evidence-based study strategies as well as how to adapt these for the classes they are currently taking.

Level 3

Recognizing they learn and develop in diverse ways, the learner collaborates with others in utilizing multiple evidence-based active learning strategies to help support their learning and development, and they can articulate how they have adapted these strategies to fit with the classes they are currently taking.

Level 3 for this guideline is similar to Level 3 for other guidelines in that it is more collaborative and draws from multiple sources. The learner should be able to demonstrate clear evidence of using multiple active learning strategies. They should be able to articulate/demonstrate which strategies they are utilizing, and they should be able to point to specific evidence-based literature for each of these (similar to Level 2). Beyond this, the learner should also be observed working with others to select and adapt these strategies such that they increase their competencies in ways that are relevant for the classes they are currently taking. Collaboratively, they should work to ensure that these individualized pathways are congruent with evidence-based recommendations as well as the student's learning goals.

Similar to the previous guideline at Level 3, the learner's discernment processes expand in at least two substantive ways. First, they work more intentionally with others to engage in their discernment of which evidence-based active study strategies to engage with as well as how to adapt these strategies to their current situations. Again, we should see the development of the learner's collaborative spiritual discernment processes. Second, following the previous guideline's Level 3 discussions, the learner will recognize that the inherent complexity of KSAs as well as learning processes necessitates the use of multiple study strategies. Theologically, it can be asserted that God's infinite life and complexity recognizes and adapts to the implicit uniqueness of each learning situation. As a result, different study strategies will be needed to better partner with God's ever-adapting life for each KSA, class, and context. A Level 3 learner for this guideline will therefore strive to collaboratively identify and adapt multiple evidence-based study strategies in discerning response to God's ever-changing invitations.

Examples of this might include:

- The learner actively participates in two or more evidence-based class activities.
- The learner can identify two or more evidence-based learning strategies they are using as well as how they have collaborated with others to adapt these for their current classes.
- The learner is observed participating in a study group that uses two or more evidence-based learning strategies.
- The learner attends a workshop where they learn about and then use two or more evidence-based study strategies and how to adapt these in ways that will help them be more successful in the classes they are currently taking.

Guideline #3—Course/Study Strategy Development Methods

Learner is able to demonstrate the processes/methods by which they develop their learning strategies and there is alignment among their courses and their own learning goals, study strategies, and how they assess these goals and strategies.

ADDIE, backward design, universal design for learning, and learner-centered are all examples of the many instructional design methods that students can use to help them develop their study strategies. While learners may not know the details of these specific methods, they should still be able to articulate the processes by which they are designing, implementing, and evaluating their learning approaches. This guideline is therefore intended to capture these self-regulated learning abilities. Overall, there are two trends: 1) from individually following some method to develop their study strategies towards collaborating with others and looking to evidence-based literature for help with this, and 2) there being close alignment between some of their learning theories/approaches and their classes towards this alignment existing for most of their courses' modules/units. In other words, this guideline becomes more collaborative and complex as one moves towards higher levels.

Decision-making processes, at their best, do not happen in haphazard ways. The clearer that one is about how they come to the choices they make, the greater the likelihood of making better decisions. Such is the case with one's spiritual discernment processes. When we more clearly understand the processes by which God seeks to lead us into the decisions that we make on a daily basis, the more fully we can partner with God's ever-leading life in these discernment methods. As they relate to developing one's learning strategies, the learner is therefore admonished via this guideline to articulate their discernment processes. In doing so, they will be improving their spiritual self-regulated learning skills as they continually identify, adapt, and evaluate the various study strategies that God is striving to lead them through. Successful engagement with these skills and processes should lead to strategies that are more tightly aligned and integrated with their current learning journey.

Level 1

The learner follows some process to design, implement, and evaluate their learning strategies. There is direct alignment between their courses and their own learning goals, study strategies, and how they assess these goals and strategies.

At Level 1 for this guideline, the learner should be able to clearly articulate some process or set of steps they are using to design, implement, and evaluate their study strategies. These steps might include reflecting on their own performance in past classes, looking to discipline-specific educational literature for insights into how they can learn better, or following prescribed study strategies. If a learner states they are using one or more of the instructional design methods found in the literature (e.g., ADDIE, backward design, etc.), then they should also be able to state how they are applying these to their study strategies in detailed ways. In addition, there should be clear evidence that their learning goals, study strategies, and how they assess the effectiveness of their strategies are directly aligned with the courses they are taking. For example, if one of their courses requires that they are able to demonstrate their abilities to conduct a research project, then the learner should adopt study goals and strategies that will better help them learn these methods as well as continually assess their competencies in these research project skills.

Spiritually speaking, the learner at this foundational level is essentially able to articulate how they are discerning the strategies through which God is laboring to work with them through. While the level of detail for these decision-making processes may be simple, clarity of the major steps is essential. In effect, the learner is outlining how they believe they are discerning and responding to God's invitations as they choose, adapt, and evaluate the learning strategies they are utilizing. They should also be able to articulate how these strategies are aligned to their current courses. Not only will such awareness and alignment help ensure greater impact of the strategies, theologically, this alignment is an incarnational manifestation of God's harmonizing and integrating life with and to the student. The learner should therefore be able to outline these discernment processes as well as how these processes are resulting in strategies that are closely aligned with their current classes in general ways.

Examples of this might include:

- The learner is able to clearly articulate some process or set of steps they are using to design, implement, and evaluate their study strategies.
- The learner is observed closely following a prescribed study strategy to guide their learning approaches.
- The learner is able to state how a specific study strategy/activity is directly related to one or more of the courses that they are currently taking.

Level 2

The learner draws from evidence-based literature and data to develop (e.g., design, implement, and evaluate) their learning strategies. There is direct alignment between the modules/units of their courses and their own learning goals, study strategies, and how they assess these goals and strategies.

Level 2 continues to extend the previous level. The study strategy development process articulated by the learner should now also include external evidence-based resources. There are at least two kinds of these resources: 1) external literature (e.g., educational research on learning, experts in the field), and 2) data from their own learning experiences. The learner should be able to clearly state which evidence-based resources they are utilizing and how these directly impact the learning strategies that they are using. Alignment is also further extended at this level with the module/units of their courses being directly aligned with their learning approaches. Following the framework developed for these guidelines, alignment between these course modules/units and the following elements should be verified: learning goals, study strategies, and how they are assessing the impact of these goals and strategies. In other words, the learner should be able to articulate the steps they are following to adjust their learning strategies for each week, module, or unit of their classes.

Pulling together Level 2 for the two previous guidelines, the learner at this level is spiritually seeking to partner with God's more impactful evidence-based educational life. Their spiritual discernment processes should draw upon such evidence-based resources as they strive to adapt the successful strategies and theories that God has used elsewhere to empower their own learning journey. As a result, the articulation of their discernment processes should include these evidence-based resources.

Furthermore, these processes should now also include aligning their strategies with their classes in more detailed ways. At Level 1, the learner would align these with their classes in general ways (i.e., course level objectives, assessments, activities). At this level, however, the learner will labor with God to align their strategies with the current week, modules, or units in each of their courses. As stated above, God adapts to each uniquely different learning context and the learner is therefore admonished by this guideline to continually align their learning strategies with these Spirit adaptations. As a result, the learner's discernment processes should clarify how the learner will continually respond to these adaptations as their course modules/units change.

Examples of this might include:

- The learner is observed working to improve their learning goals and study strategies by drawing upon evidence-based resources to support these improvements.
- The learner is able to identify specific evidence-based resources that they are using to support the development of their study strategies.

- The learner participates in a workshop on how to use evidence-based learning strategies.
- The learner is able to describe how their learning goals and study strategies are directly related to the modules/units of the classes that they are currently taking.

Level 3

The learner collaborates with others in evidence-based design, implementation, and evaluation of their learning strategies. There is direct alignment between the modules/units of their courses and the following: learning goals, study strategies, how they assess these, their understanding of learning processes, and their own unique background and interests.

Similar to other guidelines for this area, Level 3 builds directly upon Level 2 in more collaborative and complex ways. The learner should still be able to articulate the evidence-based steps by which they are developing their learning strategies, but these steps should now include collaboration with others. The learner should be able to clearly state which people they are working with and how these collaborations are directly impacting their ongoing evidence-based changes to their learning approaches. Alignment of their study strategies at this level is also extended to now include their classes' module/unit/weekly levels too. For example, if one of their classes is focusing on learning how to conduct a literature review, then their study strategies that week might incorporate practicing these skills, as well as better understanding why these reviews are essential for research methods. Following the framework developed for these guidelines, alignment between these course modules/units and the following elements should be verified: learning goals, study strategies, and how they are assessing the impact of these goals and strategies, their own understanding of learning processes, and their own unique interests, capabilities, and experiences. Overall, the goal is to help ensure that their learning approaches are working in close connection with the classes that they are currently taking as these classes unfold week-by-week.

Complexity of spiritual discernment at this level flourishes. In line with Level 3 for other guidelines, these discernment processes will be more collaborative at this level. Theologically, we can assert that learning is rarely, if ever, an individual and isolated event as God works holistically within and all around the student to help them learn and develop. As a result, spiritual discernment is better engaged in cooperation with others as the community collectively strives to identify where and how God is trying to work with the learner. As they do so, the discernment of the learner's engagement should now include more elements of the student's learning processes as the group works to ensure closer alignment with the learner's classes. Not only should they discern how closely aligned the student's strategies, goals, and evaluations of their strategies are with their courses, but they should also consider the learner's understanding of learning processes as well as the student's unique background and current interests. Again, such claims are built on the theological assumption that God is most effective when all elements of the learner's educational life are fully aligned with the work that God is doing with the student via their courses. At this higher level, then, the learner's spiritual discernment processes will necessarily be more collaborative and complex.

Examples of this might include:

- The learner participates in a study group for a specific class and can state how their study approaches directly relate to what they are learning about in the course for a specific week/unit/module.
- The learner can describe the evidence-based processes by which they developed their study strategies and these steps include working with others at various stages.
- The learner is observed working with a staff member to closely follow a prescribed evidence-based study strategy to guide their learning approaches.
- The learner is able to state how a specific evidence-based study strategy/activity is directly related to what they are learning in a current week/unit for one or more of their courses.

LEARNER-BACKGROUND GUIDELINES

As will be pointed out in the next chapter, educational systems in the U.S. have generally favored certain groups of students over others, particularly along race and class lines. In addition, no single curriculum or set of teaching/learning strategies can work for all students in all times and places. As a result, each learner must take the initiative to continually develop and adapt their learning to better fit with their own unique combination of prior experiences, interests, and cultural influences. They are also encouraged to help others do likewise, particularly with those for whom our U.S. school systems and society has and continues to marginalize. Theologically, following God's immanence, we can assert that God works with each and every student in infinitely unique ways. Students are therefore called by these guidelines to discern where and how God is uniquely seeking to work with them.

Guideline #1—Learner Capabilities

The learner adapts study strategies to their own relevant prior knowledge, interests, skills, and capabilities; Americans with Disabilities Act (ADA) considerations are addressed if needed (Core Guideline).

This guideline is one of the most consistently emphasized across evidence-based literature, assessments, and theories.[14] At its core, education might be simply conceived of as a process of students moving from where they currently are in relation to course KSAs towards the higher levels of competency that are defined by their learning goals. This therefore requires the learner adapt learning strategies and course materials in accordance with their own unique backgrounds in order to help better themselves to progress towards these objectives. This is particularly important for learners with ADA considerations as many courses and schools have not been developed for such diversity of differences. The overall trajectory of this guideline therefore spans from the learner modifying their learning approaches to meet their unique background towards collaborating with others in continually developing multiple goals, activities, and materials.

Theologically, the learner is invited to understand that every infinitesimal part of creation—every person, every organism, every atom, every subatomic particle—contains the infinite fullness of God's life and love. In every minute place and instance in time and space, God adapts his expansiveness to help each part of creation to continually grow in him. As this relates to learning, the student can realize that God is laboring moment-by-moment to help them continually progress towards their spiritually-discerned educational goals. God does this, it may be asserted, by working with and through each part of the learner and their supporting communities. This can mean that God empowers the learner through their unique personality, skill sets, and interests to achieve these educational ends. As a result, the learner is admonished via this guideline to discern how to adapt their study strategies to better align with the work that God is seeking to do with and through their unique characteristics, knowing that God infinitely cherishes them for who they are.

Level 1

Drawing on past experiences and external resources, the learner seeks to adjust their learning strategies to better meet their own prior knowledge, interests, skills, and capabilities. If appropriate, the learner utilizes ADA interventions, modifications, and accommodations.

At this level, the learner should be able articulate/demonstrate what past experiences they are drawing from, and/or what specific external resources they are utilizing to modify their own approaches to learning. There should be clear evidence of the

---

14. See the references for this guideline in the next chapter.

learner working to adjust these approaches in light of their own unique need, interests, and capabilities. These experiences and/or resources should therefore be directly related to the learner's own knowledge, interests, skills, and/or capabilities.

A significant part of partnering with God as he strives to work with and through us involves growing in self-understanding. The more we better understand our own unique passions and capabilities which God has been working to develop, the better we can partner with God through these to help us progress on our learning journey. Resultingly, the learner is invited to continually cultivate such spiritual self-understandings, so they can better adapt their study strategies to align with God's lifelong work with and through them. This is particularly important for students with "disabilities" as Western culture has a long history of undervaluing the implicit and God-given gifts, beauty, and capabilities of these socially marginalized individuals and communities.[15] This level is therefore focused on the learner being able to articulate what their inherent and enduring gifts are as well as how they are working to discerningly adapt their study strategies in light of their sacred gifts.

Examples of this might include:

- The learner can state what they believe their learning style is and how they have adjusted their study strategies to better fit with this style.
- The learner is observed making use of their school's ADA support to help them be more successful in their classes.
- The learner is able to state how they have reflected on their performance in previous classes and has modified their study strategies to better fit with their own needs and capabilities.
- The learner participates in a class activity that requires them to identify their own interests and prior knowledge/skills in relation the course and then adjust their learning strategies in light of this background.

Level 2

In light of their own relevant prior knowledge, interests, skills, and capabilities, the learner uses multiple learning strategies to pursue and demonstrate their achievement of learning goals. The learner adapts and uses modified ADA resources to address their own learning needs.

At Level 2, the learner will differ from Level 1 by seeking out multiple pathways to engaging with the course KSAs. These multiple pathways, similar to the previous level, should match their unique prior knowledge, current interests, capabilities, and skills. For ADA-related resources, whether they are ADA-identified or not, the learner

---

15. For more on this topic, see Black, *A Healing Homiletic*; Hubach, *Same Lake, Different Boat*; Reynolds, *Vulnerable Communion*; Swinton, "Restoring the Image."

should use and modify these in order to better fit with their unique learning needs and capabilities. This is important because studies on ADA resources/accommodations are revealing that non-ADA as well as ADA-identified students benefit from using well-designed ADA resources.[16]

Expanding upon the previous level, the learner will realize that their unique combination of capabilities and interests requires a unique and diverse set of study strategies. Given that humans are extremely complex and ever-changing organisms, we can expect God's work within and through us to be multitudinous and adaptive as well. The learner is therefore invited at this level to spiritually discern which combination of study strategies will more ideally fit their unique and God-shaped learning background and characteristics. Overall, the goal is to better partner with God's educational life as God works with the learner via a variety of strategies.

Examples of this might include:

- Self-identifying with a specific learning style, the learner can articulate how they have engaged with two or more learning activities to help them learn a key concept in one of their classes.

- The learner is observed turning on the closed captioning for a video in an effort to help them better understand the concepts/skills that the video is presenting.

- The learner can identify two or more sources (e.g., books, websites, online videos, mentors) that have helped them to better learn core concepts/skills in one or more of their classes. The learner is then able to articulate how these sources match their unique needs, interests, and capabilities.

- The learner participates in multiple class activities for a key concept/skill that requires them to identify their own interests and prior knowledge/skills in relation this concept/skill.

Level 3

The learner collaborates with others in adapting their multiple learning goals, strategies, activities, resources, and/or assessments to build upon their relevant prior knowledge, interests, skills, and capabilities. The learner collaborates with others to expand the range of ADA resources that address their own and/or others' learning needs and enables themselves and/or other students to exceed high standards.

At Level 3, the learner is much more involved with others than the previous two levels in that they will be observed collaborating to construct multiple ways of engaging with their learning trajectories—ways that are more in line with their backgrounds. Here, and working with others, the primary focus is on the learner becoming more self-directed in their own learning and development and better able to adapt

---

16. Katz, "Three Block Model."

their study strategies to meet their own prior knowledge, skills, interests, and capabilities. While some of this work might be done in their courses, the learner should also look to peers and other external resources to aid them in these collaboratively discerned learning approaches. Collaborative modifications can affect every part of their learning process including their learning goals, the activities that they engage in, and how they seek to self-assess their proficiencies for specific KSAs. The learner may also be a proactive part of initiatives to incorporate and adapt ADA resources/support in an effort to help all students in the class or at the school be more successful.

Continuing with the Level 3 theme of collaborative spiritual discernment, the learner will be found working closely with others to develop and utilize study strategies that are better tailored to their own unique backgrounds and characteristics. Self-understanding often comes via the reflections of others and God, it may be asserted, can and does work through our community to help us become better learners. There is also an emphasis on the learner working with others to help improve the quality of education, particularly for students with disabilities. Overall, the goal is for the learner to become a more proactive part of helping God to foster learning environments that are empowering for all students.

Examples of this might include:

- The learner is observed meeting with an instructor or staff member to develop an individualized learning plan for one of their classes.
- The learner is part of a study group that uses self- and/or peer-assessments to evaluate their progress and then develop personalized study strategies.
- The learner is an active participant in a class that is observed collaboratively engaging in Universal Design for Learning (UDL) processes to develop an upcoming unit for the course.
- The learner is part of a course that contains an activity where small groups create their own service-learning project that is of direct interest and relevance to them.

Guideline #2—Cultural Considerations

Learner is able to appropriately modify their learning strategies in light of their own cultural locations (e.g., Socioeconomic status [SES], ethnicity, gender, age, etc.).

Somewhat similar to the previous guideline, this one is more directly centered on the cultural considerations of the learner whereas the previous guideline was more related to their unique prior knowledge, interests, and capabilities. Recognizing that a student's culture deeply influences learning and development, this guideline focuses on identifying how the learner is adapting their learning strategies in light of their own cultural considerations. A student's cultural location can include one or more of the following: ethnicity, gender, age, SES, educational level, sexual orientation, religious tradition, geographic location, or political affiliations. These and other cultural factors influence many of the considerations named in the previous guideline. As a result, developing their study approaches to be more aware of these cultural factors and intentionally engaged with them should result in greater gains in achievement. Trends for the levels of this guideline range from the learner simply working to be more aware of how their cultural location might influence their learning to the student working directly with peers as well as community members to modify their learning approaches to be more culturally responsive.

Theologically, the previous guideline emphasized the work of God at more of an individual level. This guideline, however, focuses more on the work of God within and among groups of people. While it is true that each individual is infinitely unique, being not only one-of-a-kind but also lying at the intersection of multiple social-cultural groupings at any given time in their life, it has been and continues to be observed that there still seem to be general behavioral patterns among specific cultural groupings.[17] Spiritually, we might assert that God's life works through these cultural commonalities and patterns to help members of these groups grow in specific ways. Just as God's infinite life is dynamically present and active within and through each individual, we can assert that this all-loving life equally works through cultural groupings of people. If these research-based and theological assertions are accurate, then it behooves the learner to better know how God has been and continues to work with and through the various cultural groups that they might be associated with. Doing so should further empower them to better partner with God's culturally manifesting life, particularly as it relates to their own educational journey.

Level 1

The learner accesses resources to expand their understanding of their own and their communities' cultural locations (e.g., SES, ethnic, gender, age, etc.) and then modifies their learning strategies in light of this.

At this beginning level, the learner should be able to identify some of the various cultural locations for themselves and the communities that they are a part of based on ethnicity, age, gender, SES, and so on. The learner should also be able to identify resources that they are using to help them to better understand one or more of these cultural factors and how these might influence their own learning and development. The learner then uses this knowledge to modify their learning approaches. At this level, then, learners will be able to: 1) identify their own and their communities' cultural locations, 2) state which resources they are relying on to inform their understandings of these cultural locations and how these might influence their own learning and development, and 3) articulate/demonstrate how they are adapting their learning strategies based on these understandings. The primary aim at this level is the learner

---

17. See the references for this guideline in the next chapter.

develop a beginning understanding of their cultural locations and then make changes to their study strategies to be more aligned with these locations.

At this foundational level, the learner will essentially be striving to identify some of the general ways that God works through the various cultural groupings that they are a part of. In particular, the learner should seek to identify specific learning goals, strategies, and assessments that have been successfully used by others in these cultural groups. Given this information, they should spiritually discern how to adapt these successful approaches for their own unique needs (see the previous guideline.) A fundamental theological assumption here is that God works in different ways with different cultural groupings. The learner is therefore admonished at this level to try and identify these cultural patterns of the educational Spirit so that they can better partner with this life in their learning journey.

Examples of this might include:

- The learner is able to accurately identify one or more of their own cultural locations (e.g., SES, ethnicity, gender, age) and can state how they have adapted their learning strategies in light of this awareness.

- The learner can identify one or more resources (e.g., articles, books, instructors, mentors, websites) that they have used to help them better understand their own cultural locations.

- The learner is part of a class that contains resources that helps them better understand their own cultural location and how to better learn course concepts/skills.

- The learner is observed discussing with an instructor how course concepts/skills might vary based on their own cultural location.

Level 2

In light of their own cultural locations (e.g., SES, ethnicity, gender, age), the learner utilizes multiple culturally appropriate learning strategies in pursuing and demonstrating their achievement of learning goals.

Similar to the previous guideline, a learner at Level 2 differs from Level 1 when they seek out and engage multiple and culturally relevant pathways to engaging with their learning and development. These multiple pathways, however, should match the cultural location of the learner as well as the wider communities that they are likely to work with in the future. These multiple pathways should lead the student to achieving their learning goals in ways that are congruent with their cultural heritage.

Here, we continue to see more of the infinitely complex ways that God works with the learner. Every individual is a complex intersection of multiple cultural groupings at any given time, ones which change across the lifespan: we age, move, make new friends, attend different schools, are given a raise, or lose a job. Each cultural group that we are currently a part of may have different ways that God works with them. With so much cultural intersectionality, how can the learner discern which group(s) to focus on? There are at least two ways to respond: 1) choose one group (or small subset of cultural groups) to focus on and adapt one's learning approaches based on these, or 2) discerningly select and continually adapt a range of learning approaches based on multiple cultural groups. The former is a Level 1 strategy while the latter is a Level 2 approach. The learner at this level is therefore invited by God towards a more flexible and multitudinous approach to developing their learning approaches based on cultural groupings. Realizing that God educationally works through their multiple cultural groups in powerful ways, the learner will select a range of learning approaches to help them more closely partner with God in their ongoing educational journey.

Examples of this might include:

- The learner chooses a class project that is relevant to their own ethnic heritage.
- The learner is observed finding multiple e-learning modules online that help them better understand course concepts/skills in relation to one or more of their own cultural locations.
- The learner can state how they have located supplemental culturally appropriate articles on a topic for one of their courses.
- The learner is able to identify multiple resources that have helped them better know how the KSAs of one of their classes needs to be adapted for their community's culture.

Level 3

The learner collaborates with a broad range of peers, specialists, and/or community members in developing culturally appropriate learning strategies, resources, practices, and perspectives in their pursuit of learning goals.

Similar to many other guidelines, Level 3 will show evidence of the learner working directly with peers as well as outside instructors/staff and community members to adapt learning strategies to better meet their own diverse cultural locations. The learner should therefore be able to demonstrate evidence of engaging with multiple learning pathways that have been developed in collaboration with others. Also, a learner at this level will seek to broaden their diverse cultural perspectives via their learning materials and activities. Overall, this level is very similar to the previous guideline, but has a more specific emphasis on collaborative cultural engagement with course KSAs.

Again, the learner is beckoned by God to engage in their culturally-focused spiritual discernment processes in communal ways. Based on the core assumption that

God works in different ways within and to different cultural groups, it seems logical that the learner should turn to others for guidance. Collectively, these discernment collaborators should labor with the learner to engage in the processes outlined by the previous levels. They should help them better understand how God works through different yet relevant cultural groups, as well as how the learner is being invited by God to synthesize and adapt these learning approaches to the learner's unique situation and background. Such collective discernment should therefore greatly empower the learner to more fully partner with God to improve their learning strategies in more culturally relevant ways.

Examples of this might include:

- The learner is observed working with culturally diverse community members to develop a project that is relevant for the community.
- The learner is observed working with one of their classes to identify culturally diverse resources that will become required reading for a course unit.
- The learner joins a study group that seeks to create study strategies that are culturally appropriate for everyone in the group.
- The learner works with a mentor to identify multiple resources that will help them better know how the KSAs of one of their classes needs to be adapted for their community's culture.

Guideline #3—Preferential Option for Vulnerable Populations

Mission-Centered Focus: In pursuit of learning goals, the learner engages in diverse cultural experiences with underrepresented and marginalized communities and proactively works to reduce biases and increase justice for these populations (Core Guideline).

Educational studies in the U.S. continue to document a significant gap in achievements between at least two sets of groups: 1) middle/upper and lower SES students, and 2) Euro-American and Non-Euro-American students. In response, nationwide PK-16 initiatives have been launched in an attempt to close these gaps. This guideline is reflective of these initiatives and is intended to help ensure that each learner is helping to address the needs of marginalized, under-resourced, and lower performing students. Furthermore, following this guideline, classes should help to prepare students to proactively engage with marginalized and under-resourced communities in positively transforming ways. Doing so should not only help these communities, but it should also help to deepen learning for the student by making their education more meaningful, relevant, and real-world related. Overall, the trends from Level 1 to 3 are from the learner being more aware of diverse perspectives to actively engaging with diverse people and communities. It also entails the learner not only address their own personal biases, but also help others to do likewise.

Clearly, we live in a world not fully intended by God. Marginalized communities are one of the many clear indicators of this, and we can assert that God works tirelessly to help these persons and populations. While some religious communities adhere to a belief that God will eventually and miraculously right these wrongs, the theological claim reflected in this guideline is that God will most directly accomplish this by working through each one of us. Following this claim, the learner is therefore invited by God to learn and grow in their abilities to help under-resourced and marginalized groups, whether they themselves are a part of these communities or not. The levels of this guideline therefore outline the developmental stages that a learner might traverse with God in pursuit of these self-transforming and world-changing goals.

Level 1

The learner seeks out multiple cultural perspectives and experiences of underrepresented and marginalized communities as part of their pursuit of learning goals. The learner explores how their own personal biases can affect perceptions and actions, particularly as these biases relate to underrepresented and marginalized communities.

Level 1 for this guideline is primarily focused on the learner exposing themselves to diverse perspectives (locally, regionally, nationally, and/or globally) as part of their pursuit of learning goals. In line with the aims of this guideline, a specific emphasis is given to the lived experiences and perspectives of under-resourced and marginalized communities. The second part of this level involves the learner actively becoming more aware of their own biases and how these might be affecting their actions personally, civically, and professionally. The student should be able to: a) articulate/demonstrate awareness of some of their potential biases; b) state/demonstrate how these biases might be affecting their learning path, professional work, and/or civic engagement; and c) reflect on concrete steps that they can take to prevent these biases from adversely affecting themselves and others.

At this foundational level, it might be asserted that God works with the learner to help them better understand the diverse lived experiences of oppressed communities. This learning is intended not only to help the learner better understand these experiences, but also the empowering work that God has and continues to do with these communities. A central part of this learning, however, is not only focused on the communities but also on the learner themselves. Living as part of inequitable systems, each of us bears the biological and enculturated habits of bias towards non-dominant groups, even those who are members of these marginalized communities. As a result, it can be asserted that God seeks to work with each of us to become more aware of these implicit and explicit biases so that we can better partner with God in the lifelong journey of repatterning these personal biases. At this level, God therefore seeks to help the learner foundationally grow in their awareness of how oppressive systems and biases are impacting our world, as well as how God continues to work diligently for their transformation.

Examples of this might include:

- The learner shows evidence of participating in anti-racism programs.
- The learner is able to state how one or more of their own biases can potentially influence their interactions with classmates, co-workers, and/or people in the community.
- The learner is observed interacting with a classmate's viewpoints and then comparing these perspectives with someone from an under-resourced and/or marginalized background.
- The learner actively participates in a course that contains materials (e.g., readings, videos, etc.) from diverse perspectives of under-resourced and/or marginalized communities.

Level 2

In pursuit of learning goals, the learner engages in experiences that helps them directly work with diverse people from underrepresented and marginalized populations. The learner proactively assists others in exploring how their own biases can affect perceptions and actions, particularly as these biases relate to underrepresented and marginalized communities.

At this level, there are two primary considerations. The first extends upon Level 1 when the learner seeks to engage more directly with marginalized and under-resourced communities. Here, the interactions are more immersive and direct rather than simple exposure to their perspectives as it is with Level 1. For the second consideration, the work of identifying and transforming biases also expands at this level when the student now works with others in these areas. While it might at first appear that multicultural engagement from the previous guideline includes transformative reflections on biases, this is not always the case. Learners at this level therefore explicitly and directly address these kinds of personal reflections with others. This work involves the learner helping them towards a deeper awareness of their own biases and how these might be affecting their perceptions of and engagement with diverse people and communities—particularly marginalized and underrepresented ones. There should therefore be clear evidence of these kinds of engagement on the part of the learner as they continue to pursue their learning goals.

The learner's progress with God at this level will be reflected via their direct interactions with diverse marginalized and under-resourced groups. This progress should help the learner continue to progress in relation to their educational journey as God seeks to help them improve in their KSAs as a result of these direct interactions. While their involvement with these communities may be required as part of a class, it may be asserted that God is holistically striving to transform the student's heart and motivations towards empathy with and commitment to oppressed populations. Such affective transformations may be reflected not only in how they interact with these diverse communities, but also in the learner's work to help others to further recognize their own biases. Theologically, we see God's life of love and justice expanding as the learner at this level interacts more directly with marginalized communities, as well as in the learner's efforts to help broaden other's awareness of biases.

Examples of this might include:

- The learner is observed participating in a study group that regularly discusses how course content relates to under-resourced and marginalized communities.
- The learner is observed completing a service-learning project that requires them to connect with local and global peers from marginalized backgrounds.
- The learner is part of a course that includes community-based projects that expose students to under-resourced communities.
- The learner is part of a student organization that helps to facilitate events and discussions on sexism, racism, etc.

Level 3

In alignment with their learning goals, the learner engages in activities that help them develop advanced intercultural and civic engagement competencies, particularly with underrepresented and marginalized communities. The learner engages in opportunities to proactively work for equity and justice in solidarity with underrepresented and marginalized communities.

Level 3 continues with both of the considerations from Level 2. The learner will intentionally seek out interactions with people/communities in ways that deepen their ability to work with diverse cultures. Again, a central emphasis is given to marginalized and under-resourced populations. Students learn how discipline-specific concepts/skills directly relate and can be applied to working for change in solidarity with these communities. As they engage in this work, attention should be given to developing their own civic engagement and intercultural competency KSAs at higher levels as they relate to under-resourced and marginalized communities. Numerous standards are available online that outline these KSAs, and the learner should identify and integrate the most appropriate ones for their own purposes.

At this highest level, we might claim that God is working to achieve more advanced levels of harmonization and integration of his transforming work. Here, God helps the learner continue to progress along their educational journey. This is done, following God's work via this guideline, by having the learner collaboratively engage with oppressed peoples in an effort to bring about greater justice, equity, and community. In doing so, God's transforming life can have an impact simultaneously in multiple ways. Not only is the learner ideally advancing in their course KSAs, they should also deepen their intercultural competency and civic engagement KSAs. In addition, God's work to positively impact marginalizing systems and their ill effects on people and their neighborhoods can progress through this work. God's incarnationally transforming life (i.e., God's work within and through people, communities, and creation more generally) may therefore be seen at this level to not only more deeply impact biases, but also work to transform people and the larger systems that continue to propagate marginalization and oppression in our world.

Examples of this might include:

- The learner is an active participant in a course that contains social justice projects where students are required to work with a local advocacy group.
- The learner is part of a student organization that works with lower income community members to complete neighborhood improvement projects.
- The learner is able to articulate civic engagement and/or intercultural competency standards that they are working to develop in.
- The student volunteers with a community organization that works with policy makers to bring about changes that influence marginalized populations.

PROFESSIONAL DEVELOPMENT, LEADERSHIP, AND EVIDENCE-BASED PRACTICE GUIDELINES

While some administrators might not want them to know this, in almost every school, students are the majority population. If we, as U.S. citizens, really embrace democratic values and processes, then it stands to reason that we should be helping students learn how to engage in democratic processes in their own lives as well as in their communities. As a result, students should take on proactive leadership roles in their schools that are aimed at improving the quality of teaching and learning. They should also seek out additional learning opportunities to help them further develop. It is also helpful if students approach their learning in evidence-based ways as well as to participate in scholarly projects in different disciplines. Through all of these means, God works to help not only students learn more deeply, but also to improve the schools and communities that learners are a part of.

Guideline #1—Professional Development

Learner engages in and supports professional development (PD) opportunities related to improving their discipline-specific competencies (Core Guideline).

The craft of any discipline is a lifelong pursuit, one that can be continually improved upon. Whether one is in healthcare, education, management, sciences, or law, there is always more that can be learned and developed. As a result, what is being taught in one's classes is only a small foundational fraction of what can be known for each field of study. In order to help foster ongoing growth, then, the learner needs to also be involved in co- and/or non-curricular professional development opportunities. These opportunities should help the learner to identify and become more competent in the KSAs that are integral to their specific discipline. This guideline is therefore intended to help ensure that learners are engaging in PD in significant ways beyond what they are learning about in their classes. Not only should their PD help better prepare them for their chosen career, it should also help them establish a habit of continual learning that will serve them throughout their lifetime. At lower levels, this involvement can be simply participating in PD sessions, whereas at the higher levels the learner will help to develop these sessions. Overall, the learner should be found continually and proactively pursuing deeper, broader, and more expert levels of proficiency in their discipline-specific craft.

At its core, a theology of this guideline can assert that God seeks to work with the learner through multiple avenues to help them continue developing in the vocational craft that God is inviting them into. While God, as this text asserts, is abundantly active with and through the educational system(s) that the student is a part of, we can also assert that God strives to help the learner vocationally grow via other means as well. For primary and secondary students, this might mean looking to external resources or attending local events that are related to the classes they are taking. For higher education students, this will likely include reading discipline-specific journals and attending conferences. If the learner truly wants to partner with God's educational life in fuller ways, then they will seek out co- and non-curricular (i.e., not offered by the school) opportunities to help them along their learning journey. Through this guideline, we can see God laboring to work with the learner via avenues that extend well beyond the classroom.

Level 1

The learner engages in structured individual and/or group professional learning opportunities (co- and/or non-curriculum) that help them to stay current with essential KSAs in their discipline.

At this level, the learner will be found participating in co- and/or non-curricular PD opportunities that are readily available to them. These might include attending lunch-and-learns offered by their school, participating in regional trainings in their discipline, or accessing online webinars on new findings in their field. These PD offerings should help the learner stay current in a specific discipline, particularly in the area(s) of focus that they are interested in. Regardless of the PD that they engage with, these should help the learner be better prepared for a possible future career beyond what they are learning in their classes.

For this level, we can find God working with the student to engage in readily available opportunities beyond their courses that help them further develop in discipline-specific KSAs. Opportunities can abound when the student begins to look for additional ways to help them continue to learn and develop in a specific discipline. Each one of these identified opportunities theologically represents an invitation from God to broaden and deepen their KSAs. Spiritual discernment therefore is essential as the learner strives to determine which of these PD offerings to pursue. At this foundational level, however, such discernment will be more simplistic, with the learner participating in what is readily available more out of convenience than as a result of discerning what they really need (a Level 2 characteristic). Here, then, we find God working with the learner to begin broadening the educational avenues through which God can help them progress.

Examples of this might include:

- There are records of the learner attending lunch-and-learns offered by their school.
- The learner can show evidence of attending regional trainings in their discipline.
- The learner is observed accessing online webinars on emerging trends in their area(s) of interest.
- The learner subscribes to and regularly reads journals and new texts in their field.

Level 2

Based on personal reflections and feedback from peers and mentors, the learner identifies needed areas of ongoing discipline-specific PD and participates in co- and/or non-curriculum learning experiences that address these identified areas of improvement.

This level continues the previous one with the learner continually engaging with co- and/or non-curricular PD that helps them improve in a specific discipline. However, rather than attending PD events as they become available, a learner at this level will be more intentional with assessing their current competencies and identifying areas where they need improvement. To help with this, the learner will look to various sources and support systems such as asking peers and/or mentors to help them assess their knowledge and skills or attending workshops that help them to identify areas for improvement. Based upon these intentional evaluations, the learner will then seek out co- and/or non-curricular PD opportunities that directly address these areas—ones that continue to improve noted strengths and/or helps with weaknesses that they have. In essence, the learner is demonstrating the self-regulated learning skills that they will need to help them to continually improve across the whole of their career.

As a result, increased achievement in their courses should be a measurable outcome of these efforts.

As mentioned in the previous level, the student's spiritual discernment of which additional learning opportunities to engage will be more sophisticated at this level. Here, the learner will essentially be attempting to discern which additional opportunities will best help them to continue to develop in their KSAs. Basing this discernment on authentic assessments of their current capabilities and background, the learner will seek out opportunities that potentially have the greatest impact on their learning journey. Through these endeavors, we might assert that God is striving through these discernment processes as well as these opportunities to help the learner progress in line with his long-term educational plans for them. This level is therefore focused on the learner working to spiritually discern these plans and engage in these opportunities so that they can more closely harmonize with God's educational work with and through them.

Examples of this might include:

- The learner can describe how they have worked with a study group to assess their knowledge/skills and then identify co- and/or non-curricular PD opportunities to help them address areas noted in these evaluations.
- The learner asks an instructor to help them better understand what is going well and what might be improved in their discipline-specific KSAs and then identify PD events that help them to improve in these areas.
- The learner uses evidence-based guidelines to self-assess their discipline-specific KSAs and then identifies resources that will help them address noted areas for improvement.

Level 3

In addition to Level 2, the learner collaborates with others to collectively create, reflect upon, analyze, and improve co- and/or non-curriculum PD opportunities that address Levels 1 and/or 2.

While this level continues to build upon the previous one, it is also characteristically different. Here, the learner will be found not only engaging in relevant PD opportunities, they will also help to develop these. Following Level 3 for many other guidelines, these development efforts should be collaborative in nature as they work with others to design, implement, and evaluate PD offerings. These co- and/or non-curriculum PD efforts might occur at their school or with discipline-specific organizations that they are a part of. The PD events that they help to create should aid others in their own ongoing journey to continually improve in discipline-specific competencies.

Similar to the previous guideline, we find God's transformative educational work extend beyond the learner out into the community. Here, theologically speaking, the learner will be a more responsive and participatory part of God's efforts to develop such PD opportunities for the community. Working with others, the learner will strive to discern not only where God is wanting them personally to grow through co- and/or non-curricular opportunities, but which opportunities they are being invited to help develop with and for others. Again, we can see God working at multiple levels with and through the learner, laboring to have an impact on them individually, but also on the communities of which they are a part. In doing so, the learner is becoming a more intimate part of God's incarnational educational life that continually strives to help our world learn and grow.

Examples of this might include:

- The learner serves on a student government group and they actively work with others to develop PD events for the student body.
- The learner is an active participant in a discipline-specific organization and they work with peers to deliver workshops and develop resources that help colleagues improve their proficiencies.
- The learner works with student retention efforts on campus to identify best practices and help faculty, other students, and staff align their courses and programs with these practices.
- The learner collaborates with a peer to offer training sessions to colleagues on discipline-specific KSAs.

Guideline #2—Educational Leadership

Learner actively participates in leadership roles and responsibilities that improve the school's education and culture.

As may be seen by these guidelines, the institution's culture greatly influences the quality of education. Level 3 for most guidelines are highly collaborative in nature and educational research studies are finding that the more positive and interactive a school is, the higher the student achievement.[18] This culture is at least partly, if not largely, determined by the roles and responsibilities that students, faculty, and staff have. As a result, it is imperative that each individual play an active part in helping continually shape and guide the organization's actions, attitudes, and policies. This means that learners should therefore be found taking on leadership roles at their institution. At lower levels, this involvement will entail supporting positive and collaborative initia-

---

18. Hattie, *Visible Learning*, 80.

tives. At higher levels, the learner will be found leading quality improvement projects and actively mentoring others. The basic premise here is that the more committed to quality learning and development a student is, the better the education will be for them.

Theologically, it may be asserted that God is active with and through each and every part of the educational system. In order for the system as a whole to manifest God's life, then each part must be fully responsive to God's movements by actively participating in the community. For the learner, this means taking on roles and responsibilities that help the school continue to improve. By doing so, the learner will be participating more fully in God's continual work to increase the impact that the school has on students and staff as well as the wider community. In order for God's kin-dom to be more fully realized in every part of the school, every part of the school must be more fully involved.

Level 1

The learner participates in schoolwide efforts to implement a shared vision and they actively contribute to a supportive and collaborative school culture.

At this level, the learner will be aware of initiatives at their school that relate to supporting its vision and mission. The learner may serve on committees, attend events related to the school's mission, and intentionally work to develop collegial friendships with peers. Here, the learner is an active part of already existing initiative and behaviors of the school. They positively support the institution's culture and work to develop collaborative relationships with other students, faculty, and staff.

At this foundational and beginning level, the learner will respond to God's invitations to participate in the types of activities described above. While being more of a participant than a leader, the learner nevertheless will be found responding to God's invitations for this guideline by their positive and proactive support of existing schoolwide initiatives. They will also be found working to develop stronger relationships with other students and staff at the school, thereby participating more fully in God's work to foster closer collaboration. We might therefore see God laboring at this level to help the learner become a more integral and proactive part of God's transforming work at the school in beginning ways.

Examples of this might include:

- The learner is observed actively serving on committees and contributing to the committee's work.
- The learner is observed attending events related to the organization's mission.
- There is evidence of the learner intentionally working to develop collegial friendships with other students, faculty, and staff.

- The learner is able to articulate the organization's vision and can state how they intentionally work to support and implement this vision in their classes and with peers.

Level 2

The learner engages in schoolwide decision-making processes with others to identify common goals, develop strategies for pursuing these goals, and evaluate progress towards them. The learner actively and consistently contributes to the growth of others through mentoring and feedback.

Level 2 builds upon Level 1 when the learner is found participating in school initiatives that work to achieve specific goals. These projects may be part of a task force that the learner is on, ventures that their department is leading, initiatives that are being led by discipline-specific organizations, curriculum rewriting efforts, or accreditation-related improvements. At Level 1, the learner may simply take part in these as a participant. At this level, however, the learner will be an integral part of the core planning and implementation team that is leading these projects. In addition, the learner will also be found at this level mentoring others. Such mentoring can happen formally via structured programs, or informally as the learner works with a peer to improve in their courses. Overall, this level is characterized by the learner taking on roles at the school where they help implement organizational projects and more proactively mentor others.

Spiritually speaking, it might be asserted that God helps the learner progress from a participant role to a team player role. Here, the invitation is for the learner to be a part of groups that are striving to discern and implement institutional improvement projects. As an active part of these teams, the learner will be developing in their spiritual leadership abilities as they work with others to more holistically and collectively discern what their team is being called to work on. The more learners who take on such roles, the more fully and efficiently God can work with and through the school to improve its educational impact. The learner at this level is therefore invited to seek out and participate in such roles, while the school is invited to make these opportunities available to students.

Examples of this might include:

- The learner is observed taking an active part on a task force that is leading a curriculum rewriting effort.
- The learner proactively works with faculty and staff at their school to support initiatives that are being led by discipline-specific organizations.
- The learner actively contributes to a committee that is assessing accreditation-related improvements.

- The learner participates in a structured peer mentoring program.

Level 3

The learner is a leader in identifying and advocating for continuous evaluation and improvement of schoolwide vision, mission, and goals that support quality teaching and learning. The learner actively mentors and motivates others to participate in institutional leadership roles.

Extending the work of the previous level, a learner at Level 3 will be found taking a more proactive role in identifying and initiating institutional change projects at their school. At Level 2, the learner was an active participant on already existing leadership teams that designed and carried out these kinds of projects. At this level, however, there will be strong evidence of the learner taking the initiative to identify opportunities for schoolwide improvement that are intended to increase student achievement. A learner at this level will also be found working to empower others to be more actively involved in leadership roles at their school. Overall, the learner is committed to continuous improvement of their institution as evidenced by this kind of mentoring as well as by the initiatives that they take a lead role in launching.

At this highest level, it could be claimed that God is working with the learner to flourish as a spiritual leader at the school. God will work with the learner to develop their abilities to listen deeply with God for the school's identifiable strengths and areas of improvement via their active engagement with the community. The learner will then be found responding to God's motivations to help further support some of these identified strengths and/or address some of the noted areas for improvement. Engaging in spiritual discernment and implementation of such initiatives necessarily involves collaboration with others. As a result, and in parallel with these initiatives, the learner will be found partnering with God's work to continually mentor others into such spiritual leadership capabilities and projects. If each student and staff member were involved in such spiritual leadership at the school in wisely coordinated and well-harmonized ways, imagine the impact that God would be able to bring about in the community.

Examples of this might include:

- The learner is observed starting a quality improvement project to address the lack of tutoring support at their school.
- The learner shows evidence of conducting their own analyses to identify additional community-based volunteer opportunities for students to be involved in.
- The learner is observed bringing others together to identify challenges at their school and brainstorm solutions.

- The learner starts a peer mentoring program that empowers new students to be more involved in leadership roles at the school.

Guideline #3—Evidence-Based Practice

Learner conducts evidence-based practice and/or scholarly projects that improve their discipline-specific competencies (Core Guideline).

In any field of study, improvements often come incrementally via an integrated combination of learning, action, and reflection. In other words, we learn about our discipline, we try what we learn, and then we can reflect on how things are going. This basic cycle is the foundation of evidence-based praxis, which should be applied to every discipline. This guideline is therefore intended to encourage learners to engage in these kinds of approaches to help improve their discipline-specific competencies. Learners need to establish habits of continually learning how to engage in their fields of study better, apply what they are learning, and then gather data that helps them identify areas of strength as well as improvement. Such endeavors can be done informally as they engage in these activities, or more formally via scholarly projects where they follow structured research methods that assess their KSAs. This work might come as an integral part of their classes, via co-curricular activities, or in jobs or internships that they have. At lower levels, learners will be found working individually to improve their own capabilities whereas at higher levels they will be found collaborating with others to have a wider impact on their institutions or disciplines more broadly. Overall, learners should intentionally and continually use evidence/data to help improve their discipline-specific capabilities.

This guideline directly aligns with a core theological claim of this text: those theories and strategies that lead to positive and genuinely progressive changes, as documented by evidence-based methods, and that align with the better parts of one's religious tradition, can be labelled as more genuine incarnational movements of God. This guideline is therefore intended to help the learner approach their own growth in discipline-specific areas in these ways. By identifying those models and practices that are helping them make sustained progress in discipline-specific KSAs, the learner is finding those means through which God is helping them progress more effectively. If God is working to help the learner to make substantial KSA progress, then it stands to reason that such progress should be empirically observable. Evidence-based practice should therefore be, following this guideline, an integral part of the learner's spiritual discernment processes.

Level 1

The learner works to improve their discipline-specific practices through evidence-based practice and/or scholarly projects.

At this level, the learner will have clear habits of gathering data on their course-related competencies and then continually working to improve the quality and effectiveness of their KSAs based upon the data that they have gathered. The essential component of this level is the learner intentionally gathering data that will help them to better assess and subsequently improve their discipline-specific competencies from an evidence-based perspective. The learner should therefore be able to identify the data that they are gathering as well as how they are using this data to guide incremental improvements to their KSAs.

At this foundational level, we might assert that God is working with the learner to develop the basics of evidence-based practice (EBP) as part of their spiritual discernment processes. In essence, EBP is an integration of some of the other guidelines (e.g., using multiple assessments, study strategy development processes, etc.) as they are focused on helping the learner to develop specific KSAs. Here, God invites the learner to more clearly understand where and how God is working with them to develop in these specific and more narrowly focused KSAs. To make these God movements clear, the learner can look to evidence/data to help them discern how God is working with them more efficiently and effectively to grow in relation to the specific KSAs that they are working on at the time. As a result, the learner is invited to begin adopting EBP and thereby more clearly identify how God is effectively working with them.

Examples of this might include:

- There is evidence of the learner using formal and informal assessments from one or more of their classes to help evaluate and improve their capabilities.
- The learner conducts a formal EBP research project that provides insights into what they are doing well (or not).
- The learner is observed meeting with instructors, mentors, and peers to help them better understand how they are doing and what they might do differently.
- The learner is able to identify specific data that they are gathering as well as how they are using this data to guide incremental changes to their own course-related KSAs.

Level 2

The learner collaborates with others to jointly conduct EBP and/or scholarly projects that improve discipline-specific practices for themselves and/or others.

This level builds upon the previous one when the learner teams up with others to work towards evidence-based improvements in their course related competencies. As with the previous level, these efforts can be more informal ones where the learner and their collaborators use data to improve one or more of their core KSAs. Or they can work together to complete more formal scholarly projects that provide insights into the theory and/or practice of a specific discipline. The learner at this level will therefore be found actively partnering with others to complete EBP and/or scholarly projects that are intended to improve their competencies in specific disciplines.

Following trends from other guidelines, the theological progression is from engaging in EBP-based spiritual discernment on their own towards collaborating with others in these endeavors. It represents both a maturation of their understanding of how God is working with them through their community as well as God's efforts to integrate them more fully into this community. Working through close friends and mentors, God strives to help the learner utilize clear evidence to help guide their growing competencies. At this level, then, the learner better sees the ways in which God works to lead them through such evidence-based progress in close connections with their community.

Examples of this might include:

- The learner is observed participating in a study group that is focused on continually reflecting on and improving one another's KSAs in one or more of their classes.

- The learner works with peers to formally study specific skills that are more effective for their field of study (e.g., engineering design methods, hygiene habits in healthcare, chemistry lab procedures).

- The learner actively participates in a persistence and completion committee that gathers and uses data to improve pass rates in difficult classes at their school.

- The learner is a part of an apprenticeship program where they meet regularly with a mentor to observe the learner's abilities and brainstorm possible improvements.

Level 3

The learner works collaboratively with others to conduct EBP and/or scholarly projects that have an impact on one's discipline-specific theories, practices, and/or policies more broadly. The learner works to disseminate the results of these projects via presentations and/or publications.

Level 3 further extends the work of the two previous levels. There should still be strong evidence of the learner collaborating with others to engage in EBP and/or scholarly projects that are intended to improve discipline-specific practices. At this level, however, there will be two significant additions. First, the learner will be found working on projects that have a broader impact on discipline-specific theories/practices. An example of this would be studying the practices that are being used by experts in a specific discipline in an effort to help improve the field. Second, the learner will then work to widely disseminate the results of these projects with peers at their institution and/or beyond. This dissemination can take the form of campus-wide presentations, poster presentations at a conference, journal articles, book chapters, policy making, and so on. At this higher level, the learner therefore works to maximize the impact of their evidence-based and/or scholarly projects.

As the learner continues to grow with God in their understanding and effectiveness of core KSAs and what is helping to foster these, God's invitation may be asserted to shift. If the learner and their supportive community really are finding better ways to develop and engage with these KSAs, then an obligation begins to arise in their needing to document and share these better ways others. Based on the theology that God works as efficiently as possible, it stands to reasons that what God has revealed to work very well in one community might work just as effectively in other contexts. As a result, we can expect that God would therefore motivate the learner and their colleagues to share the more effective, evidence-based ways of developing and utilizing the KSAs that they are focusing on. Theologically, this level therefore represents God's efforts to foster local transformation not just for the learner and their school, but for the wider community as well. A learner who has achieved this level of EBP and/or scholarly projects may therefore be asserted to be responding to and supportive of God's continuing movements to transform our world.

Examples of this might include:

- The learner is an active participant on a research team that is studying the specific strategies that are being used by experts in a specific discipline.
- The learner attends a discipline-specific conference and presents the results of an EBP that they completed with colleagues.
- The learner is an active participant on a discipline-specific organizational committee that is reviewing and revising its policies and standards based on assessment data.
- Drawing on evidenced-based literature, the learner works with others to develop revised theories and/or strategies that they share with others via presentations and/or publications.

CLOSING REFLECTIONS

Through the guidelines in this chapter, we therefore learn of a God who cares for each individual student, a God who has long been working within each person from their beginning, and a God who has a preferential option for empowering each student to take more ownership over their own learning processes and strategies. As students, when we more deeply listen for God's movements in our educational lives, we discover a God who is dynamic in nurturing our learning and development in a myriad of ways. Overall, these guidelines help us realize just how actively God ever strives to pursue God's educational aims with each student. It is, therefore, each learner's vocational calling to develop in partnership with this dynamic educational Spirit. A student who is responsive to God's educative life in these ways, is someone who, for example, seeks out interactions with other learners, pursues complexity of thought, uses interactive technologies, strives for real-world engagement, scaffolds their own progress, and helps nurture caring learning environments. These are qualities that most educators would openly applaud in their learners and these guidelines can help students intentionally grow in these directions. From these guidelines, then, we learn more fully about a God who is dynamically involved in the learning lives of students. It is therefore up to each student to respond to these dynamic invitations in each step of their educational journey.

2

Teaching the Teachers
The Instructor Tier

HAVING EXPLORED THE LEARNER Tier and with the theological foundations found in Appendix A, we are now ready to unpack the guidelines for the Course/Instructor Tier. As with the Learner Tier, following the categories depicted in Appendix C, we will provide a detailed description for each level of each guideline. Throughout these descriptions, similar to the previous chapter, we will be providing bottom-up theological assertions that are intended to help us better understand where and how God acts in our classes based on each guideline. These theological reflections are more extensive than for the other two tiers because these guidelines were originally developed for this tier. In addition, since these guidelines were primarily developed by drawing on educational research studies at this tier, we will be providing extensive lists of resources for each guideline. While the sheer number of references presented in this chapter can seem overwhelming, they are intended to not only provide further evidence of the validity of these guidelines, but also act a body of literature that the reader can turn to for further insights and guidance. By the end of this chapter, then, we should have a much clearer understanding not only of what high impact classes look like, but also how we can more closely partner with God's educational life as theistic educators.

OBJECTIVE GUIDELINE

This guideline helps to provide the horizons towards which God is inviting teachers and students in a specific class. Knowing how to develop and utilize these objectives is essential for education as they help focus our efforts and thereby improve the effectiveness of our classes. In doing so, we are better able to identify where God is leading us so that we can follow the master throughout our educational journeys.

Guideline #1—SMART Objectives

Objectives describe observable and measurable levels of proficiency that are aligned with accreditation, institutional, and/or discipline-specific standards (Core Guideline).

Setting clear objectives is generally considered to be essential for education. Meta-analyses as well as evidence-based assessment rubrics affirm this. As a result, this guideline highlights the importance of having both measurable objectives and communicating these clearly to students. Both sets of criteria for this guideline have similar trends from Level 1 to Level 3 in that they both become more collaborative at higher levels. For the first criteria, the growing emphasis is on learners taking a more proactive part in helping to develop and/or refine measurable course objectives for themselves. For the second set of criteria, learners are tasked with being able to articulate course objectives in ways that are more meaningful and relevant to them. It must be noted, however, that these criteria are mutually independent. In other words, learners may be able to articulate objectives in their own words that have been provided to them by the instructor. In studies involving more than 45,000 students, the average effect size on student learning has been noted to be around 0.47, which is higher than Hattie's 0.4 h-point.[1] As this guideline states, these observable and measurable objectives should also align with accreditation, institutional, and/or discipline-specific standards.[2]

In order to better partner with God's educative Spirit in our courses, it greatly helps to know the directions that God is inviting us and our learners towards. Deciding upon and establishing course objectives is essentially an act of spiritual discernment in which we are attempting to clarify these holy invitations. The history of Western Christian spiritual formation has a broad and vibrant array of goals to pursue which

---

1. Hattie, *Visible Learning*, 121–24, 63–68. Supporting evidence-based assessments: CCSSO, *Intasc Model Core Teaching Standards*, Standards 1 & 2—Indicator 2, Standard 3—Indicator 1, Standard 6—Indicator 1 & 3, Standard 7—Indicator 1, Standard 8—Indicator 1 & 2; MarylandOnline, "Quality Matters Rubric Standards," Standards 1.2, 2.1, 2.2, 2.3, 2.4, 2.5, 3.1; Pianta, La Paro, and Hamre, *Classroom Assessment Scoring*, Behavior Management, Instructional Learning Formats.

2. Supporting references include: Ambrose, *How Learning Works*, 112, 47–48, 204; Barzansky et al., "Continuous Quality Improvement"; Bruning, Schraw, and Norby, *Cognitive Psychology*, 34–35, 130; Diamond, *Designing and Assessing*, 16, 40, 79, 115, 50, 53–54, 264–65; Friedman and Fisher, *Handbook on Effective Instructional Strategies*, 20, 161, 288; Gagnon and Cator, "Mapping HIV"; García de Leonardo et al., A Latin American"; Gorski et al., "Nursing Education Transformation"; Jagt - van Kampen et al., "Impact of a Multifaceted Education"; Moreau and Eady, "Connecting Medical Education; Sawyer, *Cambridge Handbook*, Kindle locations, 8158–94, 217–41; Searing and Kooken, "Relationship Between California Critical Thinking"; Slavin, *Educational Psychology*, 152, 406–9; Woolfolk, *Educational Psychology*, 457–58; Zhao et al., "Identifying Competencies of Doctors"; Zupanc et al., "A Competency Framework."

can help us see the breadth and depth of growth that God yearns for us all.[3] The challenge for our class is to therefore discern which directions God is seeking to journey with our current students. This discernment of direction is not only one that should happen before the course begins but also as it unfolds. The Levels of Development described can therefore help to encourage us to work more closely with our students to discern these unfolding invitations and goals.

For example, in Genesis 17, God makes promises to Abraham regarding the future of Israel. These promises included the land that they would inherit, the flourishing of their population, and the birth of many nations. These promises, in effect, became goals that the Israelites held front and center. These promises were repeated for many others such as Isaac (Gen 26:24), Moses (Exod 3:7–10), and Isaiah (Isa 44:1–5). Throughout the history of Israel, God reminds the people of these promises and works with them to help them to journey towards these and other goals.

In systematic theology, there is a concept known as "teleology." In essence, it is the concept that parts of creation can be understood in terms of their end goals or purposes. God is asserted by theologians, such as Thomas Aquinas, to be the author of these divine ends.[4] In this scheme, it may be asserted, God works with each part of creation to help all creation to find its fulfillment in God by continually pursuing these innate goals and ends. As with the Israelites' unfolding journey, we find in the Christian understanding of teleology a God who sets clear objectives and works with us to pursue these ends.

Didache communities, as a final example, were early Christian communities who articulated and worked towards very clear objectives.[5] Believing quite literally that the last days were upon them, these communities had very specific rules and ways of living. The purpose of this "way" was almost single-minded: to prepare their disciples for Christ's coming. They believed that by living this very well-defined way, they were directly pursuing the goal that God had for them. Their systematic apprenticeship process was therefore designed around this very focused objective as they sought to purify themselves and one another in preparation for Christ's return. *Didache* communities are therefore another example of the centrality of having clear goals in Western Christianity.

Of course, we must also realize that our objectives are always going to be a narrower and more limited version of the work that God is doing in each of our lives and communities. The *Didache* text, for instance, issued lists of "shoulds" and "should nots." While many areas of life are addressed in these lists, they are not a comprehensive compilation for every part of life.[6] As it relates to this guideline, the point is

---

3. Kyle, *Sacred Systems*, 284–85.
4. Thomas Aquinas, *Summa Theologica*, Article 3, Question 2.
5. Milavec, *Didache*.
6. Kyle, *Sacred Systems*, 62.

to realize that no set of objectives can ever capture all that we might want to do with students; in other words, objectives are inherently narrow.

Such a narrow focus, however, is one of the key factors that will help our classes be more effective if we direct time and energies towards achieving these ends. When there is a clarity and concreteness in regard to these objectives, then we can be more proactive in helping our students work towards them and thereby be more aware of and response to the directions that God is seeking to lead us in via our course. Rather than trying to address everything, which is not possible in a given course, objectives empower us to discern which divine teleological ends God is wanting us to focus on with our students. Overall, we learn from this guideline that God has very specific and measurable directions as well as levels of competency that God desires for all of our students to achieve in our class. The clearer and more concrete we can be with these objectives, just as the *Didache* communities were, then the more fully we can focus our class towards these sacred ends.

Level 1

The instructor uses given accreditation, institutional, and/or discipline-specific standards to develop measurable learning objectives. The instructor refers to course/module objectives in general ways.

The emphasis at this level is on having objectives that are observable and measurable, clearly identifying what learners will need to demonstrate by the end of the course/unit as measured by course assessments. There should be clear evidence that these objectives align with accreditation, institutional, and/or program-specific outcomes. There are numerous examples of measurable objectives that are available online as well as rubrics that can help assess the quality of objectives. In addition, while objectives in the course/modules may be present, the instructor may not spend an adequate amount of time helping learners understand them. Overall, the concern is twofold: 1) the objectives may not have a central role in the design and implementation of the course/module, and 2) the students are not being adequately directed as to where they should focus their efforts and/or what the overall purpose of the course/module and its activities are. At this level, then, the objectives should be present but are not observed as being given a central role/emphasis in the course/unit. Regardless, the given objectives should be aligned with accreditation, institutional, and/or discipline-specific standards.

Theologically, this foundational level is focused on helping the instructor spiritually discern and develop objectives that clearly articulate the directions that God is likely inviting the class towards. Drawing from existing standards, the instructor will work to discern how these might apply to their course. Spiritually speaking, using these existing standards is an affirmation of the work that God has and continues to do in other contexts. It is also based on the discerned assumption that God is likely striving to work in similar ways in the instructor's course. Once discerned, the instructor must then labor with God's guidance to ensure that these objectives are well-integrated into their course. This means that these holy objectives are used to help develop the class and that students are made aware of these teleological directions. In doing so, the instructor will be responding to God's invitations to head in these directions.

Examples of this might include:

- Course objectives are listed in one or more of the following: syllabus, course site, presentation slides, course materials, written on the board, etc.

- Source(s) of course/module objectives is clearly identified in the syllabus and/or course materials (i.e., from discipline-specific accrediting bodies, discipline-specific organizations, organization's department/division/program, textbook publisher, etc.)

- Instructor is able to state what the source(s) of course/module objectives are (i.e., from discipline-specific accrediting bodies, discipline-specific organizations, organization's department/division/program, textbook publisher, etc.)

- Instructor generally refers to the objectives by having them on presentation slides, discussing them in general ways, etc.

Level 2

While retaining alignment with accreditation, institutional, and/or discipline-specific standards, the instructor refines learning objectives based on current students' professional, civic, and/or personal lives. The instructor clearly communicates/presents learning objectives and effectively supports learners' sustained attention on the objectives.

Accreditation and discipline-specific expectations are typically more global in nature and need to be adjusted for one's local context. At this level, objectives should be adapted to the backgrounds and capabilities of learners in the class, and the instructor can articulate how they have adjusted the objectives in these ways and/or they are observed explaining these adjustments to learners. For example, objectives may need to be adjusted for specific cultures (such as immigrant populations), ADA learners, and/or learners who are accelerated. Instructors should therefore be able to articulate/demonstrate how they have adjusted the objectives in the course to meet the needs of the learners that they have in the current class.

Also, moving beyond Level 1, a course at this level clearly demonstrates adequate and focused attention on the course/module objectives. The instructor should be observed explaining the objectives to students as well as their relevance for the course. Objectives should be referred to regularly throughout the course/module and they might be presented in a variety of ways (e.g., explanation, graphic organizers, etc.).

Based upon a theology that asserts that God infinitely adapts to each person and each local context, the instructor is encouraged at this level to adjust their objectives. Such adjustments should be discerningly made in light of their current learners. Significant student factors to consider in this discernment include each learners' prior knowledge and skills, their motivations and self-efficacies, and their cultural and social contexts.[7] At the core of this spiritual discernment is how to modify the objectives so that they are better aligned with the educational trajectories that God continues to journey with each unique student on. As these objectives are altered to be more relevant and meaningful for students, the instructor should also be found at this level emphasizing them more often in the course. In doing so, they will essentially be helping learners become more aware of the educational directions that God has been and continues to personally work with them towards. This will ideally empower them to more closely partner with God on their own educational journeys.

Examples of this might include:

- Instructor is able to state how they have adjusted course/module objectives for the current learners in the course, particularly their personal, professional, and/or civic lives.
- Instructor is observed explaining to learners how they have adjusted course/module objectives for the current learners in the course, particularly their personal, professional, and/or civic lives.
- Course materials (e.g., syllabus, handouts, course site, announcements, emails, etc.) that explain how they have or will adjust course/module objectives for the current learners in the course, particularly their personal, professional, and/or civic lives.
- Learners are able to state what the course/module objectives are.
- Learners are able to state the relevance of course/module objectives for their personal, professional, and/or civic lives.

Level 3

The instructor collaborates with learners and external resources in identifying personalized learning objectives to reach long term goals that align with accreditation, institutional, and/or discipline-specific standards and are relevant for learners' professional, civic, and/or personal life. Learners are able to articulate the learning objectives in their own words and can describe how the activities in the course relate to these objectives.

At this level, instructors will collaboratively work with learners to further adapt given objectives to align with their own personal, professional, and/or civic goals. This might include taking a more nuanced and focused view of the current objectives and/

---

7. Hattie, *Visible Learning*, 41, 43, 45–47, 49–50, 57–58, 61, 104–5.

or developing new ones altogether. This level is therefore focused on helping learners to take more ownership and responsibility in the course. As a part of these processes, instructors and students might additionally turn to community resources (such as mentors, family members, or experts in the field) to help shape these learner-crafted objectives in ways that still align with accreditation, institutional, and/or program-specific outcomes. There should therefore be evidence of activities where learners create/adapt their own objectives for the course/module to better fit with their own personal, professional, and/or civic goals.

Following the first criteria at this level, learners should be able to articulate course/module objectives in their own words. The emphasis here is on learners having internalized and made sense of the objectives in their own ways. There should therefore be evidence of learners being able to articulate the objectives of the course/module using terms and examples that differ significantly from the given objectives but in ways that are still congruent with them. Learners should also be able to state why they are engaging in given course activities and how these relate to the course/module objectives.

Throughout these guidelines and the three tiers, and primarily at Level 3, an image of God's kin-dom in the classroom will emerge. This image is one that is predominantly collaborative, democratic, and communal in nature and is founded on an incarnational theology that asserts that God works with and through each and every part of the community. As a result, spiritual discernment must include every relevant member of the community. In relation to this particular guideline, this means that students and faculty will work together to modify the course/module objectives. Similar to the previous level, the goal of these alterations is to develop objectives that more closely align with the ongoing educational work that God continues to do in the lives of each student. As each student's life is intimately connected to others beyond the classroom, such discerned modifications might therefore need to include community members such as learner's family and friends. Once discerned, these desired outcomes should be intentionally and meaningfully embraced by the student as they then work diligently to achieve these objectives in the class/module. In doing so, the community will ideally be partnering with God's educational life as it works with each student as well as in the class as a whole.

Examples of this might include:

- Instructor and learners collaboratively work to adapt given objectives to align with learners' personal, professional, and/or civic goals.
- Course materials (e.g., syllabus, course site, emails, etc.) provide evidence that instructor and learners have collaboratively worked to adapt given objectives to align with learners' personal, professional, and/or civic goals.
- Instructor can state how course/module objectives have been (or will be) collaboratively developed with learners and align with: 1) learners' personal,

professional, and/or civic goals, and 2) accreditation, institutional, and/or program-specific outcomes.

- Instructor collaboratively works with colleagues to modify objectives and ensure that these align with: 1) learners' personal, professional, and/or civic goals, and 2) accreditation, institutional, and/or program outcomes.

ASSESSMENT GUIDELINES

In secular educational settings, this is one of the most emphasized of all of the course elements. In religious circles, however, it is one of the least discussed according to our studies.[8] Spiritual discernment processes and course development methods are more ideally founded upon data that we gather about the people and communities that we are working with. As a course is unfolding, assessments can provide us with such data as we work with our students. Theologically, they are the means by which God can help us and our students more clearly see where and how God is able to work with our students for their learning and development. We must therefore choose these assessments wisely so that they yield the kinds of information that we and our students need in order to better discern where and how God is moving in our classes. The following guidelines are therefore intended to not only to help with developing these assessments, but also how to engage our students with them.

Guideline #1 – Varied Assessments

The course utilizes varied assessments (e.g., formative and summative, formal and informal) to establish learners' levels of proficiencies in relation to the stated course objectives as well as to guide the course's development (Core Guideline).

Using assessments is central to education. In the course, following this guideline, assessments should play a central role in at least two ways. First, multiple assessments and types of assessment should be used to help ensure that learner proficiencies are being more accurately measured. Each type of assessment (e.g., exams, research papers, portfolios, etc.) is inherently limited in the kinds of information that it can give and using multiple types of assessments helps to provide a more robust picture of learners' actual capabilities in relation to course concepts/skills as defined by the objectives.

Secondly, assessment data should be used to continually modify course elements (e.g., objectives, activities, resources, etc.) to better meet the needs and performances of current learners. Addressing this guideline, according to numerous studies presented in Hattie's book that include more than 46,000 students, will likely have an overall average effect size of 0.62, which is one of the highest effect sizes for all of the

---

8. Kyle, *Sacred Systems*.

guidelines.⁹ Overall, the trend for this guideline is from individual to collaborative analyses and from being instructor-driven to learner-generated assessments.[10]

Holistic spiritual discernment ideally relies on multiple sources to inform the decision-making processes.[11] When these discernment processes are applied to course settings, the results are multiple and varied types of assessments that can help guide the discernment of teaching and learning as it unfolds across the class. In essence, this guideline is a necessary part of the foundation for high quality spiritual discernment. Such assessment-based discernment, as the levels of development outline below, should be communally collected, analyzed, and used for guiding instruction. From this guideline, we again learn that God seeks to guide the course in holistic ways via multiple assessment sources. Our goal as theistic educators is therefore to communally use these multiple and varied assessments to help us better move with God's ever-active educative life in our midst.

In the Gospels, we see many instances of Jesus using different kinds of assessments to guide his interactions with the disciples. For instance, in Matthew 16:13–20, we see Jesus questioning his followers about their understanding of who he was. He then uses this assessment information to build upon these understandings and help them see more clearly how God is at work within them. In Luke 9:46–48, we find Jesus listening to an argument among the disciples about who is the greatest. Based upon this listening, Jesus takes the opportunity to teach them about childlike humility. Looking next to Mark 9:14–29, Jesus responds to a situation that his disciples were unable to deal with: a young child possessed by a spirit. After helping this child, the disciples ask for insights into why they were unable to deal with this issue. Based on his assessment of the situation, Jesus points them towards a deeper life of prayer.

---

9. Hattie, *Visible Learning*, 181, 204–7. Supporting evidence-based assessments: CCSSO, *Intasc Model Core Teaching Standards*, Standards 1 & 2—Indicators 1 & 2, Standard 4—Indicator 1, Standard 5—Indicator 2, Standard 6—Indicators 1 & 3, Standard 7—Indicators 2 & 3, Standard 8—Indicator 1, Standard 9—Indicator 2, Standard 10—Indicators 1 & 2; MarylandOnline, "Quality Matters Rubric Standards," 3.1, 3.4; Pianta, La Paro, and Hamre, *Classroom Assessment Scoring*, Teacher Sensitivity, Regard for Student Perspectives, Behavior Management, Instructional Learning Formats, Quality of Feedback.

10. Supporting references: Abbott, "Learning from Errors"; Ambrose, *How Learning Works*, 64, 87, 146, 50, 81, 205; Aronsson et al., "Understanding of Core Pharmacological Concepts"; Bradshaw and Lowenstein, *Innovative Teaching Strategies*, 491, ch. 31; Bussard, "Nature of Clinical Judgment"; Chepulis and Mearns, "Evaluation of Nutritional Knowledge"; Diamond, *Designing and Assessing*, 16, 79, 150, 77; Fluit et al., "Understanding Resident Ratings"; Friedman and Fisher, *Handbook on Effective Instructional Strategies*, 68–69, 80, 161, 289, 91–92; Goodwin and Machin, "How We Tackled the Problem"; Hamrin et al., "Teaching a Systems Approach"; Hendry, White, and Herbert, "Providing Exemplar-Based 'Feedforward'"; Ingham et al., "ARCADO"; Kelly et al., "Can Less Be More?"; Lee and Wimmers, "Validation of a Performance Assessment"; Morrison et al., *Designing Effective Instruction*, 252–56, 320–21, ch. 13; Nie et al., "Evaluation of Oral Microbiology"; O'Rourke and Zerwic, "Measure of Clinical Decision-Making"; Reiser, "What Field Did You Say?," 96, 97; Sawyer, *Cambridge Handbook*, 5512–32, 8137–58, 217–41, 289–311, 393–414, 18929–75, 75–96, ch. 13; Slavin, *Educational Psychology*, 153, 208, 13, 412, 15, 18, 21–22; Woolfolk, *Educational Psychology*, 455, 95–96, 511.

11. Kyle, *Living Spiritual Praxis*, ch. 1; Kyle, *Sacred Systems*, 290–93.

Again and again, we see Jesus using multiple and varied kinds of assessment to help his followers grow in the ministries to which they have been called.

Such effective use of assessments as the basis for nurturing learning and development was also integral to early monastic communities. For example, in Cassian's *Conferences*, we find a number of discussions related to the importance of community and watching out for one another.[12] A central part of these vital relationships was mentoring and guidance.[13] Through these close connections, monks would compare notes on their unfolding spiritual journeys, offer guidance and advice, and help each other judge what is right and wrong.[14] Such feedback was central to their discernment processes and were an integral part of their growing life with God.[15] These discernment processes also incorporated self-reflections, comparisons with virtues, and other sources of assessment.[16] In these early monastic communities, then, we find assessments to be an important part of how God worked with these monastics as they continued to develop spiritually.

We can therefore see how God uses multiple and varied kinds of assessments to guide our learning and development. It can be asserted that God does not try to hide the directions that he is seeking to lead us in, but rather strives to make these known to us as plainly and clearly as possible. Assessment data is one reliable source, when used appropriately, that we can use to help us discern these directions. In our classes, then, we can trust that God is working to help us see more clearly where our students are struggling as well as progressing via the different assessments that we have discerningly adopted. When we use these diverse and multiple sources of evaluation, we are in a much better position to know where and how God is laboring for the learning and development of our students in real-time as the course unfolds. When we seek such assessment-based clarity, we are in a much better position to discern how to harmonize our efforts with the educational spirit that is ever alive and active in our courses, be these in-person or online.

Level 1

The instructor uses multiple types of assessments to draw conclusions about learner progress towards the learning objectives.

At this most basic level, the instructor will work individually to gather and analyze assessment data. The instructor should be able identify the multiple types of assessments that they are gathering, whether these assessments are formal (e.g., exams, papers, etc.), or informal (e.g., observations, passing conversations with students,

12. Cassian, *John Cassian*, 263, 557–58.
13. Cassian, *John Cassian*, 90–91, 93, 99, 512.
14. Cassian, *John Cassian*, 506–7, 13, 19, 64.
15. Cassian, *John Cassian*, 84, 90–91, 93, 99, 102.
16. Kyle, *Sacred Systems*, 84.

email/correspondence, etc.). Instructors might also use data from previous experiences in teaching the course to inform their ongoing reflections and revisions to the course.

Foundationally, the instructor will work to engage in holistic approaches to spiritual discernment in their courses. In doing so, they will be seeking multiple assessment sources upon which to more accurately evaluate how their students are doing. Such assessment data, theologically speaking, provides insights into where and how God might be working with each student. At this level, then, the instructor will therefore develop and utilize multiple types of assessments to better inform their discernment of how God is working with each student, as well as the progress that God has been able to make with them.

Examples of this might include:

- Instructor is observed using two or more assessments (formal and/or informal) to assess learners' competencies in relation to specific module/unit KSAs.
- Course materials (e.g., syllabus, handouts, course site, announcements, emails, etc.) demonstrate that the course uses two or more assessments to assess learners' competencies in relation to specific module/unit KSAs.
- The instructor can identify two or more assessments (formal and/or informal) that they are using to assess learners' competencies in relation to specific module/unit KSAs.
- Learners can identify two or more assessments that were used to assess their competencies in relation to specific module/unit KSAs.

Level 2

Based on Level 1 data, the instructor uses this information to adjust instruction in real-time as the course unfolds to provide additional and/or alternative supports for current learners.

At this level, a similar kind of process is present as with Level 1: gathering and analyzing data by utilizing multiple types of assessment. However, at this level, the instructor will additionally be observed working to further improve the quality and effectiveness of the course for their learners as the course unfolds. The emphasis here is on continually modifying the course in real-time based upon learner performance on assessment data. At this level, course elements (e.g., activities, materials, assessments, etc.) are more fluid as the instructor adjusts these in an effort to further maximize student learning and development as learners are working through the course/modules.

With the foundational data in place from Level 1, at this level the instructor moves from discernment to action. Having discerned how God is working with each student and the progress (or lack of) that is being made, the instructor works to adjust their course in real-time to be more in tune with God's work. This might mean, for instance, slowing down or accelerating the pace in response to a student's performance. Overall, the goal is to use the information gleaned from multiple assessments to help make the class more adaptive to God's work with students thereby catalyzing the Spirit's educational initiatives.

Examples of this might include:

- Instructor is observed using assessment data to modify course/module activities and/or resources in real-time as their course unfolds.
- Instructor is able to state how they are using assessment data to modify course/module activities and/or resources.
- Course materials are observed being updated in response to course assessments.
- The course site is observed to be updated in response to course assessments.
- Course announcements state that course resources and/or activities have been modified as a result of student performance on assessments.

Level 3

The instructor works with colleagues and learners to select and analyze a variety of assessments that will help them better understand what is influencing learner progress. The instructor and learners then use this data to help scaffold individual learner development towards the learning objectives.

Level 3 continues with the work of Levels 1 and 2, only now the instructor is observed to be working with learners and colleagues on many of these tasks. In addition to the previous levels, the instructor continually works with learners to expand upon the range of assessments that are utilized as well as to analyze the data that is collected from these assessments. The instructor and learners are also observed working together to decide how learners can continue to improve in relation to course KSAs based upon assessment data. Being more collaborative, the culture of Level 3 classes for this guideline are characteristically different from the previous levels as the instructor works directly with students to identify and analyze assessments as well as to modify course elements in light of this assessment data.

Here, we continue to see a clearer picture of what God's kin-dom in the classroom (on-ground or online) might more ideally look like. Being more collaborative and democratic in nature, the instructor will work directly with students and colleagues to engage in the spiritual discernment processes of the previous levels. As a result, the course should be more closely attuned to God's high impact educational movements as the group works together to adjust the course in response to assessment data. In doing so, students themselves are invited by God to take more ownership and responsibility for their own and one another's learning, thereby allowing God to further develop their self-regulated learning capabilities. Courses at this level are therefore more spiritually organismic as faculty, students, and staff cooperatively work to draw on multiple assessments to adapt the course in real-time to student performance.

Examples of this might include:

- Instructor and learners are observed working together to select, analyze, and/or develop strategies and plans for how learners can continue to improve based upon assessment data that has been gathered to date.

- Instructor is observed working with colleagues to select, analyze, and/or develop strategies and plans for how learners can continue to improve based upon assessment data that has been gathered to date.

- The syllabus, course site, and/or other course materials have evidence of instructors and learners working together to select, analyze, and/or develop strategies and plans for how learners can continue to improve based upon assessment data that has been gathered to date.

- Instructors, colleagues, and/or students are able to state how they have worked with one another to select, analyze, and/or develop strategies and plans for how learners can continue to improve based upon assessment data that has been gathered to date.

Guideline #2—Intentional and Focused Feedback

Feedback to learners is: a) positive, b) related to specific objectives and criteria, c) provides suggestions for how learners can continue to progress, and d) are conducted in a "timely" manner, providing learners with feedback that can be implemented in subsequent activities (Core Guideline).

Numerous studies continue to show that learners benefit from detailed feedback that aids them in better knowing where and how they can continue to improve in the course. Studies involving almost 222,000 students reveal an effect size for this guideline of 0.54, which is much higher than Hattie's h-point of 0.4.[17] As this guideline clearly states, this feedback should be directly related to the course/module objectives, and it should be provided to learners close enough to the completion of the assignment so that they can implement the feedback on similar and subsequent activities. It should also be chronologically close enough to the assignment's completion such that it is still relatively memorable and meaningful to learners (e.g., within about a week's time or before moving onto to other major course/module concepts and skills).

---

17. Hattie, *Visible Learning*, 121–24, 44–45, 70–71, 73–79. Supporting evidence-based assessments: CCSSO, *Intasc Model Core Teaching Standards*, Standard 3—Indicator 1, Standard 6—Indicators 1, 2, & 3, Standard 7—Indicator 2; MarylandOnline, "Quality Matters Rubric Standards," 3.1, 3.3, 3.5, 5.3; Pianta, La Paro, and Hamre, *Classroom Assessment Scoring*, Positive Climate, Teacher Sensitivity, Behavior Management, Analysis & Inquiry, Quality of Feedback, Instructional Dialogue.

Overall, the trend for this guideline is from the instructor simply providing effective feedback to their working with learners to help them identify strategies that will improve their performance in the course.[18]

The history of Western Christian spiritual formation repeatedly emphasizes the importance and centrality of receiving detailed feedback in order to help guide ongoing growth in God.[19] Theologically, what we are essentially attempting to do with this feedback is to help direct students to God's educational work with them. If well-discerned, we can affirm that God is seeking to help learners make tangible progress towards the objectives. Our feedback should therefore help them better understand how they are doing in relation to these God-centered standards, as well as how they can partner more fully with God's educational life to continue to progress (i.e., what study strategies they can use, how they might alter their study strategies, etc.). Following the theological claim that embodying God's loving nature in our journey to achieve God's aims is just as important as the aims themselves; our feedback should be positive, affirming, and constructive. The importance of such feedback can be seen in God's ongoing work within and to the Western Christian tradition.

For instance, in the story of Moses, we see God being depicted and providing direct and ongoing feedback that was intended to help Moses lead the people of Israel through their desert wanderings. Beginning with Moses' attempts to free the Hebrews from Egyptian bondage, we can see in Exodus chapters 7–12 God counseling Moses each step of the way. This feedback is not only timely, it is very specific and aimed at continually working towards the goal of Israelite liberation. Later, in Exodus 16, we find the Israelites complaining about their difficult journey in the wilderness and especially hunger. Again, God is depicted as providing specific feedback and guidance to Moses and the Hebrew people. Throughout Moses' life and journey until his death, God is asserted to provide continual feedback and guidance to Moses, ever striving to help the Israelites to cultivate and live holier lives.

In the charismatic traditions, as in many other Christian sects, a central emphasis is given to continually seeking to know God's will for our lives.[20] In their discernment processes, charismatic Christians are asserted as giving preference to more intuitive, semi-conscious movements of God within as the basis for feedback and guidance.[21] With there being three potential sources of influence ("the Holy Spirit, oneself, a

---

18. Supporting references: Ambrose, *How Learning Works*, 87–88, 149–50, 206; Bruning, Schraw, and Norby, *Cognitive Psychology*, 87–88; Clark and Mayer, *E-Learning*, 263–67; Diamond, *Designing and Assessing*, 116, 92; Friedman and Fisher, *Handbook on Effective Instructional Strategies*, 144; Gauthier et al., "Deliberate Practice"; Johnson et al., "Identifying Educator Behaviours"; Morrison et al., *Designing Effective Instruction*, 231–32; Sawyer, *Cambridge Handbook*, 8765–87; Slavin, *Educational Psychology*, 134, 52, 213, 303–4, 19; van de Ridder et al., "Framing of Feedback."

19. Kyle, *Sacred Systems*, 293–95.

20. Parker, *Led by Spirit*, 34.

21. Parker, *Led by Spirit*, 108, 11.

diabolical influence[s]"), according to this tradition,[22] the goal is to seek direct feedback from the Holy Spirit as to how one is doing and where one should go next.[23] In charismatic religious living, we can therefore see the centrality that God gives to our relying on feedback from God to help continually guide our growing spiritual lives.

Overall, this guideline can help us see that God does not just set out goals for us to pursue, but ever seeks to provide ongoing, detailed, and constructive feedback and guidance to help us all along the way. In our classrooms, we can expect God to be laboring to provide such detailed feedback to our students. As theistic educators, then, our craft should include discerning the kinds of God-manifesting feedback that learners need in order to continually progress towards the objectives that have been identified. The evidence-based educational literature is finding that such feedback should: a) be positive, b) be related to specific objectives and criteria, c) provide suggestions for how learners can continue to progress, and d) be conducted in a "timely" manner, providing learners with feedback that can be implemented in subsequent activities. This is precisely the kind of feedback that we find embodied in parts of the Western Christian tradition. As a result, we need to listen ever more deeply to what God is trying to say to our students as they learn and develop in our classes.

Level 1

Using objective-generated criteria, the instructor points out strengths and weaknesses in performance and offers positive and concrete suggestions for how learners can improve their work on subsequent assignments.

Level 1 involves the instructor following the details given for this guideline. Feedback is not negative, deconstructive, or judgmental, but rather encouraging, affirming, and positively framed. This feedback also continually compares specific portions of student work to the course, module, and/or assignment objectives, noting where the work is being done well in relation to these objectives as well as where adjustments and improvements may be needed. Finally, instructor feedback should also provide suggestions and strategies for how the learner can improve on subsequent activities. Overall, learners should be able to act on this feedback in ways that are better than before they received the feedback.

Spiritually speaking, the foundational level is focused on the instructor discerning the kinds of feedback that God is striving to give each student. Following best practices for formative assessments, we can assert that God is working to provide each one of God's beloved learners with the information they need in order to continue to progress in the course. As a result, building upon the theology articulated above, such spiritual feedback should help the student more clearly know what they are doing well, where they still need to improve, and how they might more closely work with

22. Parker, *Led by Spirit,* 34.
23. Parker, *Led by Spirit,* 105.

God to help them grow. Overall, the instructor is essentially God's agent in the work to help students receive the kinds of feedback that they need to help them to continue to progress in course KSAs.

Examples of this might include:

- Instructor is observed to be verbally providing students with timely, detailed, and constructive feedback.
- Instructor is able to state when and how they have provided students with timely, detailed, and constructive feedback.
- Students are able to state when and how they have received timely, detailed, and constructive feedback from the instructor.
- Course assessment data (formal and/or informal) show evidence of the instructor providing students with timely, detailed, and constructive feedback.
- Course site (e.g., discussion boards, announcements, etc.) shows evidence of the instructor providing students with timely, detailed, and constructive feedback.
- Course materials (e.g., handouts, course presentation slides, etc.) show evidence of the instructor providing students with timely, detailed, and constructive feedback.

Level 2

In addition to meeting Level 1, the instructor then designs learning experiences that will help learners to apply this feedback and thereby improve their competencies.

Following the previous level, Level 2 for this guideline continues to provide very detailed feedback to learners. However, the course also has activities that help students act on the feedback and thereby work to further improve their competencies in relation to relevant KSAs. Examples might include revising a draft of a paper, allowing students to research correct answers to exam questions that they have missed, and further practicing and/or re-taking a skills test. This level is therefore distinguished by activities that explicitly empower students to act on the suggestions that have been made for how they can improve their performance.

In each of the examples provided from the Western Christian tradition above, God's continual feedback and guidance resulted in concrete actions taken by the people involved. For example, in many of the instances that Moses sought feedback from God and was provided with guidance, Moses worked to carry out these directions. As it relates to our classes, if an instructor really has clearly discerned the feedback that God wants to provide each student, then steps should also be taken to then help students to implement this spiritual guidance. Based upon a theory that asserts that we learn in part via actions and experiences, the instructor is invited to develop activities that guide students in applying the feedback. In doing so, these activities are essentially empowering each learner to partner with God in these subsequent activities and thereby continue to develop in response to the feedback.

Examples of this might include:

- Students are observed completing an activity that has them apply the instructor feedback that they received previously.

- Assessment data (formal and/or informal) shows evidence of students being required to complete an assignment where they had to apply instructor feedback.

- Instructor can state how they have had students apply feedback that they have provided on previous assignments to subsequent assignments.

- Learners can state how they have applied feedback that they have received on previous assignments to subsequent assignments.

- Course materials and/or site (e.g., syllabus, discussion boards, drop boxes, etc.) state how students are and/or will be required to complete an assignment where they have to apply instructor feedback on previous assignments to subsequent assignments.

Level 3

Extending Level 2, the instructor works with learners to build self-regulated learning skills, helping them use feedback to reflect on their own performance to then develop and apply concrete strategies for how they will continue to improve in the course.

Further building upon Level 2, at this level instructors will work with learners to help them identify and utilize strategies that will help them improve their learning and development based upon the feedback they have been provided. This level is more cooperative as well as self-directed as students are guided in reflecting on their performance in relation to the feedback that has been provided, as well as in determining steps that learners might take to improve. Level 3 is therefore more collaborative between the instructor and learners as they work to find more effective strategies for improvement in light of the specific feedback that has been provided. This level is intended to not only improve student learning and development in relation to key course concepts/skills, but to also build metacognitive, critical thinking, and problem-solving skills.

Continuing to develop the democratic and collaborative view of the kin-dom in the classroom (on-ground and/or online), this level invites faculty and students into a closer relationship in relation to course feedback. Here, students will not only be an integral part of determining how to respond to the feedback that has been provided to date, they might also be a part of helping to generate this feedback as they reflect on their own work (see the guideline below on self-assessments). Theologically, the invitation is towards more collaborative approaches to spiritual discernment in terms of the feedback and how it might be used to improve learning achievements. Working together, students, staff, and faculty are called to discern what kinds of feedback God is seeking to provide as well as how God intends this feedback to be utilized going forward. In doing so, they will be cooperatively laboring together to build a learning environment that is ever more responsive to God's ever-unfolding feedback and guidance.

Examples of this might include:

- Instructor is observed empowering students to review feedback that has been provided, and to develop concrete plans for how to continue to improve in the class.

- Students complete an assignment where they have to review feedback that has been provided by the instructor to then develop a concrete plan for how they will use this feedback to continue to improve in the class.

- Students are able to state how they have been guided by the instructor(s) and/or staff to use feedback that has been provided by the instructor(s) to modify their study strategies to continue improving in the class.

- Course materials (e.g., course site, syllabus, handouts, etc.) have directions that guide students in using the feedback that has been provided by the instructor to develop concrete plans for how to continue to improve in the class. Students are then required to follow these directions for one or more assignments.

Guideline #3—Evidence-Based Assessments

Assessments are utilized in accordance with evidence-based recommendations and, whenever possible, their reliability and validity are established.

Clearly, assessments are a necessary and integral part of any course, and there are numerous kinds of assessments that one can use. It is therefore imperative, with so many possibilities, that a course utilize assessments that are most appropriate for its content, learners, institutional setting, and so on. Overall, course assessments should be used in accordance with evidence-based recommendations. Instructors should also collaborate with others to reduce bias and establish the validity and reliability of these assessments. Doing so will help ensure that the information gleaned from these assessments is providing the kinds of insights that instructors need in order to make decisions related to course design and student achievement.[24] When instructors do

---

24. Supporting references: Ambrose, *How Learning Works*, 31, 148; Bruning, Schraw, and Norby, *Cognitive Psychology*, 130–31; Clark and Mayer, *E-Learning*, 266; Diamond, *Designing and Assessin*, 40, 79, 177; Kunina-Habenicht et al., "Assessing Clinical Reasoning"; McGill, van der Vleuten, and Clarke, "Construct Validation"; Norgaard, Draborg, and Sørensen, "Adaptation and Reliability"; Reiser and Dempsey, *Trends and Issues*, 97; Sawyer, *Cambridge Handbook*, 8217–41; Slavin, *Educational Psychology*, 419, 22, 44, 73–75; Woolfolk, *Educational Psychology*, 497–99, 513–14, 17–18.

this, the effect size can be close to 0.34, according to studies that have included almost 136,000 students.[25]

As this book has asserted, when subjected to theological reflection, evidence-based recommendations can be viewed as God's guiding life in our classrooms. Such recommendations can therefore also apply to our assessments. Theologically, establishing the reliability and validity of our assessments helps to ensure that the data being gleaned from them is providing us with a consistent and accurate picture of what is unfolding at the educational intersection of God and our students. In other words, we need to be sure that the assessments we are using are telling us what we think they are telling us in relation to God's work in our class. Additionally, conducting bias analyses helps to ensure that our assessments are accurate and consistent for all students regardless of their SES, gender, ethnicity, etc. God values and works equitably and appropriately with all learners and our assessments therefore need to provide us with an accurate depiction of this spiritual work for each student.

When we look to the Western Christian tradition, we find support for the use of evidence-based assessments that establish their reliability and validity. For instance, writers on spiritual discernment emphasize the importance of seeking confirmation of the discernment process before acting upon any decision that we have made.[26] The goal of this confirmation is to help ensure that the direction we believe God is leading us in is accurate and can be affirmed via additional processes. This is one way to think about evidence-based guidelines for specific assessments. When we look to how others have effectively utilized the assessments that we are considering for our class, we are seeking confirmation for the use of these specific assessments.

Similarly, in his work *Religion within the Limits of Reason Alone*, eighteenth century German philosopher Immanuel Kant articulates an approach to religion that is oriented towards freely choosing moral principles that can be clearly discerned based primarily on reason.[27] Essentially, Kant argues that our faculties of reason are a valid and reliable source for discerning how to live our lives. It is this emphasis on reliability and validity for discernment that this guideline is pointing towards when it comes to the assessments that we use in our courses.

Overall, this guideline helps us to know that God is seeking to ensure that our methods of data collection and evaluation are of sufficient quality so that we can have a clearer picture of the work that God is actually doing in our courses. By looking to evidence-based guidelines for the specific assessments that we are using, we are looking for further confirmation of the reliability and validity of these tools that are intended to help us better know where and how God is impacting our students.

---

25. Hattie, *Visible Learning*, 178–79. Supporting evidence-based assessments: CCSSO, *Intasc Model Core Teaching Standards*, Standard 6—Indicator 1 & 3, Standard 9—Indicator 2; MarylandOnline, "Quality Matters Rubric Standards," 3.4.

26. Kyle, *Living Spiritual Praxis*, 51.

27. Kant, *Religion Within Limits*, 105–6, 20, 23, 43, 55–56, 69.

However, just because the specific assessments we are using have been successfully utilized elsewhere does not automatically mean that they will work equally as well for our classroom. As a result, we too must measure these assessments when we apply them as the basis of our reason, as well as additional validity and reliability confirmation processes, in order to be sure that they are providing an accurate picture of student learning and development for each one of our learners. In doing so, we will be in a much better place to more accurately and clearly discern the educational work that God is doing so that we can partner more closely with God in this work.

Level 1

The instructor follows evidence-based recommendations for developing, implementing, interpreting, and applying specific assessments.

At this level, instructors should be able to identify and/or be observed using evidence-based recommendations that they are relying on to help guide the design and implementation of the assessments being used in their course. They should also be able to articulate how they are interpreting assessment results, as well as how these interpretations align with the evidence-based recommendations that they are drawing from. Overall, the goal of this foundational level is for the instructor to incorporate more evidence-based assessments into their courses.

Theologically, using evidence-based resources is an effort to acknowledge and integrate the work that God has done in other contexts into one's own. If these assessments have successfully worked for others, then based on the evidence-based argument developed previously, it can be asserted that this is also possibly the work of God in our own classes. In other words, if God has used these assessments in other contexts then there is a possibility that God may also act with and through these assessments in our own. Of course, this is not necessarily the case, so we must be ready to adapt evidence-based resources to our own unique contexts. At this foundational level, then, we are invited to identify and adapt evidence-based assessments that have been utilized in other contexts that are similar to our own. In doing so, we are increasing the likelihood of partner with God's ongoing educational work via these assessments.

Examples of this might include:

- Instructor is observed using an evidence-based assessment strategy (e.g., team-based learning, rubrics that have been validated by others, etc.).
- Course materials (e.g., course site, syllabus, handouts, etc.) show evidence of the use of an evidence-based assessment strategy (e.g., team-based learning, rubrics that have been validated by others, etc.).
- The instructor is able to articulate which evidence-based assessment strategy they are utilizing.

- The instructor can identify specific evidence-based literature to support the assessments that they are using in their course (e.g., literature on writing good multiple-choice questions, processes for developing higher quality rubrics, etc.)

- Assessments and assessment data are observed to align with specific evidence-based best practices (e.g., discrimination indices on multiple choice questions are within acceptable limits, rubrics used in the course align with best practices, etc.).

Level 2

The instructor works to minimize bias for specific evidence-based assessments and to establish their validity and reliability based on course data.

Across the class, as well as across multiple offerings of the course, the instructor should work to establish the reliability and validity of the evidence-based assessments that they are using in the course. Assessment data is useless at best and misguided at worst if the assessments are unreliable and/or invalid. Furthermore, there should be evidence that the instructor has and continues to conduct bias analyses on their assessments to help ensure that one group of students (based on age, gender, SES, ethnicity, etc.) is not consistently and unjustifiably outperforming other groupings of students.

The product of one's spiritual discernment is only as good as the data and evaluations that this discernment is based upon. As a result, we must continually work to establish the reliability and validity of the assessments that we are using with each group of students. In essence, we are seeking to ensure that the information being gleaned from these assessments is providing the most accurate picture of how our students are doing in relation to course outcomes. Furthermore, as many assessments have been found to favor certain groups of students over others such as with some standardized tests,[28] we must ensure that our assessments are unbiased. Through these reliability and validation processes, we will be striving to develop the clearest picture possible of the educational progress that God is making with each and every student.

Examples of this might include:

- The instructor can state how they have reviewed assessment data to determine if the assessments are reflective of students' actual abilities (e.g., verify assessment validity).

- Instructor is able to articulate the process(es) by which they have validated and established the reliability of their assessment strategies.

---

28. Kruse, "Cultural Bias in Testing"; Rodolfo, "A Social Psychological Perspective"; Shuttleworth-Edwards, "Generally Representative."

- The instructor invites others to assess student achievement on one or more course assignments and reliability/validity are established based upon these multiple assessments.

- Assessment results do not show evidence of similar student performance receiving significantly different assessment scores (e.g., check for biases and/or lack of reliability).

- Instructor selects assessments to use in the course that have already been found to be reliable and valid for similar populations.

Level 3

The instructor collaborates with learners and/or others to engage in Level 1 and 2 activities.

Building upon the previous levels, at Level 3 the instructor proactively works with learners and/or others to improve evidence-based assessments in their course in terms of their reliability, validity, and non-bias. Such collaboration should focus on analyzing assessment data as well as adapting the assessments so that they provide greater congruence with the evidence-based recommendations. In addition, the instructor should work individually and/or with others to continually modify the assessments as a result of the gathered data.

In line with the democratic view of the educational kin-dom articulated at Level 3 for many other guidelines, this level encourages collaborative engagement with the work of the two previous levels. Here, the holy invitation is for faculty, students, and others to work together to adapt evidence-based assessments to their own contexts. Striving to develop a clearer picture of the educational work that God has been doing, they will also work together to ensure the validity and unbiased reliability of these assessments. From the development of these evaluative tools to the use of the data that they generate, learners and instructors are invited to cooperatively discern how to best engage with these assessments. Overall, their democratic kin-dom work will be to ensure the best possible utilization of these tools.

Examples of this might include:

- The instructor is observed working with students to review assessment data and collaboratively determine if the assessments are reflective of students' actual abilities (e.g., verify assessment validity).

- The instructor is observed working with students to choose, use, and reflect on the results of specific evidence-based assessments.

- The instructor is observed working with colleagues to reflect on assessment data to collaboratively decide how to use these results to help improve student achievement in the course.

- Instructor and/or their peer(s) can show evidence that they worked together to develop reliable, validated, and/or non-biased assessments.
- Course materials (e.g., course site, handouts, presentation slides, announcements, etc.) show evidence of the instructor(s) and students working collaboratively to develop, implement, and/or analyze assessments that align with evidence-based standards.

Guideline #4—Self- and Peer-Assessments

When appropriate, self- and/or peer-assessments and reflections are utilized that are intended to lead to improved learning and development.

Across many of the guidelines, there is a distinct emphasis on collaborative approaches to course development. In alignment with these aims, self- and peer-assessments can be a central part of one's courses. The primary purposes of these kinds of assessments are to help learners not only continue to progress in relation to course KSAs, but also to take more responsibility for their own and one another's learning and development. These kinds of assessments are also intended to foster deeper learning by having students engage more directly in their educational processes. Self- and peer-feedback should follow the other assessment guidelines given above. When these kinds of assessments are done well, they can result in an average effect size of 0.56, which is significant according to studies with more than 3,300 students.[29] Overall, the trend for these levels is from more instructor-centered and structured assessment activities towards more self-directed and learner-driven improvements across the course.[30]

This guideline helps us better understand how God seeks to work through students themselves to help foster their own and one another's growth. Related to the learner-learner interaction guideline (Guideline #1 in the Activities, Organization, and Resources section below), we find a theology of God working both within and among the class, which is characteristic of at least one of Christ's assertions about the kin-dom of God.[31] The overall movement of the Spirit here is to help learners take

---

29. Hattie, *Visible Learning*, 186–87, 203–4. Supporting evidence-based assessments: CCSSO, *Intasc Model Core Teaching Standards*, Standards 1 & 2—Indicator 2, Standard 6—Indicator 2, Standard 7—Indicator 2, Standard 8—Indicator 1; MarylandOnline, "Quality Matters Rubric Standards," 3.5, 5.2, 6.2; Pianta, La Paro, and Hamre, *Classroom Assessment Scoring*, Analysis & Inquiry, Quality of Feedback.

30. Supporting references: Ambrose, *How Learning Works*, 29, 151, 206; Bartlett-Ellis, Carter-Harris, and MacLaughlin, "Preparing Students"; Bruning, Schraw, and Norby, *Cognitive Psychology*, 88, 307; Clark and Mayer, *E-Learning*, 315; Friedman and Fisher, *Handbook on Effective Instructional Strategies*, 131; Gibbs and Taylor, "Comparing Student Self-Assessment"; Maas et al., "Critical Features"; Matlin, *Cognition*, 34, 202; Schoo et al., "Teaching Health Science Students"; Woolfolk, *Educational Psychology*, 368.

31. Luke 17:20–21.

more ownership of learning and development in the class. Such a central emphasis on personal transformation has been integral across Western Christian history.[32]

In 2 Samuel 12, for example, we find a story about the prophet Nathan being sent by God to reprimand King David for committing adultery and murder. In this passage, Nathan initially guides David through a peer-assessment by telling him a story about a rich man's exploitation of a poor man and his lamb. David responds with rage at the rich man's actions and uses criteria of justice and empathy to base his condemnations of the rich man. Nathan then helps David to apply a self-assessment to see how his own actions are essentially the same as the rich man's. David's eyes are opened, and he subsequently seeks repentance for his own behaviors, thereby applying the results of these peer- and self-assessments. In this passage, we can see how God uses these approaches to assessment to help us to grow in our spiritual lives.

While not explicitly theistic, Yale University's *Spiritual Self-Schema* program is one in which both self- and peer-assessments are an integral part of spiritual growth and development. In this program, participants use self-identified goals that they would like to work towards and then engage in regular self-evaluation in relation to these criteria.[33] The purpose of these self-assessments are to help one see where they are becoming derailed from their desired spiritual development so that they can then create interventions that will help them continue to grow. As a part of these continual self-reflections, they also encourage participants to seek outside support and feedback.[34] Utilized intentionally and mindfully, these self- and peer-assessments are an integral part of the means through which a fuller spiritual life can be realized according to the developers of this program.[35]

As educators, then, the invitation that we find God leading us towards with this guideline is to empower students to respond to the educational Spirit via self- and peer-assessments. It is an invitation to help students better learn how to listen and respond to God's educative work with them and each other. By doing so, our classes are helping to foster increased self-regulated learning skills which, from a theological stance, essentially are students' own abilities to discern where and how God is leading them to learn and develop. As a result, self- and peer-assessments can be asserted to be an important part of how God's educative life works with and through our classes.

Level 1

The instructor provides learners with criteria for an assignment to guide performance. The instructor then assists each learner in examining their own and/or each other's work in relation to these criteria.

32. Kyle, *Sacred Systems*.
33. Avants and Margolin, *Spiritual Self Schema*, 13–17, 56.
34. Avants and Margolin, *Spiritual Self Schema*, 34.
35. Avants and Margolin, *Spiritual Self Schema*, 7.

At this level, the instructor will provide most of the guidance for learners to engage with self- and/or peer-assessments. These kinds of assessment activities are highly structured as learners are taken, step-by-step, through these processes. A course at this level should not only have these kinds of activities, but also detailed criteria (e.g., rubrics, info sheets, guidelines, etc.) which learners are instructed on how to use.

At this foundational level, the instructor is called to discern where and how God may be inviting them to integrate self- and/or peer-assessments in their course. Such activities not only generate assessment data, they also help students to develop through them. As stated above, self- and peer-assessments invite the learner into the evaluative processes with God more directly. As these processes may be new for many, the instructor will guide learners through them in a step-by-step manner at this beginning level. Once students are more accustomed to these processes, they will be able to partner with God's assessing life more fully at higher levels.

Examples of this might include:

- Instructor is observed guiding students in evaluating their own and/or one another's work using a set of guidelines that the instructor has provided.
- Course assignment(s) require students to use a rubric to assess their own and/or each other's work.
- Discussion boards and/or other course materials show evidence of students critically reflecting on their own and/or each other's work in relation to a set of standards that they have learned about in class.
- Students and/or instructor(s) can state how they engage in self- and/or peer-assessments in relation to course concepts/skills.
- Course utilizes teaching/learning strategies that require students to evaluate their own and/or each other's work (e.g., team-based learning, self-regulated learning activities, etc.).

Level 2

Building on Level 1, the instructor helps learners apply the results of self- and/or peer-assessments in order to strengthen their performance.

Level 2 is similar to the previous level in that students will utilize criteria to complete self- and peer-assessments to improve and deepen their learning and development. Courses at this level, however, will then intentionally have students use the results of these assessments. An example might include revising a draft of a paper that has been self-assessed or improving their discussion board posts based on replies they have received from peers. This level is therefore distinguished by activities that explicitly empower students to act on the suggestions that have been gathered from self-/peer-assessments.

With assessment data being asserted to be the bedrock foundation for spiritual discernment in a course, acting on what is discerned is equally important. In doing so, we will be responding to God's movements to help us continue on our educational journey. As this relates to this guideline, the instructor is invited to work with students to apply the holy invitations that have been discerned from the self- and/or peer-assessments. By comparing their work with the given standards and having identified their own and/or one another's strengths/weaknesses, students will be in a position to better know what they might need to do in order to continue improving in the class. The instructor is therefore called to guide students in taking concrete steps to respond to these God-centered invitations based upon self- and/or peer-assessments.

Examples of this might include:

- Students are observed completing activities that guide them in applying the results of self-/peer-assessments, such as revising a draft of a paper.
- The course site has assignments that require students to use feedback received from peers to revise/improve their work.
- Course materials (e.g., syllabus, handouts, presentation slides, etc.) contain directions that guide students in applying the results of peer-/self-assessments and students are required to follow these directions in the course.
- Instructor is able to articulate how they guide students in a step-by-step manner to use self-/peer-assessment data to revise assignments, improve on exams, etc.
- Students are able to articulate how they have been guided by their instructor in a step-by-step manner to use self-/peer-assessment data to revise assignments, improve on exams, etc.

Level 3

The instructor and learners work collaboratively to generate assessment criteria. The course then helps to build learners' self-regulated learning skills by guiding them in analyzing and applying the results of self- and/or peer-assessment data to improve their performance.

At this level, there will be evidence of the instructor working with learners to generate self-/peer-assessment criteria. The primary shift, then, is from instructor-driven criteria at previous levels to collaboratively-generated assessment criteria at this level. In addition, similar to Guideline #2 for this area, classes at this level will require students to reflect on self-/peer-assessment outcomes, develop plans/strategies to improve, and then implement these plans. Level 3 therefore extends the work of Level 2 by more explicitly engaging students in reflecting on, learning from, and responding to self- and/or peer-assessments. These kinds of assessments are therefore intended to help increase students' self-regulated learning skills as they reflect more deeply on what a course assignment requires, work to complete and assess the assignment for themselves and/or one another, and finally work to improve their performance on similar and subsequent assignments. In courses at this level, instructors can be observed to work with learners to identify more effective learning strategies that will help them continue to improve in the course.

At this highest level, we again find the democratic and cooperative nature of God's work in the course. Here, students and teachers work together to more closely partner with God on Level 1 and 2 endeavors. Rather than the instructor solely designing and implementing these kinds of assessment activities, they work with learners to discern these evaluative tools as well as how their resulting data might be subsequently utilized. Of course, these assessments should still adhere to the previous guideline, so students and instructors must ensure the evidence-based validity and reliability of these self- and peer-assessments. In doing so, it can be asserted that they will therefore be partnering more closely with God's work to improve learning through these types of assessment activities.

Examples of this might include:

- Students are observed working in groups to create self-/peer-assessment criteria.

- An assignment that guides learners in developing self-/peer-assessment criteria has them apply these assessments, requires them to reflect on the results of these assessments, and then directs them to develop strategies for revisions and/or improvements.

- Course materials (e.g., syllabus, handouts, presentation slides) contain directions that guide students in developing, implementing, and analyzing self-/peer-assessments. Students are required to follow these directions and then develop strategies for increasing their competencies in the course.

- The instructor is observed guiding students through self-regulated learning processes (e.g., goal setting, developing learning strategies, evaluating progress, revising strategies) and requires students to engage in these via self-/peer-assessments that have been collectively developed by the class.

- Instructor(s) and/or students are able to articulate how they have (or will) collaboratively engaged in creating self-/peer-assessments, analyzed the results of these, and then developed strategies to improve in the course.

ACTIVITIES, ORGANIZATION, AND RESOURCE GUIDELINES

Theologically, a course's activities, how it is organized, and the resources that it utilizes are the means through which God directly enacts the kinds of transformation that he is striving to bring about for the people and communities that we are working with. "God" as a concept is often thought of in more abstract and other-worldly terms. But in our courses, God's educative life is very incarnational and concrete, and the activities, organization, and resources (AORs) are where the theological rubber meets the educational road. The following evidence-based guidelines are intended to help us to know what kinds of AORs that God can be asserted to have been able to effectively and consistently act within and through.

Guideline #1—Learner-Learner Interactions

Activities and resources intentionally foster learner-learner interactions (Core Guideline).

Social-cultural learning theories assert that students learn as much through their interactions with one another as they do on their own. Evidence-based studies and assessment tools have confirmed the substantial impact that learner-learner interactions have on student achievement.[36] Collectively, based on numerous studies involving more than 85,000 students, the average effect size of interventions related to this guideline is 0.51, which is significantly higher than Hattie's hinge point of 0.4.[37] This guideline therefore seeks to articulate the kinds of student interactions that different classes might have. The general trend with these levels is from simpler and more instructor-guided activities toward ones where learners are helping determine the directions that their projects/tasks should go in. As a result, learner-learner interactions are deeper and more intentional at higher levels and require more complex collaboration and group work skills as well as higher order thinking.[38]

---

36. Supporting references: Bradshaw and Lowenstein, *Innovative Teaching Strategies,* ch. 17, 19, 21; Bruning, Schraw, and Norby, *Cognitive Psychology,* 234, 306; Clark and Mayer, *E-Learning,* 184, ch. 13; Diamond, *Designing and Assessing,* 79, 194; Friedman and Fisher, *Handbook on Effective Instructional Strategies,* 92, 144; Myers et al., "Building a Community"; Sawyer, *Cambridge Handbook,* 13079–102; ch. 23, 24; Slavin, *Educational Psychology,* 247, 338; Woolfolk, *Educational Psychology,* 50, 314, 69.

37. Hattie, *Visible Learning,* 94–95, 104–5, 86–87, 210–14; CCSSO, *Intasc Model Core Teaching Standards,* Standard 3—Indicators 1 & 2, Standard 5—Indicator 2, Standard 6—Indicator 2, Standard 8—Indicators 1 & 2; MarylandOnline, "Quality Matters Rubric Standards," 1.9, 5.2, 5.4; Pianta, La Paro, and Hamre, *Classroom Assessment Scoring,* Positive Climate, Regard for Student Perspectives, Content Understanding, Quality of Feedback, Instructional Dialogue, Student Engagement.

38. Specific learner-learner references: Peer teaching and tutoring, collaborative learning, etc.: Hattie, *Visible Learning,* 186–87, 203–4, 12–14; Burgess et al., "Peer Tutoring"; Chua et al., "Effectiveness of a Shared Conference"; Diamond, *Designing and Assessing,* 79, 116–17, 93; Donovan and McCumber, "Interprofessional Collaborative Practice"; Dumas et al., "Expanding Simulation Capacity"; Ford, "Development of Nurse Self-Concept"; Friedman and Fisher, *Handbook on Effective Instructional Strategies,* 92; Kan et al., "How We Developed"; Knowlton and Jones, "Student-Led Clinical Orientation"; Lorio et al., "Power of Peer-Assisted Learning"; Manyama et al., "Improving Gross Anatomy Learning"; Moore, Westwater-Wood, and Kerry, "Academic Performance and Perception"; Morrison et al., *Designing Effective Instruction,* 211–14; Sawyer, *Cambridge Handbook,* 843–66, 2631–56, 4810–51, 5209–34, 381–405, ch. 12; Slavin, *Educational Psychology,* 273; Valente-Ferreira, Nunes Aranha, and Faria Ornellas de Souza, "Academic Leagues"; Wong et al., "An Integrative Review."

Classroom discussions, debate, etc.: Hattie, *Visible Learning,* 182–83; Boyd, Baliko, and Polyakova-Norwood, "Using Debates"; Bradshaw and Lowenstein, *Innovative Teaching Strategies,* ch. 11; Bruning, Schraw, and Norby, *Cognitive Psychology,* 212; Leslie, "Improving Class Discussion";

Interactions among Christians for the purposes of nurturing spiritual growth and development has been central to this religious tradition from the very beginning and continues to be a core value and means of transformation. For instance, Jesus is depicted as sending out the disciples to practice ministry in pairs.[39] In Luke's version of this dispensation, the seventy disciples return to Jesus joyfully because of the good works that had been done and experienced by them.[40] While these passages do not explicitly address this, these passages can be taken as emphasizing the importance of working with one another in our ministries such that we learn and grow together. Indeed, such learner-learner interactions are emphasized throughout the history of Western Christian spiritual formation and have been integral to Christian views of human growth and development across the centuries.[41]

Furthermore, Western Christian theology has long had a concept called "koinonia." Mel Lawrenz, a writer on spiritual formation, states that this term includes such elements as "sharing material goods, sharing in ministry, and being partners in the Gospel."[42] In essence, this theological concept is intended to capture the spiritual benefits of the fellowship that happens among disciples. Spiritual growth, Lawrenz asserts, is not to happen in complete isolation but must involve our intimate interactions with other sojourners. It is through our sustained interactions, according to the concept of koinonia, that we continue to grow in God together.

Following this, we can expect that God's educational life actively and effectively (as evidence by educational research) works through the relationships in our classes to help students learn and grow. As the levels below depict, the more intentional and intense these interactions are, the more extensively God works with and through them to foster learning and development. As teachers, we should therefore work to foster these kinds of holy interactions in our classes in order to enable God to deepen learning and development among our students more fully.

Sawyer, *Cambridge Handbook*, ch. 12, 26.

Role-playing: Beaird, "Care on a Continuum"; Bradshaw and Lowenstein, *Innovative Teaching Strategies,* ch. 13; Fossen and Stoeckel, "Nursing Students' Perceptions"; Hart and Chilcote, "'Won't You Be My Patient?'"; Leslie, "Expanding Moral Imagination"; Sittikariyakul, Jaturapatporn, and Kirshen, "Acting as Standardized Patients."

Games, game-based learning: Bradshaw and Lowenstein, *Innovative Teaching* Strategies, ch. 12; Clark and Mayer, *E-Learning,* ch. 16; Kaylor, "Fishing for Pharmacology Success"; Laine et al., "Science Spots AR"; Pitt, Borman-Shoap, and Eppich, "Twelve Tips for Maximizing Effectiveness."

39. Mark 6:7; Luke 10:1.

40. Luke 10:17–20.

41. Kyle, *Sacred Systems*, 288; Kyle, *Spiritual Being & Becoming*, 48.

42. Lawrenz, *Dynamics of Spiritual Formation*, 99.

Level 1

The course intentionally structures simple interactions among learners to support learning and development.

At this level, learner interactions are shorter and more superficial, requiring little more than common social skills. As a result of these kinds of interactions, learners will be learning more about one another and engaging with content/skills in simpler ways. Examples of these kinds of activities might include brief and more general class discussions, short think-pair-shares, quick game-based activities, simple role-playing, and collaborative activities that do not require more than a simple engagement with course content/skills. Overall, this level is focused on having students interact in simpler ways.

At this foundational level, God can be asserted to help students to develop the basic interaction skills they need to help each other engage with course KSAs in beginning ways. Here, following this guideline, God can also be found helping students to build simpler relationships with one another. Through these beginning relationships, course KSAs can then be nurtured by God in simpler and shorter ways. While we might want our students to interact in more substantive ways, God molds these beginning interactions into the strong foundations that God needs in order to help students achieve higher levels.

Examples of this might include:

- Students are observed to work in short-term groups on simpler activities, problems, etc. related to course concepts and skills.
- The course site has evidence of assignments where students are required to collaborate on short-term activities.
- The instructor and/or students are able to describe group-work activities that they have (or will) engaged that were of shorter duration.
- Assessment data shows evidence of learners working together for brief periods to complete the assessment.
- Groups in the class are typically formed using random selection such that members of each group only work with one another for brief periods.

Level 2

The course facilitates students learning about each other's diverse perspectives, critically reflecting on these, and/or helping one another to engage with relevant KSAs in improved ways.

This level has learners engage with one another in deeper and more intentional ways. Here, learners are encouraged to better understand the diverse perspectives that their classmates have in relation to course KSAs and to engage with these perspectives in more critically constructive ways. Examples might include peer teaching/tutoring, small and large group debates, group problem-solving assignments, and small group analyses of case studies. Learners at this level will also be more supportive of one another's educational journey by intentionally helping each other to engage with course KSAs in deeper ways.

As students continue to interact with one another, God's relational life is able to emerge in more complex and sustained ways. Being the very essence of the glue that binds learners together, God is able to help leaners to engage with each other via constructive critical reflection. Here, God may be found helping each person reflect on the potential strengths and limits of one another's KSAs and thereby learn more about themselves in the process. This level is therefore theologically characterized by God's work to help students engage with each other as well as course KSAs in deeper and more sustained ways.

Examples of this might include:

- Learners are observed cooperatively engaging with course content in more critically reflective and long-term ways.

- Learners are observed questioning their own and one another's assumptions, exploring how/why they understand course content in the ways that they do, providing constructive feedback and support to one another, etc.

- There is evidence of students being assigned to long-term groups where they are required to engage with course content and one another in increasingly complex ways (e.g., applying, evaluating, analyzing, etc.).

- The instructor is able to describe how they have designed group activities that require students to engage with course content and one another in increasingly complex ways (e.g., applying, evaluating, analyzing, etc.).

- Assessment data has evidence of students working in groups in ways that result in their engaging with course content and one another in increasingly complex ways (e.g., applying, evaluating, analyzing, etc.).

Level 3

Building on Level 2, the course facilitates long-term group projects/activities where groups are required to collaborate in substantive ways (e.g., decision-making, problem solving, exploration, invention, etc.).

This level extends beyond the previous one by requiring learners to collaboratively engage in long-term decision-making, problem solving, real-world projects, and so on. These kinds of activities typically require learners to engage with both one another as well as course KSAs in ways that require more responsibility. Examples of activities might include small groups completing extended service-learning projects, design projects for ill-defined problems, long-term peer-assessment partnerships, and semester-long group research projects. Groups should be observed and supported in their transitions through normal group development processes (e.g., forming, norming, storming, performing, adjourning) as they engage in these activities over an extended period of time.

At this highest level, God may be asserted to have fostered a genuine team. Whether this is with only two students or an entire class, God's relational life with and through these groups may be clearly seen in the positive and productive ways that they work with one another. These highly effective groups are therefore able to engage with projects that are more in-depth and advanced than teams at previous levels can handle. They are, spiritually speaking, able to respond to God's movements of collaborative creativity, mutual support and affirmation, group reconciliation, and restorative processes. Such teams, of necessity, work closely together over an extended period of time and usually require close mentoring from the instructor to help them to continually respond to God's team-building movements. Though they require quite a bit of effort, these teams typically engage with KSAs in substantially deeper ways than at previous levels thereby manifesting God's educational life more completely.

Examples of this might include:

- Assessment data shows clear evidence of students engaging in activities that have required them to demonstrate their abilities to collaborate on long-term problem-solving, research, service-learning, etc. projects.
- Groups are observed to transition through typical group development processes (e.g., forming, norming, storming, performing, adjourning) across the course.
- Students and/or instructor(s) are able to articulate and present evidence of how groups have been working together in long-term ways on projects that have required them to collaborate on activities such as service-learning projects, design projects for ill-defined problems, long-term peer-assessment partnerships, and semester-long group research projects.
- Course materials (e.g., syllabus, handouts, course site, etc.) show clear evidence of students completing activities that have required them to demonstrate their abilities to collaborate on long-term problem-solving, research, service-learning, etc. projects.

Guideline #2—Higher Order Thinking

Activities and resources help learners progress in higher order thinking to improve learning and development (Core Guideline).

Similar to the first guideline, the effect size for this one is around 0.50, based on studies including almost 457,000 students.[43] Critical thinking skills are widely acknowledged to be essential competencies that students need to develop. This guideline is therefore intended to help instructors focus on these skills in relation to course KSAs. The trend from Level 1 to Level 3 is from learners being guided through simpler critical thinking activities towards their having to use more complex higher order thinking. At the highest level, learners take more control and initiative in developing these kinds of activities. These increasingly complex skills may build gradually across the course or they may be engaged from the very beginning with scaffolded support being provided along the way. Overall, the goal is to help students continue to develop in these very important capabilities while deepening their learning in the process.[44]

Theologically, being present within, to, and beyond all that is, God can be asserted to be the very Source and Essence of complexity.[45] One of the great benefits of being able to process things in increasingly complex ways is that it allows one to appreciate and understand the complexity of God more fully. If it really is God's desire that we better know and come to be more like God,[46] then it stands to reason that God would seek to foster such higher order thinking and complex capabilities in our classrooms. In the Christian testament, 1 Corinthians 13 for instance, we hear Paul of Tarsus speaking of such life-long development. Nestled within a passage about the importance of love, Paul points out the kinds of changes that come as we grow into adulthood when he writes, "When I was a child, I talked like a child, I thought like a child, I reasoned like a child. When I became a man, I put the ways of childhood behind me."[47] In these scriptures, Paul is working to help his readers develop a deeper, more complex, and nuanced understanding of love and its centrality for Christians. Such writings also speak to the importance of our calling to continue growing in our

---

43. Hattie, *Visible Learning*, 101–2, 47–49, 55–56, 58–59, 88–93, 203–4, 08–14. Supporting evidence-based assessments: CCSSO, *Intasc Model Core Teaching Standards*, Standards 1 & 2—Indicator 2, Standard 4—Indicator 2, Standard 5—Indicators 1 & 2, Standard 6—Indicators 1 & 2, Standard 8—Indicators 1 & 2; MarylandOnline, "Quality Matters Rubric Standards," 2.5, 5.2; Pianta, La Paro, and Hamre, *Classroom Assessment Scoring*, Regard for Student Perspective, Content Understanding, Analysis & Inquiry, Quality of Feedback; Instructional Dialogue.

44. Supporting references: Ambrose, *How Learning Works*, 62, 117; Aronsson et al., "Understanding of Core Pharmacological Concepts"; Boyer, Tardif, and Lefebvre, "From a Medical Problem"; Bradshaw and Lowenstein, *Innovative Teaching Strategies*, 338, ch. 3, 5, 7; Bruning, Schraw, and Norby, *Cognitive Psychology*, 233, 307; Bussard, "Nature of Clinical Judgment"; Diamond, *Designing and Assessing*, 117, 92; Chamberland et al., "Does Medical Students' Diagnostic Performance?,"; Clark and Mayer, *E-Learning*, 17, 242–44, ch. 15; Kulasegaram et al., "Mediating Effect"; Kunina-Habenicht et al., "Assessing Clinical Reasoning"; O'Rourke and Zerwic, "Measure of Clinical Decision-Making"; Raterink, "Reflective Journaling"; Sawyer, *Cambridge Handbook*, 522–45, 90–605, 1430–554, 4538–609, 9538–58; Slavin, *Educational Psychology*, 255; Woolfolk, *Educational Psychology*, 367, 459, ch. 8.

45. Kyle, *Sacred Systems*, 279.

46. Kyle, *Sacred Systems*, 285.

47. 1 Cor 13:11.

understanding of God's infinite mysteries, something which requires higher order and more complex thinking patterns to grasp.

Such increasing complex lifespan developments may also be found in the research conducted by James Fowler and his research team. The results of some of these studies are outlined in his well-known book, *Stages of Faith*.[48] One of the key findings, based upon interviews with thousands of people, is that as we grow across our lifetime, our understanding of God appears to grow through distinct stages. It is interesting to note that in the childhood stages, our theological conceptions are more primal, undifferentiated, and intuitive. However, as many people grow throughout their life, according to Fowler's research, these understandings become more personally reflective and one is better able to deal with complex paradoxes related their theological and religious understandings.

Within the Western Christian tradition, we can see God working to help many of us develop higher order and more complex thinking skills. Contemporary educational research has subsequently found that when we help students to utilize complex thinking patterns in relation to course content/skills, their learning is deeper, longer-lasting, and more meaningful. This guideline therefore helps us better understand that God's educational life seeks to foster such complexity of thought, not only for the sake of deeper learning, but also so that we might come to know and respond to God's infinitely complex life more fully. As a result, we should work with our students to help them develop their higher order thinking skills, for in doing so, we are likely helping them to be more responsive to God's more complex movements within and among them.

Level 1

The course guides learner engagement with simpler critical thinking skills (e.g., apply, analyze, and evaluate) for course KSAs.

At this level, learners are intentionally guided by the instructor in their understanding and application of more basic critical thinking skills such as evaluating information based upon given criteria, comparing and contrasting course concepts, and inductive/deductive reasoning skills. This level is therefore distinguished by: 1) the instructor providing most of the structure and resources for learners to operate within and utilize, and 2) engagement with more basic levels of critical thinking skills. Examples of this level might include students learning basic methods of inquiry that are common for the discipline, simpler gather-organize-analyze-report projects, and having learners evaluate information based upon given criteria.

Moving beyond simpler recall of factual information, it can be asserted that God works with students at this level to help them engage with KSAs in more complex ways. Knowing that long-term memory is supported by more complex encoding

48. Fowler, *Stages of Faith*.

processes,[49] God may be found inviting students to engage in these learning strategies. In doing so, students are not only learning KSAs in deeper ways, they are also developing the basic critical thinking skills they will need in order to use these KSAs in world-changing ways. We can therefore find God working with students at this level to develop these higher order thinking skills so that students can more fully become change agents with God in their communities.

Examples of this might include:

- Instructor is observed facilitating a class discussion where students critically evaluate course knowledge/skills.
- The course has assignments that require students to analyze a case study using concepts from the class.
- Students are able to state how they have applied specific skills they are learning to a real-world situation.
- The class has a project where students are required to compare-contrast course KSAs.

Level 2

The course facilitates more complex higher order thinking skills (e.g., synthesizing, creating, innovating, etc.) and/or guides learners in challenging assumptions inherent in concepts, skills, materials, theories, methods, activities, etc.

For Level 2 courses, learners will be expected to engage with higher order thinking skills that are more synthesizing, integrative, and multi-dimensional in nature. Instructors should therefore be observed to model these kinds of thinking skills, and there should be activities that require learners to actively engage in and apply them. These courses might also have learners question and critically reflect on the course itself. Here, students might question a textbook's position, the instructor might encourage students to challenge the instructor's claims, or a theory that is being presented might be analyzed for its inherent limits and/or biases. Overall, courses at this level empower students to engage in more complex higher order thinking skills in relation to course KSAs.

Continuing with the critical thinking development of the previous level, we might claim that God is inviting students at this level to enter into more complex kinds of engagement. As asserted above, God's life and movements are infinitely complex, intricately integrated, and multidimensional in nature. Following the beliefs of some panentheistic theologians,[50] even simple-celled organisms can respond to God's life at some level. However, the more complex an organism's capacities are, the better able

---

49. Matlin, *Cognition*, ch. 5.
50. See Appendix A.

they will be able to respond to God's more complex orchestrations and manifestations. At this level, then, we can assert that God is working with our students to reach toward higher levels of complex thinking, feeling, doing, relating, organizing, etc. In doing so, God is helping learners develop their fuller capabilities to partner with God's infinitely complex life in our increasingly complex world.

Examples of this might include:

- Instructor is observed facilitating small group activities that require students to use course concepts to create, innovate, design, etc.

- Course assignments require learners to identify and critically analyze assumptions that are inherent in course readings.

- Students in the class complete a semester-long project where they have to propose novel solutions to real-world problems.

- The instructor is observed demonstrating and explaining how to synthesize specific course knowledge and/or skills and then requires students to do likewise with different parts of the course.

Level 3

The course helps learners to design and implement higher order thinking experiences that are aligned with learning objectives, result in a variety of outcomes and artifacts, and that build on learners' interests and backgrounds.

Being more learner-driven, at this level the instructor collaborates with students to develop activities that engage in the higher order thinking skills described for the two previous levels. In contrast to the instructor providing structure and resources as they would at Levels 1 and 2, learners are instead guided in identifying methods, resources, and theories they might utilize themselves. As a result, learners are not only using higher order thinking skills in the activities they are helping to develop, but they are also using these skills as part of the activity development process itself. The primary focus at this level, then, is having learners take primary responsibility for the development of higher order thinking activities to support their ongoing educational journey.

Here we find a continually emerging image of Level 3 courses as being God's educational kin-dom that is democratic, collaborative, and inherently relational. If God really is seeking to help students develop higher order thinking skills, then it might stand to reason that God would invite students into the complex and critically reflective process of developing these kinds of activities. With each student being infinitely unique, such invitations are therefore more likely to result in activities that are better matched to their current capabilities when well-planned and facilitated. As a result, the instructor is called to help students discern what kinds of critical thinking activities to engage in and how these might be used to deepen learning. In doing so, the class will be collectively participating in God's work to continually nurture higher order thinking for the purposes discussed above.

Examples of this might include:

- The course requires students to identify and address an ill-defined problem in their local community.

- The instructor(s) and learner(s) are observed collaborating to develop a semester-long research project that is directly related to course concepts/skills.

- Students are required to develop a rubric to assess a course paper and then make revisions based upon self-/peer-assessments using this rubric.

- The instructor can describe course activities where students had to develop their own inquiry-based projects/experiments.

Guideline #3—Use of Technologies

Course intentionally integrates relevant and interactive technologies to improve learning and development.

The use of technology in courses can span from simpler applications to using it in ways that redefine the activities that the technology is being used with. Models such as SAMR (Substitution, Augmentation, Modification, and Redefinition) provide further insights into these kinds of technology integration.[51] Overall, one of the primary aims of technology integration is to help our students gain the competencies they will need in order to more effectively utilize relevant technologies in their personal, civic, and/or professional lives. Another primary aim is using these technologies in ways that genuinely help improve student learning and development in the course. As a result, when assessing technology integration, we must consider how reliant on the technology an activity is (i.e., how easily can the activity be completed with or without the specific technology) as well as the competencies that such technology use requires.

Educational studies on technology have included more than 8,000,000 students and have shown an overall effect size of 0.33, which is less than Hattie's recommended h-point of 0.4.[52] One of the primary messages that has emerged from these many studies is that it is not so important as to which technology one is using as it is on how the technology is being utilized. In other words, pedagogy matters far more than the technology itself. With an effect size of less than 0.4, then, why include it as one of the

---

51. Romrell, Kidder, and Wood, "SAMR Model as a Framework."

52. Hattie, *Visible Learning*, 179–81, 207–8, 20–33. Supporting evidence-based assessments: CC-SSO, *Intasc Model Core Teaching Standards*, Standard 3—Indicator 2, Standard 5—Indicator 2, Standard 6—Indicator 2, Standard 7—Indicators 1 & 2, Standard 8—Indicators 1 & 2; MarylandOnline, "Quality Matters Rubric Standards," 1.5, 1.7, 6.1, 6.2, 6.3, 6.4, 8.2, 8.5; Pianta, La Paro, and Hamre, *Classroom Assessment Scoring,* Regard for Student Perspectives.

guidelines? First, it is now difficult to pick up an educational research journal and not find numerous articles that are related to the use of technology in some way. Indeed, technology has become all pervasive in our society. Second, and more importantly, there is growing evidence that those who do not know how to effectively use science and technology will increasingly have more difficulty finding employment and/or jobs that pay living wages.[53] As a result, this guideline has been included to ensure that technology integration is being given proper attention in our educational systems.[54]

From a simple view, turning now to our theological reflections, technology may be seen as nothing more than a tool. Tools are used by many species to help accomplish tasks that are needed in order to better thrive as beautiful manifestations of God's life in creation.[55] Most religious traditions utilize tools to help their disciples continually grow in their spiritual lives—sacred texts, incense, worship bulletins, houses of prayer—are all tools that God can be asserted using to help us achieve these holy ends. For instance, in Exodus 35:30—39:43, we hear of God calling Bezalel and Oholiah, and many other skilled craft persons who were blessed with the "divine spirit, with skill, intelligence, and knowledge in every kind of craft" (Exod. 35:31), to build such sacramental artefacts as the tabernacle, the ark of the covenant, lampstands, altars, incense, and others. These are a testament to the purposes and ways that God works through these to foster religious living.

Translating this theology of tools to a more contemporary era, digital technologies can also be viewed through this more simplistic lens. From this perspective, our role as educators is therefore to integrate such technologies as social media, apps, and websites into our courses to better enable our students to deepen their educational engagement with God. When done discerningly, they will be partnering with God's life as God works to achieve educational outcomes through the use of these technologies.

However, there is also a more deeply profound theological view of technology that may be developed. Building upon an incarnational view of God, it can be asserted that God's transformative life also exists within and through the technologies themselves. This is a radically different view of the physical world than what most westerners have of "inanimate objects." Generally, most view them as dead, lifeless,

---

53. Blow, "A Future Segregated?"

54. Supporting references: Alqahtani et al., "Live Demonstration Versus Procedural Video"; Bradshaw and Lowenstein, *Innovative Teaching Strategies*, 12, 18, 19, 21; Bellack and Thibault, "Creating a Continuously Learning Health"; Bruning, Schraw, and Norby, *Cognitive Psychology*, 308; Chen et al., "Resolving Bottlenecks"; Clark and Mayer, *E-Learning*, 31; Diamond, *Designing and Assessing*, ch. 18; Duke et al., "Preserving Third Year"; Hortsch, "'How We Learn'"; Irwin and Coutts, "A Systematic Review"; Keegan et al., "Use of Mobile Device Simulation"; Khandelwal et al., "How We Made Professionalism Relevant"; Morrison et al., *Designing Effective Instruction*, ch. 10; Park and Park, "Effectiveness"; Peacock and Grande, "An Online App Platform"; Reiser and Dempsey, *Trends and Issues*, 201; Sawyer, *Cambridge Handbook*, 771–96, 5089–103, 13622–38, ch. 25, 30; Schlegel et al., "Use of Video"; Vaccani, Javidnia, and Humphrey-Murto, "Effectiveness of Webcast"; Woolfolk, *Educational Psychology*, 336–40; Zitzelsberger et al., "Using Wikis."

55. Jacobs, von Bayern, and Osvath, "A Novel Tool-Use Mode."

and devoid of any kind of energetic life. Yet, the field of quantum physics is helping us to see just how dynamic subatomic life really is.[56]

Some scientists/religionists, such as Jesuit paleontologist/geologist and theologian Pierre Teilhard de Chardin have developed theologies to accompany these revised understandings of the physical world. Challenging his own enculturation into the lifeless view of inanimate objects, Teilhard de Chardin proclaims a radically different theological view of them and God's active life within and through them in his well-known Hymn to Matter. For Teilhard de Chardin, basic matter, the stuff from which tools are made, are manifestations of God's very own life. In this text, he writes,

> I bless you, matter, and you I acclaim: not as the pontiffs of science or the moralizing preachers depict you, debased, disfigured—a mass of brute forces and base appetites—but as you reveal yourself to me today, in your totality and your true nature . . . I acclaim you as the divine milieu, charged with creative power, as the ocean stirred by the Spirit, as the clay moulded and infused with life by the incarnate Word.[57]

From this perspective, technology may no longer be seen from a human-centered perspective as a mere tool whose sole purpose is to help us achieve our personal and/or communal goals. Instead, each technology is viewed as a unique manifestation of God with whom we are invited to partner with in order to help God achieve his aims in the world. From this incarnational perspective, every technology is inherently sacred, as is our role as theistic educators to help our students learn to better appreciate and partner with these manifestations of God in their personal, professional, and civic lives.

For many, this theology of technology may seem ridiculous because our Western culture has unfortunately cultivated a very low, unsacred, and human-centered (anthropomorphic) view of the material world. Nevertheless, we assert that this theology of technology is more in line with the most recent advances in both science and systematic theology.[58] As a result, theistic educators should therefore: 1) help students better appreciate the technologies that we have, 2) discerningly use them to help our students learn and develop more deeply, and 3) empower our students to learn how to use these technologies more effectively in their own personal, professional, and civic lives. This means that educational systems must help our students continually develop the KSAs to more successfully do so. As a result, our classrooms need to intentionally integrate them in pedagogically sound and evidence-based ways. For when we do, we are better partnering with God to fulfill his aims in our world—not only for our students, but also within and through the technologies themselves.

56. Pickover, *Physics Book*.
57. Chardin, *Hymn of Universe*, 69–70.
58. See panentheistic authors such as: Bracken, *Divine Matrix*; Clayton and Peacocke, *In Whom We Live*; Cobb, Jr. and Griffin, *Process Theology*; McGrath, *A Fine-Tuned Universe*; Peacocke, *Paths from Science Towards God*; Smith, *God, Energy and the Field*.

Level 1

The course provides opportunities for learners to use relevant technologies in simpler ways that support but do not fundamentally change the learning experiences. Only very basic technology skills are needed by learners.

Level 1 technology integration in a class will typically involve more basic and supportive uses. For example, technology might be used to enable learners to track their grades, access resources, submit assignments on the learning management system (LMS), conduct simple internet searches, use email, and take notes electronically. Only basic technical skills (such as accessing and navigating) are required and the activities themselves are not impacted by the technology in significant ways (i.e., the activity could be completed fairly easily via non-technology ways if necessary). At this level, then, technology is more of a convenient "means-to-an-end" rather than being integral to the learning process itself.

Theologically, it might be asserted that God is working at this foundational level to help students develop the basic technology skills they need to partner with God's educational work. In a sense, this could be viewed as an introduction to how God works with and through these digital technologies to help foster learning. In order to do so, students therefore need to begin using technologies to support their learning activities. At this level, such use is simpler and more for convenience sake than it is for impacting learning processes more directly. Overall, God works at this level to help students gain familiarity and begin establishing the habits and skills they will need for the more advanced levels.

Examples of this might include:

- Students are observed downloading and submitting assignments via the course learning management system (LMS).
- Course assignments require students to conduct an internet search to find information.
- Students are observed taking notes and accessing the course site during face-to-face sessions.
- The course site contains discussion boards that students are required to participate in.
- The syllabus contains technology use expectations that encourage technology in the class but also outline the etiquette related to this use.

Level 2

The course expands the options for learners' responsible use of relevant and more interactive technologies to improve learning. The technologies are integral to engagement with learning experiences and intermediate technical skills may also be required of the learner.

For this level, technology integration is more sophisticated and requires more technical skills for learners. The learning activities themselves are modified as they rely more heavily on the technology that is being utilized. Examples might include using a spreadsheet to conduct analysis and generate charts, using interactive digital games/apps to help prepare for a test, creating a digital photo collage to illustrate important course concepts, and using online survey software to collect large samples of data. Also, learners must sometimes (but not always) have a better understanding of the technologies they are using in order to be able to complete the activities in ways that foster deeper learning. As a result, this level may require learners to have and/or develop more sophisticated technological skills in order to be able to effectively use the technologies to further enhance their learning.

God's work with learners, it might be asserted, continues to complexify at this level. With advanced computer coding, God is able to do more with and through technologies. As a result, God's educational aims through these technologies can be more sophisticated. The instructor is therefore invited to spiritually discern which technologies God is calling them to integrate into the course. At this level, these technologies will play a more central role in the learning activities, making these activities more difficult to engage without the specific technology. Similar to the previous guideline, learners' technological capabilities may also need to be more complex and of a higher order.

Examples of this might include:

- The course requires learners to use interactive digital games/apps to help them better learn concepts.
- Learners are observed submitting digital storytelling projects in place of written papers for an assignment.
- The instructor is observed demonstrating how learners can use a virtual patient/client to practice skills.
- The course site contains interactive e-learning modules that students must complete.

Level 3

The instructor collaborates with learners in identifying relevant interactive technologies that redefine course activities in significant ways. The technologies are essential in order to engage in learning experiences and advanced technical skills may also be required.

The integration of technology at Level 3 is much more sophisticated than the previous two levels. In general, the activity would be extremely difficult to complete without the use of technology and the technology itself redefines the nature of the activity. Examples of such technology enhanced activities at this level might include online collaborative projects with communities from other parts of the nation/world, online team-based mind maps, use of intelligent tutoring systems, and immersive 3D digital simulations. Learners are also often required to develop and utilize more advanced technical skills, which are needed in order to effectively use these kinds of technologies to improve their learning. In addition, as with other guidelines, there should be some evidence of instructors collaborating with learners in choosing and implementing these technologies and/or developing their technology skills sets.

Further extending Level 3's democratic view of God's kin-dom, the instructor will collaborate with students in selecting technology-enhanced learning activities. These activities should not only help to facilitate learners' deep engagement with core KSAs, they should utilize advanced technologies. These advanced technologies, as asserted above, may be considered manifestations of God, a part of whose purpose it is to help students to learn more deeply. Students and faculty are therefore invited at this level to discern which advanced technologies they can best partner with to help achieve the learning outcomes. In doing so, learners will also likely need to further develop their own technical skills in order to more closely respond to God's educational life with and through these complex technologies.

Examples of this might include:

- The instructor(s) and students are observed working together to create interactive e-learning modules they will complete.
- The course site contains links to (or has embedded in it) virtual 3D software/simulations that are used to help students better understand course concepts.
- Students and the instructor(s) collaborate using online technologies with a school from another part of the world to complete a real-world project together.
- The instructor(s) and students use HTML to collaboratively create a website as part of the course.

Guideline #4—Real-world Applications

The course helps learners to adapt relevant KSAs to address real-world issues in authentic contexts.

Similar to the previous guideline, the effect size of this one is below Hattie's hinge point value of 0.4. Based on studies with almost 61,000 students, the average effect size is 0.34.[59] Again, one might ask the question as to why we therefore would include

---

59. Hattie, *Visible Learning*, 208–12, 30–31. Supporting evidence-based assessments: CCSSO,

this guideline. Cognitive psychology studies have repeatedly shown that there is better recall of information when the context for recall more closely matches the context in which the information was initially learned. In addition, preparing students to be competent co-workers and civically engaged community members is a central part of the mission of education according to many authors.[60] As a result, our classes should help learners to be able to apply course KSAs in real-world situations. Doing so will not only help with their transference of KSAs to these situations it will also aid in helping these KSAs to be more relevant and meaning to students, which is an important part of fostering deeper learning.[61]

As a course moves from Level 1 to Level 3, learners move from more simply engaging course KSAs within authentic settings/scenarios towards more actively identifying and directly addressing real-world problems. The transition is therefore twofold: 1) from instructor-driven to collaborative, and 2) from simple presence in an authentic setting/scenario towards engaging more directly with real-world issues in a local context. Overall, courses should therefore prepare learners to be able to develop

---

Intasc Model Core Teaching Standards, Standard 5–Indicators 1 & 2, Standard 8–Indicator 2; Pianta, La Paro, and Hamre, *Classroom Assessment Scoring*, Regard for Student Perspectives, Content Understanding.

60. Real-world simulations, clinical simulations, etc. references: Bradshaw and Lowenstein, *Innovative Teaching Strategies*, ch. 14–17; Eggenberger, Krumwiede, and Young, "Using Simulation Pedagogy"; Garnett, Weiss, and Winland-Brown, "Simulation Design"; Gude et al., "Can We Rely on Simulated?"; Jeffries, "The Good News"; Jorm et al., "Large-Scale Mass Casualty"; Landeen et al., "Exploring Student and Faculty Perceptions"; Makransky et al., "Simulation Based Virtual Learning"; Rue and Doolen, "Pseudostandardized Patients"; Zimmermann et al., "Inter-Professional in-Situ Simulated."

Real-world projects, project-based learning, service-learning, community-based pedagogies, etc. references: Amalba et al., "Effect of Community"; Barnes, "Impact of Service-Learning"; Bradshaw and Lowenstein, *Innovative Teaching Strategies*, ch. 28; Bruning, Schraw, and Norby, *Cognitive Psychology*, 233; Chuang et al., "Medical and Pharmacy Student Concerns"; DeBonis, "Effects of Service-Learning"; Fitzwater and Tong, "Clinical Policy Evaluation"; Gavin-Knecht and Fischer, "Undergraduate Nursing Students' Experience"; Landheer-Zandee et al., "Impact"; Matlin, *Cognition*, 370; Sawyer, *Cambridge Handbook*, 8808–30, ch. 19.

Workplace experiences, clinicals, immersion experiences, etc.: Bradshaw and Lowenstein, *Innovative Teaching Strategies*, ch. 23, 24, 26, 27; Braniff et al., "Assistantship Improves Medical Students' Perception"; Gilliland, "Effects of Community-Based Hospice"; McGettigan and McKendree, "Interprofessional Training"; Park et al., "A BEME Systematic Review"; Piquette, Moulton, and LeBlanc, "Creating Learning Momentum"; Ritten, Waldrop, and Wink, "Nurse Practitioner Students"; Teunissen, "Experience, Trajectories, and Reifications"; von Pressentin, Waggie, and Conradie, "Towards Tailored Teaching."

61. Additional supporting references: Ambrose, *How Learning Works*, 23, 83, 117–18, 19; Bradshaw and Lowenstein, *Innovative Teaching Strategies,* ch. 14, 15, 16, 17; Bruning, Schraw, and Norby, *Cognitive Psychology,* 88, 104; Clark and Mayer, *E-Learning,* 21, 240–42, 62–63, 260–61; Diamond, *Designing and Assessing,* 192, 96; Friedman and Fisher, *Handbook on Effective Instructional Strategies,* 131; Diogo, Barbosa, and Ferreira, "A Pilot Tuning"; Laine et al., "Science Spots AR"; Matlin, *Cognition,* 174, 370; Sawyer, *Cambridge Handbook,* 590–605, 5319–58, 876587–87, 13591–611, ch. 20; Slavin, *Educational Psychology,* 217; Woolfolk, *Educational Psychology,* 16, 259, 314.

KSAs in ways that are directly related to the authentic settings of their personal, professional, and/or civic lives.

One of the most significant aspects of Jesus' work with his disciples that has been noted was the very real-world mentoring and experiences that he continually provided them with. For instance, Jesus sent many of his followers out two-by-two to minister; he encouraged his disciples to directly minister to people who sought their help; he brought some of his disciples with him during times of prayer and struggle; he helped them struggle with difficult questions about his divine nature; and he worked with them to solve problems such as how to feed more than 5,000 people.[62] In each of these cases, and many others, we find Jesus working with his followers to continually adapt their knowledge and skills to address the real-world situations they found themselves in.

Western Christian spiritual formation practices generally resonate with these kinds of approaches by collectively asserting that our life and growth in God should include engaging with real-world issues.[63] Mission trips, for instance are a common way that many Christian communities strive to help their congregants grow in their life in God while at the same time addressing real needs in the world.[64] Such projects can be powerful ways through which the participants, as well as the communities they work with, learn and develop together more fully with God—individually, socially, economically, and politically.

Overall, this guideline depicts a spirituality of personal, professional, and civic life that God ever invites us into, one in which we seek to more fully partner with God's life in real-world ways. In our classes, then, the holy invitation is to discern how God is inviting us and our students to engage with course KSAs in these diverse and real-world environments. Some, such as John Dewey, have asserted that education is not solely intended for the sake of knowledge acquisition but so that the information and skills can be applied in ways that have a tangible impact on daily life.[65] Theologically, we might assert that God seeks to lead us in these directions and we are therefore called to help our students to more directly learn course KSAs for these ends. As a result, the holy invitation is twofold: 1) partnering with God's educational life in diverse and real-world environments so that our students learn and develop more deeply, and 2) helping them to learn how to discerningly use course KSAs to address real-world problems and issues in positive and productive ways. What we find, then, is that God is not just seeking to transform the lives of our students but also their communities. Our task as theistic educators is to discern which classroom and community transformations God is ever inviting us towards.

---

62. Luke 10:1–23. Matt 10:1–20, 26:36–46. Mark 8:27–30, 9:14–29. John 6:5–9.
63. Kyle, *Sacred Systems*, 288.
64. Wilder and Parker, *Transformission*, 14.
65. Dewey, *Democracy and Education*, 8.

Level 1

The course engages learners in applying course KSAs in authentic contexts/scenarios in direct and unmodified ways.

Level 1 courses for this guideline seek to place learners within the authentic settings/scenarios that are most likely to apply the central course KSAs. Exposure to such diverse and real-world settings is key at this level, and the application of the KSAs will be direct and unmodified. This means that learners are only expected to apply the KSAs in exactly the same way as they were taught without any kind of adaptations or modifications to the KSAs (adaptations and modifications are a Level 2 competency according to this guideline). In addition, such applications will have the primary purpose of helping the student better learn the KSAs rather than attempting to address a specific real-world problem/issue (this is a Level 2 competency). Learners in these courses therefore have the added benefit of engaging with course KSAs in similar contexts/scenarios as they will need to apply them in their professional, civic, and/or personal lives.

At this foundational level, God may be asserted to work with students to become familiar with the more authentic situations/scenarios that the KSAs are intended to address. By learning and applying KSAs in these contexts, God seeks to help the student begin to make the relevant and real-world connections that God will need them to make in order to enact change later on in their life. In essence, God is laying the essential foundations for students to be able to respond to God's movements at higher levels in more direct and transformational ways. At this beginning level, then, God may be asserted to be helping learners to become familiar and more comfortable with these situations/scenarios and the KSAs that are related to them.

Examples of this might include:

- The class is observed meeting in real-world settings (e.g., hospitals, public schools, community centers).
- Students are observed engaging in role-playing activities that mimic real-world situations.
- The course has an immersion trip as part of the course that has the primary purpose of exposing students to specific contexts, but not addressing specific issues/problems in the community.
- Students are observed practicing a skill in a real-world setting (e.g., taking blood pressures at a community center, learning how to collect water samples from a local creek).

Level 2

The course guides learners in adapting relevant KSAs for authentic contexts/scenarios in order to address a given real-world problem or issue.

This level is somewhat similar to Level 1 in that course KSAs are engaged in authentic and real-world contexts/scenarios. However, at this level learners are provided with a problem or they will engage with a real-world issue they might be expected to find in such a context. In order to address this given issue/problem, learners should also be expected to adapt key KSAs in significant ways. This requires a higher level of competency on the part of the learner as compared with Level 1, where learners merely had to apply what they had learned in direct and unmodified ways. This level is therefore distinguished from the previous level by: 1) having learners address real-world issues that are provided by the instructor and/or community partner(s), and 2) being required to modify the relevant KSAs in significant ways in order to address these problems/issues.

As will be discussed below, helping students grow in a step-by-step and scaffolded manner is central to how God works with learners, according to evidence-based educational research. For this guideline, we can assert that God is now helping students to partner with God's work in the community in more transformative ways. At the previous level, God worked to help learners become more familiar and comfortable with real-world situations. At this level, God now works to help the student engage more directly with these settings. In doing so, God may be asserted to be nurturing students' capabilities to work more effectively in these contexts. As they become more proficient in adapting course KSAs to these scenarios, learners can be more responsive to God's transformative life in the community. At this level, however, such proficiencies are intermediate as the instructor provides real-world issues to be addressed.

Examples of this might include:

- Course requires students to complete a service-learning project in the community where they adapt course concepts as part of their analyses and planning.
- Students are observed adapting course skills (such as healthcare skills, conflict mediation, strategic planning, and web development) to help a non-profit organization.
- Syllabus shows evidence of the course having highly structured internships where students are required to adapt the skills they are learning in class to these workplace settings.
- The course has an assignment where learners collect and analyze data in the field in order to help address a local problem.

Level 3

The course helps learners identify a real-world problem or issue in an authentic context/scenario that requires relevant KSA adaptations and requires them to carry out a plan that directly addresses this issue.

Level 3, like many other guidelines, is more collaborative in nature wherein the instructor(s) and community members work with learners to identify significant real-world problems or issues and then engage with these within authentic contexts/scenarios. This level therefore differs from Level 2, where learners are provided with a real-world issue by the instructor. However, these projects also build upon Level 2 by still requiring significant adaptations to be made to relevant KSAs. Activities for this level should include the following: 1) they are collaboratively generated by students, community members, and the instructor, and 2) require significant modifications to course KSAs in order to effectively address the real-world issue. Overall, the focus for this level is therefore on learners having more collaborative responsibility and leadership with instructors and/or community partners in identifying real-world issues, and then working to find effective ways of addressing these issues by adapting KSAs to authentic contexts.

At Level 3, students will have more fully developed into spiritual agents of change with God. This level is based upon a core theology that asserts that God is ever and proactively involved in fostering positive transformations in every part of creation. As a result, it can be asserted that God labors with students to learn how to use course KSAs to address one or more of the significant real-world problems that God has been working on. Discernment of these problems as well as engagement with them is one that is best achieved via close collaboration with those who have long been working with God on these problems. As a result, the course will help learners develop the capabilities they need in order to cooperatively discern and collectively address these issues in genuinely transformative ways with God using core course KSAs.

Examples of this might include:

- There is evidence of students working with a community partner to conduct an asset/needs assessment and create a plan to address identified assets/needs via adapting relevant course KSAs.

- Course activities include student-generated case studies that require learners to use modified versions of course KSAs in order to complete them.

- The class is observed partnering with an organization to complete a Continuous Quality Improvement (CQI) project that aligns with learning objectives and results in recommendations being made to the organization.

- Students complete an advocacy project they are passionate about where they identify relevant organizations who are working on the topic and then work with these organizations to strategize and/or work towards making change.

Guideline #5—Scaffolding Guidance

The course has learners engage in activities in ways that consistently scaffolds their increasing competencies for key KSAs (Core Guideline).

While the other guidelines above were more focused on specific course activities, this one identifies aspects of a course/module's overall organization and structure. All courses, according to this guideline, should minimally guide students through their learning and development in a step-by-step manner. Concepts and skills should build upon previous ones and the instructor should work to ensure that students are generally competent in core KSAs before moving on to subsequent ones. Based on studies with almost 153,000 students, the overall average effect size for this guideline exactly matches Hattie's hinge point of 0.40.[66] It is also one that is repeatedly and prominently noted in other evidence-based course assessment tools,[67] as well as in a broad range of educational literature.[68]

At higher levels, instructors will partner with learners in developing and selecting varied pathways that support their growth in core course KSAs. These pathways should allow for learner choice and be tailored to better match current students' diverse backgrounds. They should also support scaffolding wherein learners' progress to more advanced KSAs is dependent upon the demonstration of predetermined levels of competency for the more basic KSAs that these advanced topics/skills are founded upon. Overall, this guideline is therefore focused on how the course guides learners to engage in their learning experiences.

It is common place for Christian authors to talk about "God's plan/will" for their life. Throughout Western Christian history, God has been asserted as continually and

---

66. Hattie, *Visible Learning*, 125–26, 67–72, 78–79, 84–86, 208, 31–32.

67. CCSSO, *Intasc Model Core Teaching Standards*, Standards 1 & 2–Indicators 1 & 2, Standard 3–Indicator 2, Standard 4–Indicator 2, Standard 5–Indicator 2, Standard 7–Indicator 1, Standard 8–Indicators 1 & 2; MarylandOnline, "Quality Matters Rubric Standards," 1.1, 1.2, 2.2, 3.4, 4.2, 4.6, 5.1, 8.1; Pianta, La Paro, and Hamre, *Classroom Assessment Scoring*, Teacher Sensitivity, Productivity, Instructional Learning Formats, Content Understanding, Analysis and Inquiry, Quality of Feedback, Instructional Dialogue.

68. Albanese and Case, "Progress Testing"; Ambrose, *How Learning Works*, 38, 59–62, 114–16, 46–47; Blissett, Cavalcanti, and Sibbald, "ECG Rhythm Analysis"; Bradshaw and Lowenstein, *Innovative Teaching Strategies*, 225; Bruning, Schraw, and Norby, *Cognitive Psychology*, 34–35, 63, 87–88, 106, 78, 211–12, 34, 357; Burkhardt et al., "Engagement and Creation"; Chan et al., "Part Versus Whole"; Chen et al., "Sequencing Learning Experiences"; Clark and Mayer, *E-Learning*, 13, 37, 39, 97, 106–7, 17, 34, 40–41, 53, 226–30, 38, 56–57, 317, 29–33, 44–45; Chs. 10, 12; Diamond, *Designing and Assessing Courses and Curricula*, 17, 115, 50, 94; El Hussein, Jakubec, and Osuji, "The Facts"; Elias et al., "Evolving the Picot Method"; Friedman and Fisher, *Handbook on Effective Instructional Strategies*, 6, 53, 68, 80, 101, 15, 44, 91, 99, 288–89; Keegan et al., "Use of Mobile Device Simulation"; Kiernan and Hazard-Valleland, "Cancer as a Platform"; Kok et al., "Systematic Viewing in Radiology"; Kostiuk, "Can Learning ISBARR Framework Help?"; Matlin, *Cognition*, 177, 81–84; Morrison et al., *Designing Effective Instruction*, 72–74, 124, 62, 66, 69–72, 91–92; Sawyer, *Cambridge Handbook*, 909–30, 1430–59, 506–31, 2744–91, 5234–57, 448–71, 8194–217, 9480–87, 538–58, 12835–59, 3379–401, 3450–79, 8192–219; Slavin, *Educational Psychology*, 152–53, 73–74, 203–7; Woolfolk, *Educational Psychology*, 50, 255–56, 316, 54, 429, 33, 54.

intimately acting with our lives, ever-seeking to help us to grow and be transformed in God's life.[69] The Israelites' journey through the wilderness, after being liberated from Egypt by Moses, is one example of how God has been depicted as leading communities step-by-step towards a growing life in and with God.[70] Throughout this journey, the Bible has many stories of God performing miracles, providing counsel, and chastising the Hebrew people as they falter many times in their struggles to learn what it means to be a people for and with God.

The Spiritual Exercises, which were created by Ignatius of Loyola, are another example of Western Christianity's emphasis on providing scaffolding to its disciples for their spiritual journeys.[71] In essence, the Spiritual Exercises are intended to be a very personal and intense journey wherein the participant comes to better know Jesus. This is done by a combination of the participant using their imagination to prayerfully enter into biblical texts about Jesus' life, death, and resurrection along with reflective conversations with a spiritual director. In its original form, the spiritual director will choose passages that seem most appropriate for where the participant currently is in their journey with Jesus. In this way, the participant is met where they are while being gently guided by an experienced director. Such scaffolding is therefore considered central to the Spiritual Exercises.

Applied to our classes, this means that we should seek to partner with God's scaffolding life as it attempts to lead both us and our students in a step-by-step manner towards deeper learning and development. Such discernment of these step-by-step leadings must be both communal and individualized. Since no two students are alike, the work that God is doing in and with each student may vary greatly. Acknowledging our inherent limitations, this guideline theologically asserts that God will only invite each student to do what they are able to at the present moment and that progress may unfold in gradual and stepwise or spiral ways across the course. As theistic educators, we are therefore called to structure our classes in ways that help our students respond to these scaffolding invitations from God. In doing so, we will be helping deepen their competencies in the course KSAs over time and with repeated engagement as led by our experienced and carefully discerned guidance.

Level 1

Learners are clearly and intentionally guided through activities across the course that has them repeatedly engage key KSAs and scaffolds their growing competencies in these areas (i.e., ensures achievement before moving on to new KSAs).

Numerous educational research studies have and continue to show that repeated and distributed engagement with key KSAs is better than engaging with these KSAs in

---

69. Kyle, *Sacred Systems*, 280.
70. See Exod 15–40.
71. For an overview of the Spiritual Exercises, see Barry, *Letting God Come Close*.

a very intense and shorter period of time. As a result, there should be clear evidence of continual engagement across the course/module(s). A class at Level 1 will therefore guide students through key course KSAs in scaffolding ways. This means that learners are aided in grasping foundational KSAs in deeper ways before moving onto to newer and more complex ones. Overall, then, a course at this level will show evidence of guiding students through key KSAs in scaffolded ways.

At this level, God may be asserted as working the establish patterns of continually progressive learning and development for key KSAs. While cognitive learning is not necessarily always linear, it does appear to build upon prior knowledge and competencies (see the Learner Background guidelines below). As a result, we can expect God to be laboring to lay the solid foundations now upon which future learning will rest. Recognizing that such learning may unfold in non-linear ways for different students and groups of students, the instructor must continually discern where and how God is moving through learning processes and progress in real-time. In doing so, they will be partnering with God's efforts to build these solid foundations in scaffolded ways.

Examples of this might include:

- The course contains e-learning modules that help students master foundational concepts before moving onto more advanced ones.

- Students are required to complete a series of self-check quizzes throughout the course and the results are used by the instructor to more closely work with students who are struggling with core concepts/skills.

- The course site is set up so that students are not allowed to progress to the next unit until they have demonstrated a certain level of achievement on previous units.

- The instructor is observed working with individuals/groups to ensure they understand foundational topics before moving the class onto subsequent topics.

Level 2

The instructor plans a variety of sequenced resources and learning experiences that scaffold competency in key course KSAs and are matched to the experiences, needs, and interests of learners and allow for learner choice.

Level 2 builds upon the expectations of Level 1 but does so in more varied ways. Here, a greater emphasis is given to matching course pathways to the unique backgrounds and needs of current learners. This level is therefore similar to the first level in that it still meets the same standards of scaffolding but differs in that it is more varied with multiple pathways. Central to this level, then, is that the course allows for multiple paths to engage with and demonstrate course competencies, with pathways that are matched to the diverse backgrounds, capabilities, and interests of current learners in the class.

While all of these guidelines should be seen in close relationship to one another, this one is particularly connected to the Learner Background guidelines. Here, God may be found working to help the instructor develop multiple paths to learning core KSAs. These paths should ideally be tailored for the diversity of learners that are in the class. What is of most importance for this particular guideline and level is that these different learning pathways embody the scaffolded approach articulated in the previous level. Theologically, we can see God working to create educational systems that allow for God to guide learners in a variety of directions. Each of these paths should therefore be designed for scaffolded progress since this is how God is asserted to better work with students according to this guideline.

Examples of this might include:

- The course offers multiple activities for completing an assignment (e.g., written paper, digital storytelling project, formal presentation).
- The course allows students to choose from among several different ways to demonstrate their competencies on key course concepts/skills (e.g., multiple choice quiz, oral exam).
- The course site has multiple e-learning modules for the same unit that students can choose from to support their learning in scaffolded ways.
- The instructor is observed providing multiple ways of explaining and representing a core concept/skill (e.g., lecture, demonstration, use of videos).
- The instructor is observed helping students choose an assignment to complete that better matches the students' backgrounds and interests from among a set of given course activities.

Level 3

The instructor works with learners to identify sustained and varied pathways in the development of key course KSAs using a range of resources, learning experiences, and ways of demonstrating scaffolded progress towards these relevant KSAs.

Similar to Level 2, courses at Level 3 for this guideline allow for multiple pathways to engage with course concepts and skills. At this level, however, learners have a more proactive role in developing these varied pathways. For example, Level 3 courses may involve learners in developing specific projects and activities, guiding them in creating assessments (such as rubrics and test questions), helping them in locating and utilizing resources, and/or mapping out learning pathways that enable them to meet course/module objectives. Here, there is a much greater emphasis on self-directed learning and the instructor empowers learners to identify their own strengths and weaknesses in relation to course KSAs and to then develop learning paths in response to these. The instructor will also ensure that these student-generated paths to learning are scaffolded (as outlined by Level 1) and that they align with course objectives.

Across these guidelines, one of the primary invitations of Level 3 is towards developing more democratic and collaborative educational systems. Theologically, this is asserted to be a fuller embodiment of God's educational kin-dom. For this guideline, we can see how such spiritually democratic classrooms emerge. By first developing multiple scaffolded trajectories that are tailored to students' uniqueness in the two previous levels, God is in a better position to help faculty and students work together to develop new and better pathways. These already existing scaffolded pathways will provide the necessary guidance that learners and instructors need in order to democratically discern new ones. This highest level is therefore focused on encouraging them to cooperatively discern these new scaffolded paths in light of already existing ones. Overall, God can therefore be seen working to greatly expand and improve upon these already existing paths in a myriad of ways.

Examples of this might include:

- The instructor is observed working with students to decide upon their own learning path from a given set of possibilities.

- Instructor(s) and students are observed collaboratively developing specific projects and activities for the course that scaffold each student's competencies for course concepts/skills.

- There is evidence of students and instructors creating a rubric that outlines the scaffolded progress (i.e., different levels of competency) that learners will need to demonstrate across the course.

- The class contains an assignment that requires students and the instructor(s) to work together to identify the articles, videos, books, etc. that each learner will use to develop their course competencies.

Guideline #6—Caring Learning Environment

Mission-Centered Focus: *The class environment is one that is experienced by learners to be safe, inclusive, and caring.*

These kinds of environments are to be expected in any context. Some cognitive science and educational studies have shown that we learn and retain more when we are less stressed, so these environments are particularly important for educational settings (be they online or face-to-face environments).[72] Learning, as may be seen by

---

72. Bradshaw and Lowenstein, *Innovative Teaching Strategies*, 100; Clark and Mayer, *E-Learning*, 189–90; Duke et al., "Preserving Third Year"; Diamond, *Designing and Assessing*, 203; Sawyer, *Cambridge Handbook*, 17615–81, 8192–217; Young, Williamson, and Egan, "Students' Reflections."

these Educational System Guidelines, is an iterative process of trial-and-error, continuous feedback, and ongoing efforts to continually improve. As a result, classes should be safe spaces that allow for risk-taking without fear of failure, they should encourage free and positively supported exploration of ideas and diverse perspectives, and they should be ones in which participants support and challenge one another in affirming and constructive ways. In order to help facilitate such learning environments, there needs to be clear expectations that students are not only coached on but also have a part in developing.

Involving more than 130,000 students, the average effect size is 0.36, which is close to Hattie's hinge point.[73] As we shall see below, these considerations are particularly important from a theological perspective. Overall, the trend across these levels is from instructor-generated expectations towards collaborating with learners to set such expectations and then engaging them in interactions in ways that embody the expectations. When assessing a course for this guideline, we can therefore look at the extent to which learners are involved in both setting these expectations and then being guided to act in accordance with them.

Across Western Christian history, there has been and continues to be a central emphasis on Christians working to establish God's reign of love, care, respect, and values in the world.[74] In John's Gospel and epistle writings in the Bible, for instance, love is repeatedly emphasized. It is from John (John 3:16) that we hear of Jesus' life on earth being the result of God's love for the world. We find John's version of the last supper (John 13:1–17) being centered on serving one another out of love. In his letters (1 John 4, 2 John 1:5–6, and 3 John 1:20–23), John stresses the importance of love and caring as being essential for Christian life. Again and again, John admonishes his hearers to root themselves firmly within love, which God is the source of.

In contemporary U.S. society, with the rise of cities and the social, political, and economic disparities that are a central part of this country, urban ministries continue to be at the forefront of restoration and renewal in lower income and marginalized communities.[75] These ministries have been involved in such movements as helping African American migrants from the South to settle in northern cities in the first half of the twentieth century, working with marginalized communities to deal with the political and economic repercussions of the "white flight" that happened after World War II, the civil rights movement in the 1960s, and many other initiatives. Overall, the goal of many of these urban ministry organizations is to work towards greater political equity and justice, redistribution of resources, and building communities of safety, af-

---

73. Hattie, *Visible Learning*, 49–50, 78–79, 102–4, 83–84. Supporting evidence-based assessments: CCSSO, *Intasc Model Core Teaching Standards*, Standard 3—Indicator 1; MarylandOnline, "Quality Matters Rubric Standards," 1.9, 5.4; Pianta, La Paro, and Hamre, *Classroom Assessment Scoring*, Positive Climate, Negative Climate, Behavior Management, Teacher Sensitivity.

74. Kyle, *Sacred Systems*, 285.

75. Green, "History in Service," 6–16.

firmation, and love. Such work is founded on the belief that spiritual growth can only develop to its fullest when such environments of love are nurtured.[76]

In light of these assertions, this guideline should come as no surprise to theistic educators. If our goal is to help foster the life of God in our courses, then it stands to reason that our classes should embody God's values of love, respect, care, and safety. Secular educational research confirms this theological claim: the more fully our classes embody and enable such ideals as safety, love, care, and respect, the more deeply our students will learn and develop. Another one of our primary aims as educators is to therefore intentionally foster course environments that manifest God's life of respect, love, positivity, and room for errors as John and urban ministries assert. To do so is to help create a culture in which God's educational life can more fluidly and effectively work.

Level 1

The course has explicit expectations for a safe and positive learning environment and there is evidence of behavior that includes respect and caring for one another.

Level 1 for this guideline involves the instructor setting expectations for a safe, inclusive, and caring class environment. These expectations should not only be stated in the beginning of the class but also explicitly addressed throughout the course. At this level, there will therefore be clear evidence of learners interacting with one another in ways that are congruent with the course's behavioral expectations. There will also be evidence of the instructor positively and proactively working to ensure that they are adhered to.

At this initial level, God can be asserted to be laying the necessary foundations for compassionate and caring classes. Recognizing that these kinds of environments do not create themselves, especially given the many negative influences in Western society, God might be expected to encourage the instructor to discerningly create clear expectations. Similar to Judeo-Christianity's Ten Commandments,[77] these expectations can describe the kinds of general behaviors that student should and should not engage in. By doing so, they will essentially be helping the community to know which kinds of behaviors God is more likely to move through in fuller ways as well as those that are less God-manifesting. This level is, theologically speaking, focused on providing spiritual guidance to students and faculty in the form of course behavioral expectations.

Examples of this might include:

- The syllabus clearly states behavioral expectations.

---

76. Smith, "To Be Untrammeled," 55.
77. See Exod 20 and Deut 5.

- The instructor is observed correcting students when they act in ways contrary to these expectations (e.g., asking a student to put their phone away, redirecting a student who is off-task).

- Students are observed affirming one another's efforts (e.g., saying "good job," thanking others for their help).

- The instructor is observed encouraging students to take risks by attempting difficult problems or answering complicated questions, and then positively affirms their efforts when they do.

- The class shows clear evidence of positively supporting trial-and-error approaches to learning (e.g., students are positively supported while repeatedly working on a skill until they achieve competency).

- The instructor is observed affirming students for sharing their diverse beliefs, viewpoints, answers, etc.

Level 2

In addition to Level 1, the course has activities and assessments that require respectful interaction, mutual support, and individual/group responsibility for the class environment.

Level 2 includes the previous level's recommendations of having clear behavioral expectations for the class. It then goes beyond this by having activities that intentionally facilitate learners' safe, inclusive, and caring interactions. Overall, the goal here is to have students intentionally practice these expectations via the activities and assessments that they are required to complete in the course. It is one thing to have clear expectations that students must minimally comply with (Level 1), but quite another to help them intentionally utilize these expectations in course activities (Level 2).

Simply knowing where and how God is more likely to move is not the same as responding to these spiritual movements in our lives and communities. In our classes, therefore, we must move beyond simply having God-centered behavioral expectations to helping students intentionally act in accordance with them. By developing activities that encourage such engagement, we are essentially helping our students respond to God's movements within and among them. This level is therefore focused on spiritually discerning activities that help students to develop the God-responsive habits they will need for environments of caring, inclusivity, and safety.

Examples of this might include:

- Learners are required to participate in a class debate where they are led by the instructor in positively and constructively engaging with viewpoints and opinions that are different from their own.

- Small groups are required to report how they have followed the behavioral expectations of the course as they have worked together to complete a project.

- Students are observed participating in a peer tutoring activity in ways that explicitly conform to the class' behavioral expectations.
- The instructor is observed coaching students in relation to the expectations as they work on a small group activity.

Level 3

Building on Level 2, the instructor collaborates with learners in developing and applying expectations for a learning climate that includes openness, mutual respect, and positive peer relationships in the course.

This level includes the previous levels' recommendations for having and utilizing clear behavioral expectations. However, for courses at this level, the instructor will be found working with learners to define and implement these expectations. Activities and interactions at this level might include the instructor leading students through a brainstorming process to generate expectations, small groups setting their own ground rules for how they will interact, the instructor modeling the collaboratively developed expectations, and incentives being offered to learners who clearly demonstrate the expectations (though research has shown that the impact of such external/extrinsic rewards are limited and they follow a law of diminishing returns). A class at this level is therefore one that is more collaborative in relation to this guideline and should result in expectations that are more meaningful to learners.

With our spiritual theme of democratic and collaborative engagement being firmly established at Level 3 for more guidelines, this one adds to this version of kindom centered education. Here, we may assert that God strives to work through students and teachers to collaboratively discern the God-manifesting expectations that will be used throughout the course. These expectations should align with the ones outlined in the previous two levels, but they should also be more meaningful and relevant for students. In essence, we find God working through the whole of the class in order to establish these expectations as well as embody them in all that the class does. It is a whole community engagement and commitment that is at the core of sustainable community building.[78] Our classes are therefore invited by God to respond to these cooperative practices in the establishment of safe, caring, and inclusive environments.

Examples of this might include:

- The instructor is observed leading students through a brainstorming process to generate behavioral expectations for the class.
- The class has an activity that leads small groups through a process of setting their own ground rules for how they will interact and resolve conflicts.

---

78. Kretzmann and McKnight, *Building Communities*.

- The instructor is observed modeling the expectations that were developed collaboratively by the class.
- The instructor is observed encouraging students to modify class expectations if they need to be changed.

TEACHING/LEARNING THEORY GUIDELINES

Learning theories and teaching strategies are always based upon the experiences and studies of practicing educators and/or researchers. Theologically, they essentially are models for how God's educative life effectively works within and through our courses. Of course, they must always be used with caution and discerned modification because the contexts in which they were formulated may not match our current ones. Nevertheless, they are intended to help us and our students better know the possible means and methods through which learning and development happens with and in God. The following guidelines provide details for the kinds of theories and strategies that we should consider as well as how to modify and apply them.

Guideline #1—Holistic Teaching and Learning Theories

Instructor is able to articulate: a) specific and holistic teaching and learning theories that they might utilize, and b) when and how these theories might apply (Core Guideline).

With an average effect size of 0.57 that is based on educational research studies involving more than 1,600,000 students, this guideline is one of the more prominent and influential ones to focus on. These studies have included both general educational theories[79] as well as more holistic development theories.[80] What instructors believe about student learning and development and how to shape it can greatly influence how they will design and implement a course in terms of their learning processes,[81]

---

79. Hattie, *Visible Learning*, 109–10, 12–15, 19–21, 99–203. Supporting evidence-based assessments: CCSSO, *Intasc Model Core Teaching Standards*, Standards 1 & 2—Indicators 1 & 2, Standard 3—Indicator 2, Standard 4—Indicator 1, Standard 9—Indicator 2; MarylandOnline, "Quality Matters Rubric Standards," 1.2, 2.5.

80. Hattie, *Visible Learning*, 152–53, 87–88, 207–8, 12–14, 29–30. Supporting evidence-based assessments: CCSSO, *Intasc Model Core Teaching Standards*, Standards 1 & 2-Indicator 1; Pianta, La Paro, and Hamre, *Classroom Assessment Scoring*, Instructional Learning Formats.

81. Ambrose, *How Learning Works*, 15, 19–20; Balmer, Richards, and Varpio, "How Students Experience and Navigate"; Bradshaw and Lowenstein, *Innovative Teaching Strategies*, 26, ch. 1; Bruning, Schraw, and Norby, *Cognitive Psychology*, 86; Chen et al., "How We Used a Patient"; Clark and Mayer, *E-Learning*, 24, 35, 121, 60–61, 282; Curtin et al., "Exploring the Use"; Diamond, *Designing and Assessing*, 40, 191–92; Elander and Cronje, "Paradigms Revisited"; Haji et al., "Measuring Cognitive Load"; Jacobs et al., "Impact of Institute"; Joseph, Rhodes, and Watson, "Preparing Nurse Leaders"; McLellan et al., "Preparing to Prescribe"; Morrison et al., *Designing Effective Instruction*, 144–45, 350, 53–62; Preusche and Lamm, "Reflections on Empathy"; Roberts and Kumar, "Student Learning"; Sandars et al., "Importance of Educational Theories"; Sawyer, *Cambridge Handbook*, 522–45, 648–70, 885–905,

as well as their holistic development.⁸² For instance, an instructor who believes that learners are an empty bucket that simply needs to be filled with information will likely approach their course differently from someone who thinks that learners already come with basic knowledge upon which they need to construct new concept/skills. As a result of this claim, this guideline is intended to help instructors reflect upon these teaching and learning theories as well as how they are using them to improve their classes. Overall, the trend is from simply being more explicit about these theories to drawing from multiple ones to help guide the course's development.

When we reflect theologically on this guideline, a map is a helpful analogy. With the objectives providing us with clear directions that God is inviting us to journey towards with our students, learning theories can provide us with more detailed insights into what this journey might look like and how we might begin to engage with it. Like a map, they can provide an overview of the different pathways that God might work with our students through in order to achieve the same destination. Western Christian history is filled with numerous theories and strategies that are intended to help inform our formation ministries.⁸³

For instance, there have been numerous theologians and spiritual cartographers throughout Western Christian history who have sought to articulate a deeper theological understanding of human nature. Augustine of Hippo asserted that people are a conflicted dichotomy of body and soul with human will standing between these two and needing to choose which one's desires to act upon.⁸⁴ Thomas Aquinas shared some of these views of Augustine, but had a much more positive view of the body, emphasizing its goodness and necessity for the soul's development in God.⁸⁵ More contemporarily, Karl Rahner emphasized the wholeness and transcendental nature of humanity and its relationship to God.⁸⁶ Again and again, theologians have continually sought to articulate a clearer understanding of who we are as human beings so

---

1176–203, 5164–89, 10224–48, 20030–55; Slavin, *Educational Psychology*, 215; Wijma, Zbikowski, and Brüggemann, "Silence, Shame and Abuse"; Woolfolk, *Educational Psychology*, 49, 455, 62–72.

82. Al-Eraky, "Twelve Tips"; Bradshaw and Lowenstein, *Innovative Teaching Strategies*, ch. 18; Bruning, Schraw, and Norby, *Cognitive Psychology*, 255; Clark and Mayer, *E-Learning*, ch. 4, 5, 6; Delany et al., "Replacing Stressful Challenges"; Diamond, *Designing and Assessing*, 193; Holmes et al., "Harnessing Hidden Curriculum"; Lucieer et al., "Development of Self-Regulated Learning"; Matlin, *Cognition*, 184; Mikkonen, Kyngäs, and Kääriäinen, "Nursing Students☒ Experiences"; Morrison et al., *Designing Effective Instruction*, 172–74; Paek, Hoffman, and Black, "Perceptual Factors"; Rougas et al., "Twelve Tips"; Sagasser et al., "GP Supervisors' Experience"; Sawyer, *Cambridge Handbook*, 628–48, 5381–405; Slavin, *Educational Psychology*, 178–79; St Clair-Thompson et al., "Mental Toughness and Transitions"; Woolfolk, *Educational Psychology*, 98–100, 90, 254.

83. Kyle, *Living Spiritual Praxis*, 79–87; Kyle, *Sacred Systems*; Kyle, *Spiritual Being & Becoming*, ch. 1.

84. Augustine, *Trinity*, 131, 55, 210–11, 76, 80, 311, 61, 74.

85. Aquinas, *Summa Theologica*, Part Ia, Question 75, Answer 73, Reply 71, Part Ia, Question 76, Answer 71, Answer, Part Ia, Question 76, Answer 78, Answer; Torrell, *Saint Thomas Aquinas*, 4, 8, 253, 55–59.

86. Rahner, *Foundations of Christian Faith*, 28, 31, 75, 94, 138, 82, 84, 435–36.

that we might better know how to work with ourselves and one another for our growing life with God.

One of the specific challenges as theistic educators, however, is not only to learn how to adapt such theological anthropologies for our classroom purposes, but also to be able to theologically reflect on the secular learning theories that we are utilizing. As this book illustrates, secular evidence-based findings can greatly help in better understanding how to work with our students. Taking the extra step to theologize these secular theories and guidelines can empower us to better understand God's nature and actions in our classes. Overall, theologized learning theories have the primary purpose of helping us better understand God's educational efforts with our students and therefore empower us to partner with this sacred life more closely before, during, and after the course (i.e., design, implementation, and evaluation). The fundamental theological claim for this guideline, then, is that God continually helps humanity create these learning theory maps so that we might know and partner with God more closely. The invitation is to therefore utilize and theologically adapt the maps that have been revealed to us so that our courses are more successful in attaining God's educative aims for our students.

As it relates to holism, Western Christianity has had a rich and vibrant history of theological anthropologies that depict the holistic interconnectedness of human nature in relation to creation.[87] In fact, I believe that it is one of the distinct advantages that religious and theistic formators have over Western secular educators as educational research confirms the importance of engaging students holistically. Theologically, such holism is inherent: if God really is present within every part of creation and God is infinitely and inseparably interconnected within God's self (i.e., God is not a fragmented being), it therefore stands to reason that every part of creation is holistically interconnected through God. Such holistic views of creation run throughout the history of Western Christianity.

For instance, in his book, *Body, Soul, and Human Life*, Joel Green thoroughly explores views of human nature that are depicted in the Bible.[88] One of Green's main claims is that the human person is primarily understood as an integrated whole.[89] Contrary to contemporary scientific moves to dissect and categorize parts of humanity, Green claims that such approaches are lacking in both the Hebrew and Christian testaments of the Bible. Instead, he claims, "segregating the human person into discrete, constitutive 'parts'" is not as important as considering each person in their completeness and wholeness.[90]

Similarly, Maximus the Confessor, who lived in the sixth and seventh centuries, placed a central emphasis on the integration and unity of individuals in their journeys

---

87. Kyle, *Sacred Systems*; Kyle, *Spiritual Being & Becoming*, ch. 1.
88. Green, *Body, Soul, and Human Life*.
89. Green, *Body, Soul, and Human Life*, 8, 69.
90. Green, *Body, Soul, and Human Life*, 49, 69.

with God. While Maximus did identify and articulate insights into body, mind, and soul,[91] one of his primary assertions was that the spiritual life is fundamentally a journey of internal integration and external unity with God.[92] Looking to Christ as the mediator between God and humanity, Maximus also asserted that one's journey with God is one of a holistic reintegration of one's fragmented parts.[93] The more fully one works with Christ to do this, Maximus claims, the more fully Christ becomes manifest in them through such holism.[94] Holistic integration and development can therefore be seen as being a part of Christianity's views of God's goals and methods for working with humanity.

In our classes, this can therefore mean that God is not just interested in cognitive growth and development. The Spirit is additionally seeking to shape the whole of our students as well as the communities of which they are a part. If this is the case, then our courses need to be developed to be responsive to God's holistic transformations with our students and the wider world. Granted, in the relatively short time that we have with our students, there are limits to what we and God can do. However, from the very beginning, this guideline helps to remind us that we need to be listening for and responding to the more holistic aims and approaches that God has for our classes.

Level 1

The instructor is able to articulate their own understanding of holistic student learning and development and seeks to adjust the course's teaching strategies in light of these understandings.

At this level, instructors will work to be able to explicitly state what their own views of student holistic learning and development are and how they are using these models to inform and guide the course's development. Instructors do not necessarily need to be able to label these learning theories (e.g., constructivism, cognitive science models, etc.). Rather, it is more important that they are able to clearly articulate: 1) the processes by which they believe students holistically learn/develop, 2) strategies that can be used to help students to grow along these paths (i.e., align with their understandings of learning processes), and 3) how they have designed their course to support such learning and development (i.e., that align with their theories). Overall, inconsistencies between these theories and how the course is designed should be pointed out at this level.

Theologically, at this foundational level God can be asserted to help faculty to bring to their awareness their current understandings of learning processes. In doing so, instructors can further identify their own misconceptions about these processes

---

91. Thunberg, *Microcosm and Mediator*, 97–98, 106–7, 52, 76, 96, 209–12.
92. Thunberg, *Microcosm and Mediator*, 111–12, 70–71, 76, 331, 430.
93. Thunberg, *Microcosm and Mediator*, 112, 70–71, 97, 331, 73, 80–83, 91–92, 400, 6, 30.
94. Thunberg, *Microcosm and Mediator*, 171, 231, 330, 430.

as well as how God might be working with and through them. As they gain clarity in these areas, instructors can then see more clearly how their courses align or misalign with their own understandings of learning processes. Where there are misalignments, faculty can adjust their courses. Where there is alignment, they will be able to partner with God's educational life in these processes more closely. Overall, the goal at this level is for instructors to articulate their own spiritualized learning theories and then work to ensure that they are teaching in congruence with them.

Examples of this might include:

- Instructor is able to state the general processes by which they believe learning happens.
- Instructors can describe how the activities in their class directly support students' learning processes.
- The syllabus contains a statement that briefly describes the general learning theories that the course is based upon.
- The instructor articulates how the general learning theories they are using for their class help students to learn more effectively.

Level 2

The instructor uses observations of students as well as evidence-based resources to inform their own holistic teaching and learning theories. Based upon this information, they adjust their course.

Level 2 extends beyond Level 1 when the instructor reflects upon the actual learners in their course and how they seem to be holistically learning and developing in relation to course concepts/skills. These reflections can be based upon assessment data that they have gathered and/or conversations with learners about this topic (via class discussions, one-on-one meetings with students, and/or indirectly via papers, journals, or discussion board posts). The instructor should then be able to compare this information with their own views of holistic learning and development and note similarities and differences. Finally, by additionally drawing from evidence-based holistic teaching and learning theories, the instructor should then be able to articulate how they are using this synthesized knowledge to modify and improve their course.

As instructors clarify their own understandings of learning processes, following evidence-based practice principles, they should then strive to identify a data-driven basis for these understandings. In doing so, they are essentially seeking confirmation and clarity of the processes through which God is working with their students to learn and develop. This can be done in at least two ways as discussed above, both of which should be utilized at this level: by looking to evidence-based educational resources and by examining data gathered about their students, past and present. Both avenues should provide insights into how God is more effectively working with their students. As with Level 1, once these evidence-based processes have been identified and confirmed, the instructor should modify their course to better align with them. By doing this, they are essentially empowering God's educational life to blossom through these learning processes.

Examples of this might include:

- The instructor can state how they have used assessment data to better understand how their students learn best in their class.

- The instructor can identify specific evidence-based learning theories to inform their understanding of learning processes.

- The instructor is observed using a specific evidence-based learning theory to inform the teaching strategies being used in their course.

- The instructor can articulate how their understanding of learning processes is based upon both evidence-based theories and their observations of students in their classes.

Level 3

Recognizing that students learn and develop in diverse ways, and building on Level 2, the instructor collaborates with others to develop and utilize multiple evidence-based holistic teaching and learning theories to help guide course development. They are also able to articulate when and how each theory is being utilized.

This more complex level further builds upon the previous level when the instructor is able to articulate how the diversity of students in their course necessitates the use of multiple theories to support holistic learning and development. In addition, an instructor at this level will recognize that different course KSAs likely require different theories in order to maximize learning for each KSA. This level therefore represents an intellectual advancement for instructors in relation to these teaching and learning theories when they come to realize that one holistic theory is not sufficient to provide the kinds of nuanced and more complex insights and guidance that are needed when working with diverse learners and varying KSAs. Instructors should therefore be able to clearly articulate why multiple holistic theories are needed to direct their course and how each of these are being used to guide course development. Finally, and related to other guidelines, Level 3 here is intended to support more collaborative classes where there are many different pathways to achieving course objectives. The instructor should be able to explain how each of the pathways is related to one or more of the evidence-based teaching/learning theories that they are using.

Again, as with Level 3 for other guidelines, we see the democratic/collaborative view of God's kin-dom in the classroom emerge. Such collaborations will likely be necessary as the instructor works with others to develop and implement multiple evidence-based learning theories in their course. Spiritually speaking, this level essentially asserts that God works through different processes for different KSAs, students, pathways, objectives, and activities. If this assertion is accurate, then the instructor will need numerous theoretical maps to help them more closely partner with God's multiple movements in their course. Such an endeavor is an advanced competency but will also enable the instructor to more effectively move with God's multitudinous and ever-adapting educational life.

Examples of this might include:

- The instructor is able to identify two or more evidence-based teaching/learning theories that have worked with others to help guide their course development.
- The instructor can state how they have worked with others and used assessment data in addition to two or more evidence-based teaching/learning theories to better understand how their students learn best in their class.
- The syllabus contains a statement that briefly describes two or more general theories that the course is based upon.
- The instructor can explain how they have worked with others to use different evidence-based teaching theories to develop multiple pathways for students in their course.

Guideline #2—Active Teaching and Learning Strategies

Course utilizes active teaching and learning strategies (Core Guideline).

Increasingly over the past few decades, educational literature has given a central emphasis on the use of active teaching and learning strategies.[95] In particular, the following active strategies are repeatedly highlighted in the literature (if known, the effect size is noted for each): elaboration and self-reflections (0.64);[96] self-regulated learning and study strategies (0.6);[97] direct instruction or modeling followed by

---

95. Bradshaw and Lowenstein, *Innovative Teaching Strategies*, 130; Clark and Mayer, *E-Learning*, 17, 43, 253–54; Diamond, *Designing and Assessing*, 79, 115, 93, 263; Gonsalvez, Ovens, and Ivanusic, "Does Attendance?"; Sawyer, *Cambridge Handbook*, 5209–34.

96. Hattie, *Visible Learning*, 192–93. Additional supporting literature: Ambrose, *How Learning Works*, 37, 210; Bruning, Schraw, and Norby, *Cognitive Psychology*, 86, 105, 332; Chamberland et al., "Does Medical Students' Diagnostic Performance?"; Clark and Mayer, *E-Learning*, 230–33, 42, 355; Curtin et al., "Exploring the Use"; Harvey, "Connecting Theory to Practice"; Matlin, *Cognition*, 173–74; Morgan et al., "How We Use Patient Encounter Data"; Morrison et al., *Designing Effective Instruction*, 143, 94; Raterink, "Reflective Journaling"; Sawyer, *Cambridge Handbook*, 545–66, 692–715, 909–53, 2791–857, 5358–81, 8194–217, 765–87, 10454–74, 2859–83; Shapiro et al., "Medical Students' Creative Projects"; Slavin, *Educational Psychology*, 189; Sukhato et al., "To Be or Not to Be"; Wheeler et al., "Storytelling"; Woolfolk, *Educational Psychology*, 316.

97. Hattie, *Visible Learning*, 188–92. Additional supporting literature: Ambrose, *How Learning Works*, 88, 210–11; Bruning, Schraw, and Norby, *Cognitive Psychology*, 86–87; Clark and Mayer,

learner practice (0.59);[98] peer teaching/tutoring (0.54);[99] concept mapping (0.46);[100] class discussions, debate, etc. (0.46);[101] problem solving, problem-based learning, etc. (0.35);[102] real-world and clinical simulations (0.33);[103] inquiry-based pedagogies (0.31);[104] real-world projects, service-learning, etc.;[105] workplace experiences, internships, etc.;[106] role-playing;[107] and game-based strategies.[108] As this list suggests, there are numerous strategies that instructors can draw from to use in their course. The challenges in using these strategies are twofold: 1) choosing which strategy(ies) to use, and 2) how to adapt them for one's course. Overall, the trend for this guideline is from using these strategies in basic ways towards developing multiple evidence-based strategies in collaboration with learners. In addition, as one moves to higher levels, the strategies should more closely match the background, interests, and capabilities of learners while simultaneously ensuring that these strategies foster genuine progress towards the learning outcomes. The overall average effect size for these studies is 0.47 for more than 6,400,000 students, which is above the 0.4 hinge point.[109]

E-Learning, 318, 56, 63; Diamond, *Designing and Assessing*, 194; Friedman and Fisher, *Handbook on Effective Instructional Strategies*, 101, 31; Matlin, *Cognition*, 185; Sawyer, *Cambridge Handbook*, 522–45, 930–53, 1459–85; Slavin, *Educational Psychology*, 153; Woolfolk, *Educational Psychology*, 123, 270–71.

98. Hattie, *Visible Learning*, 172–73, 204–7. Additional supporting literature: Ambrose, *How Learning Works*, 214; Bruning, Schraw, and Norby, *Cognitive Psychology*, 87, 177–78; Clark and Mayer, *E-Learning*, 357–59, ch. 11; Friedman and Fisher, *Handbook on Effective Instructional Strategies*, 80; Morrison et al., *Designing Effective Instruction*, 147–49, 98; Sawyer, *Cambridge Handbook*, ch. 4, 5; Slavin, *Educational Psychology*, 147–48, 207.

99. See references already cited in the Learner-Learner Interaction Guideline above.

100. Hattie, *Visible Learning*, 167–69. Additional supporting literature: Ambrose, *How Learning Works*, 30, 59; Booker and Peterson, "Use of Knowledge Tree"; Bradshaw and Lowenstein, *Innovative Teaching Strategies*, ch. 25; Hendrix et al., "Integrating Mental Health Concepts"; Hung and Lin, "Using Concept Mapping"; Orique and McCarthy, "Critical Thinking."

101. See references already cited in the Learner-Learner Interaction Guideline above.

102. Hattie, *Visible Learning*, 210–12. Additional supporting literature: Bradshaw and Lowenstein, *Innovative Teaching Strategies*, ch. 10; Bruning, Schraw, and Norby, *Cognitive Psychology*, 331; Clark and Mayer, *E-Learning*, 351–52; Friedman and Fisher, *Handbook on Effective Instructional Strategies*, 218; Hung and Lin, "Using Concept Mapping"; Orique and McCarthy, "Critical Thinking"; Reiser and Dempsey, *Trends and Issue*, 199–200, ch. 7; Wood et al., "Twelve Tips"; Woolfolk, *Educational Psychology*, 278–88.

103. See references already cited in the Real-World Guideline above.

104. Hattie, *Visible Learning*, 208–10. Additional supporting literature: Ambrose, *How Learning Works*, 37; Andrews et al., "How We Implemented"; Bradshaw and Lowenstein, *Innovative Teaching Strategies*, 361; Kharraz et al., "Perceived Barriers"; LeDuc, "An Instructional Strategy"; Sawyer, *Cambridge Handbook*, ch. 11, 21; Smith et al., "Stimulating Research Interest"; Woolfolk, *Educational Psychology*, 316–21.

105. See references already cited in the Real-World Guideline above.

106. See references already cited in the Real-World Guideline above.

107. See references already cited in the Learner-Learner Interaction Guideline above.

108. See references already cited in the Learner-Learner Interaction Guideline above.

109. Hattie, *Visible Learning*, 49, 88–89, 143–44, 47–49, 54–57, 68–69, 72–73, 82–93, 203–14,

Active strategies are basically any strategy that engages students beyond mere passive listening and absorption of information. They guide them in actively processing and applying what they have seen, heard, or experienced. In essence, this guideline is a step in the direction of more holistic and comprehensive approaches to education, which was elaborated on in Guideline #1 above for this area. Theologically, this guideline presents an image of God as being dynamically engaged with our students and many of the different spiritual formation strategies from Western Christian history very much align with this guideline.[110]

Francis of Assisi, who was known for his works of charity amongst the poor, held such practices to be central for one's growing spiritual life.[111] With a philosophy of giving one's entire self to others, Franciscan spirituality is one that is dynamically engaged with the world.[112] In addition to lives of service, Francis expected his disciples to share the Christian gospel with others through both word and deed.[113] Central to this way of life, then, was an active life of both being and doing good in the world.[114] Active formation strategies may therefore be seen in this strand of Christianity.

Looking more broadly, following Richard Foster's book *Streams of Living Water*, we find the following six traditions outlined that have been a core part of Western Christian history: contemplative, holiness, charismatic, social justice, evangelical, and incarnational. For the contemplative tradition, Foster asserts that there is a central emphasis on solitude, praying with sacred texts, and taking time to reflect on daily life.[115] The holiness tradition holds structured spiritual disciplines as being essential to one's growing life in God.[116] For the charismatic tradition, Foster recommends seeking out an experienced mentor grow in the ways that are central to this tradition.[117] Founded on themes of justice, compassion, and unity, the social justice tradition is one of the most socially active and politically engaged streams in the Western Christian tradition.[118] The evangelical tradition proactively interacts with the world

---

28–31, 34–35. Supporting evidence-based assessments: CCSSO, *Intasc Model Core Teaching Standards*, Standards 1 & 2—Indicator 2, Standard 3—Indicator 2, Standard 5—Indicator 2, Standard 7—Indicator 1, Standard 8—Indicators 1 & 2; MarylandOnline, "Quality Matters Rubric Standards," 5.2, 6.2; Pianta, La Paro, and Hamre, *Classroom Assessment Scoring*, Regard for Student Perspective, Instructional Learning Formats, Content Understanding, Analysis and Inquiry, Instructional Dialogue, Student Engagement.

110. Kyle, *Sacred Systems*, 285–90.
111. Bonaventure, "Major Life," 635, 37, 39, 91.
112. Bonaventure, "Major Life," 639, 41, 44, 85, 737.
113. Bonaventure, "Major Life," 647, 722, 24.
114. Bonaventure, "Major Life," 729.
115. Foster, *Streams of Living Water*, 56–57.
116. Foster, *Streams of Living Water*, 88.
117. Foster, *Streams of Living Water*, 131.
118. Foster, *Streams of Living Water*, 167–71.

through proclamation.[119] Finally, the incarnational tradition seeks to find and be with God in our everyday life.[120] In each one of these strands of Christian spirituality we find active engagement with God, ourselves, and the world around us to be a central theme. Western Christianity therefore helps us to realize that spiritual growth and development requires each individual's active participation and it is through such active engagement that the Spirit transforms us as well as the world.

In our classrooms, then, we are invited to discern the kinds of active teaching and learning strategies that God is wanting us and our students to enact so that the learning and development that is captured by the spiritual discerned objectives can be achieved. We are invited to utilize those strategies that have repeatedly shown themselves to be more effective (i.e., evidence-based strategies), and to involve our students in the collective discernment of these strategies. The more we can actively engage and immerse our students in the KSAs of our class, this guideline asserts, the more God's educational life will be able to transform our students. Stated differently, it is our students' active engagement with God's educative life that will deepen learning and foster development for them more deeply. Our goal, as theistic educators, is to therefore discern which active teaching and learning strategies to utilize and how to adapt them for and with our students.

Level 1

Drawing on specific active teaching and learning strategies, the instructor seeks to apply these to the course.

Level 1 is achieved with the acknowledgement of active teaching and learning strategies in the course. The instructor should be able to articulate/demonstrate what strategy(ies) they have chosen and how these are being used in the course to help students achieve the learning objectives. These strategies can involve individual, small group, or whole class activities, and they should clearly help learners actively engage with course KSAs. In addition, following other guidelines, these strategies should clearly align with the course's learning objectives.

Foundationally, the instructor will seek to discern which active teaching/learning strategies that God is inviting the class to engage in. Discernment of these strategies, at this level, may or may not include one or more of the following considerations: course learning outcomes, learner background, resources available, etc. In essence, the instructor is striving to allow God to lead them towards the active strategies that are likely to engage students most deeply with the KSAs given the existing contextual constraints and considerations. Once discerned, it is the instructor's job to continually discern where and how God is working with the class as they engage with the activities. In its most spiritual and ideal form, the instructor will be helping the class move

---

119. Foster, *Streams of Living Water*, 219.
120. Foster, *Streams of Living Water*, 263.

with God's educational life as God labors to lead them into deeper learning via these active strategies.

Examples of this might include:

- The instructor is observed engaging students in course discussions/debates that requires each student to be actively involved.
- The course contains assignments where learners must reflect on their own progress and develop a plan for improving their competencies.
- The course site shows evidence of students being required to conduct a peer-assessment.
- The class is observed to have a rhythm of lecturing/demonstrating for fifteen to twenty minutes followed by learners practicing and actively engaging with the concepts/skills that were just presented.

Level 2

The instructor utilizes one or more evidence-based active teaching and learning strategies and is able to articulate how they have adapted these strategies for the current course.

This level further extends upon the previous one when the instructor is able to articulate/demonstrate how they are using specific evidence-based active teaching and learning strategies (see a beginning list of such strategies above). Ideally, they should be able to present specific evidence-based literature that they are relying on as well as articulate/demonstrate how these strategies are being applied to their course. Finally, the instructor should be able to state/demonstrate what adaptations they have made to these strategies in light of the current course, given its unique content, students, and learning environment(s).

Following the theistic view of educational research articulated in this text, evidence-based active strategies are approaches that God has successfully been able to foster learning through in other contexts. These are therefore strategies that the instructor can initially consider as part of their discernment of which ones God may be inviting the class to engage in. However, just because a particular strategy was effectively used in another context does not mean that God will seek to work through it with one's current class. As asserted throughout this book, God ever-adapts to each infinitely unique place and time. For Level 1 above, the instructor may simply find and utilize an active strategy without many discerned adaptations. At this level, however, the instructor will labor to discern not only which evidence-based strategies God is wanting to work through, but also how God needs these strategies to be modified for the current cohort of students. This level is therefore focused on greater clarity of discernment of which evidence-based strategies God is inviting the class towards as well as how these might need to be adapted for current students.

Examples of this might include:

- The instructor can state which evidence-based strategies they are using in their course and can name which evidence-based source(s) support the use of these strategies and how they are adapting them for their current course.
- The syllabus contains a statement regarding the active teaching strategies that are being used in the course and identifies which evidence-based source(s) support the use of these strategies.
- The instructor is observed facilitating an active learning strategy with students and they explain to students the evidence-based reasons for engaging with these activities.
- The instructor is able to explain how and why they have adapted a specific evidence-based strategy for the class.

Level 3

Recognizing that students learn and develop in diverse ways, the instructor collaborates with learners and others in utilizing multiple evidence-based active teaching and learning strategies to help guide course development. The instructor empowers learners to choose and/or develop their own active ways of engaging with course KSAs and ensures that these varied pathways align with course objectives.

Level 3 for this guideline is similar to Level 3 for other guidelines in that it is more collaborative and draws from multiple sources. The course should have clear evidence of multiple active teaching and learning strategies. The instructor should be able to articulate/demonstrate which strategies they are utilizing, and they should be able to point to specific evidence-based literature for each of these (similar to Level 2). Beyond this, the course should also have clear evidence of learners being empowered to choose and/or develop their own active ways of increasing their competencies with course KSAs as defined by the objectives. The instructor should work with students to ensure that these individualized pathways are congruent with evidence-based recommendations as well as the course objectives.

The democratic educational view of God's kin-dom in the classroom continues to emerge at this level for this guideline. Here, students and the instructor will work collaboratively to spiritually discern which evidence-based active strategies God is seeking to move with and through. Given the unique complexities of each student's educational journey, multiple strategies should be cooperatively developed at this level. In doing so, faculty and students will be developing a highly engaged, multi-path course that is very meaningful and relevant for learners' current civic, professional, and/or personal lives. Such multitudinous and spiritually discerned active engagement will therefore likely result in closer alignment between God's formative work in each student's life within and beyond the course. The actively engaged class at this level is therefore one that fosters transformation on a wider scale than is intended by the course objectives.

Examples of this might include:

- The instructor is observed working with students to select and adapt evidence-based activities for an upcoming unit.

- The instructor can identify two or more evidence-based active strategies that they are using as well as how they have collaborated with students to adapt these for the course.

- The class is observed to have two or more evidence-based active teaching strategies being used.

- The class has an assignment where learners must reflect on their own progress and develop evidence-based learning strategies for improving their competencies.

Guideline #3—Course/Study Strategy Development Methods

Instructor is able to demonstrate the processes/methods by which they develop their course and there is alignment among course elements (Core Guideline).

ADDIE, backward design, universal design for learning, learner-centered, and rapid prototyping are all examples of the many instructional design strategies that can be used to help guide course development. While instructors may not know the details for these specific strategies, they should still be able to articulate the processes by which they are designing, implementing, and evaluating their course. This guideline is therefore intended to capture these abilities.

When instructors are able to do this, the effects are tremendous. According to studies gleaned from Hattie's research, the average effect size for this guideline is by far the most significant, being 0.69, which higher than any other guideline presented herein. This effect size is based on studies involving more than 54,000 students.[121] Overall, there are two trends: 1) from individually following some course development process/strategy towards collaborating with others and looking to evidence-based literature for help with this; and 2) close alignment among some of the course's major elements towards this alignment existing for all course elements at both the

---

121. Hattie, *Visible Learning*, 94–95, 109–10, 12–13, 19–21, 81. Additional evidence-based assessments: CCSSO, *Intasc Model Core Teaching Standards*, Standards 1 & 2—Indicator 1, Standard 6—Indicator 1, Standard 7—Indicators 1, 2, & 3, Standard 8—Indicator 1, Standard 9—Indicator 1 & 2; MarylandOnline, "Quality Matters Rubric Standards," 2.1, 2.2, 3.1, 4.1, 5.1, 6.1; Pianta, La Paro, and Hamre, *Classroom Assessment Scoring*, Concept Understanding, Instructional Learning Formats, Regard for Student Perspectives.

course and weekly/module/unit levels. In other words, similar to others, this guideline becomes more collaborative and complex as one moves towards higher levels.[122]

In the book, *Living Spiritual Praxis*, I presented a somewhat complicated and very detailed way to engage in spiritual formation course/program development.[123] The hallmark of these methods, which distinguishes them from secular instructional design methods, is the centrality of spiritual discernment that is given to them. Unfortunately, such methodologies have been historically and widely neglected in Western Christian religious education and spiritual formation.[124] Yet, as the effect size for this guideline demonstrates, it is one of the most important processes that we can engage in to significantly improve learning and development in our courses. There has been some throughout Christian history, however, who have sought to provide guidance on these methods.

For instance, *The Philokalia* is a collection of writings compiled from Eastern Christianity that is intended to provide detailed guidance on the road to "purification, illumination, and perfection."[125] These texts provide insights into the nature of humanity as well as the reality of God as understood and experienced in this tradition.[126] Several authors outline their theories of change and views of spiritual development.[127] Setting spiritual goals to strive for,[128] these authors provide details on spiritual practices that can help to achieve these goals.[129] Overall, these writings can help one not only better understand the nature of one's growing life with God for this tradition, but

---

122. Supporting references: Ambrose, *How Learning Works*, 85, 89; Close et al., "Shared Curriculum Model"; Darabi et al., "Learning How"; Diamond, *Designing and Assessing*, 40-41, 79, 196; Eychmüller et al., "Undergraduate Palliative Care"; Friedman and Fisher, *Handbook on Effective Instructional Strategies*, 161-62, 289-90; Gagnon and Cator, "Mapping HIV"; Garnett, Weiss, and Winland-Brown, "Simulation Design"; Gooi and Sommerfeld, "Medical School 2.0"; Gorski et al., "Nursing Education Transformation"; Herr et al., "An Interprofessional Consensus"; Holden et al., "'Men's Health"; Hsih et al., "Student Curriculum Review Team"; Kool et al., "Goal Orientations"; Lypson et al., "Optimizing Post-Graduate Institutional Program"; Morrison et al., *Designing Effective Instruction*, 2-3, 5, ch. 3; Nasser, Saad, and Karaoui, "Mapping of Biomedical Literature Evaluation"; Nicola et al., "How We Did"; Sawyer, *Cambridge Handbook*, 8194-217; Slavin, *Educational Psychology*, 152-53, 221; Stringfellow et al., "Defining Structure"; Taylor et al., "How We Implemented"; Tiruneh et al., "Systematic Design"; Wijnen-Meijer et al., "Vertically Integrated Medical Education"; Woods, "Exploring Unplanned Curriculum Drift"; Woolfolk, *Educational Psychology*, 368, 456-62; Zimmermann et al., "Inter-Professional in-Situ Simulated Team"; Bradshaw and Lowenstein, *Innovative Teaching Strategies*, 11; Bruning, Schraw, and Norby, *Cognitive Psychology*, 130; Castanelli, Smith, and Noonan, "Do Anaesthetists Believe?"; Chen et al., "Resolving Bottlenecks"; Clark and Mayer, *E-Learning*, 137, ch. 3.

123. Kyle, *Living Spiritual Praxis*.

124. Kyle, *Sacred Systems*.

125. Saint Nicodemus and Saint Metropolitan, *Philokalia*, 11, 13.

126. Saint Nicodemus and Saint Metropolitan, *Philokalia*, 25, 36, 60, 70, 110, 17, 68, 201, 53, 69.

127. Saint Nicodemus and Saint Metropolitan, *Philokalia*, 25, 57, 119, 22, 30, 42, 233, 77, 93.

128. Saint Nicodemus and Saint Metropolitan, *Philokalia*, 23, 36, 57-58, 113, 45, 90.

129. Saint Nicodemus and Saint Metropolitan, *Philokalia*, 24, 39, 48, 63, 71, 120, 40, 55-56, 68-69, 228, 46, 92.

also how to go about developing a journey that deepens one's relationship with our creator.

More contemporarily, John Elias has sought to articulate an approach to thinking about and designing religious education systems for local congregations.[130] Elias seeks to detail views of and approaches to adult religious education that may be utilized in churches. Addressing such areas as adult psychology, social contexts, and faith development, Elias provides a solid theoretical foundation upon which to develop religious education programs. Elias also provides crucial insights into planning, organizing, and managing these programs along with specific strategies that may be used at individual, group, and institutional levels of a religious community. Resources such as these are essential for successful formation program development work.

For theistic educators, it is imperative that we engage in well-discerned, wisely educated, and systematic course development. Why? Theologically, the very core of theistic approaches to education (and the whole of one's spiritual life) is to discern where and how the Spirit of teaching and learning is inviting us to partner with God so that our students learn and develop in the ways that the Spirit would like them to. This guideline is therefore not just significant in terms of its effect size—it really is the heart of this book and the center of all spiritually-discerned education. Contrary to what we might think, discerning God's life and invitations for our classrooms is not an impossible and impenetrable mystery. Why would a God who desires for this beloved creation to grow in God not clearly make these invitations and intentions known and discernable to us? Such a God could be considered to be impotent at best and sadistic at worst. This guideline can therefore be embodied in spiritually discerning ways so that we can more fully know and respond to God's ever-unfolding and transformative life in our classes. Overall, then, this guideline invites us to be more intentional with our spiritually discerning course development methods.

Level 1

The instructor follows some process to design, implement, and evaluate the course. There is direct alignment among the course's objectives, activities, and assessments.

At Level 1 for this guideline, the instructor should be able to clearly articulate some process or set of steps that they are using to design, implement, and evaluate the course. Such course development might include reflecting on student performance in past classes, looking to discipline-specific educational literature, analyzing assessment data, or following standardized curriculum to help guide these processes. If an instructor states that they are using one or more of the common instructional design methods found in the literature (e.g., ADDIE, backward design), then they should also be able to state how they are applying these to the current course in detailed ways.

---

130. Elias, *Foundations and Practice*.

In addition, there should be clear evidence of course level objectives, activities, and assessments being aligned with one another. For example, if one of the course objectives involves learners being able to demonstrate their abilities to conduct a research project, then there should be activities that guide students through these methods as well as assessments that verify their competencies in these research project skills. Such alignment could be verified by both reviewing course materials (e.g., syllabus, course site, observations) as well as via discussions with the instructor and/or students.

Here, the instructor will be found engaging in the basics of spiritually discerning course development methods. Theologically, they will understand that God is well-organized and continually strives to work with them to develop clear and well-thought-out plans for their class. Ideally, they will be able to articulate the processes they have engaged to develop their course in spiritually discerning ways. The results of such discernment at this level should include a close alignment between general course objectives, activities, and assessments as stated above. Such close alignment, and its documented high impact on student achievement, is evidence of God's tendencies to work in well-structured and coordinated ways. The instructor at this level will therefore be found responding to God's invitations and guidance to help ensure a tightly aligned class.

Examples of this might include:

- The instructor is able to clearly articulate some process or set of steps that they are using to design, implement, and evaluate the course.
- The instructor is observed closely following a prescribed curriculum to develop their class.
- There is close alignment between the course objectives that are listed in the syllabus and the activities and assessments that are used.
- The instructor is able to state how a specific course activity or assessment is directly related to one or more course objectives.

Level 2

The instructor draws from evidence-based literature and data to support course development (e.g., design, implementation, and evaluation). There is direct alignment among courses as well as module/unit/weekly objectives, activities, and assessments.

Level 2 continues to extend the previous level. The course development process articulated by the instructor should now also include evidence-based resources. The instructor should be able to clearly state which evidence-based resources they are utilizing and how these directly impact their course development processes. There should be two sources of evidence-based resources: 1) external resources (e.g., educational research literature, experts in the field, etc.), and 2) data from their own courses. There should therefore be evidence of the instructor using one or both of these sources to support their course development processes.

Alignment at this level is also extended to include not only course level objectives, activities, and assessments, but also the course's module/unit/weekly levels as well. For example, the research project skills mentioned in Level 1 might be distributed across several units/weeks in the course. If so, there should be clear evidence of each unit's objectives, activities, and assessments that not only align with each other but also with the course level. Overall, the goal is to help ensure that these course elements are working as closely together as possible to support student learning and development.

As has been discussed many times already, the use of evidence-based resources to support education may be viewed as an attempt to more clearly identify God's high impact work in other contexts. Knowing this, a teacher is then possibly in a better position to discern whether God might be seeking to act in their own class in similar ways. Data gathered from their course can then provide further clarity and guidance to these spiritually discerning endeavors. As a result, such evidence-based practices should be a central part of the instructor's course development methods. Further extending upon the previous level, we will also find educators at this level understanding that God's movements of alignment extend to the unit/weekly level as well as the course level. As a result, they will work to ensure spiritual synchronicity at these more detailed levels.

Examples of this might include:

- The instructor can identify data from their class that they are using to help develop course objectives, activities, and assessments.

- A review of the course site and/or materials reveals close alignment among course and module/weekly elements.

- The instructor is able to identify specific evidence-based resources that they are using to support their course development processes.

Level 3

The instructor collaborates with learners, colleagues, and external sources to engage in evidence-based course development. There is direct alignment among courses as well as module/unit/weekly objectives, activities, assessments, teaching and learning theories, and learner background considerations.

Similar to other guidelines for this area, Level 3 builds directly upon Level 2 in more collaborative ways. The instructor should be able to articulate the evidence-based steps by which they are developing their course, but these steps should now include collaboration with others. Such collaborations should be intended to further aid the instructor in their course's development. Examples of this might include turning to colleagues for ideas on how to adapt specific evidence-based instructional strategies, reviewing assessment data together and deciding which direction(s) the course should go next, and meeting to redesign the course based on past experiences. The instructor should be able to clearly state who they are working with and how these collaborations are directly impacting their evidence-based course development work.

Alignment is also further extended at this level with all course elements being directly aligned at all levels of the course. Following the framework developed for these guidelines, alignment for the following course elements should be verified: objectives, activities, assessments, teaching and learning theories, and learner background considerations. Again, this alignment should be affirmed by course materials and/or in discussions with the instructor and should exist at the modules/units/week levels as well.

Continuing our Level 3 theme of collaborative and democratic views of the course kin-dom, this guideline encourages cooperative engagement with course development methods. In essence, the group will be seeking to spiritually discern how God is wanting to structure and implement the course. Including students in these discernment processes can be considered as essential since God is seeking to develop the course for them and learners may provide insights that are needed for these processes. In addition, the course's alignment is also extended to include all of the course's elements as discussed above. Theologically, seeking such comprehensive alignment is acknowledging God's educational life within and through each of these elements. It is also reflective of the belief that, ultimately and ideally, God's life and movements are internally consistent and perfectly coordinated. This level is therefore the fulfillment of a collaboratively discerned, evidence-based, and comprehensively aligned class. It is therefore no wonder as to why this guideline yields the highest documented impact on student achievement, as God is able to guide the development of well-designed course.

Examples of this might include:

- The instructor can describe the evidence-based processes by which they developed their course and these steps include working with others at various stages.
- The instructor is observed meeting with peers to discuss how one or more of their classes are going and what might be done to continually improve them.
- There is close alignment between the weekly/module/unit objectives that are listed in the syllabus or on the course site and the activities and assessments that used in these weeks/modules/units.
- The instructor is able to state how a specific activity or assessment is directly related to one or more course objectives and learning theories as well as the unit that this activity/assessment is a part of.

LEARNER-BACKGROUND GUIDELINES

As we shall shortly see, the following guidelines are focused on helping us connect more deeply with the backgrounds and lived experiences of our students and their communities. Deeply rooted in a theology that asserts God's presence within and through all of creation, our course development processes must be squarely founded upon an intimate knowledge of what God has and continues to do educationally and culturally in the life of our students. If we are to partner with God's transformative life with our students, then we will need to be aware of the work that God has been and continues to with them. These guidelines are therefore intended to help us with this data gathering and subsequent chapters will help us better know what kinds of data to gather about our students and how this data can be used to design, implement, and evaluate our courses.

Guideline #1—Learner Capabilities

Course is adapted to learners' relevant prior knowledge, interests, skills, and capabilities, and ADA considerations are addressed (Core Guideline).

This guideline is one of the most consistently emphasized across evidence-based literature, assessments, and theories. In studies involving more than 1,700,000 students, the average of effect size of address factors related to this guideline is around 0.54, which is well above the 0.4 h-point.[131] So, why is this guideline so important? At its core, education might be simply conceived as a process of taking students from where they currently are in relation to course KSAs towards the levels of competencies that are defined by the objectives. This therefore requires engaging with learners' current backgrounds, knowledge, and interests in order to help better them to progress towards these objectives. This is particularly important for learners with ADA considerations as many courses have not been developed for such diversity of differences. The overall trajectory of this guideline therefore spans from the instructor developing the course to meet these diverse backgrounds based upon their experiences with previous classes towards collaborating with students in continually adapting the course as it unfolds in real-time. As with other guidelines, the movement is from more instructor-centered initiatives at Level 1 to more collaborative approaches at Level 3.[132]

---

131. Hattie, *Visible Learning*, 41–51, 89–91, 99–101, 71–72, 93–98. Supporting evidence-based assessments: CCSSO, *Intasc Model Core Teaching Standards*, Standards 1 & 2—Indicators 1 & 2, Standard 4—Indicators 1 & 2, Standard 6—Indicator 3, Standard 7—Indicators 1 & 2, Standard 8—Indicator 1; MarylandOnline, "Quality Matters Rubric Standards," 1.6, 1.7, 2.3, 7.2, 8.3; Pianta, La Paro, and Hamre, *Classroom Assessment Scoring*, Teacher Sensitivity, Regard for Student Perspectives, Content Understanding, Analysis & Inquiry, Quality of Feedback, Instructional Dialogue.

132. Supporting References: Ambrose, *How Learning Works*, 13, 15–18, 27, 29–30, 31–34, 85–87, 114–15, 45, 82, 204–5, 11–13; Bok et al., "Feedback-Giving Behaviour"; Bruning, Schraw, and Norby, *Cognitive Psychology*, 34–35, 62–63, 86–87; Clark and Mayer, *E-Learning*, 23, 172, 291, 308, 22–27; Diamond, *Designing and Assessing*, 40, 98, 115, 17, 93, 262–63, 64; Friedman and Fisher, *Handbook*

One of the core assertions of Western Christian theology is the claim that God infinitely and intimately loves all of creation.[133] At an individual level, this means that God knows and works with each student to help them to grow in unique, individual, and wholly appropriate ways based upon their background, traits, and capabilities. This can be seen clearly in how Jesus worked with each of his disciples, responding appropriately to each and assigning tasks and responsibilities to fit with their unique backgrounds and characteristics. For instance, in John 4:1–42, we find a story about Jesus meeting a Samaritan woman at a local well. Through this encounter, Jesus is depicted as having an ability to know some of the personal details of this woman's life and her relationships. In response to this very personal knowledge, Jesus is shown to tailor his advice and message to her unique situation.

More broadly, in the book, *Sacred Systems*, after exploring fifteen different spiritual formation systems, I argued (among other things) that each system was uniquely adapted to their local time and place.[134] Each system, from early Christian monastic communities to medieval mendicant movements right on up until today, were reflective of the common beliefs and practices of their generation. Rather than seeking to create a "one size fits" approach to spiritual formation, I asserted, these fifteen different sacred systems from across more than 2,000 years of Christian history seem to suggest that God ever-adapts God's transformative movements to the local context that are situated in time and space.

As theistic educators, then, a big part of our vocation is discerning where and how God has been and continues to work with each of the individual learners in our class. This requires coming to know our students on a personal level, particularly in relation to course KSAs. What we are interested in is how God has been shaping their prior knowledge, interests, skills, and capabilities prior to the course. From a faith perspective, we can then trust that these are the necessary foundations that we are being invited to work with and build upon.

In the grander scheme of God's plan for each learner, the overall invitation is to discern where and how God wants to help each student progress from where they currently are to where he wants them to be by the end of the course as outlined by the spiritually discerned objectives. This is so that our course can better become a more

---

on Effective Instructional Strategies, 6, 20, 68, 80, 92, 131, 44, 61, 91, 289, 91; Gannon-Tagher and Robinson, "Critical Aspects of Stress"; Harley et al., "Comparing Virtual"; Khandelwal et al., "How We Made Professionalism"; Kool et al., "Goal Orientations"; Lin and Huang, "Examining Charisma"; Matlin, *Cognition*, 178–81, 370; Morris and Chikwa, "Audio Versus Written Feedback"; Morrison et al., *Designing Effective Instruction*, 11, 55–56, 112–13, 38–39; Reiser and Dempsey, *Trends and Issues*, ch. 9, 17; Sawyer, *Cambridge Handbook*, 545–66, 1578–600, 2112–55, 5164–209, 448–92, 8263–89, 765–87, 9480–87, 13978–4002, 7594–615, ch. 7, 16, 29; Slavin, *Educational Psychology*, 116–18, 52, 205, 409, ch. 10, 12; Woolfolk, *Educational Psychology*, 49, 253, 455, 384, 477, ch. 7.

133. Placher, *A History of Christian Theology*, 15.

134. Kyle, *Sacred Systems*, 299–300.

integral part of God's plans and unfolding life with each student both now and in the future.

Level 1

Drawing on past experiences and/or external resources, the instructor seeks to adjust the course appropriately to meet the diverse prior knowledge, interests, skills, and capabilities of learners. The instructor applies interventions, modifications, and accommodations based on ADA requirements.

At the level, instructors will tend to rely more heavily on past experiences and/or external sources to adapt the course to meet the diverse backgrounds and/or ADA needs of learners. The instructor should be able articulate/demonstrate what past experiences they are drawing from and/or what specific external resources they are utilizing to support the course's modified development. These experiences and/or resources should therefore be directly related to the learners' knowledge, interests, skills, and/or capabilities (including ADA, if relevant).

At this foundational level, the instructor is invited to turn their attention more directly towards learners in more general ways. In education, there can be a tendency to focus solely on the course KSAs and neglect any considerations of the diversity of students in the class. As argued above, such narrow KSA/curriculum foci are not fully responsive to God's educational movements as God ever works to adapt to each community in time and place. At this level, then, the instructor should be found thinking about past students that they have had and how they might adapt their course to better fit with learner backgrounds. The instructor might also be found looking to external resources, such as on differentiated instruction, learning styles, and ADA accommodations to help them to begin tailoring their course for a diversity of preferences, experiences, and capabilities. In doing so, theologically, they are essentially responding to God's efforts to more closely match the course to the educational work that God has been and continues to do in the lives of students.

Examples of this might include:

- The instructor is observed using ADA checklists or guidelines from the internet to help develop their course.

- The instructor is able to state how they have reflected on student performance in previous classes and have modified their course to better fit with learners' needs and capabilities.

- The instructor is observed working with a colleague to develop a course based upon their combined experiences of prior students.

- The instructor is able to identify specific resources that they have used to help them better understand how their students learn and articulate how they have used these resources to develop one or more of their classes.

Level 2

In light of learners' relevant prior knowledge, interests, skills, and capabilities, the instructor plans multiple learning experiences and assessments that allow for learner choice in pursuing and demonstrating their achievement of course objectives. The instructor adapts instruction and uses modified ADA resources to address the learning needs of all current learners in the course.

Courses at Level 2 differ from Level 1 by allowing for multiple pathways to engage with the course. These multiple pathways, however, should match the diversity of students that are or are likely to be in the class based upon learners' prior knowledge, current interests, capabilities, and skills. They should also closely align with course objectives. For ADA-related resources, the instructor should modify these in order to better fit with all of the current learners in their course. Studies on ADA resources/accommodations are revealing that non-ADA as well as ADA students benefit from well-designed ADA compliant courses. Instructors at this level should therefore show evidence of developing their course to meet ADA best practices in ways that benefit all students.

As was asserted above, God seeks to adapt God's formative work to each unique community, time, and place. Looking at the history of Western Christianity, such spiritual adaptations have resulted in a variety of spiritual formation approaches for this religious tradition. This level essentially replicates such diversity of approaches in the class. By developing multiple paths and allowing learners some freedom of choice, God is better able to guide students along varying trajectories that are better suited to their unique interests, experiences, and capabilities. These pathways must be ADA empowering not only because of the ongoing marginalization of students with disabilities, which is not reflective of God's work, but also because such ADA designed pathways often facilitate learning in deeper ways for all students. This level therefore embodies God's multiple and varied paths to learning in our courses.

Examples of this might include:

- The instructor is observed helping students choose from a number of given assessment options, which are better suited to learners' capabilities, to demonstrate their competencies in specific course concepts or skills.
- The course allows students to choose a research project that better meets their current interests.
- The instructor is observed presenting multiple representations of key course concepts/skills in an effort to address current learners' diverse needs.

- The instructor can state how they developed multiple pathways (e.g., two or more modules, sets of course materials, videos, etc.) to help students achieve learning outcomes.

Level 3

The instructor collaborates with learners in adapting multiple course objectives, activities, resources, and/or assessments to build upon learners' relevant prior knowledge, interests, skills, and capabilities. The instructor collaborates with learners and colleagues to expand the range of ADA resources that enables all learners to exceed high standards.

Level 3 courses are much more participatory for students than the previous two levels in that instructors will be observed collaborating directly with learners in the class to construct multiple pathways to the objectives that are more in line with learners' backgrounds. Here, the primary focus is on helping students become more self-directed in their own learning and development and better able to adapt the course to meet their own prior knowledge, skills, interests, and capabilities. While much of this work is done directly with students in the course, the instructor should also look to colleagues and other external resources to aid them in these collaborative modifications, particularly for ADA resources. The incorporation and adaptation of these ADA resources/support should have the purpose of helping all students in the class to be more successful. Collaborative course modifications can affect every part of the class including more nuanced and refined objectives, the activities that learners engage, and how students demonstrate their proficiencies (i.e., assessments).

The democratic view of God's kin-dom in the class is more fully realized in classes at this level. Here, learners work directly with the instructor to develop course elements that are relevant and meaningful for them personally. It must be noted, however, that such collaborative development will ideally build directly upon the previous level. This means that students and faculty will look to the multiple pathways that have already been developed at Level 2 and then work to further expand and/or modify these spiritually discerned trajectories. Student engagement is essential because it will be very difficult to know how God is seeking to act in each student's life without their input and feedback. This is especially important for students with disabilities as ADA empowered pathways will likely need to be continually altered for each new group of students. Overall, we find God facilitating a class that is continually adapting to each student and group of students via the democratically discerned and developed multiple pathways.

Examples of this might include:

- The instructor is observed meeting with students one-on-one to develop individualized learning plans for the course.

- The course contains an activity where small groups create their own service-learning project that is of direct interest and relevance to them.
- The instructor can state how they have worked with students to select ADA-compliant resources to better support all students in the class.
- The class is observed collaboratively engaging in Universal Design for Learning (UDL) processes to develop an upcoming unit for the course.

Guideline #2—Cultural Considerations

Instructor is able to appropriately modify the course in light of learners' diverse cultural locations (e.g., SES, ethnicity, gender, age, etc.).

Somewhat similar to the previous guideline, this one is more directly centered on the cultural considerations of each learner whereas the previous guideline was more related to their individual prior knowledge, interests, and capabilities. Recognizing that one's culture deeply influences learning and development, this guideline focuses on identifying how instructors are adapting their course in light of cultural considerations. A student's cultural location can include one or more of the following: ethnicity, gender, age, SES, educational level, sexual orientation, religious tradition, geographic location, political affiliations, and so on. These and other cultural factors influence many of the considerations named in the previous guideline. As a result, developing classes to be more aware of these factors and intentionally engaged with them (i.e., culturally responsive teaching) should result in greater gains in student achievement.[135] When we do, according to studies that have involved almost 10,700,000 students, the effect size is on average 0.37, which is close to Hattie's hinge point of 0.4.[136] Trends for the levels of this guideline range from the instructor simply working to be more aware of how learners' cultural location might influence learning to their working directly with students as well as community members to modify the course to be more culturally responsive.

Theologically, this guideline would assert that God is active within and through entire cultures across time and space. The idea here is that God works differently

---

135. Supporting literature: Batley et al., "Cynicism and Other Attitudes"; Bradshaw and Lowenstein, *Innovative Teaching Strategies*, 24–25, 27, ch. 6; Bruning, Schraw, and Norby, *Cognitive Psychology*, 156–57, 212, 356, 57; Diamond, *Designing and Assessing*, 347–48; Hallam et al., "Do Commencing Nursing and Paramedicine"; Matlin, *Cognition*, 453; Morrison et al., *Designing Effective Instruction*, 56–57; Reiser and Dempsey, *Trends and Issues*, 352–53, ch. 17; Sawyer, *Cambridge Handbook*, 1273–319, ch. 29; Slavin, *Educational Psychology*, 285, ch. 4; Woolfolk, *Educational Psychology*, 51, 188, 262, 387–89, 455, ch. 5.

136. Hattie, *Visible Learning*, 52–53, 57, 61–70, 124–25. Supporting evidence-based assessments: CCSSO, *Intasc Model Core Teaching Standards*, Standards 1 & 2—Indicators 1 & 2, Standard 3—Indicator 1, Standard 4—Indicator 2, Standard 7—Indicator 3, Standard 8—Indicator 1, Standard 9—Indicator 3, Standard 10—Indicator 1; MarylandOnline, "Quality Matters Rubric Standards," 2.3; Pianta, La Paro, and Hamre, *Classroom Assessment Scoring*, Regard for Student Perspective.

through each culture that is historically located in time and space through the symbols, beliefs, and values of each culture. For instance, in Acts 17:16–34 we find a story about Paul of Tarsus interacting with both Greek and Jewish culture. In this story, Paul is challenged by Greek philosophers and asked to explain his message about Jesus to them in ways that they can understand. In response, Paul affirms their religiosity and makes several references to their own poets, beliefs, and practices to tell them more about who he personally believed Jesus to be.

While it is possible to read this story and assert that one way to evangelize in other cultures is to identify similarities between their beliefs and practices and our own and then use these commonalities to encourage conversion, there is an alternative viewpoint. If we believe that God was working through Paul in this event, then we might claim that God was affirming the work that God had already been doing in both cultures and then working to build upon this work. As the story goes, Paul spent some time learning more about the Athenian culture and he learned from it as a result. In turn, Paul then shares from his own cultural beliefs, and some of the people learned from him. One thing that we might therefore conclude from this encounter is that God works uniquely in every culture to continually further the growth of God's kin-dom in all times and places.

Contextual theologians, such as Angie Pears, argue this point. It is an understanding of religious expression as being "radically contextual."[137] With this understanding, we can more clearly see and affirm the work that God is doing within and through each moment in time and space. When it comes to culture, it is an affirmation of the goodness, beauty, love, and truth that God has been working from before the dawn of time to manifest within, to, and beyond each community. It is an effort to see God as already being present within each unique culture, to find and affirm God's image in the current culture, in whatever forms that holy image might take. This is what Black theologians, such as Kelly Brown Douglas, assert as being essential for developing an understanding of the Black Christ.[138] Rather than trying to force a set of beliefs, images, and practices on another culture, it is one that first seeks to affirm the God that is already there. Overall, it is a theological claim that God values, affirms, and works through each culture in infinitely wise and magnificent ways.

If this is true, then as theistic educators we can trust that there are sacred pearls of wisdom and collective experiences in our students' cultures that our classes can benefit from as well as contribute to. Just as our students come to class with prior knowledge and capabilities that we can build upon, so too do their communities and cultures have much to offer in our courses. The holy invitation, then, is to proactively know the cultural locations and backgrounds of our students and to then discern how these can be integrated more fully into the class. At its highest levels, this is a mutual discernment process with our students and their communities which should result in

137. Pears, *Doing Contextual Theology*, 2.
138. Douglas, *Black Christ*, 6.

the entire class benefitting from the educational blessings that God is laboring to birth in our midst in each passing moment. Overall, the cultural backgrounds and communities to which our students are inseparably connected is therefore another avenue through which God seeks to shape the directions of our courses and the student learning and development that it is intended to help foster.

Level 1

The instructor accesses resources to expand their understanding of the SES, ethnic, gender, age, and other differences among learners and their communities and then modifies the course in light of this.

At this beginning level, the instructor should be able to identify some of the various cultural locations of learners based on ethnicity, age, gender, SES, etc. The instructor should also be able to identify resources that they are using to help them to better understand one or more of these cultural factors and how these might influence learning and development. The instructor then uses this knowledge to modify the class. At this level, then, instructors will be able to: 1) identify the cultural locations of learners in the course, 2) state which resources they are relying to inform their understandings of these cultural locations and how these might influence learning and development, and 3) articulate/demonstrate how they have adapted course elements based on these understandings. The primary aim at this level is the instructor developing a beginning understanding of their students' cultural locations and then making changes to the course to be more aligned with these locations.

The foundational invitation at this level is for the instructor to acknowledge the already existing presence of cultural diversity in their class. U.S. educational systems, in particular, are guilty of embracing a monocultural view of classrooms, curriculum, teaching strategies, and assessments. These culturally dismissive perspectives have resulted in the achievement gaps as stated above. Theologically, such perspectives are reflective of God's ever contextualizing movements. As a result, the instructor at this level will be found not only being aware of the cultural diversities in their class, but also seeking out resources and support to help them better understand these diversities. In doing so, they will be striving to better understand how God works through such cultural diversity in relation to the course's KSAs and thereby labor to be more culturally responsive to his ever-adapting educational life.

Examples of this might include:

- The instructor is able to accurately identify one or more cultural locations (e.g., SES, ethnicity, gender, age, etc.) of students in their class and can state how they have developed the course in light of this awareness.

- The instructor can identify one or more resources (e.g., articles, books, students, mentors, websites, etc.) that they have used to help them to better understand their current students' cultural locations.
- The class contains resources that accurately represent the cultural diversity of students in the course.
- The instructor is observed discussing with students how course concepts/skills might vary based on one's cultural location.

Level 2

In light of learners' relevant cultural locations (e.g., SES, ethnicity, gender, age, etc.), the instructor plans multiple culturally appropriate pathways of learning experiences and assessments that allow for learner choice in pursuing and demonstrating their achievement of course objectives.

Similar to the previous guideline, courses at Level 2 for this guideline differ from Level 1 by allowing for multiple and culturally responsive pathways to engage with the course. These multiple pathways, however, should match the cultural diversity of students and the wider communities that are currently or are likely to be in the class based upon learners' ethnicity, age, gender, SES, and so on. These multiple pathways should also lead students to achieve the course/module objectives.

Following the theological claims for this guideline, as well as Level 2 from the previous guideline, the holy invitation here is for the instructor to spiritually discern and develop multiple ways for students to engage with course KSAs. Each of these pathways should be developed in light of the cultural education that the instructor worked to build in Level 1. Theologically, the instructor should be working to discern where and how God has and continues to work with each identified culture, in relation to the specific KSAs in the course. For instance, does God work differently with lower SES students, as documented by evidence-based educational literature, to learn math than God does with upper SES students? If so, then the instructor should work to develop various ways of engaging with the math concepts in the course for these and other cultural diversities that are present in the class. As stated in the previous guideline, by developing such a course, the instructor will be empowering God to work with each student in various ways along a variety of learning trajectories—ones that are more culturally relevant and responsive.

Examples of this might include:

- The course empowers students to choose a class project that is relevant to their own ethnic heritage.
- The course site contains multiple e-learning modules that students can choose from and are tailored to one or more cultural locations.

- The instructor requires students to find additional culturally appropriate articles on a topic.
- The class contains an activity that requires students to identify a specific culture that they are likely to work with in the future, one that they know very little about, and complete a project in relation to this culture.

Level 3

The instructor collaborates with learners to develop course elements and provide different culturally appropriate pathways to engage with the course. The instructor collaborates with a broad range of colleagues, specialists, and/or community members to understand and address learners' cultural needs and to integrate diverse cultural resources, practices, and perspectives into the class.

Similar to many other guidelines, a Level 3 course will show evidence of the instructor working directly with learners as well as outside colleagues and community members to adapt course elements to better meet learners' diverse cultural locations. The course should therefore have evidence of multiple pathways to engage with course KSAs that are developed in collaboration with students. Also, courses at this level will integrate diverse cultural perspectives via course materials and activities. Overall, this level is very similar to the previous guideline but has a more specific emphasis on the cultural locations of students as well as diverse cultural engagement with course KSAs.

The notion of a democratically engaged kin-dom class is further expanded by this guideline. The instructor will be found working directly with students in the course to spiritually discern and develop the multiple culturally relevant pathways. In addition, however, the instructor will seek to include community members and experts from the various cultures represented in the class. In doing so, the instructor will essentially be moving towards developing a community-based course wherein students interact with others as they collaboratively develop these culturally relevant paths. Theologically, Level 3 courses for this guideline are intentionally harmonizing the progressive work that God continually labors to do with various cultures both within and beyond the class.

Examples of this might include:

- The instructor is observed working with students and community members to develop a class project that is relevant for the community.
- There is evidence of the instructor working with students to identify culturally diverse resources that will become required reading for a unit in the course.
- The instructor empowers student groups to create a summative course assessment that is culturally appropriate for everyone in the group.

- The instructor is observed working with students to develop personalized learning goals that encourage them to adapt course concepts/skills to their own and/or their community's cultural location.

Guideline #3—Preferential Option for Vulnerable Populations

Mission-Centered Focus: *In pursuit of learning objectives, the course engages learners in diverse cultural experiences with underrepresented and marginalized communities that proactively reduce biases and increase justice for these populations* (Core Guideline).

Educational studies in the U.S. continue to document a significant gap in achievements between at least two sets of groups: 1) middle/upper and lower SES students, and 2) Euro-American and Non-Euro-American students. In response, nationwide PK-16 initiatives have been launched in an attempt to close these gaps.[139] According to studies contained in Hattie's meta-meta-analysis, an overall effect size for these kinds of programs, which have included more than 196,000 students, is 0.44.[140] This guideline is reflective of these initiatives and is intended to help ensure that each class is adequately addressing the needs of marginalized, under-resourced, and lower performing students. Furthermore, following this guideline, classes should help prepare students to proactively engage with marginalized and under-resourced communities in positively transforming ways. Overall, the trends from Level 1 to 3 are from having students be more aware of diverse perspectives to actively engaging with diverse people and communities. It also entails having the instructor not only address their own personal biases, but also help their students to do likewise.

---

139. Supporting literature: Alnassar et al., "Clinical Psychomotor Skills"; Ambrose, *How Learning Works*, 182; Amoako-Sakyi and Amonoo-Kuofi, "Problem-Based Learning"; Aponte et al., "Mentoring Hispanic"; Barnes, "Impact of Service-Learning"; Blanchet-Garneau, "Critical Reflection"; Bradshaw and Lowenstein, *Innovative Teaching Strategies*, 467–69, ch. 2; Bruning, Schraw, and Norby, *Cognitive Psychology*, 212; Clark and Mayer, *E-Learning*, 82, 127, 200, 61; Cowan, Weeks, and Newsome-Wicks, "Promoting Success"; Diamond, *Designing and Assessing*, 193, 279–80, ch. 21; Chuang et al., "Medical and Pharmacy Student Concerns"; Gavin-Knecht and Fischer, "Undergraduate Nursing Students' Experience"; Mahmoud, Al-Zalabani, and Abdulrahman, "Public Health Education"; Martins et al., "How We Enhanced"; Morrison et al., *Designing Effective Instruction*, 166; Murray, "Culture and Climate; Murray,"Factors That Promote and Impede"; Peltzer et al., "Strategies for Building Advocacy Skills"; Hole et al., "Educating Change Agents"; Read, Pino-Betancourt, and Morrison, "Social Change"; Ritten, Waldrop, and Wink, "Nurse Practitioner Students"; Sawyer, *Cambridge Handbook*, 1407–30, 9345–67, 18125–73; Slavin, *Educational Psychology*, 102–3, 11–12; Stroup and Kuk, "Nursing as a Career Choice"; Van Schalkwyk, Bezuidenhout, and De Villiers, "Understanding Rural Clinical Learning Spaces"; Woolfolk, *Educational Psychology*, 190, 335–36; Zaidi et al., "Gender, Religion, and Sociopolitical Issues."

140. Hattie, *Visible Learning*, 58–60, 63–64, 95–96, 149–51. Supporting evidence-based assessments: CCSSO, *Intasc Model Core Teaching Standards*, Standards 1 & 2—Indicator 2, Standard 3—Indicator 1, Standard 5—Indicators 1 & 2, Standard 6—Indicator 3, Standard 7—Indicators 1 & 3, Standard 8—Indicator 1, Standard 9—Indicator 3, Standard 10—Indicator 1; Pianta, La Paro, and Hamre, *Classroom Assessment Scoring*, Teacher Sensitivity, Concept Understanding.

It has been noted by several authors that the God of the Hebrew and Christian Scriptures is a God of justice and mercy, particularly for underrepresented and marginalized communities.[141] Furthermore, in the Gospels, Jesus is depicted as having a preferential option for poor and marginalized persons. Throughout his ministry, we find Jesus helping people who were born blind, those stricken with leprosy, eating with "sinners," and Samaritans who were shunned by Jews.[142] Over and over, Jesus is seen spending much of his time and energies in solidarity with people and communities who were oppressed, overburdened, and under-resourced.

In her book, *Mujerista Theology*, Ada Maria Isasi-Diaz asserts her brand of Latina theology as being "a liberative praxis—reflective action that has as its goal the liberation of Hispanic women."[143] It is an approach to spirituality, religion, and theology that takes as one of its central pillars working for equity and justice for this community. It is one that takes seriously the lived experiences of Latinas and their ways of knowing, relating, loving, and living. In short, Isasi-Diaz has presented God as working deeply and continually within and through Hispanic women, empowering them towards greater liberation while in the very midst of *la lucha*, the "ability to deal with suffering without being determined by it."[144] It is works such as these that are a continual testimony of Jesus' ongoing work within and through marginalized and oppressed communities.

As it relates to our classrooms, we can therefore expect God to be proactively working with struggling students, yearning for the very highest and best both for and from them. This does not mean that God neglects higher performing, middle/upper class, or dominant group students. These higher achieving students, educational research has repeatedly shown, generally do well within the educational system as it currently is—likely because mainstream educational systems (at least in the U.S.) have been largely created by and sustained for these dominant group members. Marginalized, under-resourced, and lower performing students, however, need more support, intentional focus, and sometimes different kinds of strategies in order to be more successful.

As we have seen with Jesus' ministry, where there are needs, there is God. God, it can therefore be asserted, continually beckons us to be his more direct and proactive support for struggling students. In addition, since educational systems are a major part of the formation of the world's citizens, this guideline further asserts that we should also be working with our students to develop the skills that they will need to continually transform marginalizing, inequitable, and unjust political, social, and economic systems. It requires helping our students, as well as ourselves, for instance,

---

141. Brown, *Spirituality and Liberation*, 16; Isasi-Díaz, *Mujerista Theology*, 106–7; Soelle, *Silent Cry*, 193.

142. Mark 9:1–12; Luke 17:11–19; Matt 9:10–13; John 4:4–26.

143. Isasi-Díaz, *Mujerista Theology*, 192.

144. Isasi-Díaz, *Mujerista Theology*, 129.

to allow the Spirit to raise awareness of the implicit and explicit biases that each of us personally has so that we can collectively work to grow beyond them. There is no place in God's kin-dom for such distortions, it may be asserted, and if we are truly open to God's yearnings in us for a world of justice, peace, love, and prosperity, then our educational systems must proactively work with our students towards these ends. Overall, this guideline challenges us to move beyond our comfort zones in directions where marginalized and under-resourced populations become a thing of the past.

Level 1

The course includes multiple cultural perspectives and experiences of underrepresented and marginalized communities that align with course objectives. The instructor explores how their own personal biases can affect perceptions and actions, particularly as these biases relate to underrepresented and marginalized communities.

Level 1 for this guideline is primarily focused on exposing learners to diverse perspectives within the class as well as in the community (locally, regionally, nationally, and/or globally). In line with the aims of this guideline, a specific emphasis is given to the lived experiences and perspectives of under-resourced and marginalized communities. The second part of this level involves the instructor actively becoming more aware of their own biases and how these might be affecting their actions personally, civically, and professionally. Of particular importance for this guideline are instructor biases that are related to lower performing students, as well as learners from marginalized and under-resourced communities. The instructor should therefore be able to: a) articulate/demonstrate awareness some of their potential biases, b) state/demonstrate how these biases might be affecting their work as an educator, and c) reflect on and take concrete steps to prevent these biases from adversely affecting their students. Instructors might also conduct self-analyses on their course to identify and help them better address gaps among groups of students in their class (e.g., based on SES, ethnicity, gender, GPA, performance in the class, etc.).

At this level, we can assert that God is working to lay the foundational groundwork needed to help students become more aware of the lived experiences of marginalized communities. By integrating resources that expose students to these lived experiences, the instructor is essentially allowing God to develop consciousness in them. Awareness can give way to empathy, which can then lead to action. Through these processes, the Spirit of justice and mercy shifts the mind, molds the heart, and ultimately transforms actions at higher levels. These foundational levels are therefore the beginning steps that God is attempting to take towards these ends.

A significant part of such facilitation, as noted above, is the instructor becoming aware of their own implicit biases. Theologically, these biases may be view as socially enculturated distortions of God's life in one's psyche. At higher levels, the instructor will be called upon to work with students to help mitigate their biases. Before this can happen, however, God strives to help the instructor mitigate their own biases according to this guideline. Overall, this level is therefore focused on establishing the strong foundations that God will need in order to enact the more difficult work of subsequent levels.

Examples of this might include:

- The course contains materials (e.g., readings, videos, etc.) from diverse perspectives of under-resourced and/or marginalized communities.
- Learners are observed interacting with one another's viewpoints and then comparing these perspectives with someone from an under-resourced and/or marginalized background.
- The course hosts guest speakers from marginalized groups.
- The instructor is able to: a) articulate awareness of some of their own potential biases that are related to age, gender, ethnicity, etc.; b) state how these biases might be affecting their interactions with specific students in the class; and c) identify concrete steps that they are taking to prevent these biases from adversely affecting their students.

Level 2

In pursuit of learning objectives, the course has learning experiences that facilitate learners' direct engagement with diverse people from underrepresented and marginalized populations. The instructor assists learners in exploring how their own biases can affect perceptions and actions, particularly as these biases relate to underrepresented and marginalized communities.

At this level, there are two primary considerations. The first extends upon Level 1 by having learners engage more directly with marginalized and under-resourced communities. Here, the interactions are more immersive and direct rather than simple exposure as it was with Level 1. For the second consideration, the work on identifying and transforming biases also expands at this level when the instructor now works with learners in these areas. While it might at first appear that multicultural engagement from the previous guideline includes transformative reflections on biases, this is not always the case. Courses at this level therefore explicitly and directly address these kinds of personal reflections with learners, scaffolding them towards a deeper awareness of their own biases and how these might be affecting their perceptions of, and engagement with, diverse people and communities. The class should therefore have clear evidence of these kinds of reflective activities across the course, particularly as they relate to under-resourced and marginalized populations.

Having established some level of consciousness of the lived experiences of marginalized communities at the previous level, it might be asserted that God now seeks to deepen this in significant and more personal ways. At this level, students are immersed more directly in these lived experiences by talking and working directly with these populations. Through such intimate and personal encounters, God can have a greater impact on one's heart as students see and experience, to some extent, what life is more truly like for marginalized persons.

An important part of this work, however, must include students becoming more aware of their own explicit and implicit biases and stereotypes. If unaddressed, these biases can be reinforced and result in negative experiences that are damaging for students as well as the communities/people that they are in relationship with.[145] Here, God therefore labors intensely to transform these biases and deepen the empathic relationships that students have with marginalized populations. With such emotional and intercultural maturity in place, God can then help students to move to the next level of solidarity-based action.

Examples of this might include:

- The course includes community-based projects that expose students to under-resourced communities.

- The course contains assignments where students are required to: a) articulate awareness of some of their own potential biases that are related to age, gender, ethnicity, etc.; b) state how these biases might be affecting their interactions with others; and c) identify concrete steps that they are taking to prevent these biases from adversely affecting their personal, professional, and/or civic lives.

- Learners are observed completing a service-learning project that requires them to connect with local and global peers from marginalized backgrounds.

- Students are required to complete an Implicit Association Test (IAT) and reflect on the possible implications of the results.

Level 3

In alignment with learning objectives, the course has activities that facilitate learners' development of advanced intercultural and civic engagement competencies, particularly with underrepresented and marginalized communities. The course provides opportunities for learners to proactively work for equity and justice in solidarity with underrepresented and marginalized communities.

Level 3 continues with both the considerations from Level 2. The course intentionally facilitates interactions among learners as well as with other people/communities in ways that deepen their ability to work with diverse cultures. Again, a central emphasis is given to marginalized and under-resourced populations, and students learn how course KSAs directly relate and can be applied to working for change in

---

145. Reed-Bouley and Kyle, "Challenging Racism."

solidarity with these communities. As they engage in this work, attention should be given to developing students' civic engagement and intercultural competency KSAs at higher levels as they relate to under-resourced and marginalized communities. Numerous rubrics are available online that outline these KSAs, and the instructor should identify and integrate the most appropriate ones for their class. A review of course materials should clearly identify these resources.

At this highest level, God's transformative impact moves from class to community. Here, students work in solidarity with leaders of marginalized communities. Rather than following a service model where outsiders decide what a community needs, God instead strives to connect students with these local community leaders. In doing so, students are providing additional support, skills, and resources that these leaders have identified that they need to help further augment and empower the work that God has been and continues to do in the community.

God will be able to do this more effectively when students possess more sophisticated and mature intercultural and civic engagement competencies. The instructor is therefore called to ensure such competencies by preparing and thoroughly assessing students before such solidarity-based actions are engaged. Central to such preparations, following our democratic Level 3 views of the kin-dom, are collaborative spiritual discernment processes between the instructor, community leaders, and students. In doing so, God will be able to help coordinate all parties involved in the project(s) and ensure the greatest likelihood of success.

Examples of this might include:

- The course contains social justice projects where students are required to work with a local advocacy group.
- Students in the course are observed partnering with families and community members from underrepresented backgrounds to complete a neighborhood improvement project.
- A course assignment requires students to work with policy makers to bring about policy changes that influence marginalized populations.
- The instructor is observed using a civic engagement and/or intercultural competency rubric to help guide the development of the course.

PROFESSIONAL DEVELOPMENT, LEADERSHIP, AND EVIDENCE-BASED PRACTICE GUIDELINES

While each of the categories above were directly related to what happens within our classes, this category is more focused on what happens outside of them. Here, the invitation from God is for teachers to ensure that they are continually responding to God's call to improve as educators. It is also a calling for instructors to be proactively involved in institutional leadership positions that improve educational quality in their schools. Finally, it is a calling to develop evidence-based approaches to education that are to be foundational for their spiritual discernment processes. The following guidelines are therefore intended to help theistic educators continually support and develop the quality of education for themselves and others.

Guideline #1—Professional Development

Instructor engages in and supports professional development (PD) opportunities related to improving their educational competencies (Core Guideline).

The craft of education is a lifelong pursuit, one that can be continually improved upon. In order to help foster such ongoing growth, instructors need to be involved in professional development opportunities. Doing so can have a tremendous impact on student achievement as the instructor's teaching competencies improve. These opportunities can cover how to write better objectives, how to create more reliable and valid assessments, keeping up with the latest educational technologies that are available, and so on. This guideline is therefore intended to help ensure that instructors are engaging in PD in significant and ongoing ways. At lower levels, this involvement can be simply participating in PD sessions, whereas at the higher levels, the instructor will help to develop these sessions. Overall, the instructor should be found continually and proactively pursuing deeper, broader, and more expert levels of proficiency in their educational craft. In studies including more than 47,000 people, the effect size is 0.65, which is not only well above Hattie's 0.40 hinge point, but also one of the highest for all of these guidelines.[146] Ongoing PD of educators is therefore an important factor for improving student achievement.

Just as God may be asserted to work with students to continually learn and develop, so too might it be claimed that God labors with instructors. Theologically, education is a craft of continually discerning and responding to God's movements with and through the class. Such a discipline, like most others, is one that can be continually improved upon and cultivated across the lifespan. As a result, each instructor is invited to not only discern where and how God is wanting them to improve but to also work with and for other educators to help them develop as well.

We can see the importance of this guideline through the many examples from Western Christian history provided for the other guidelines above. So much of the Christian ministry work is twofold in its foci. First, it is intended to help others come to know more intimately and live more fully with God. In doing so, individuals and communities are transformed as they manifest more of God's life of love, justice, harmony, truth, beauty, peace, and organization. However, as we can see from Jesus'

---

146. Hattie, *Visible Learning*, 109–13, 19–21. Supporting evidence-based assessments: CCSSO, *Intasc Model Core Teaching Standards*, Standard 4—Indicators 1 & 2, Standard 6—Indicator 1, Standard 7—Indicator 1, Standard 9—Indicators 1 & 3, Standard 10—Indicator 1.

work with his own followers in preparing them to go out and minister themselves, we can see a second central focus for Christian ministry. This religious tradition has often and largely been evangelizing in nature. Not satisfied with merely transforming an individual/community and being finished, Christianity has additionally sought to then equip its disciples to go and do likewise for and with others. It is a self-replicating model of global transformation that continues to spread the unending gospel of God's life of love.

As a result, Western Christian spiritual formation has often had, and continues to have, a focus on equipping the saints for ministry to others across one's lifespan. As theistic educators, then, we can learn from this religious tradition the importance of continually engaging in opportunities that empower us to teach others more effectively. In doing so, we are responding to God's unending efforts to improve the quality of ministers on this planet. Education is, we assert, a central part of God's ongoing and transformational ministries and it is therefore a core part of our calling to continually improve in this vocational craft.

Level 1

The instructor engages in structured individual and/or group professional learning opportunities that help them to stay current with essential KSAs in their discipline as well as to provide all learners with effective curriculum and learning experiences.

At this level, the instructor will be found participating in PD opportunities that are readily available to them. These might include attending lunch-and-learns offered by their school, attending regional trainings in their discipline, and accessing online webinars on educational technologies. These PD offerings should help the instructor to stay current in their own field of study and/or help them better understand how to teach more effectively. Regardless of the focus of the PD that they engage with, these should help the instructor be better prepared to help their students learn and develop in their classes.

At this foundational level, God may be asserted to be inviting each instructor to participate in PD offerings that God needs them to engage with. It might be further asserted that God has an ongoing series of such opportunities planned for each faculty member as they engage in their educational craft. At regular intervals, the instructor is therefore invited to discern which offerings are available and are likely to be most meaningful and relevant to their current situation. In doing so, they are allowing God to continually work to mold and shape them into the best possible educator they can be each step of the way.

Examples of this might include:

- There are records of the instructor regularly attending lunch-and-learns offered by their school.

- The instructor can show evidence of attending regional trainings in their discipline.
- The instructor is observed accessing online webinars on emerging technologies in education.
- The instructor subscribes to and regularly reads journals and new texts in their field, particularly those that are related to teaching and learning in their discipline.

Level 2

Based on personal reflections and feedback from students, peers, and mentors, the instructor identifies areas of ongoing PD and participates in learning experiences that address these identified areas of educational improvement.

This level continues the previous one with the instructor continually engaging with PD that helps them improve as a professional educator. However, rather than attending PD events as they become available, an instructor at this level will be more intentional with assessing their current competencies and identifying areas where they need improvement. To help with this, the instructor will look to various sources and support systems such as student course evaluations and having colleagues observe their classes and provide feedback. Based upon these intentional evaluations, the instructor will then seek out PD opportunities that directly address these areas—ones that continue to improve noted strengths and/or help with weaknesses that they have. In essence, the instructor is demonstrating the self-regulated learning skills that they will need to help them continually improve across the whole of their educational career. As a result, increased student achievement in their courses should be a measurable outcome of these efforts over the long-term.

Deepening the foundational work of the previous level, God invites the instructor to intensify their discernment processes. Just as with students, who are called to reflect and act upon the educational feedback they have received, so too are instructors invited to seek out and wisely utilize feedback on their own teaching competencies. Without such assessment data, it will be difficult for the instructor to clearly know which areas God is calling upon them to improve. The educator therefore needs to discern: 1) what types of assessment sources are likely to be most valid and helpful for them; 2) who should conduct these assessments of their teaching, be this themselves or others; and 3) how to best interpret assessment results so they can choose the PD offering(s) that are likely to be most timely and impactful for them. Throughout these discernment processes, the instructor can expect God to be striving to guide them clearly each step of the way.

Examples of this might include:

- The instructor can describe how they have met with a colleague to review student course evaluations and then identify PD opportunities to help them address areas noted on these evaluations.

- The instructor invites a staff member to talk with their class about what is going well and what might be improved, and then the instructor participates in PD events that help them improve based on the class' feedback.

- The instructor uses evidence-based guidelines to assess their own course and then identifies resources that will help them address noted areas for improvement.

- The instructor participates in a workshop that helps them assess one or more of their teaching competencies and then improve in these areas.

Level 3

In addition to Level 2, the instructor collaborates with colleagues to collectively create, reflect upon, analyze, and improve PD opportunities that address Levels 1 and/or 2.

While this level continues to build upon the previous one, it is also characteristically different. Here, the instructor will be found not only engaging in relevant PD opportunities, they will also help to develop these. Following Level 3 for many other guidelines, these development efforts should be collaborative in nature as they work with others to design, implement, and evaluate PD offerings. These PD efforts might occur at their institution or with discipline-specific organizations that they are a part of. The PD events that they help to create should aid others in their own ongoing journey to continually improve in discipline-specific educational competencies.

At this level, God can be asserted to be trying to maximize the PD endeavors of each faculty member. In line with Western Christianity's self-propagating foci, the instructor at this level is called to seek out PD offerings to improve their own competencies. In addition, they are invited to be a more integral part of helping discern and develop these offerings for and with others. Here, the democratic and collaborative educational kin-dom is extended as faculty collectively helps to decide what to offer in the form of PD. Through these efforts, God maximizes both the efficiency and effectiveness of ongoing PD ministries.

Examples of this might include:

- The instructor serves on a faculty development committee and they actively work with others to develop PD events for instructors.

- The instructor is an active participant in a discipline-specific organization and they work with peers to deliver workshops and resources that help colleagues improve their teaching proficiencies.

- The instructor works with student retention efforts on campus to identify best practices and help instructors and staff align their courses and programs with these practices.
- The instructor collaborates with a peer to offer training sessions to colleagues on discipline-specific KSAs.

Guideline #2—Educational Leadership

Instructor actively participates in leadership roles and responsibilities that improve the institution's education and culture.

As may be seen by these guidelines, the institution's culture greatly influences the quality of education. Level 3 for most guidelines is highly collaborative in nature and educational research studies are finding that the more positive and interactive a school is, the higher the student achievement. This culture is determined by the roles and responsibilities that students, faculty, and staff have. As a result, it is imperative that each individual play an active part in helping to continually shape and guide the organization's actions and attitudes. This means that instructors should therefore be found taking on leadership roles at their institution. When they do, the effect size on student learning is around 0.36, based on studies involving more than 1,100,000 people.[147] At lower levels, this involvement will entail supporting positive and collaborative initiatives. At higher levels, the instructor will be found leading quality improvement projects and actively mentoring others. The basic premise here is that the more committed to quality learning and development an organization's members are as a whole, the better the education will be within its classes/programs.

This guideline is very much in line with the democratic and collaborative views of God's kin-dom articulated by Level 3 for most guidelines. In order for educational systems to embody this kin-dom, its constituents need to be directly and substantively involved in its operations. This means that instructors are not only encouraged to voice their opinions, desires, and needs in relation to decisions, but their voices should also have a measurable impact on these decisions.

Such a view is based on the theology that God is active with and through each and every member of the school. As have been presented for many of the other guidelines above, the Western Christian tradition has numerous examples of God seeking to empower individuals and communities for leadership engagement. From the Gospel-spreading initiatives of the early Christian communities to the ongoing work for justice today, God can be asserted to labor to work with and through humanity. In order to more fully actualize this sacred life, each member must therefore be proactively responsive to God's leadership invitations within and around them. For

---

147. Hattie, *Visible Learning*, 83–85. Supporting evidence-based assessments: CCSSO, *Intasc Model Core Teaching Standards*, Standard 3—Indicator 1, Standard 5—Indicator 1, Standard 6—Indicators 1 & 3, Standard 7—Indicators 2 & 3, Standard 9—Indicators 1, 2, & 3, Standard 10—Indicators 1 & 2.

instructors, this means being engaged in leadership positions and decision-making bodies that have an impact on the educational quality of the school directly or indirectly. This guideline therefore outlines the roles that God may be asserted to be inviting instructors into.

Level 1

The instructor participates in schoolwide efforts to implement a shared vision and they actively contribute to a supportive and collaborative institutional culture.

At this level, the instructor will be aware of initiatives at their school that relate to supporting its vision and mission. The instructor may serve on standing committees, attend meetings or trainings related to the organization's mission, or intentionally work to develop collegial friendships with co-workers. Here, the instructor is an active part of already existing initiatives and behaviors of the school. They positively support the institution's culture and work to develop collaborative relationships with others.

At this foundational level, the instructor is invited to identify and participate in existing initiatives that support God's general work at the school. Ideally, the mission and vision of the educational institution has been well-discerned, and the instructor is called to proactively help fulfill this mission. The instructor should have faith that God has specific ways that he is inviting the instructor to participate in these institutional initiatives. As a result, the instructor's spiritual discernment should focus on where and how they are being called to support the school's mission and vision.

Examples of this might include:

- The instructor is observed actively serving on standing committees and contributing to the committee's work.

- The instructor is observed attending meetings related to the organization's mission.

- There is evidence of the instructor intentionally working to develop collegial friendships with co-workers.

- The instructor is able to articulate the organization's vision and can state how they intentionally work to support and implement this vision in their classes, with co-workers, etc.

Level 2

The instructor engages in institutional-wide decision-making processes with colleagues to identify common goals, develop strategies for pursuing these goals, and evaluate progress towards them. The instructor actively and consistently contributes to the growth of others through mentoring, feedback, and sharing of practices.

Level 2 builds upon Level 1 when the instructor is found participating in initiatives that work to achieve specific goals. These projects may be a part of a task force that the instructor is on, ventures that their department is leading, initiatives that are being led by discipline-specific organizations, curriculum rewriting efforts, or accreditation-related improvements. At Level 1, the instructor may simply take part in these as a participant. At this level, however, the instructor will be an integral part of the core planning and implementation team that is leading these projects.

In addition, the instructor will also be found at this level mentoring others on how to improve their educational craft. Such mentoring can happen formally via structured programs or informally as the instructor works with a colleague to reflect on and improve their course(s). Overall, this level is characterized by the instructor taking on roles where they help to lead organizational projects as well as more proactively mentor others.

As the instructor continues to gain experience at Level 1 with institutional policies, process, and cultures, they can gradually develop the ability to move into more influential leadership roles. Level 2 for this guideline is an acknowledgment of such development as God invites the teacher to take on roles where they are a central part of the planning and implementation teams. Central to these roles, the instructor should engage in spiritual discernment with others as to which goals to pursue as well as how they will go about this work. As the faculty member engages in these leadership roles, they will likely be more well-known in the community. Another holy invitation that often comes with such social standings is the calling to actively mentor and support others. At this level, the instructor will therefore also be found responding to these mentoring invitations.

Examples of this might include:

- The instructor is observed taking an active part on a task force that is leading a curriculum rewriting effort.
- The instructor proactively works with colleagues at their school to support initiatives that are being led by discipline-specific organizations.
- The instructor actively contributes on a committee that is assessing accreditation-related improvements.
- The instructor participates as a mentor in a structured mentoring program for new employees.

Level 3

The instructor is a leader in identifying and advocating for continuous evaluation and improvement of institutional-wide vision, mission, and goals that support student learning and development. The instructor actively mentors and motivates colleagues to participate in institutional leadership roles.

Extending the work of the previous level, an instructor at Level 3 will be found taking a more proactive role in identifying and initiating institutional change projects. At Level 2, the instructor was an active participant on already existing leadership teams that designed and carried out these kinds of projects. At this level, however, there will be strong evidence of the instructor taking the initiative to identify opportunities for institutional improvement that are intended to lead to increased student achievement. Examples of these might include the instructor starting quality improvement projects, conducting their own asset-needs or SWOT analyses to identify areas for growth at the school, or bringing groups together to identify challenges and brainstorm solutions. An instructor at this level will also be found working to empower others to be more actively involved in leadership roles at their school. Overall, the instructor is committed to continuous improvement of their institution as evidenced by this kind of mentoring as well as by the initiatives that they take a lead role in launching.

At this highest level, we can assert that God is calling the faculty member to take one of the most central roles in an institution that there is: personal ownership of and commitment to continuous quality improvement of the school. It should be noted that this follows the view of these guidelines that asserts that each subsequent level necessarily builds upon the previous one(s). For this guideline, theologically, this means that God has been working to imbue the instructor with the knowledge, experiences, skills, and sense of timing that they will need to more effectively analyze and facilitate such institutional change processes. Someone who is brand new to the school and is motivated towards organizational change will likely not be as effective as someone who has progressed through the previous levels at the school. Such sacred transformations require an intimate knowledge of, and experiences with, the institution's complex social, political, and economic dynamics. As part of this work, the instructor is also called to intentionally and proactively help others develop in their spiritual leadership abilities and participation. This highest level is therefore characterized by the faculty member's abilities to partner with God to leverage innovative change in their organization as well as in other individuals at the school.

Examples of this might include:

- The instructor is observed starting a quality improvement project to address the lack of technology support at their school.
- The instructor can show evidence of conducting their own SWOT (strengths, weaknesses, opportunities, and threats) analyses to identify areas for growth in their department.
- The instructor is observed bringing students together to identify challenges at their school and brainstorm solutions.

- The instructor starts a faculty mentoring program that empowers new instructors to be more involved in leadership roles at the school.

Guideline #3—Evidence-Based Practice

Instructor conducts evidence-based practice and/or scholarly projects that improve the quality of education (Core Guideline).

In any field of study, improvements often come incrementally via an integrated combination of learning, action, and reflection. In other words, we learn about our discipline, we try what we learn, and then we can reflect on and subsequently change how things are going. This basic cycle is the foundation of evidence-based practice, which should be applied to education just as it should to every field. This guideline is therefore intended to encourage instructors to apply these kinds of approaches to their educational craft.

Instructors need to establish habits of continually learning how to teach better, apply what they are learning to their own classes, and then gather data that helps them identify areas of strength as well as improvement. Such endeavors can be done informally as they teach each class more formally, via scholarly projects, where they follow structured research methods. At lower levels, instructors will be found working individually to improve their own course, whereas at higher levels, they will be found collaborating with others to have a wider impact on their institutions or teaching-oriented disciplines more broadly. Overall, instructors should intentionally and continually use evidence/data to help improve the art and science of teaching. With almost 140,000 people participating in these kinds of education studies, the effect size is approximately 0.56 for this guideline.[148]

This text is founded on the theological premise that research methods can be used to document God's tangible and effective movements within and to educational systems. Educational research studies often document these holy transformations at macro-levels, with hundreds or even thousands of students being a part of these studies. This guideline essentially represents an extension of these assertions at the micro-level. Here, the invitation is for the instructor to continually seek evidence that confirms their spiritual discernment of where and how they are being invited to respond to God's movements.

In Christian history, such evidence-based confirmations can be seen in how many have viewed miracles. For instance, as we can see in Jesus' ministry, oppositional

---

148. Hattie, *Visible Learning*, 112–13, 15–18, 78–79, 81. Supporting evidence-based assessments: CCSSO, *Intasc Model Core Teaching Standards*, Standards 1 & 2—Indicators 1 & 2, Standard 3—Indicator 1, Standard 4—Indicator 1, Standard 5—Indicator 2, Standard 6—Indicators 1, 2, & 3, Standard 7—Indicators 1, 2, & 3, Standard 8—Indicator 1, Standard 9—Indicators 1, 2 & 3, Standard 10—Indicators 1 & 2; MarylandOnline, "Quality Matters Rubric Standards," 1.9; Pianta, La Paro, and Hamre, *Classroom Assessment Scoring*, Teacher Sensitivity, Instructional Learning Formats, Content Understanding, Analysis & Inquiry, Quality of Feedback, Instructional Dialogue.

community leaders challenged Jesus to demonstrate his authority through miraculous healings.[149] The manifestation of these miracles was often viewed as affirming God's work through Jesus. In essence, these miracles can be seen as evidence-based confirmation of Jesus' life and work.

As it relates to one's classroom, such evidence-based perspectives can be applied in perhaps less "miraculous" ways—though learning processes are complex and amazing. Based on the theological assertion that God continually and proactively labors with and through our classes to help students learn and develop, we can view their significant and measurable progress as evidence-based confirmations of God's work in the course. As a result, we are called to not only engage in ongoing spiritual discernment and implementation, but also evaluative reflections on the impact of our teaching. This guideline is therefore focused on helping instructors theologically approach their teaching processes in evidence-based and/or scholarly ways.

Level 1

The instructor works to improve their instructional practices through evidence-based practice and/or scholarship projects.

At this level, the instructor will have clear habits of gathering data on their classes and then continually working to improve the quality and effectiveness of these based upon the data that they have gathered. Examples of this kind of work might include using formal and informal assessments of their students to help evaluate the impact of specific class activities, conducting formal educational research projects that provide insights into what is working well in their classes (or not), or holding focus groups with students to help the instructor better understand how their class is being perceived or engaged with. The essential component of this level is the instructor intentionally gathering data that will help them better assess and subsequently improve their educational competencies. The instructor should therefore be able to identify the data that they are gathering as well as how they are using this data to guide incremental changes to one or more of their courses.

Foundationally, evidence-based practice involves identifying, gathering, analyzing, and then applying the results of data from one's course. The sacred invitation at this level might therefore be focused on discerning what kinds of data to gather, where and how to gather this data, what analysis processes to engage, and then how to best utilize the results of these analyses. Even for a single activity, massive amounts of data can be gathered on everything from individual cognitive and affective dynamics to small and whole group processes. God is, it is asserted, to be working at all of these levels, and one can therefore turn their attention to any one of these areas. As a result, the instructor must continually discern where God is inviting them to focus now so that they can partner more closely with God in these focused areas. Overall, it is a

---

149. For example, see: Matt 16:1–4.

spiritual invitation for the educator to develop evidence-based and/or scholarly habits in relation to their classes' ongoing improvements.

Examples of this might include:

- The instructor is found using formal and informal assessments of their students to help evaluate the impact of specific class activities.
- There is evidence of the instructor conducting formal educational research projects that provide insights into what is working well in their classes (or not).
- The instructor is observed holding focus groups with students to help the instructor better understand how their class is being perceived or engaged with by students.
- The instructor is able to identify the data that they are gathering as well as how they are using this data to guide incremental improvements in one or more of their courses.

Level 2

The instructor collaborates with colleagues at their institution to jointly conduct evidence-based practice and/or scholarly projects that improve teaching/learning for their own classes and/or the institution as a whole.

This level builds upon the previous one when the instructor teams up with others to work towards evidence-based educational improvements. As with the previous level, these efforts can be more informal ones where the instructor and their collaborators use data to improve one or more of their courses. Or they can work together to complete scholarship of teaching and learning (SoTL) projects that provide insights into the theory and/or practice of education. Examples at this level might include the instructor participating in a community of practice that is focused on continually reflecting on and improving one another's classes, working with colleagues in their discipline to study teaching strategies that are effective for their field, or actively participating in an institutional committee that gathers and uses data to improve persistence and completion rates in difficult classes. The instructor at this level will therefore be found actively partnering with others to complete evidence-based practice and/or scholarly projects that are intended to improve the quality of education.

Supporting the collaborative view of God's kin-dom in our educational systems, this level emerges when the instructor partners with others to engage in Level 1 evidence-based practices. Cooperative projects are more likely to be successful as God works with and through each participant's varying backgrounds and capabilities. The scope of these projects may also be expanded as God strives to have a broader educational impact beyond a single class or instructor. These projects might therefore involve several classes and faculty members as they collectively work to spiritually discern and subsequently improve teaching and learning in their courses. In doing so, God is not only improving the quality of education, he is also working to transform the school's culture as these communities of evidence-based and/or scholarly practice develop.

Examples of this might include:

- The instructor participates in an "active learning" community of practice that is focused on continually reflecting on and improving the teaching strategies in their course by using assessment data.
- The instructor is observed working with colleagues in their discipline to study teaching strategies that are effective for their field.
- The instructor actively participates in a persistence and completion committee that gathers and uses data to improve pass rates in difficult classes.
- The instructor is a part of a mentoring program where they meet regularly with another faculty member to analyze data from their classes and brainstorm possible improvements.

Level 3

The instructor works collaboratively to conduct evidence-based practice and/or scholarly projects that have an impact on one's educational discipline and/or educational theories, practices, and/or policies more broadly. The instructor works to disseminate the results of these projects via presentations and/or publications.

Level 3 further extends the work of the two previous levels. There should still be strong evidence of the instructor collaborating with others to engage in evidence-based practice and/or scholarly projects that are intended to improve the quality of education in their own classes and at their institution. At this level, however, there will be two significant additions. First, the instructor will be found working on projects that have a broader impact on educational theory/practice in their field. An example of this would be studying teaching strategies that are being used in multiple classes in their discipline in an effort to help the field more effectively teach their subject. Second, the instructor will then work to widely disseminate the results of these projects with colleagues at their institution and beyond. This dissemination can take the form of lunch-and-learns, poster presentations, journal articles, book chapters, policy revising, and so on. At this higher level, the instructor therefore works to maximize the impact of their evidence-based educational projects.

With God's collaborative kin-dom taking root and having a broader community impact at the previous level, here this kin-dom flourishes in more substantial ways. The scope and focus of these projects expand to include more than any one instructor's course. Rather, God's intentions here are to further the God-manifesting theories and practices of education that are more impactful at one's institute and in one's discipline(s). As a result, the sacred invitations are for faculty to continually conceive and engage with evidence-based and/or scholarly projects that might not only have a broader educational impact, but that might then also be disseminated more widely. In doing so, God's educational impact is amplified as others benefit from the work that God has been doing with and through the originators of these projects.

Examples of this might include:

- The instructor is an active participant on a research team that is studying the teaching strategies that are being used across multiple classes in their discipline in an effort to help the field more effectively teach their subject.
- The instructor attends a discipline-specific conference and presents the results of an evidence-based project that they completed with colleagues.
- The instructor is an active participant on a discipline-specific organizational committee that is reviewing and revising educational accreditation policies and standards based on assessment data.
- Drawing on evidenced-based literature, the instructor works with colleagues to develop educational theories and/or strategies that they share with others via presentations and/or publications.

CLOSING REFLECTIONS

Overall, each of these guidelines provide core evidence-based and theological insights into the nature and work of theistic education. For instance, the objective and assessment guidelines can help us realize the level of care and intentionality that God strives to be active within our classes. Here, we find a God who seeks to provide very clear, measurable, and achievable goals for our students; a God who provides multiple and varied kinds of feedback that are valid, reliable, and unbiased; a God who works directly with our students as well as through peer groups to provide detailed assessments.

With so much emphasis in these guidelines on using clearly defined theories, strategies, and processes, it should also be apparent that God does not engage in educational transformations in random or haphazard ways, even though creativity and spontaneity are inherent. As educational research and other human science fields have found, biological, psychological, and sociological patterns have been established in our students and our educational systems. As a result, enduring theories and methods can therefore be developed to better work with God in these patterns. These guidelines therefore also help us see that God labors to uncover these patterns, create theories and models to help clarify and better understand them, and to then develop strategies and processes to partner with God through these enduring patterns in transformative ways.

Here, we find a God who is as theoretical and rigorous just as he is creative and spontaneous. It might be asserted that God therefore seeks to help us, as instructors, utilize these theories, and strategies in an effort to better understand and more closely partner with God's work in our classrooms. Just like knowing the steps to a dance from the beginning, the more we can anticipate God's actions beforehand, the more closely we can move in harmony with God. This, of course, is the primary and ultimate aim of theistic educators, and these guidelines can empower us to achieve such an intimate partnership more completely.

3

Admonishing the Administrators
The Organizational Tier

WITHOUT TIME, RESOURCES, AND support, it can be very difficult for teachers and students to engage in the kinds of activities outlined in the two previous chapters. Administrative personnel and departments are therefore called by God to continually nurture environments where learners, instructors, and staff can thrive. The guidelines presented in this chapter provide detailed insights into some of the specific ways that administration can support students and faculty. These guidelines are directly aligned with the other two tiers so that administrators can better know where and how to focus their energies. In essence, according to these guidelines, administration is the support, training, and resources that God is striving to provide learners and instructors with. In their being and becoming in God's work in these ways, administrative personnel will be directly contributing to the development of a high impact educational system.

OBJECTIVE GUIDELINES

We have already seen that having clear objectives is essential to quality teaching and learning. With so much diversity of faculty and students within each school, however, it is easy for wander from the horizons towards which God is calling them. As a result, school administration is invited to help ensure that they continue to have clearly stated objectives that align with communally discerned directions. When administrative personnel do this, they are essentially helping ensure that learners and instructors are staying on track with God's aims.

Guideline #1—SMART Objectives

Organization ensures that instructors and learners adequately utilize objectives to guide learning and development (Core Guideline).

Setting clear learning objectives is generally considered to be essential for education. Meta-analyses as well as evidence-based assessment rubrics affirm this. As a result, this guideline highlights the importance of having both measurable objectives as well as relating these to students' personal, professional, and/or civic life. Moving from Level 1 to Level 3, there is a growing emphasis on the learner being able to articulate learning objectives in ways that are more meaningful and relevant to them personally, as well as being able to see the relationship between these personal learning objectives and the classes that they are taking. The organization should therefore be proactively involved in helping both students and instructors develop and utilize these kinds of learning objectives.

With God working with learners to help them better see where God is striving to lead them via their learning objectives, and with God helping instructors to develop more meaningful and relevant objectives for their classes, organizational administrators and staff are invited to help support these directions. In the forms of training, consultations, and objective checks, God can work through organizational leaders to help both learners and instructors develop and utilize better learning objectives. Overall, it is a work of God to cultivate an educational community that continually works to discern and refine the goals that God is seeking to lead learners and the classes that they are taking towards.

Level 1

The organization ensures that learners and instructors are aware of accreditation, institutional, and/or discipline-specific standards that can be used to develop measurable learning objectives.

The emphasis at this level is on organizations working directly with instructors and learners to be aware of objectives that are measurable and that clearly identify what learners will need to be able to demonstrate. Organizations should also work to ensure that these objectives align with accreditation, institutional, and/or program-specific outcomes. There should therefore be clear evidence at this level of the organization proactively making sure that learning objectives are being given a central role/emphasis.

At this foundational level, organizational staff will work with instructors and learners to adhere to basic best practices for objectives. Evidence-based educational literature, as argued in this book, has identified the patterns that God has worked to establish in relation to these objectives. The organization is therefore invited to help instructors and learners discern if God is working to manifest these same patterns, or best practices, for the objectives that they are using. If so, then the organization can work to help them be more aware of and responsive to these God-movements to establish higher quality learning objectives.

Examples of this might include:

- Training sessions for instructors on how to develop quality course objectives.
- Co-curricular activities that help students clarify learning goals for themselves.
- Instructors and staff are observed working with students to better understand course and/or program objectives.
- Accreditation reports that list course and/or program learning objectives and present evidence for how these programs/courses are helping students be aware of these objectives.

Level 2

The organization provides the support instructors and learners need to better understand the relevancy of learning objectives for learners' professional, civic, and/or personal life.

At this level, the organization will have evidence of working with instructors to adapt objectives to the backgrounds and capabilities of current learners in their class(es). The organization should be observed working with learners to continually clarify their own learning goals and relate these more directly to their personal, professional, and/or civic life. The organization should also proactively work to ensure that there is clear and sustained attention on institutional, program, course, and personal learning objectives across the institution.

Recognizing that God is working with each individual learner to pursue the paths that God has for them, organizational staff and leaders will help instructors and learners develop and clarify learning objectives that relate more directly to learners' personal, professional, and/or civic lives. One of the main invitations at this level is for the organization to cultivate more of a flexible and adaptable learning culture as it relates to objectives. Each new cohort of students comes with varied backgrounds and different horizons towards which God is leading them and even current students' lives shift and change from one term to the next. Through it all, God can be expected to move, shift, and flow with each student; the organization is therefore invited to continually adapt as God does. This means that organizational staff can continually work with instructors and learners to help them adjust their learning objectives to better align with the work that God is currently doing within and among them.

Examples of this might include:

- Training sessions that work with instructors to continually adapt course objectives to be more relevant for and meaningful to current learners' personal, professional, and/or civic lives.
- Organizational resources that provide guidance to instructors/learners on how to develop and refine learning goals that are more relevant for and meaningful to learners' personal, professional, and/or civic lives.

- Institutional surveys that help assess how well instructors and/or learners understand the relevancy of learning objectives for learners' personal, professional, and/or civic lives.
- Accreditation documents that outline detailed plans for ensuring that program and/or course objectives are continually revised to meet the needs of current learners' personal, professional, and/or civic lives.

Level 3

The organization works to foster a culture where instructors and learners collaborate in developing personalized learning objectives that align with accreditation, institutional, and/or discipline-specific standards and are relevant for learners' professional, civic, and/or personal life. The organization provides support to instructors and learners on how to ensure that learners are able to articulate how the activities in courses relate to these personalized objectives.

At this level, the organization will help learners and instructors collaboratively work with one another to further adapt given course objectives in ways that align with learners' own lifelong personal, professional, and/or civic goals. Resources and support from the organization will help ensure that learners take more ownership and responsibility for their lifelong learning goals. Level 3 organizations will also work to help instructors and students turn to community resources (such as mentors, family members, experts in the field, etc.) to help shape learner-crafted learning objectives in ways that still align with accreditation, institutional, program-specific, and/or course outcomes. The organization will also provide support so that learners and instructors better understand how curricular and co-curricular courses and programs directly support learners' lifelong personal, professional, and/or civic goals. Overall, organizations at this level intentionally work to foster a culture of relevant personalized learning objectives that help students exceed high expectations and pursue their life's goals in ways that are aligned with accreditation, institutional, program-specific, and/or course standards.

Building on the previous level, organizational leadership will continue to foster a spiritually adaptive learning objective culture but in ways that are more communal. Built on a theology that God can work more directly and effectively through collaborative discernment and action, the organization will intentionally support instructors, learners, and others as they work together to ensure that learning objectives are as relevant and meaningful to the current learners as they can be. Recognizing that God works just as diligently through accrediting bodies, these communally adapted learning objectives should be aligned with such expectations as well. Overall, the organization should work to help all relevant parties to continually adjust these objectives to better align with the work that God is and will be doing in the lives of current and future learners.

Examples of this might include:

- Organizational staff are observed helping instructors and learners collaboratively work together to adapt given objectives to align with learners' personal, professional, and/or civic goals.

- There is documentation that members of the organization have helped to arrange for instructors and/or students to collaboratively work with colleagues and/or community members to modify learning objectives and thereby ensure that these align with: 1) learners' personal, professional, and/or civic goals, and 2) accreditation, institutional, program-specific, and/or course outcomes.

- Curricular and/or co-curricular programs that help learners better understand how course objectives and activities are related to their own personalized learning goals and are supported by the organization as evidenced by the tangible resources that have been provided (e.g., money, release time to develop these programs, sending staff to training, etc.).

ASSESSMENT GUIDELINES

As anyone who has worked with assessments on any level knows, these data collection and analysis processes can quickly become overwhelming. In addition, extensive training is needed to ensure the validity, reliability, and usefulness of these assessment processes and information. Administrative staff can therefore provide much needed support, resources, and guidance on this. In doing so, they will essentially be teaching faculty and students how God works with and through these processes to help guide teaching and learning. Such help is therefore a central spiritual discernment component for each educational organization, and administrative staff are called to be a core part of this calling.

Guideline #1—Varied Assessments

The organization supports instructors and learners in utilizing varied assessments to support learning and development (Core Guideline).

Using assessments is central to education. Organizational units should therefore support the use of assessments in at least two ways. First, the organization should ensure that multiple assessments and types of assessment are being used to help confirm that learner proficiencies are being more accurately measured. Each type of assessment (e.g., exams, research papers, portfolios) is inherently limited in the kinds of information that it can give, so the organization should support the use of multiple types of assessments to help provide a more robust picture of learners' actual capabilities in relation to course concepts/skills as defined by the objectives. Secondly, organizations should provide training and resources on how assessment data can be used to continually modify teaching and study strategies to better meet the needs and performances of current learners.

Given the inherent complexities of human learning and development, it really does take a village to assess a student. As a result, God might be expected to be working to help support a school culture that is positively and constructively focused on a variety of assessments. Organizational leaders are therefore encouraged by this guideline to discerningly respond to these God-centered invitations. By working with students and instructors to more effectively adapt and utilize a range of assessments, the organization can help them use assessments to collectively provide the kinds of comprehensive insights needed to make evidence-based decisions in relation to teaching and learning. Overall, theologically speaking, the goal is to generate data that may be used to provide a clearer picture of where and how God is laboring to help learners and instructors continually improve.

Level 1

The organization provides training and support to instructors and learners on how to use multiple types of assessments to draw conclusions about learner progress towards learning objectives.

At this most basic level, the organization will work with learners and instructors to gather and analyze assessment data. The organization should help learners and instructors be able to identify the multiple types of assessment that they are gathering, whether these assessments are formal (e.g., exams, papers) or informal (e.g., observations, passing conversations with students, emails/correspondence). The organization will also help learners and instructors use data from previous experiences in teaching/learning (e.g., prior classes) to inform their ongoing reflections on assessments.

Organizational staff at this level will be found working with instructors and learners to continually expand their understandings of the broad range of assessments that are available. Each one of these types of assessments is, from a spiritual perspective, another lens through which to identify God's work in the school. Built on a theology of God's infinite life being at work with and through the near-infinite complexities of learning and development, no single type of assessment can provide the kinds of nuanced and detailed insights that are needed to more clearly discern where and how God is working in our educational systems. The organization will therefore be found helping learners and instructors adapt a wider variety of assessments in an effort to provide a broader picture of what God might be doing with current learners. Based upon the data derived from these diverse types of assessments, learners, instructors, and staff will be in a far better position to spiritually discern what God has and continues to do educationally at the school.

Examples of this might include:

- There is evidence of the organization providing training and/or support to learners and instructors on how to use multiple types of assessments to draw conclusions about learner progress towards learning objectives.

- As a result of organizational training and/or support, instructor(s) can identify two or more assessments (formal and/or informal) that they are using to assess learners' competencies in relation to specific module/unit KSAs.

- As a result of organizational training and/or support, learner(s) are observed using assessments (formal and/or informal) to assess their own competencies in relation to specific KSAs,

- There is evidence of the organization assessing how well learners and instructors can use multiple types of assessments to draw conclusions about learner progress and then provide training/support as a result.

Level 2

The organization helps instructors and learners use assessment information to modify their teaching/study strategies in real-time as courses unfold to better support learner progress in their courses.

At this level, a similar kind of process is present as with Level 1: the organization supporting the gathering and analyzing of data from multiple types of assessment. However, at this level, the organization will additionally be observed working with learners and instructors to further improve the quality and effectiveness of their teaching/study strategies as their courses unfold. The emphasis here is on continually modifying these strategies in real-time based upon learner performance on assessment data. At this level, these strategies are therefore more fluid as the learners and instructors adjust these in an effort to further maximize student learning and development.

Once learners and instructors have utilized multiple types of assessments to gain a better understanding of the potential impact that God's educational life has been having, they are now in a position to engage in discernment that leads to modified action. Organizational support can therefore take the form of not only teaching such action-oriented discernment processes, but also in providing close consultations where staff help instructors and learners apply them. The ultimate theological goal here is for students and faculty to develop the spiritual capabilities to use assessment results to help them discern what God wants them to do next.

Theistic education is fundamentally focused on our becoming ever more responsive to God's educational life with and to our educational systems. At this level, then, organizational staff will be found working with learners and instructors to help them be more responsive to God's movements based upon the varied assessment data that they have collected. The organization will then support faculty and students as they strive to modify their teaching and learning strategies in real-time as a result of their spiritual responsiveness to God's ever-present movements.

Examples of this might include:

- There is evidence of the organization providing training and/or support to learners and instructors on how to use assessments to modify teaching/study strategies.

- There is evidence of the organization assessing how well learners and instructors can use assessments to modify teaching/study strategies and then provide training/support as a result.

- As a result of organizational training and/or support, instructor(s) are observed using assessment data to modify course/module activities and/or resources in real-time as their course unfolds.

- As a result of organizational training and/or support, learner(s) are observed using assessment data to modify their study strategies.

Level 3

The organization empowers instructors and learners to work collaboratively to select and analyze a variety of assessments that will help them better understand what is influencing learner progress.

Level 3 continues with the work of Levels 1 and 2, only now the organization proactively helps learners and instructors work together on many of these tasks. In addition to the previous levels, the organization provides the training and support needed for learners and instructors to continually work together to expand upon the range of assessments that are utilized, as well as how to analyze the data that is collected from these assessments. The organization helps instructors and learners collaboratively decide how learners can continue to improve in relation to course KSAs based upon assessment data. Being more cooperative in nature, the culture of Level 3 organizations for this guideline are characteristically different from the previous levels as the organization ensures that learners and instructors work together to identify and analyze assessments, as well as modify teaching/study strategies in light of this assessment data.

Building upon the village analogy above, the holy invitations at this level are for the organization to help learners and instructors work more closely together in relation to assessment gathering, discernment, and applications. Based upon an understanding of God's kin-dom as being inherently interconnected and communal, organizational staff will be found intentionally nurturing such collaborations as they relate to assessments. When these efforts are engaged, learners, instructors, and staff will be responding to God's efforts to foster communities that collectively and continually work to more clearly identify God's movements via the assessments, and subsequently respond more immediately and closely to God's invitations as they modify their teaching and learning strategies. In doing so, the organization will be encouraged to support an assessment-driven educational culture that manifests God's life more fully, which is a thriving community where learning happens more deeply.

Examples of this might include:

- Organization is observed providing training/support for learners and instructors to select and analyze a variety of assessments that will help them better understand what is influencing learner progress.

- There is evidence that the organization has provided support so that instructors and learners can name specific and multiple assessments that they have used to modify their study/teaching strategies in consultation with one another.

- As a direct result of the training/support that the organization has provided, instructors and learners are observed working together to select, analyze, and/or develop strategies and plans for how learners can continue to improve based upon assessment data that has been gathered.

- Organization actively creates and supports events where learners and instructors can work together to critically reflect on assessment data as well as modify their teaching and/or study strategies.

Guideline #2—Intentional and Focused Feedback

The organization cultivates a teaching and learning environment where quality feedback is used by instructors and learners to continually improve learner competencies and foster self-regulated learning skills (Core Guideline).

For this guideline, the organization should know that numerous studies continue to show that learners benefit from high quality and detailed feedback that aids them in better knowing where and how they can continue to improve in their courses. At the lower level, the organization will be observed working with learners and instructors to offer and utilize feedback that identifies areas of strength as well as areas of needed improvement. Beyond this, there should also be evidence of the organization providing training and support for learners and instructors on how to then use this feedback to identify and engage with learning activities that empower learners to continually improve. At the highest levels, the organization will be able to demonstrate that they are proactive in supporting the use of this feedback to foster more collaborative self-regulated learning environments.

Theologically, and ideally, feedback is an identification and affirmation of God's invitations of what the learner needs to know about themselves and where to go next. Such feedback should therefore help the learner know more clearly how they are doing in relation to specific competencies as well as how well they are responding to God's movements with and through their learning processes. The organization should therefore provide both students and faculty with the resources, training, and support that they need in order to develop and use feedback in ways that further God's educational work at the school.

Level 1

The organization empowers instructors and learners to use assessment feedback that identifies strengths and weaknesses in learner performance and offers positive and concrete suggestions for how learners can improve their achievements using objective-generated criteria.

Organizations at this level will be noted working with both learners and instructors to more effectively develop and/or use feedback. Working with instructors, the organization will strive to ensure that feedback is positive, related to specific objectives and criteria, provides suggestions for how learners can continue to progress, and conducted in a "timely" manner, providing learners with feedback that can be implemented in subsequent activities. In supporting learners, on the other hand, the organization will help them use feedback to further clarify what their own areas of strength/improvement are. Overall, at this level there should be evidence of the organization providing support and resources on how to more effectively utilize feedback to improve learning.

One of the questions at the very core of theistic religious traditions is, "What is the will of God?" This foundational level is an attempt to answer this question for learners through the feedback that they are provided. Not wanting to leave us with confusion, it might be asserted that this feedback should be reflective of God's life and values: positive, constructive, detailed, and timely. Organizational staff therefore needs to work with instructors to help them better learn how to discern what God is wanting the student to know so that they can continue to respond to God's educational life in increasingly intimate ways. Learners, on the other hand, can be guided by staff on how to receive, reflect on, and use this detailed feedback. Overall, this foundational level is therefore focused on the organization working with students and faculty to better learn how to discern, provide, and receive the kinds of feedback that God is striving to communicate.

Examples of this might include:

- The organization hosts lunch-and-learns for instructors on how to create more effective feedback.
- Organizational staff are observed working directly with students to reflect on feedback they have received in an effort to identify areas of strength/improvement.
- As a result of organizational training/support, instructors are observed providing their students with timely, detailed, and constructive feedback.
- Learners taking part in a student success event are able to state how they have used feedback from others to improve in one or more of their courses, being able to highlight the areas of strength/improvement that were identified by the feedback that was provided.

Level 2

Building on Level 1, the organization supports learners and instructors in developing learning experiences that will help learners apply this feedback and thereby improve their competencies.

Working to improve upon the previous level, Level 2 organizations will help learners and instructors develop the competencies that they need to be able to engage with activities that will help learners continue to improve. These activities should directly relate to the feedback that has been generated at Level 1. In other words, these learning experiences should help learners address noted areas of strength/improvement. Organizations at this level will therefore be observed working with both learners and instructors to continually develop activities that are based upon feedback.

It can be argued that God's guidance is rarely ever solely for informational purposes; God often tends towards action and transformation. As it relates to assessment feedback, organizational staff should therefore work with learners and instructors to adapt their teaching and learning strategies based upon the feedback that has been discerned. In doing so, the organization is becoming a tangible part of God's transformative actions in the school. In order for this to happen most fully, faculty and students need training and support in being able to discern how to use the feedback to better respond to God's educational invitations.

Examples of this might include:

- The organization provides learners and/or instructors with resources that talk about how to identify activities that can help learners improve using feedback.
- As a result of attending an event on how to use feedback to improve learning, students are observed engaging in learning experiences that help them improve in their courses based upon feedback that they have received.

- Learners can state how organizational staff have worked with them to learn how they can apply feedback they have received on previous assignments to subsequent assignments.
- Course materials (e.g., syllabus, discussion boards, drop boxes) of instructors who have completed training on feedback will show evidence of requiring students to complete an assignment where they have to apply instructor feedback from previous assignments to subsequent assignments.

Level 3

Extending Level 2, the organization cultivates an environment where instructors and learners work together to build self-regulated learning skills, helping learners use feedback to reflect on their own performance and to then develop and apply concrete strategies for how they will continue to improve their progress towards learning goals.

This level is intended to not only improve student learning and development in relation to key course concepts/skills, but to also build their metacognitive, critical thinking, and problem-solving skills. As a result, the organization should be observed providing learners and instructors with the close support they need as well as the necessary training and resources to use feedback to foster self-regulated learning. Instructors should therefore be able to work with learners in identifying and utilizing strategies that will help learners improve their learning and development based upon the feedback that they have been provided. As with Level 3 for other guidelines, the organizational culture in relation to feedback should be more collaborative in nature. Learners should, in response to this culture, also be observed taking more ownership of their learning as a result of organizational interventions. This collaborative and self-regulated learning culture, when carefully tended to by the organization, should therefore be one in which noted areas of strength/improvement give rise to learning activities that directly address these areas.

At this highest level, we might find a truer version of a learning organizational culture. With learners and instructors working together with one another as well as staff to utilize feedback in the most effective ways, the school can become a collaborative, self-assessing, and continually adaptive learning environment. In a sense, it becomes a living and learning organism of God. Here, we might assert that God works with learners to use feedback in close consultation with others to assess not only their own competencies, but also their learning processes. Instructors, too, should be supported by the organization in their collaborations with students as they work together to modify their classes in response to the feedback. Throughout the school, then, we would find God working to nurture a self-regulated learning culture that continually adjusts and adapts itself based upon the cooperatively discerned feedback.

Examples of this might include:

- There is evidence of the organization providing training to instructors on how to work with learners' in building self-regulated learning skills.

- The organization hosts events where students collaboratively reflect on feedback that they have received and then identify strategies that will help them improve in their courses.

- Institutional site(s) contain resources that help learners collaboratively utilize feedback in ways that guide the development of more effective study strategies.

- Organization provides tutors who are trained to help students continually review assessment feedback with instructors and/or other students and then modify their study habits.

- Organization supports a mentoring system where instructors learn to develop students' self-regulated learning skills in relation to course feedback that they provide.

Guideline #3—Evidence-Based Assessments

The organization intentionally works to ensure that assessments are utilized in accordance with evidence-based recommendations and, whenever possible, their reliability and validity is established.

As most educational institutions know, assessments are an integral part of ensuring high quality teaching and learning processes. However, there are numerous kinds of assessments that can be used. It is therefore imperative, with so many possibilities, that the organization works with learners and instructors so that they utilize assessments that are most appropriate for their applications. This means, following this guideline, there will be clear evidence of the organization providing training and support on how to use assessments in accordance with evidence-based recommendations. At higher levels, the organization should be observed proactively empowering learners and instructors to consistently collaborate with one another to reduce bias and establish the validity and reliability of these assessments. The organization should also help to ensure that the information gleaned from these assessments is providing the kinds of insights that learners and instructors need in order to make decisions related to improving their teaching/learning strategies.

As a further example of the theological basis of this book, educational research studies that have documented how assessments can be effectively used can be theologically interpreted as purer manifestations of God's educational life with and through them. Organizational staff should therefore be knowledgeable in how to use assessments so that they can better assist students and faculty. Working with students, this might mean helping them interpret assessment results as well as helping them develop and utilize their own assessments in spiritually discerning ways. In supporting instructors, staff can provide ongoing training, resources, and support as they develop and use a wide variety of assessments. Again, a spiritual goal of assessments is to help the community more clearly discern where and how God is acting so that we can better partner with and respond to God's educational movements. As a result, the organization needs to work with learners and instructors to help ensure that these assessments are reliably and validly being used.

Level 1

The organization provides ongoing training to instructors and learners on evidence-based practices in developing, implementing, interpreting, and applying specific assessments to improve learning.

At this level, the organization should be able to identify and/or be observed using specific interventions that are designed to help learners and instructors utilize evidence-based recommendations to help guide the use of assessments. For instructors, the organization will work with them to continually be aware of evidence-based findings related to assessments as well as providing them with the support that they need to implement them in accordance with these recommendations. Working with learners, and following best practices, organizational staff will help them better understand what their assessment results mean and how these results might be used to help learners modify their study strategies and continue to improve. Overall, organizations at this level are focused on helping learners and instructors more successfully use assessments to improve learning and development as outlined by current evidence-based best practices.

As stated above, when using evidence-based recommendations for assessments, it might be asserted that the organization is essentially helping learners and instructors more closely partner with God in their development and use. While adaptations to these assessments will likely be needed, based on the assertion that God adjusts to each unique situation, we can start with the evidence-based findings to help us better understand how God has successfully used similar assessments elsewhere. Organizational leaders are therefore encouraged to help learners and instructors continually be aware of these recommendations so that they can more closely partner with God's life and invitations through the assessments.

Examples of this might include:

- There is evidence of the organization hosting training sessions for learners on how to interpret and use results from quizzes, papers, portfolios, clinicals, etc. to improve their study strategies.
- As a direct result of support that has been provided by the organization, instructors are observed using evidence-based assessment strategies (e.g., team-based

learning, rubrics that have been validated by others, etc.) in one or more of their courses.

- Organizational staff are able to articulate which evidence-based assessment strategies that they have worked with instructors and/or learners to use.

- Learners, after attending an event on effectively using assessments, are observed using specific recommendations that provide insights into how to interpret and/or apply assessment results to improve their study strategies.

Level 2

The organization works with learners and instructors to minimize bias for specific evidence-based assessments and to establish their validity and reliability in helping improve learning and development.

This level builds upon and is inclusive of the previous level. Here, there will be strong evidence of the organization supporting learners and instructors in their work to establish the reliability and validity of the assessments they are using to help improve learning and development. Working with learners, the organization will provide training, mentoring, and resources that help them to verify that the changes they are making to their learning strategies (based upon assessment results) really are improving their achievement. For instructors, the organization will proactively work to guide them on how to perform reliability, validity, and bias checks for the assessments that they are using in their courses.

While evidence-based findings can theologically document the successful assessment work of God in other contexts, some work still needs to be done in discerning God's life in our own school. Organizational staff are therefore invited to support faculty and students in establishing the reliability and validity of the assessments they are utilizing. Spiritually speaking, the organization will be helping them to verify the extent to which they are responding to God's movements through the assessments. This is based on the theological assertion that God's educational actions can be verified repeatedly (i.e., reliably) and via multiple means (i.e., validity). We would also expect that God's work through assessment would not favor any one group of students over another, which would render the assessment at least partially invalid. In other words, these assessments should be unbiased. Overall, then, organizational staff should be found working to help learners and instructors more reliably and validly work with God via the chosen assessments.

Examples of this might include:

- The organization provides training and/or one-on-one consultations with instructors on how to perform reliability, validity, and bias checks for the assessments they are using in their courses.

- Instructor are observed, with direct organizational support, working to review assessment data and determine if the assessments are consistently reflective of students' actual abilities (e.g., verify assessment validity, reliability, and non-bias).

- Learners can describe how they have worked directly with organizational staff to verify that the improvements they have made to their study strategies (in response to their performance on quizzes, papers, etc.) are leading to positive improvements in their achievement (i.e., validity checks).

- The organization hosts events where instructors, learners, and/or their peers can work to develop evidence-based assessments and verify their reliability/validity.

Level 3

The organization proactively empowers a culture of collaboration to help learners and instructors engage in Level 1 and 2 activities.

Level 3 organizations will be found to have interventions that directly foster a culture of collaboration in relation to the evidence-based use of assessments. There will be strong indicators of the organization proactively working with learners and instructors as both of these groups continually work together to interpret and capitalize on the information that assessments are providing in reliable, valid, and unbiased ways. At this level, the organization moves beyond working with learners and instructors individually and/or as distinct groups, and instead strives to bring them together to more effectively utilize assessment data in congruence with current best practices. Intentionally working to build a collaborative culture, the organization will therefore be found working to create and support opportunities for learners, instructors, staff, and administrators to engage in this work together.

Here, we can again find God working to foster a collaborative kin-dom culture for Level 3 with most of the other guidelines. As it relates to this guideline, organizational leaders may be asserted to respond to God's invitations to help students and faculty partner together in the evidence-based development and use of assessments. Here, staff will be found working with these groups to cooperatively ensure the validity and reliability of the assessments they are using. Ideally, it will be a collective spiritual discernment process wherein the community works together to try and clarify where and how God is successfully working with and through their assessments. Being a process of continual discernment, refinement, and adaptation, the community will essentially become a more cohesive spiritual organism of God's life and educational work through these assessments.

Examples of this might include:

- The organization hosts events where learners, instructors, and staff collaborate on developing, implementing, and/or interpreting evidence-based assessments.

- As a direct result of institutional support, instructors are observed working with students to choose, use, and reflect on the results of specific evidence-based assessments.

- Learners can articulate, after attending a training session, how they have worked with others to modify their study strategies based upon specific assessment results in reliable and valid ways.

- An organizational site is observed to have opportunities for online collaboration in developing, implementing, and/or interpreting evidence-based assessments and this site is actively being used for these purposes by learners and/or instructors.

Guideline #4—Self- and Peer-Assessments

The organization supports the use of self- and peer-assessments to improve learning and development.

Across many of the guidelines, especially at higher levels, there is a distinct emphasis on collaborative approaches to course development. In addition, educational research has repeatedly shown that students learn a great deal when working with their peers. Peer tutoring, for example, has been found to be one of the more effective means to foster learning.[1] Organizations should therefore intentionally work to support both learners and instructors in their collaborative use of these kinds of assessments and teaching/learning strategies. Overall, the primary purposes of self- and peer-assessments are to help learners not only continue to progress in relation to course KSAs, but also to take more responsibility for their own and one another's learning and development. As organizations work with learners and instructors, following the levels for this guideline, there should be an increasing trend towards developing collaborative self-regulated learning skills via self- and peer-assessments.

Theologically, we might assert that God works educationally through self- and peer-assessments in effective ways. For peer-assessments, peers are more likely to have a closer understanding of course KSAs with each other than they will compared to their expert instructor. As a result, God can ideally work through students as they collaboratively struggle to better understand and achieve what is expected of them. As a result, organizational staff should help both instructors and learners incorporate these teaching and learning strategies into their repertoire.

For self-assessments, it might be asserted that God labors with and through the student to discover for themselves how they are doing in relation to the learning outcomes as well as how they might progress towards them more fully. Here, staff can again help faculty and students more intentionally and successfully use these strategies. In doing so, when done discerningly, organization staff may be asserted to

---

1. Hattie, *Visible Learning*, 186–87.

respond to God's endeavors to encourage these kinds of assessments, thereby furthering the educational work of God with and through the school.

Level 1

The organization provides instructors and learners with training to use assessment criteria as the basis for self- and/or peer-assessments.

Level 1 organizations for this guideline will be able to show evidence of providing the training and/or support that learners and instructors need in order to more effectively engage with self- and peer-assessments. Organizations should be observed helping both of these groups to learn how to generate and/or utilize detailed criteria as the basis for these teaching/learning strategies. They should also be found working with leaners and instructors on how to provide high quality feedback in relation to these assessments (e.g., detailed, positively constructive, directly related to the criteria, notes areas of strength and improvement, etc.). Overall, there should be evidence of the organization taking intentional and system-wide steps to encourage and support self- and peer-assessments.

At this foundational level, organizational staff will essentially be helping faculty and students engage in the basic spiritual discernment processes that are needed to develop self- and/or peer-assessments. This discernment entails, among other things, determining which criteria God is inviting them to use, which assignments are most appropriate for these kinds of assessments, and how God wants to facilitate the implementation of them. Realizing that God can work with learners, as well as instructors, to develop and use these kinds of assessments as an integral part of their strategies, organizational staff will work with both groups. Overall, the organization will help faculty and students to better partner with God's educational life with and through these types of assessments.

Examples of this might include:

- As a direct result of events hosted by the organization, instructors are observed guiding students in evaluating their own and/or one another's work using a set of guidelines that the instructor has provided.

- Learners will be observed, while attending an organizational event or thereafter, using rubrics or guidelines that have been provided by one or more of their classes to assess their own and/or their classmates' progress.

- The organization provides documentation of training sessions that have been offered to instructors and/or learners on the effective use of self- and/or peer-assessments.

- Supporting self- and peer-assessments is explicitly addressed in organizational strategic plans, and specific interventions have been identified for providing this kind of support.

Level 2

Building on Level 1, the organization provides support to instructors and learners to help them apply the results of self- and/or peer-assessments in order to increase student achievement.

At this level, the organization will continue to support the use of self- and peer-assessments among learners and instructors alike. Beyond this, however, Level 2 organizations will help instructors and learners utilize the results of these kinds of assessments in more effective ways. For instructors, this might mean guiding them in how to develop courses that have learners apply self- and/or peer-assessment data to subsequent activities. For learners, it might entail helping them continually reflect on and modify their study strategies, as well as engage in supplemental activities based upon self- and/or peer-assessment results. This level is therefore distinguished by organizational interventions that explicitly empower students and instructors to use self-/peer-assessment results to improve teaching/learning.

When it comes to spiritual discernment, data gathering and analyses are only one part of what we might believe God is trying to do through the discernment. Ultimately, the data derived from our assessments should lead to some kind of action that positively impacts learning and development. At this level, then, one of the holy invitations is for students and faculty to better utilize the information that they are gleaning from self- and/or peer-assessments to inform their discernment of how to better partner with God's educational life going forward. Organizational staff should therefore provide resources, training, and support for these spiritual discernment processes so that learners and instructors can modify their teaching/learning strategies in light of this data. In doing so, the school will be helping to further foster a spiritual culture of continuous quality improvement, via these types of assessments, and the changes that come as a result of effectively using them.

Examples of this might include:

- There is evidence of the organization providing support and/or training to learners and instructors on how to use self-/peer-assessment results to improve teaching/learning strategies.

- As a result of attending organization events, students are observed using self-/peer-assessment results to modify their study strategies and/or engage in supplemental activities that are intended to improve their competencies.

- Instructor is able to articulate, after attending a training session, how they have guided students in a step-by-step manner to use self-/peer-assessment data to revise assignments, improve on exams, etc.

- Organization provides peer tutors that help learners critically reflect on their own and their classmates' work and then utilize this information to modify their learning strategies and/or seek out supplemental activities.

Level 3

The organization intentionally fosters a culture where instructors and learners work collaboratively to generate assessment criteria. The organization then helps them apply these criteria to self- and/or peer-assessments to improve learning and development.

For Level 3, there will be evidence of the organization working directly with learners and instructors to help them to collaboratively generate self-/peer-assessment criteria. Working with learners, this will mean helping them take more initiative to develop and implement these kinds of assessments in order to continually improve their learning strategies. On the instructor side, the organization will help them learn how to develop course modules that integrate this kind of work. For instance, helping an instructor create an activity where learners work in small groups to create a rubric that will then be used (with input from the instructor) to assess their papers. At this level, then, the organization will proactively work to foster a more collaborative and self-initiating culture when it comes to self-/peer-assessments. In other words, the organization should be found helping learners and instructors work more closely together to initiate and utilize these assessments.

Theologically, the Level 3 spiritual culture of collaboration continues to expand with this guideline. Here, organizational leaders are admonished to help learners and instructors engage in cooperative spiritual discernment processes in relation to self- and/or peer-assessments. From beginning to end, faculty and students can work together to develop, implement, and subsequently utilize the results of these assessments to improve teaching and learning. Overall, organizational staff will be working with them to collectively discern where and how God is laboring to work with and through these types of assessments for the benefit of the community.

Examples of this might include:

- The organization hosts events where learners and instructors work together to learn more about self-/peer-assessments and how they can work more closely together to develop these.

- As a result of working with staff, students are observed working in groups to create and use self-/peer-assessment criteria to improve their learning strategies.

- After attending a training session, an instructor is observed creating an assignment that guides learners in developing self-/peer-assessment criteria, has them apply these assessments, requires them to reflect on the results of these assessments, and then directs them to develop strategies for revisions and/or improvements.
- The organization hosts speakers on how to develop and use self-/peer-assessments in more collaborative and self-initiating ways.

ACTIVITIES, ORGANIZATION, AND RESOURCE GUIDELINES

With the wide diversity of activities that are outlined by these guidelines, it would be very difficult for students and instructors to effectively engage with many of them. This is particularly true of the higher levels for each guideline, as these levels require a great deal of sophistication, preparations, and coordination. Administrative staff can therefore help support God's work through these various activities. By providing guidance, training, and resources, they can further empower the transformative impact of these activities. The following guidelines are therefore intended to help administration know what specific kinds of training and support that learners and instructors need so that they can better plan for and implement these training and support systems.

Guideline #1—Learner-Learner Interactions

The organization intentionally supports learner-learner interactions to support learning and development (Core Guideline).

For this guideline, an organization will be found to intentionally support interactions among learners. Social-cultural learning theories assert that students learn as much through their interactions with one another as they do on their own. As a result, the organization will proactively work with learners as well as instructors to nurture high quality peer-to-peer interactions that encourage critical reflection and complex decision-making. Overall, following these guidelines, the organization will help faculty, students, and staff continually create collaborative micro-cultures that are geared towards improving student achievement.

"Where two or three are gathered in my name, I am there among them" (Matt 18:20). As we have asserted throughout this text, God is an integral part of learning processes. As it relates to this guideline, this means that organizational staff and leaders need to be working to help foster the kinds of healthy and interactive relationships among students that genuinely deepen learning. In doing so, the organization will be working to nurture the kinds of communal engagement that are indicative of God's kin-dom. Such engagement is not only essential for prosperous organizations, it is also conducive to quickened learning and development. Theologically, these healthy and interactive relationships empower God's educational life to not only act with each learner directly but also through their peers.

Level 1

The organization provides education for learners and instructors to know how to intentionally develop simple interactions among learners to support learning and development.

Organizations at Level 1 will be observed providing training and support to learners and instructors on how to utilize learner-learner interactions in simpler, yet more effective, ways. At this level, these kinds of activities will be shorter and more superficial, requiring little more than common social skills and a more surface level engagement with course KSAs. However, the organization will work to ensure that instructors know how to develop these kinds of activities following best practices and that learners understand the learning benefits that can be derived from them. Overall, then, this level is focused on having students interact in simpler ways.

At this beginning level, it can be asserted that God is essentially working to lay the necessary foundations for more complex relational interactions. Here, the relationships themselves are at a forming level of group process, allowing God to break the ice among learners so that they might start learning from one another in simpler ways. In essence, God may be seen at this level as metaphorically pouring the foundations of what will eventually become a building in which more complex social interactions and deeper learning can happen at higher levels. As a result, the organization is invited to spiritually discern the kinds of training and support that they need to provide to instructors and students so that they can more effectively engage with these kinds of interactions.

Examples of this might include:

- The organization provides training sessions on how instructors can facilitate and students can more effectively participate in such activities as: general class discussions, short think-pair-shares, quick game-based activities, and simple role-playing.
- Students are observed, at an organizationally hosted event, working in short-term groups on simpler activities and problems related to course concepts and skills.
- As a result of staff consultations, instructors and/or students are able to describe group-work activities that they have (or will) engaged in that were of shorter duration and helped them better understand course concepts.

- The organization maintains online resources and e-learning modules that help learners and/or instructors better utilize simple group work activities to improve teaching/learning strategies.

Level 2

The organization helps learners and instructors cultivate an environment where students learn about each other's diverse perspectives, critically reflect on these, and/or help one another to engage with relevant KSAs more extensively.

At this level, the organization will work directly with learners and instructors to engage with and/or facilitate critical and mutually supportive group work. In these kinds of learner-learner interactions, group members will be observed critically reflecting on their own and their classmates' views of course content. They will also be more supportive of one another's educational journey by intentionally helping each other engage with course KSAs in deeper ways. As a result, the organization will be observed providing resources, training, and support that helps students, staff, and faculty develop these kinds of deep engagement.

As the activities at this level are typically longer and of a more complex nature, God can work more extensively through them. Peer-to-peer interactions are important because individuals at similar stages of learning, who process things in similar ways, are better able to help one another learn and develop with the right kinds of guidance and support. The organization therefore needs to continually assess how faculty, staff, and students are engaging at this level, and then discern where God seems to be inviting them towards. In doing so, the organization is essentially discerning what kinds of infrastructure God needs to have in place in order to work more effectively with and through these more complex and critical interactions.

Examples of this might include:

- The organization provides training sessions to instructors on such teaching strategies as peer teaching/tutoring, small and large group debates, team-based learning, group problem-solving assignments, small group analyses of case studies, etc.
- As a result of training sessions, learners are observed questioning their own and one another's assumptions, exploring how/why they understand course content in the ways that they do, providing constructive feedback and support to one another, etc.
- The organization provides training to peer tutors to help them engage their classmates in more critically reflective ways.
- The instructor is able to describe, after a staff consultation, how they have designed group activities that require students to engage with course content and

one another in increasingly complex ways (e.g., applying, evaluating, analyzing, etc.).

Level 3

Building on Level 2, the organization provides training to instructors and learners so that long-term group projects/activities require groups to collaborate in substantive ways (e.g., decision-making, exploration, invention, etc.) in relation to relevant KSAs.

A Level 3, the organization will extend the guidance they are providing to learners and instructors beyond the two previous levels. Here, the organization will proactively provide opportunities for its constituency to learn more about how to develop and effectively engage with substantial group work. Examples might include small groups completing extended service-learning projects, design projects for ill-defined problems, long-term peer-assessment partnerships, and semester-long group research projects. The organization will help learners and instructors alike better understand the complexities of engaging in these kinds of activities as well as provide guidance on how to better support transitions through normal group development processes (e.g., forming, norming, storming, performing, adjourning).

At this highest level, it can be asserted that God can labor more extensively to help foster mutual growth through these long-term and more intense learning relationships. In Western Christianity, we see Jesus working for as long as three years with his disciples to help them learn and develop in preparation for their ministries—a significant part of which involved peer-to-peer learning strategies as discussed previously. Organizational leaders and staff are therefore invited to help faculty and students learn the necessary skills for developing and sustaining these kinds of interactions and projects. Theologically, the organization is helping instructors and learners develop the spiritual capacities to be more responsive to God's educational life within and to these types of intensive peer-based learning interactions. As a result, the organization must help students and faculty learn how to foster such healthy learning relationships through which God can work in fuller ways.

Examples of this might include:

- Organization provides training on how to develop such teaching/learning strategies as extended service-learning projects, faculty-student research projects, design projects for ill-defined problems, long-term peer-assessment partnerships, etc.
- There is evidence of the organization providing close support to groups as they transition through typical group development processes (e.g., forming, norming, storming, performing, adjourning).
- As a result of attending training sessions, students and/or instructor(s) are able to articulate how they will develop groups that will work together on long-term

projects as service-learning projects, design projects for ill-defined problems, and long-term peer-assessment partnerships.

- The course materials (e.g., syllabus, handouts, course site) of instructors who have consulted with staff show clear evidence of students completing activities that have required them to demonstrate their abilities to collaborate on long-term problem-solving, research, and service-learning projects.

Guideline #2—Higher Order Thinking

The organization provides support that helps learners and instructors use higher order thinking to improve learning and development (Core Guideline).

With higher order thinking skills being given a major emphasis in education, organizations need to provide resources, training, and support to both learners and instructors. This support, following this guideline, will entail helping them understand what these skills are as well as how they can be more fully integrated into their learning/teaching strategies. At lower levels, the organization will be found helping learners and instructors utilize application, evaluation, and analysis strategies to deepen learning. At higher levels, the organization will support a culture where they work both independently and together to design and implement these kinds of critically engaged activities. Overall, there should be strong evidence of the organization providing learners, staff, and instructors with the essential guidance and support that they need for these kinds of engagement.

As asserted in previous chapters, God's evolutionary life appears to be working towards fostering increasing complexity. At the level of learning, this might mean that God works to nurture increasingly sophisticated understandings of the KSAs that are the focus of attention. Organizational staff should therefore be found helping support God's work of increasing complexity and sophistication via the development of higher order thinking processes. In doing so, the organization will be allowing God to work with and through them to build the necessary training and support systems that will be needed in order for God to do this work more efficiently and effectively. This guideline is therefore intended to encourage organizational leaders and staff to discern and provide infrastructure support that empowers the development and use of a higher thinking process in pursuit of learning outcomes.

Level 1

The organization helps guide learners and instructors in how to engage with simpler critical thinking skills (e.g., apply, analyze, and evaluate) for relevant course KSAs.

Level 1 organizations will be observed proactively working with both learners and instructors to increase their understanding and application of more basic critical thinking skills. Such efforts should involve helping them not only better understand what these competencies are but also how they might use these to improve their learning/teaching strategies. One of the primary goals here is to help learners and instructors see more clearly how these important skills can be used to deepen learning in significant ways. The organization should therefore be able to present evidence on how they are working with these groups towards these ends.

When organizational staff provide these kinds of support to faculty and students, they are theologically partnering with God's work to develop these kinds of capacities at the school. At this foundational level, the organization will be working with God to further develop an institutional culture where basic higher order thinking skills are a normal part of how the organization operates in pursuit of its learning goals. With this culture in place, God can then build and expand upon this work at higher levels. Organizational staff, at this level, will therefore work to discern where, how, and to what extent God is inviting them to further build these critical thinking foundations, especially in relation to curricular and co-curricular KSAs.

Examples of this might include:

- Organization provides training sessions on basic higher order thinking skills and how to apply these to teaching/learning strategies.

- As a direct result of organizational support (e.g., training, consultations, etc.), classes have projects where students are required to compare-contrast course KSAs.

- Organizational staff are able to state how they have worked with learners to analyze, evaluate, and apply specific concepts/skills.

- Organization works with instructors and/or learners to utilize a critical thinking rubric to assess their own engagement with concepts/skills.

Level 2

The organization provides support for more complex higher order thinking skills (e.g., synthesizing, creating, innovating) and/or encourages learners and instructors to challenge assumptions in course concepts, materials, and activities.

Moving beyond Level 1, organizations at this level will be found helping learners and instructors engage with more complex higher order thinking skills. Being that these skills are more synthesizing, integrative, and multi-dimensional in nature, the organization will work to ensure that learners and instructors have the education and support they need to engage in these kinds of teaching/learning strategies. Such support might also involve funding for faculty-student research projects, hosting interdisciplinary events where student, staff, and faculty engage with real-world scenarios in innovative ways, or encouraging a culture of constructive criticism across levels of the institution. Overall, the goal is for the organization to foster curricular and co-curricular environments where more advanced higher order thinking skills are an integral part of learning processes.

Based partly on the claim that no system, concept, or skill is perfect, we can expect God to be working to help these continually improve. Towards these teleological ends, we might therefore expect God to work to develop in each of us the necessary capacities to be able to dissect, assess, and ultimately reimagine better ways of being and becoming. In our school systems, this might mean that God is therefore working to help faculty, staff, and students develop these more advanced higher order thinking competencies. As a result, organizational leaders and staff should discern and respond to God's invitations to provide the kinds of resources, training, and support that learners and instructors need to further develop and utilize these competencies. In doing so, they are more likely to be directly participating in God's efforts to advance the critical thinking culture that was established at Level 1, according to this guideline.

Examples of this might include:

- Organization provides evidence of hosting consultations with instructors on how to integrate advanced higher order thinking skills into their courses.

- After attending a training session, instructors are observed demonstrating and explaining how to synthesize specific course knowledge and/or skills and then requiring students to do likewise with different parts of their course.

- Students attend a session that is hosted by the organization where they participate in small group activities that require them to use concepts/skills to create, innovate, design, etc.

- The organization supports committees made up of faculty, staff, and students who continually and critically question the limitations, inherent biases, and underlying assumptions of curriculum materials.

Level 3

The organization helps learners and instructors collaboratively design and implement higher order learning experiences that are aligned with learning objectives, result in a variety of outcomes and artifacts, and that build on learners' interests and backgrounds.

Being more collaborative and learner-driven, at this level the organization will show evidence of helping learners and instructors collaborate on developing activities that engage in the higher order thinking skills described for the two previous levels. The overall goal is to directly support an environment where learners are not just participants in critical thinking activities but are also active authors of them in pursuit of their own learning and development. Toward these ends, the organization will therefore be found to provide ample opportunities for faculty, staff, and students to cooperatively develop these kinds of joint ventures. Through these, learners are not only using higher order thinking skills in the activities that they are helping to develop, but they are also using these skills as part of the activity development process itself.

Further expanding the spiritual kin-dom view of educational systems that has been emerging across the guidelines at all three tiers, this level is indicative of the more collaborative efforts of God. Here, organizational staff will work with faculty and students to cooperatively develop learning activities that are intended to help themselves and/or others more fully partner with God's higher order thinking educational life. As God works to continually improve learning processes, this organizational work will advance the schools' critical culture at a higher level. Rather than being more of a top-down initiative, staff will help learners and instructors at this level become a more integral part of God's learning organization as they continually and cooperatively develop these higher order thinking activities. At this level, then, the school becomes more like a living organism and manifestation of God's critically reflective educational kin-dom.

Examples of this might include:

- Organization provides resources and release time needed for faculty/staff and learners to collaborate on developing and implementing research projects that are directly related to course concepts/skills.

- Staff are able to articulate how they have worked with learners to continually assess higher order thinking study strategies and help them identify specific changes that need to be made to these that will result in higher achievements in one or more of their courses.

- Instructors, as a result of attending a training session, are observed implementing course activities where they work with students to develop their own inquiry-based projects/experiments.

- Organization can present evidence of developing projects with community partners so that students and instructors/staff can collaboratively work with these partners to identify and address ill-defined problems in the local community.

Guideline #3—Use of Technologies

Organization intentionally integrates relevant and interactive technologies to improve learning and development.

According to Hattie's book, *Visible Learning*, educational research studies involving more than 8,000,000 people have been conducted on the use and impact of technologies.[2] The volume of these studies speaks to the increasingly central role

2. See the references for this guideline in the previous chapter.

that these technologies have for educational institutions. As a result, following this guideline, organizations need to be very intentional regarding the resources, training, and support that they are providing to learners and instructors in relation to their technology use. At lower levels, the organization will help students and instructors alike learn how these technologies might be used in simpler ways to support learning both in and out of their classes. At higher levels, the organization will empower both of these populations to utilize technology in more advanced ways, such as in making use of discipline-specific software packages and skill sets (e.g., SPSS, augmented/virtual reality, and coding in HTML/CSS). Support for all levels of this guideline should be in the form of training, resources, and consultations, as well as in the technology infrastructure and help desk support that are needed to use these technologies. Overall, the institution's support for technology use should be primarily aimed at improving student achievement by working directly with students, staff, and faculty towards these ends.

A greatly expanded incarnational view of God's kin-dom is needed to fully understand the work that God labors to do with and through technologies in our schools. As argued above, God is asserted to not only use technologies to help learners progress, but God also works within and through these technologies themselves as living manifestations of God's incarnate life throughout all of creation: from the infinitesimal subatomic particle to the infinity of the whole of creation. Situated within this vast and infinitely complex incarnational life of God, organizational staff are invited to help students and faculty partner with God in order to help realize God's fullest potentials with and through each piece of technology. Stated another way, each piece of technology has some purpose that God is trying to fulfill in relation to student achievement. The organization should therefore help instructors and learners discern these God-centered purposes and thereby better choose and utilize technologies toward these ends.

Level 1

The organization provides opportunities for learners and instructors to use relevant technologies in simpler ways that support but do not fundamentally change the learning processes. The organization provides training and support for very basic technology skills.

At Level 1, the organization will be found working directly with learners and instructors in two ways. First, the organization will ensure that they know about and have access to technologies that can be used to support learning in more basic ways. Second, the organization will help instructors and learners develop the basic skills they will need in order to utilize these technologies. At this level, then, there will be evidence of the organization providing infrastructure, resources, and training for these more basic levels of technology usage to support learning and development.

At this foundational level, organizational staff will essentially be helping students and faculty further develop the more basic skills that they will need in order to help them partner with God's educational work with and through the technologies in more simplistic ways. For instance, using word processing software to type rather than handwrite a paper. Here, God's use of technology is more substitutive, meaning that the learning activities could be completed fairly easily without the technology, but the technology does provide some minor benefits (e.g., spell check functions for the word processing software). At this level, it might be asserted, God is helping instructors and learners learn how to partner with God's educational life through the technologies in more simple and fundamental ways. These foundational steps become necessary in order to progress to higher levels of this guideline where God seeks to complexify the educational work that he is doing via the technologies. The organization should therefore provide close mentoring, resources, and training to help students and instructors partner with our technologically-empowering God in more foundational ways.

Examples of this might include:

- The organization provides learners and instructors with a list of technologies that are available to them through the organization as well as additional resources that they might use to support teaching/learning in more basic ways.

- As a result of participating in a faculty development session, instructors are observed developing course assignments that require students to conduct an internet search to find information for a class project.

- Working with a staff member, learners are observed using software to manage and format citations for their course papers.

- The organization's strategic plan includes the implementation and adequate maintenance of basic technologies to support learning.

Level 2

The organization expands the options for learners' and instructors' responsible use of relevant interactive technologies to support learning. The organization provides training so that technologies are integral to engagement with learning as well as to help improve intermediate technical skills for both learners and instructors.

A Level 2 organization will be found providing the support that is needed for learners and instructors to effectively utilize interactive technologies to improve student achievement. Such usage will involve technology that is integral to the learning process by requiring more direct engagement with key KSAs via the technology. Examples might include using a spreadsheet to conduct analysis and generate charts, using interactive digital games/apps to help prepare for exams, or creating interactive e-learning modules that teach important course concepts. As with the previous level, there will be evidence of the organization taking proactive steps to ensure that its support covers infrastructure (e.g., networks, help desk support, etc.) for these kinds of technologies. At this level, however, the organization will also work to ensure that learners and instructors develop intermediate technology skills in order to more effectively use these kinds of technologies for their personal, professional, and/or civic lives.

Moving beyond the foundational level, organizational staff will work with students and faculty to further develop their abilities to discern which technologies God is inviting them to utilize, as well as to enhance their technical skills so that they may use these technologies in more effective ways. As their technical skills develop, so too will the range of technological possibilities that they can partner with God through. Organizational staff are therefore invited at this level to help learners and faculty expand these skills as well as their awareness of the vast number and wide variety of technologies that God may be seeking to advance learning through. At this level, the organization will also help faculty and students work with God via the technologies in more sophisticated and complex ways, ways in which the technologies significantly augment or modify the learning activities. Here, God's work with and through the technologies become more central to the learning processes. As a result, the organization should help to ensure that learners and faculty are able to partner with God's technologically-enhanced educational life in more central and complex ways.

Examples of this might include:

- After attending a training session, instructors are able to demonstrate their ability to create interactive e-learning modules for their courses.

- In working with staff, learners can describe online interactive sites and/or apps that they are using to help them better understand concepts and/or practice skills.

- The organization can provide evidence of having provided training on intermediate technology skills.

- At an organizational event, learners are observed creating a digital image collage to help them better understand important course concepts.

Level 3

The organization supports a culture where instructors and learners collaborate in identifying relevant interactive technologies that redefine learning processes in significant ways. These technologies are essential in order to engage in the learning experiences and the organization provides training and support for advanced technical skills.

Moving beyond the previous level, organizations at this level will provide access to more advanced technologies to support student learning. These kinds of technologies are essential to the learning processes (i.e., activities would be very difficult to complete without the use of technology), and they may require more advanced technical skills in order to utilize them. Examples of technology-enhanced activities at this level might include collaborative projects with communities from other parts of the nation/world, online team-based mind maps, creating interactive digital storytelling projects, use of intelligent tutoring systems, and immersive digital simulations. In addition, as with other guidelines, there should be some evidence of instructors collaborating with learners in choosing and implementing these technologies.

Complexity at this level may be at or near its maximum. God's work with and through the technologies themselves are complex enough to more fully support and/or facilitate the learning activity in and of themselves. The discernment and technological skills that are required to use these God-manifesting technologies are often much more advanced, requiring careful planning and sometimes coding/programming. In addition to this, the spiritual selection and use of these technologies at this level is done in more democratic and collaborative ways. As a result, organizational staff must spiritually discern what kinds of training and support that each use of technology at this level might require. Here, the organization will realize that God strives to work with and through these more complex technologies to collaboratively foster learning. Staff will therefore endeavor to discern where and how God is striving to act in these ways, and subsequently provide the kinds of training and support that students and faculty need to better partner with God through these technologically advanced avenues.

Examples of this might include:

- The organization provides training sessions to classes so that the instructor(s) and students are able to work more closely together to create interactive e-learning modules for the class.
- Staff work with instructors and students to identify virtual simulation software to help them better understand concepts and/or practice relevant skills.
- The organization provides websites where students and instructors can work together to develop sites that better support learning activities.
- As a result of attending a training session, students and the instructors are observed collaborating via online technologies with a community from another part of the world to complete a real-world project together.

Guideline #4—Real-world Applications

The organization helps learners and instructors adapt relevant KSAs to address real-world issues in authentic contexts.

Preparing students to be competent co-workers and community members is central part of the mission of education. As a result, organizations should help learners and instructors apply relevant KSAs in real-world situations. Doing so will not only aid learners with their transference of KSAs to these situations, it will also help these KSAs be more relevant and meaningful to students, which is an important part of fostering deeper learning.

As an organization moves from Level 1 to Level 3, they will be observed working with learners and instructors to move from more simply engaging course concepts/skills within authentic settings/scenarios towards more collaboratively identifying and directly addressing real-world problems. The transition that the organization should be working to support is therefore twofold: 1) from instructor-driven to collaborative, and 2) from simple presence in an authentic setting/scenario towards engaging more directly with real-world issues. Overall, the organization should therefore prepare learners and instructors to develop KSAs in ways that are directly related to the authentic settings of learners' personal, professional, and/or civic lives.

As has been asserted for this guideline at the previous tiers, God does not necessarily (or always) foster learning simply for the sake of learning itself. Yes, learning can be a fulfilling activity in and of itself, and the feelings and experiences of the fulfillment that come with new insights, abilities, and attitudes no doubt have their origins and ends in God. Yet, we can also assert that God labors to use these learnings to help our world progress in substantive ways. As a result, the organization should be found helping students and faculty develop and engage with real-world scenarios where their KSAs have an increasingly positive impact. In doing so, the organization will be helping them to respond to God's invitations to use their developing capabilities in socially, politically, and/or economically transformative ways in the community. In essence, the organization will be partnering with God more fully to help ensure that learning is not merely an end in and of itself, but also a powerful means through which educational systems themselves become God's agents of change in our world. It is, therefore, a more efficient way through which God strives to work: learning to change the world while simultaneously learning about it.

Level 1

The organization supports opportunities that help learners and instructors know how to apply relevant course KSAs in authentic contexts/scenarios in direct and unmodified ways.

Organizations at this level will be found working with learners and instructors to learn how to take relevant KSAs that they are working to develop competencies in and to apply these in real-world situations. At this level, such KSA applications will be direct and unmodified. This means that the learner will only be expected to apply the KSAs in the exactly the same way as they have been introduced to them, without any significant adaptations or modifications (KSA adaptations and modifications are a Level 2 competency according to this guideline.) In addition, Level 1 organizations will ensure that such applications will have the primary purpose of helping the learner better acquire key concepts/skills rather than attempting to address a specific real-world problem/issue (again, this is a Level 2 competency.) As a result, there will be evidence of the organization providing resources, training, and/or mentoring to help learners and instructors identify and engage with teaching/learning strategies that foster these kinds of KSAs' development. In other words, the organization should be found supporting activities that help learners to engage with KSAs in similar contexts/scenarios as they will need to apply them in their professional, civic, and/or personal lives.

With the aim of helping students and faculty progress towards real-world impact, at this foundational level, organizational staff will provide the necessary training and support that they need to begin engaging with real-world scenarios. Here, it might be asserted, God seeks to help learners and instructors see more clearly how core KSAs might apply to one or more real-world situations. Organizational staff will therefore help them to discern and utilize such situations and scenarios as they relate to core KSAs. In essence, this foundational level is a beginning stage for the kinds of real-world engagement that will emerge at higher levels. As a result, the organization will partner with God in discerning how to develop and support these necessary foundations.

Examples of this might include:

- The organization offers training sessions to learners and/or instructors on how to use simulation strategies to develop KSAs.
- Organizational budgets have funding to support immersion trips where learners are exposed to diverse real-world contexts.
- As a result of being mentored by staff, instructors are able to develop role-playing activities that mimic real-world situations.
- As part of an organizationally hosted event, students are observed practicing a skill in a real-world setting (e.g., taking blood pressures at a community center, learning how to collect water samples from a local creek, etc.).

Level 2

The organization provides training for learners and instructors on how to adapt relevant KSAs for authentic contexts/scenarios in order to address a given real-world problem or issue.

A Level 2, the organization is somewhat similar to Level 1 in that the organization will be found helping learners and instructors apply relevant KSAs in authentic and real-world contexts/scenarios. However, at this level, the organization will ensure that learners and instructors engage with specific problems/issues in these authentic situations. Doing so requires a higher level of competency on the part of the learner compared with Level 1 since they will be expected to adapt key KSAs in significant ways in order to address the given problems/issues. As a result, there should be strong evidence of the organization working to ensure that learners and instructors have the competencies and support that they will need in order to: 1) identify specific real-world issues, and 2) effectively adapt relevant KSAs in order to address these issues.

Building upon the previous foundational level, organizational staff will work with faculty and students to develop the discernment and application skills needed to better partner with God in adapting core KSAs to a given real-world situation. Theologically, it is an invitation for the organization to discern which real-world issues to partner with God on. Staff should therefore help learners and instructors to engage in this spiritual partnership and be able to creatively adapt core KSAs in the ways that God needs them to be adapted in order to more effectively address the real-world situation. Through training, mentoring, and resources, organizational staff will therefore be working with God to empower these kinds of projects and applications so that God can have a greater impact in the community.

Examples of this might include:

- Organization maintains a list of community partners and already identified real-world projects that students, faculty, and/or staff can and do work on.

- Organization has a director of community engagement, service learning, etc. on staff who works with students, staff, and faculty to identify community projects that both address local needs as well as align with learning objectives.

- Staff/faculty and students are observed working together at an organizationally hosted event to adapt relevant skills (such as healthcare skills, conflict mediation, strategic planning, web development, etc.) to help a community organization.

- After attending a faculty development training, instructors' courses have assignments where learners collect and analyze data in the field in order to help address a local problem.

Level 3

The organization helps learners and instructors to collaboratively identify real-world problems or issues in authentic contexts/scenarios that require KSA adaptations and supports them in carrying out plans to directly address these issues.

At this level, the organization will further extend their Level 2 efforts. Since Level 3 is more collaborative in nature by being centered on instructors, staff, and learners working together to identify real-world problems, the organization should be found providing the training and support that is necessary for these kinds of cooperative endeavors. This support should address at least two aspects in order to be rated at this level: 1) helping learners, staff, instructors, and/or community organizations to collaboratively identify and work on real-world problems/issues, and 2) working to ensure that these projects require learners to make significant modifications and adaptations to relevant KSAs. Overall, then, the organization's focus for this level should be on helping learners to have more collaborative responsibility and leadership with instructors and/or community partners in identifying real-world issues and then supporting their work to find effective ways of addressing these issues by adapting KSAs to authentic contexts.

We can again see the complexity of God's educational work at Level 3 increase in substantive ways. Here, organizational staff will be found partnering with God's efforts to empower faculty and students to more collaboratively and proactively engage with real-world issues. The organization will therefore provide training, resources, and support to both learners and instructors on how to discerningly identify real-world situations to engage with. The organization will also help them to use cooperative spiritual discernment processes to determine how they will go about engaging with these situations in ways that are likely to be transformative for all who are involved and impacted by the project. Overall, the organization will essentially be helping faculty and students to collectively discern where and how God is inviting them to collaboratively engage with real-world projects in genuinely transformative ways.

Examples of this might include:

- There is evidence of the organization providing resource and mentoring support to students and/or instructors as they work with a community partner to conduct an asset/needs assessment and create a plan to address identified assets/needs via adapting relevant course KSAs.

- After attending a training session, instructors require students in one of their classes to partner with an organization to complete a Continuous Quality Improvement (CQI) project that aligns with learning objectives and results in recommendations being made to the organization.

- Working with staff, students complete an advocacy project that they are passionate about where they identify relevant organizations who are working on the topic and then work with these organizations to strategize and/or work towards making change.

- The organization provides funding that allows instructors and/or staff to attend conferences on how to work with students to collaboratively develop service-learning projects.

Guideline #5—Scaffolding Guidance

The organization supports learners and instructors in developing activities that consistently scaffolds learners' increasing competencies for key KSAs (Core Guideline).

While the other guidelines in this area are more focused on the organization supporting learners and instructors with their engagement in specific teaching/learning activities, for this guideline the organization should be working to help them better organize how they engage with these activities. According to this guideline, the organization should minimally ensure that students are moving through their learning and development in a step-by-step manner. In other words, concepts and skills should build upon previous ones and the organization should help ensure that learners are generally competent in core KSAs before they are allowed to progress to subsequent ones.

At higher levels, the organization will help learners and instructors partner in developing and selecting varied pathways that support learner growth in core course KSAs. These pathways should allow for learner choice and be tailored to better match current students' diverse backgrounds. The organization should make sure that these varied pathways support scaffolding wherein learners' progress to more advanced KSAs is dependent upon the demonstration of predetermined levels of competency for the more basic KSAs that these advanced topics/skills are founded upon. Overall, this guideline is therefore focused on how the organization supports learners' progress through their learning experiences.

Further expanding upon the assertion that God works with and through evolutionary and step-by-step processes, this guideline invites organizational staff to provide the kinds of support that are needed to partner with God via these educational processes. Just as houses are built by necessity from the ground up, the neuropsychic structures upon which genuinely new learning takes place must be firmly established before proceeding on to subsequent KSAs. In these scaffolded processes, it may be asserted that God is laying the strong and holy foundations that will be needed in order for ongoing progress to sustainably occur. As a result, the organization must help ensure that learners and instructors are intentionally organizing their learning and teaching in a step-by-step manner, be this in linear or spiral learning ways. Overall, organizational staff are essentially working with faculty and students to discern how God is inviting them to organize and engage with scaffolded learning processes.

Level 1

The organization supports learners and instructors in developing activities that repeatedly engage key KSAs and scaffolds learners' growing competencies in these areas (i.e., ensures achievement before moving on to new KSAs).

An organization at Level 1 will work with learners and instructors to ensure that students are guided through key course KSAs in scaffolded ways. This means that the organization will provide resources and support to help confirm that learners grasp foundational KSAs in deeper ways before moving onto to newer and more complex ones. Overall, then, an organization at this level will show evidence of working intentionally to ensure that students' pathways to learning are guided in scaffolded ways.

At this foundational level, organizational staff will essentially be helping instructors and learners grasp the basics of spiritually discerning a well-scaffolded organization of learning processes. Organizational staff will help students and faculty establish that the current KSAs build directly on previous ones whilst simultaneously becoming the strong building blocks for the next level of learning. From this perspective, theologically speaking, the organizational staff will be helping students and faculty discern how God is seeking to guide the learning process. This foundational level is therefore centered on the organization, helping to ensure that God's strong foundations of core KSAs are in place before advancing to subsequent and more advanced KSAs.

Examples of this might include:

- The organization provides training to instructors on how to develop e-learning modules that help students master foundational concepts before moving onto more advanced ones.

- Organizational staff are observed working with students to help them study key concepts/skills repeatedly over an extended period of time.

- As a result of attending a workshop, instructors are observed working with students/groups to ensure that they understand foundational topics before moving the class onto subsequent topics.

- The organization hosts guest facilitators who help learners and/or instructors better learn how to scaffold learning activities.

Level 2

The organization provides training to learners and instructors on developing a variety of sequenced resources and learning experiences that scaffold competency in key KSAs that are matched to learners' experiences, needs, and interests and allow for choice.

Level 2 builds upon the expectations of Level 1 but does so in more varied ways. Here, the organization will work to ensure that there is a greater emphasis on learners and instructors matching course pathways to the unique backgrounds and needs of current learners. This level is therefore similar to the first level in that it still meets the same standards of scaffolding but differs in that it is more varied with multiple pathways. Central to this level, then, is that the organization proactively works with learners, staff, and instructors to develop multiple paths to engage with and demonstrate key competencies. The organization should also help ensure that these pathways are matched to the diverse backgrounds, capabilities, and interests of current learners.

At Level 1, organizational staff will help faculty and students better understand and learn the fundamentals of scaffolded learning processes. At this level, the organization will help them build upon these foundational capabilities by more closely partnering with God's ever-adaptive educational life. Knowing that learning processes vary from student-to-student and that they rarely follow a perfectly linear progression, organizational staff will help instructors and learners develop multiple pathways of learning that are better tailored to each learners' unique backgrounds and capabilities. Spiritually, the organization will be helping them more clearly discern how God is seeking to work with each learner and then develop relevant and multiple scaffolded pathways to learning core KSAs. Educational systems at this level are therefore found to more closely partner with God's multitudinous ways of organizing and guiding learning processes, ones that are appropriately tailored for the current cohort of students and faculty.

Examples of this might include:

- Staff work with instructors to offer multiple class activities for completing an assignment (e.g., written paper, digital storytelling project, formal presentation, etc.).
- The organization works with programs/departments to develop and maintain a library of e-learning modules and other resources that students can choose from to support their learning.
- As a result of attending a faculty development event, instructors are observed providing multiple ways of explaining and representing core course concepts/skills (e.g., lecture, demonstration, use of videos, etc.) to their students.
- After attending a student success workshop, learners can describe multiple learning activities that they have used to help them better understand course concepts/skills.

Level 3

The organization fosters an environment where learners and instructors work collaboratively to identify sustained and varied pathways to the development of key KSAs using a range of resources, learning experiences, and ways of demonstrating scaffolded progress towards these KSAs.

Similar to Level 2, a Level 3 organization will provide resources, training, and close support to empower learners and instructors in their development of multiple and varied pathways to engage with core KSAs. At this level, however, the organization will be found intentionally supporting faculty, staff, and student collaboration in developing these scaffolded paths. Here, then, there is a much greater emphasis on the organization enabling learners, staff, and instructors to collaboratively identify and adapt varied and scaffolded learning paths that better meet the diverse backgrounds and interests of current students.

While this level seems to be only a small change over Level 2, its implications are potentially enormous. At Level 3, the organization is essentially continuing with the work of nurturing God's schoolwide educational organism. Here, all parts of the community come together in various ways to collaboratively discern and build upon multiple scaffolded learning pathways that are relevant and meaningful for current students and faculty. In this way, with the needed support and guidance of organizational leaders, God can work in more harmonized ways to continually create and/or modify these pathways. Being more fully responsive and adaptive at this cooperative level, God's educational life can work far more effectively as learners can discerningly navigate via these multiple paths to intensify their learning processes. Achieving and sustaining success at this level, however, will likely require the close support, training, and relevant resources that this level admonishes organizational leaders to provide. When they do, they are effectively responding to God's movements to continually coordinate and synchronize these multiple pathways and learners' effective engagement with them.

Examples of this might include:

- As a result of attending a training session, instructors are observed working with students to develop their own learning path in their courses.
- Learners are observed working with institutional tutors to help them map out scaffolded study plans that will enable them to be more successful in one of their courses.
- The organization hosts study groups that help learners to use supplemental textbooks, and articles to help them study for exams.
- Program/departmental faculty, staff, and students are aided in their collaborative work to develop and maintain a library of e-learning modules and other resources that students can choose from to support their learning.

Guideline #6—Caring Learning Environment

Mission-Centered Focus: The organization works to create and sustain a learning environment that is safe, inclusive, and caring.

These kinds of environments are to be expected in any organization. Some cognitive science studies have shown that students learn and retain more when they are less stressed, so these environments are particularly important for educational settings (be they online or face-to-face environments). Learning, as may be seen by these

Educational System Guidelines, is an iterative process of trial-and-error, continuous feedback, and ongoing efforts to continually improve. As a result, the organization should work to ensure that curricular and co-curricular events are safe spaces that allow for risk-taking without fear of failure, encourage free and positively supported exploration of ideas and diverse perspectives, and are ones in which participants support and challenge one another in affirming and constructive ways. In order to help facilitate such learning environments, the organization needs to help set clear expectations that students, faculty, and staff are not only coached on, but also have a part in developing. Overall, then, the trend across these levels is from the organization having clear expectations towards supporting the collaborative development of and engagement with safe, inclusive, and caring expectations. When assessing an organization for this guideline, we can therefore look at the extent to which the organization involves staff, instructors, and students in both setting these expectations and then being expected to act in accordance with them.

The evidence-based studies that support this guideline affirm that God's kin-dom in our schools is one that manifests God's love, caring support, and constructive accountability.[3] Western culture as well as education has had an unfortunate history of punishment, negative reinforcement, and harsh criticisms. Christianity, too, has and continues to propagate these kinds of negative approaches to conversion, formation, and hierarchical control. Yet psychological, sociological, and educational studies clearly show that these negative approaches do not yield long-term positive outcomes. Following the theistic views of research followed in this text, then, we might assert that such negative approaches are actually distortions of God's formative actions. These numerous studies alternatively verify that our God of love works most effectively through loving, positive, and empowering means. Our school systems, if they are to be more responsive to and manifesting of God's kin-dom life, need to therefore establish patterns of care, inclusivity, and positive support. In continually nurturing these kinds of God-centered environments can God's educational life work more freely and effectively with our students.

Level 1

The organization has explicit expectations for a safe and positive learning environment and there is evidence of behavior that includes respect and caring for one another.

An organization at Level 1 will be observed setting clear expectations for a safe, inclusive, and caring school environment. These expectations should not only be presented whenever new students, staff, and/or faculty join the organization, but also addressed on regular occasions. At this level, there will also be clear evidence of organizational members interacting with one another in ways that are congruent with the

---

3. See the references for this guideline in the previous chapter.

school's behavioral expectations as well as the staff positively and proactively working to ensure that they are adhered to.

Working at this foundational level, the organization will help its constituents be aware of the kinds of behaviors and interactions that are more manifesting of God's kin-dom life within and among them. With God's nature being one of love, support, empathy, care, inclusivity, vitality, accountability, and structure, the organization's expectations should be reflective of these. As a result, students, faculty, and staff will not only know what these positive expectations are, but there will also be clear evidence of them embodying them in their interactions. In doing so, the organization will be helping itself to respond more fully to God's loving life as an organizational culture.

Examples of this might include:

- The institution's websites and/or other materials clearly state behavioral expectations (e.g., code of conduct, ethical guidelines, etc.).

- The organization provides mandatory syllabus statements on behavioral expectations for the institution (e.g., classroom decorum, regulations on technology usage, instructor response times, etc.).

- Administrators and staff are observed affirming one another for sharing their diverse beliefs, viewpoints, and ideas.

- Organizational behavioral expectations are listed on job descriptions and annual review forms.

Level 2

In addition to Level 1, the organization supports activities that require respectful interaction, mutual support, and individual/group responsibility for the learning environment.

Level 2 includes the previous level's recommendations wherein the organization has clear behavioral expectations for its members. At this level, however, there will be evidence of the organization going beyond this by supporting activities that intentionally facilitate safe, inclusive, and caring interactions among students, faculty, and staff. Overall, the goal here is for the organization to work directly with students, staff, and faculty in intentionally practicing these expectations. It is one thing to have clear expectations that members of the organization must minimally comply with (Level 1), but quite another for the organization to help them intentionally utilize these expectations in their activities (Level 2).

Based on the belief that God is proactively working to nurture these kinds of loving environments, organizational members will therefore discern how God is inviting them to develop activities, processes, and policies that intentionally empower these kinds of behavioral patterns. In essence, these are organizational spiritual practices in the sense that these intentional activities are anticipated to help learners, instructors, and staff be more responsive of God's caring life in habituated ways. In other words, by proactively engaging with these kinds of activities, the organization will be helping its constituents more fully manifest God's caring, supportive, and inclusive environments. The work at this level is therefore an intentional effort on the part of the organization to further establish God's kin-dom culture of love.

Examples of this might include:

- After attending an organizational event on bullying, a learner is observed positively intervening when one of their peers acts negatively towards another classmate.

- As a result of attending a workshop on positive learning environments, instructors are observed encouraging students to take risks by attempting difficult problems and answering complicated questions and then positively affirms their efforts when they do.

- There is evidence of staff working with instructors to develop class assignments that require students to positively and constructively engage with viewpoints and opinions that are different from their own.

- Administrators and staff are observed positively coaching one another in relation to one or more of the organization's behavioral expectations.

Level 3

The organization intentionally helps instructors and learners collaborate in developing and applying expectations for a learning climate that includes openness, mutual respect, and positive peer relationships.

This level includes the previous levels' recommendations for having clear institutional behavioral expectations. However, for organizations at this level, members will be found collaboratively working with one another to develop and implement these expectations. An organization at this level is therefore one that is more collaborative in relation to this guideline and should result in expectations that are more meaningful to and relevant for its members.

Further building on the Level 3 expectations for other guidelines, the work here is oriented towards drawing staff, students, and faculty together to collaboratively develop and implement the God-manifesting behavioral and interaction expectations. Founded on the assertion that God works through each member of the community to foster a culture that is genuinely loving and empowering of everyone, the organization will work to ensure that each individual participates in these processes in ways that are appropriate for them. Again, we find God's living kin-dom organism emerging as organizational leaders help continually facilitate ongoing spiritual discernment reflections and revisions to the school's culture. While it will be a never-ending "work-in-progress," due to the continually changing student body, the organization should cooperatively aim for God's culture of loving care, positive support, and all-encompassing inclusion.

Examples of this might include:

- The organization provides training to instructors on how to lead students through a brainstorming process to generate behavioral expectations for their classes.

- After participating in an organizational event, learners are observed modeling expectations that were collaboratively developed at this event.

- Staff work with instructors and students on how to help small groups work together to set their own ground rules for how they will interact and resolve conflicts together.

- The organization is observed offering incentives to those who clearly demonstrate school expectations that have been cooperatively developed.

TEACHING/LEARNING THEORY GUIDELINES

With as complex and in-depth as teaching and learning activities are, so too are the theories, strategies, and methods that can inform their implementation. While many instructors receive an education on some of these, their understanding and abilities to implement the broader range of theories, strategies, and methods is likely limited. In addition, there are very few schools that intentionally and explicitly teach students about learning theories, various study strategies, or methods that might be used to help them to develop these strategies. In either case, ongoing professional development on these topics should be an essential part of the administration's agenda for each school year. Theologically, the school will be helping faculty and students alike gain the necessary insights they will need to better know about and partner with God's educational life via teaching and learning processes.

Guideline #1—Holistic Teaching and Learning Theories

Organization helps learners and instructors articulate: a) specific holistic teaching and learning theories that they might utilize, and b) when and how these theories might apply (Core Guideline).

What instructors and students believe about learning and development and how to shape it can greatly influence which teaching/study strategies they will choose and how they engage with these. For instance, a person who believes that learners are an empty bucket that simply needs to be filled with information will likely approach their teaching/learning strategies differently from someone who thinks that people already come with basic knowledge upon which they need to construct new concept/skills.

As a result of this claim, this guideline is intended to help organizations work more closely with learners and instructors in reflecting upon these learning theories. The organization should also provide resources, training, and/or support on how learners and instructors can better use these theories to improve learning and development. Overall, the trend for the organization is from helping faculty and students be more explicit about these theories to helping them collaboratively draw from multiple theories to help guide teaching and learning.

Theologically, educational theories are ideally our best approximation of the enduring ways that God has been observed to more effectively work to foster learning. Based on the assertion that God always acts simultaneously with and through the whole of each person's life, these theories should be more holistic in nature. Their primary aim is to empower practitioners to better partner with God's educational life to help learners develop. As a result, the organization should therefore provide students and faculty with the necessary training, support, and resources to not only learn about these more holistic theories, but also learn how to more effectively utilize them. In doing so, they are providing them with the insights that they need to more fully respond to God's movements through learning processes.

Level 1

The organization provides training that helps learners and instructors articulate their own holistic understandings of learning and development and how to adjust their teaching and/or learning strategies in light of these understandings.

At this level, there should be evidence of the organization providing training, resources, and/or support to students and instructors so they are better able to explicitly state what their own views of holistic learning and development are and how they are using these models to inform and guide their teaching/learning. Here, an emphasis should be given to helping learners and instructors clearly articulate: 1) the processes by which they believe people holistically learn/develop, 2) strategies that can be used to help people to grow along these paths (i.e., strategies that align with their understandings of learning processes), and 3) how they have developed their courses/study habits to support such learning and development (i.e., ones that align with their learning theories). Overall, the organization should also be found helping learners and instructors identify and rectify inconsistencies between these theories and their study habits or course designs.

Foundationally, the organization will be found working with students, faculty, and staff to essentially be able to articulate the more effective processes through which God works to nurture learning. These understandings should be detailed enough to help them understand some of the core dynamics by which learning and development occur. They should also be able to articulate how they can more closely partner with God through these processes via the teaching/learning strategies that they are utilizing. With the holistic theories providing the roadmap for how the path of learning unfolds, the strategies provide the logistical means by which to help move with God from point A to point B on the educational journey. Spiritually speaking, this level is therefore focused on the organization helping faculty and students clarify what they believe God has revealed to them about how God fosters learning as well as how they can more closely partner with God's educational life.

Examples of this might include:

- After attending a workshop, students and/or instructors are able to state the general processes by which they believe learning happens.

- Organizational staff are observed discussing learning processes with a study group, so they can then use the best strategies to prepare for a test.

- The organization provides instructors with a selection of syllabus statements that briefly describe general learning theories that a course might be based upon.

- Staff work with an instructor to help them better understand how the activities in their class directly support students' learning processes.

Level 2

The organization supports learners and instructors in using observations as well as evidence-based resources to inform and adjust their own holistic learning theories.

Level 2 extends beyond Level 1 when the organization helps learners and instructors reflect upon how current students seem to be learning in the best ways possible. These reflections can be based upon assessment data and/or conversations with one another about this topic (directly via class discussions or one-on-one meetings between instructors and students, or indirectly via papers, journals, discussion board posts, etc.). The organization should then help learners and instructors compare this information with their own personal views of holistic learning and development and note similarities and differences. Finally, the organization should empower instructors and students to also draw from evidence-based holistic learning theories and then articulate how they are using these, along with their observations, to modify and improve their teaching/study approaches.

Moving beyond the previous level, the organization will help instructors and students reflect upon their understandings of how God works to foster learning in light of their own and others' observations of learning processes. Looking to data from their own experiences as well as evidence-based resources can help to further refine the accuracy of their educational theologies (i.e., their understanding of how God nurtures learning and development). In addition, this data can help them improve how they might partner with God's educational life. As a result, the organization should be found helping students, faculty, and staff gather, reflect on and implement the learnings that they glean from these resources. Knowing that while patterns exist biologically, psychologically, and socially (and therefore that God acts in patterned ways across contexts), the organization will help its constituency adapt these theories and how they apply them to their own infinitely unique context.

Examples of this might include:

- Staff work with study groups to help them better use a specific study strategy (e.g., distributed practice, mnemonic devices, concept mapping, etc.) based on an evidence-based learning theory.
- As a result of attending a workshop, learners and/or instructors can identify specific evidence-based learning theories to inform their understanding of learning processes.
- The organization provides consultations to instructors that help them better articulate how their understanding of learning processes can be based upon both evidence-based theories and their observations of current students in their classes.
- After participating in a training, students can state how they have used their performance on exams, papers, etc. to understand how they learn best in their classes.

Level 3

Recognizing that students learn and develop in diverse ways, and building on Level 2, the organization fosters a collaborative culture that helps learners and instructors develop and utilize multiple evidence-based holistic learning theories to help guide learning and development, as well as be able to articulate when and how each theory is being utilized.

This more complex level further builds upon the previous level when the organization works with students and instructors to be able to articulate how the diversity of students at the institution necessitates the use of multiple theories to support holistic learning and development. In addition, the organization should work with learners and instructors to recognize that different sets of KSAs require different learning theories in order to maximize learning for each KSA. This level therefore represents an intellectual advancement for students and instructors in relation to these theories when the organization helps them realize that one holistic learning theory is not sufficient to provide the kinds of nuanced and more complex insights and guidance that are needed when working with diverse learners and concepts/skills. There should therefore be clear evidence of the organization working with learners and instructors to clearly articulate why and how multiple holistic theories are needed to direct their teaching/learning. Finally, and related to other guidelines, Level 3 here is intended to support a more collaborative culture wherein students and instructors work together to identify and implement multiple evidence-based learning theories.

Theologically extending the claims of Level 2, this level asserts that while God does work in similar ways across varied contexts, different kinds of contexts will likely require different movements of God to foster learning and development. As a result, different holistic learning theories are needed in order to help clarify these categorical differences of contexts. For instance, in classes where memorization is an integral part of learning, then information processing and cognitive theories can provide spiritual insights into how God works to support learning.[4] In programs where specific skills are being developed, then neo-Piagetian skill development theories may be more insightful for students and instructors.[5] Here, then, the organization will be found working with learners and faculty to collaboratively learn about, adapt, and utilize various evidence-based holistic learning theories so that they can more closely partner with God's educational life.

Examples of this might include:

- As part of an organizationally hosted event, instructors can state how they have worked with others to use assessment data in addition to two or more evidence-based learning theories to better understand how their students learn best in their class.

- Staff can state how they have worked with study groups to improve their strategies using two or more evidence-based learning theories.

- The instructor can explain how they have worked with consultants to use different evidence-based learning theories to develop multiple pathways for students in their course.

- The organization provides funding for faculty and staff to attend trainings on how to use multiple evidence-based learning theories to improve student achievement.

Guideline #2—Active Teaching and Learning Strategies

The organization helps learners and instructors utilize active teaching and learning strategies (Core Guideline).

Increasingly over the past few decades, educational literature has given a central emphasis on the use of active teaching and learning strategies. In particular, the following active strategies are repeatedly highlighted in the literature: elaboration and self-reflections; self-regulated learning and study strategies; direct instruction or modeling followed by learner practice; peer teaching/tutoring; concept mapping; class

---

4. For instance, see Matlin, *Cognition*.
5. For example, see Morra et al., *Cognitive Development*.

discussions and debate; problem solving and problem-based learning; real-world and clinical simulations; inquiry-based pedagogies; real-world projects, service-learning; workplace experiences and internships; role-playing; and game-based strategies.[6] As this list suggests, there are numerous strategies that learners and instructors can draw from to use. As a result, the organization needs to take a proactive part in providing resources, support, and training on these active strategies. The challenge that learners and instructors face in using these strategies are twofold and organizational interventions therefore need to address both of these: 1) deciding on which strategies to use, and 2) how to adapt them for each unique application. Overall, the trend for this guideline is from the organization helping learners and instructors to use these strategies in basic ways towards helping them to develop multiple evidence-based strategies in collaboration with one another. In addition, as the organization moves to higher levels, it should help instructors and learners ensure that these strategies more closely match the background, interests, and capabilities of current learners while simultaneously ensuring that these strategies foster genuine progress towards the learning outcomes.

Organisms change in response to active engagement with their environments. Theologically, it can be asserted as a movement of God to help creation progressively evolve through mutual interactions with that which is around them. As it relates to theistic education, this means that students are invited by God to actively participate in their learning processes. As noted above, educational research studies have clearly and repeatedly shown that the more active learners are, the more deeply they learn. Organizational staff are therefore called to work with faculty and students to learn how to more effectively utilize these active strategies. Ultimately, it is a discernment of where and how God is working to help learners actively engage with their educational journeys. The organization needs to equip its constituency for these purposes as well as help them continually determine which active strategies are most appropriate.

Level 1

The organization helps learners and instructors draw on specific active teaching and learning strategies and apply these to help improve learning and development.

Level 1 is achieved when the organization intentionally seeks to acknowledge and support active teaching and learning strategies at their school. There should be evidence of the organization working with learners and instructors to articulate/demonstrate what strategies they have chosen and how these are being used to help achieve learning outcomes. These strategies can involve individual, small groups, or whole class activities, and they should clearly help learners actively engage with relevant KSAs. In addition, following other guidelines, the organization should work

---

6. See references for these guidelines in the previous chapter.

with students, staff, and faculty to help ensure that these strategies clearly align with the learning objectives.

Foundationally, the organization should work to ensure that students and faculty are aware of the wide range of active strategies through which God works to nurture learning. Staff should also provide the necessary training and support that instructors and learners need in order to spiritually discern which specific strategies God is inviting them to utilize. A central part of this discernment should be adaptions that God needs students and instructors to make in order for God to work more effectively through them. As the organization continues this work, they will be partnering with God to evolve a culture that more actively engages with God's educational life.

Examples of this might include:

- Staff are observed working with study groups to assess each other's work and offer suggestions to one another for how to improve (e.g., peer-assessment/tutoring).

- After attending a workshop, instructors are observed engaging students in course discussions/debates that require each student to be actively involved.

- The organization provides training sessions on specific active teaching/learning strategies.

- Instructors participate in an organizationally sponsored certificate program where they learn how to develop a rhythm of lecturing/demonstrating for fifteen to twenty minutes, followed by having learners practice the concepts/skills that were just presented.

Level 2

The organization provides training to learners and instructors on utilizing one or more evidence-based active teaching and learning strategies, as well as how to adapt these strategies for their current courses.

This level further extends upon the previous one when the organization is observed working with learners and instructors to more clearly articulate/demonstrate how they are using specific evidence-based active teaching and learning strategies (see a beginning list of such strategies above). The organization should help faculty, staff, and students continually learn about specific evidence-based sources, so they can continue to develop and refine their teaching/learning strategies. Finally, there should be evidence of the organization working with learners and instructors to be able to state/demonstrate what adaptations they have made to these strategies in light of their current classes.

Realizing that God has and continues to effectively work through specific and high impact active strategies to nurture learning, the organization will help students and faculty learn about these evidence-based approaches. Of course, as each situation is unique, God can be expected to work in varied ways through these strategies. As a result, organizational staff should provide students and instructors with the support and resources they need in order to adapt these evidence-based active teaching/learning strategies for each application. As they do, the organization will be helping its constituency to partner more fully with God's educational life with and through these high impact practices.

Examples of this might include:

- The organization provides training sessions on specific evidence-based active teaching/learning strategies.
- Staff are observed working with individual instructors to develop an evidence-based strategy for their class.
- After attending a workshop, learners can state which active evidence-based study strategies they are using and can name which source(s) support the use of these strategies as well as how they are adapting these for their current classes.
- Staff work with an instructor to develop a syllabus statement regarding the active teaching strategies that are being used in the course that identifies which evidence-based sources support the use of these strategies.

Level 3

The organization helps learners and instructors recognize that students learn in diverse ways and therefore collaboratively develop multiple evidence-based active teaching and learning strategies. The organization then empowers learners and instructors to select personalized and active ways of engaging with relevant KSAs to ensure that these varied pathways align with learning objectives.

Level 3 for this guideline is similar to Level 3 for other guidelines in that it is more collaborative and draws from multiple sources. The organization should therefore work with learners and instructors to cooperatively utilize evidence-based active teaching and learning strategies. The organization should ensure that students and instructors are able to articulate/demonstrate which multiple strategies they are utilizing and be able to point to specific evidence-based sources for each of these (similar to Level 2).

Beyond this, the organization should develop interventions that support instructors in empowering learners to choose and/or develop their own active ways of increasing their competencies for key course KSAs. The organization should also work with students and instructors to ensure that these individualized and active pathways are congruent with evidence-based recommendations as well as the course objectives.

God's work with and through learning processes might be asserted to be as complex as humans are. As a result, we can expect God to work in diverse and varied ways to address learners ever-changing needs and progress. In response, the organization therefore needs to help faculty and students be more proficient in partnering with God via multiple evidence-based active teaching/learning strategies. As a central part of this, building upon the collaborative kin-dom culture identified by Level 3 for other guidelines, organizational staff should proactively empower instructors and learners to partner with one another in the spiritual discernment and use of these strategies. With each student being infinitely unique, this collaborative discernment should result in learning pathways that are tailored for each person. In doing so, the organization will be partnering with God to non-dualistically realize the twofold nature of education: personalized learning and communal engagement.

Examples of this might include:

- The organization provides training sessions on multiple evidence-based active teaching/learning strategies and how these may be collaboratively developed.

- Staff are observed working with study groups to select and adapt two or more evidence-based learning strategies.

- The organization hosts an event where students learn about and then collaboratively use two or more evidence-based study strategies and how to adapt these to their current classes.

- The organization offers a workshop to help instructors to identify two or more evidence-based strategies that they can use as well as how to collaborate with students to adapt these for their courses.

Guideline #3—Course/Study Strategy Development Methods

Organization ensures that learners and instructors are able to demonstrate the processes/methods by which they develop their courses or learning strategies and there is alignment among these strategies with course elements (Core Guideline).

ADDIE, backward design, universal design for learning, learner-centered, and rapid prototyping are all examples of the many instructional design methods that can be used to help guide course development and/or study strategies. Since learners and instructors may not know the details for these specific methods, the organization should work with them so that they are able to articulate the processes by which they are designing, implementing, and evaluating their course or learning approaches. This guideline is therefore intended to capture these abilities. Overall, there are two trends for the organization: 1) from working with learners and instructors to individually follow some method to develop their study strategies or course elements (e.g., objectives, activities, assessments) towards collaborating with others and looking to evidence-based literature for help with this; and 2) from helping learners/instructors to ensure there is close alignment between some of the course elements and teaching/

learning approaches towards this alignment existing for most courses' modules/units and the teaching/learning approaches. In other words, this guideline becomes more collaborative and tightly integrated as one moves towards higher levels.

At their core, from a theistic perspective, course development methods essentially are spiritual discernment processes. They are a set of steps that one can engage to help determine what each part of the learning process might need in order to be more impactful. In essence, they are intended to help discern where and how God's educational life is likely to be acting so that we can more closely partner with God in these endeavors. Just as there are several different ways to engage in spiritual discernment according to the Western Christian tradition,[7] so too are there numerous course development processes that can be engaged. The organization therefore needs to provide learners and instructors with the resources, training, and support that they need in order to discerningly select and effectively engage with the course development methods that are more appropriate for their current needs.

Level 1

The organization provides training for learners and instructors in following some process to design, implement, and evaluate teaching/learning strategies. The organization helps ensure alignment among teaching/learning objectives, activities/strategies, and assessments.

At Level 1 for this guideline, the organization will work with learners and instructors to be able to clearly articulate some process or set of steps they are using to design, implement, and evaluate their learning strategies or courses. If a learner or instructor states they are using or would like to use one or more of the instructional design methods found in the literature (e.g., ADDIE, backward design, etc.), then the organization should help ensure that they are able to state how they are applying these in detailed ways. In addition, the organization should work to verify that there is clear evidence of alignment between learning goals, activities, and assessments. For example, if one of the course objectives involves learners being able to demonstrate their abilities to conduct a research project, then there should be course activities or study strategies that guide students through these methods, as well as assessment practices that verify their competencies in these research project skills.

Based on the theological assertion that God is actively engaged in every stage of the teaching/learning process, the organization should foundationally ensure that students and faculty have a clear set of spiritual discernment processes to help them to design, implement, and evaluate their approaches. Minimally, these course/study strategy development methods should help guide their selection of clear learning objectives, teaching/study strategies, and assessments. Theologically, these elements

---

7. For examples, see Au and Au, *Discerning Heart*; Isenhower and Todd, *Living into Answers*; Parker, *Led by Spirit*.

should be the ones that they have discerned that God is inviting them to partner with him in. These methods should also result in objectives, strategies, and assessments that are clearly and closely aligned with one another. Spiritually speaking, such close alignment is reflective of God's integrative, harmonizing, and organizing nature. At this foundational level, then, organizational staff should provide the training and support that instructors and learners need to select and engage in these course development methods to help ensure that their outcomes include close alignment among objectives, strategies, and assessments.

Examples of this might include:

- The organization conducts regular reviews of classes to see if there is alignment between course objectives, activities, and assessments.

- As a result of attending a workshop, learners and/or instructors are able to clearly articulate some process or set of steps that they are using to design, implement, and evaluate their study strategies/courses.

- The organization provides funding for instructors to attend a training session on how to adapt a prescribed curriculum for one or more of their classes, one that has close alignment between objectives, activities, and assessments.

Level 2

The organization supports learners and instructors in drawing from evidence-based literature and data to design, implement, and evaluate teaching/learning strategies. The organization helps to ensure that there is direct alignment among courses as well as module/unit/weekly objectives, activities, and assessments for the teaching/learning strategies being used by learners/instructors.

Level 2 continues to extend the previous level. The organization should help ensure that the teaching/learning processes articulated by learners and instructors now include evidence-based resources. There should be two sources of evidence-based resources: 1) external resources (e.g., educational research literature, experts in the field, etc.), and 2) data from their own experiences/courses. The organization should work with them to clearly state which evidence-based resources they are utilizing and how these directly impact the development of their teaching/learning strategies. Alignment at this level is also extended to include not only course level objectives, activities, and assessments but also the course's module/unit/weekly levels too. In other words, the organization should help confirm that the learning approaches that are being used by students and instructors are directly related to what is being expected for each week in their classes. Such organizational interventions can happen via students, staff, and/or faculty.

Moving to this higher level, we can assert that faculty and students are partnering with God in more complex ways. In addition to engaging with spiritually discerning course development methods in structured ways, the organization will help learners and instructors draw from evidence-based sources to further inform these methods. Essentially, faculty and students will be seeking to better understand how God has successfully worked in other situations so that they might more clearly discern how God might be striving to work in their current context. The organization should therefore equip and train learners and faculty for evidence-based course development. In addition, organizational staff should help them ensure alignment of learning objectives, strategies, and assessments for each week/module of their courses as discussed above. In doing so, the organization will be further empowering them to participate in God's harmonizing and organizing life in more detailed and extensive ways. Based on the theological claim that God's organizing and synchronizing efforts are active in every part of creation, the organization will help learners and instructors respond to these godly movements in relation to their teaching/learning approaches each week.

Examples of this might include:

- The organization hosts a series of workshops where learners and/or instructors are able to use evidence-based resources to design, implement, and evaluate their study strategies/courses.

- The organization conducts regular reviews of classes to see if there is alignment between objectives, activities, and assessments at both the course level as well as at the module/unit/weekly level.

- Organizational staff mentor students on how to use evidence-based learning strategies to help design their study habits.

- A staff member is able to describe how they have worked with an instructor to develop specific evidence-based parts of a course.

Level 3

The organization fosters a culture where learners and instructors collaborate with others in evidence-based design, implementation, and evaluation of teaching/learning strategies. The organization helps ensure alignment for the following teaching/learning elements: objectives, activities, assessments, teaching/learning strategies, learner/instructor backgrounds, and teaching/learning theories.

Similar to other guidelines for this area, Level 3 builds directly upon Level 2 in collaborative ways. The organization should work to ensure that learners and instructors are able to articulate the evidence-based steps by which they are developing their teaching/learning strategies, but these steps should now include collaboration with others. Overall, there should be evidence of the organization working directly with learners and instructors to collaborate with others and using these collaborations to more positively and directly impact their evidence-based teaching/learning strategies.

Alignment at this level is also further extended as the organization provides training and resources so that the following teaching and learning elements are directly related to one another: objectives, activities, assessments, teaching/learning strategies, learner/instructor backgrounds, and teaching/learning theories. Overall, the organization should be found intentionally working to increase the collaboration and direct alignment of teaching and learning processes at the school.

Building upon and beyond the previous level, and aligning with Level 3 assertions for other guidelines, the organization will help faculty and students work together, as well as with others, to engage in evidence-based teaching/learning development methods. In doing so, they will be cooperatively discerning where and how God is inviting them to partner with God in their teaching/learning processes. Again, the evidence-based sources should be used to help learners and faculty collaboratively and more clearly discern these high impact invitations. The organization therefore needs to help facilitate these communal discernment methods and ensure that students and instructors have the KSAs as well as resources and support that they need in order to effectively engage in these spiritual discernment methods. Organizational staff should also work with them so that not only is there close alignment among course/study objectives, strategies, and activities as there was at Level 2, but also alignment with teaching/learning theories and learner background considerations as well. In essence, this is a further partnering with God's harmonizing and organizing life as it works to integrate and synthesize all aspects of the teaching/learning process. The organization is therefore invited at this level to help students and faculty respond to these more extensive and complex harmonizing and synthesizing invitations of God.

Examples of this might include:

- Staff are observed working with study groups for a specific class to help them better understand how their evidence-based study approaches directly relate to what they are learning about in the course.

- The organization hosts a series of workshops where learners and/or instructors work with others to collaboratively use some evidence-based process or set of steps to design, implement, and evaluate their study strategies/courses.

- A group of students are observed working with a staff member to closely follow a prescribed evidence-based study strategy to guide their learning approaches.

- Instructors attend a workshop where they work with peers to discuss how one or more of their classes are going and what might be done to continually improve them.

- The organization conducts regular reviews of classes to see if there is alignment between course/module objectives, activities, assessments, learning theories, and learner background considerations.

LEARNER-BACKGROUND GUIDELINES

"All hands on deck!" Each student can be asserted to be their own micro-culture of diversity given their unique backgrounds, interests, and capabilities. As a result, instructors and learners alike will likely need as much help as is available to continually adapt their teaching and learning strategies to each student's unique needs. To use another common cliché, it really does take a village to teach a student, and administration is tasked by God with helping coordinate these community adaptations. These guidelines are therefore intended to provide administrators with key insights into the kinds of training and support that may be needed to adapt teaching and learning to each student's unique situations. By following these, administrators will be helping support God's infinitely adaptive educational life within and through the school.

Guideline #1—Learner Capabilities

Organization helps learners and instructors adapt teaching/learning to learners' relevant prior knowledge, interests, skills, and capabilities; The organization ensures that ADA considerations are addressed (Core Guideline).

This guideline is one of the most consistently emphasized across evidence-based literature, assessments, and theories. At its core, education might be simply conceived of as a process of taking students from where they currently are in relation to course KSAs towards the levels of competencies that are defined by the learning objectives. This therefore requires engaging with learners' current backgrounds, knowledge, and interests in order to help better them to progress towards these outcomes. This is particularly important for learners with ADA considerations as many courses and schools have not been developed for such diversity of learning capabilities. There should therefore be evidence of the organization working with students and instructors to learn how to modify their teaching/learning approaches to more closely align with learners' unique backgrounds. The overall trajectory of this guideline therefore spans from the organization helping learners and instructors to adapt these approaches to meet these diverse backgrounds towards empowering them to collaborate with one another in continually modifying their objectives, strategies, and materials.

If God really is omnipresent and all-loving, then it stands to reason that God cares intimately and passionately about each and every student and unceasingly labors for their vitality and prosperity. Based on this assertion, every educational system is therefore called to be present to the work that God has and continues to do in the life of each learner. Organizational leaders should therefore work with students, staff, and faculty to know each learner as well as they can and to then modify their teaching/learning strategies in light of this. Such adaptations are particularly important for students whom our current educational systems have not been well-designed for, such as ADA learners. Founded on the notion that many so-called "disabilities" are socially created and constructed,[8] the organization needs to help ensure that learners themselves, as well as instructors and staff, are modifying their efforts as needed to better align with the educational aims and efforts that God continues to do with and through ADA-identified students. Overall, then, the organization is invited via this guideline to help learners and instructors adapt their teaching/learning efforts to better fit with the individualized work that God continues to do with each student across their lifespan.

Level 1

The organization helps learners and instructors draw on past experiences and external resources to adjust teaching/learning strategies to appropriately meet the diverse prior knowledge, interests, skills, and capabilities of learners. The organization provides training on how to apply interventions, modifications, and accommodations based on ADA requirements.

At this level, the organization will help learners and instructors articulate/demonstrate what past experiences they are drawing from and/or what specific external resources they are utilizing to modify their teaching/learning approaches to better fit with students' backgrounds. The resources, training, and support that the organization provides should therefore enable students and instructors to better align these approaches with current learners' knowledge, interests, skills, and/or capabilities (including ADA accommodations, if relevant).

At this foundational level, organizational staff will be found working with students and faculty to reflect on their experiences, as well as additional resources to help them begin modifying their learning/teaching strategies to better fit with the needs, assets, and backgrounds of themselves/current students. Theologically, it is an invitation to become more aware of where and how God has been working with each student and to then adjust learning/teaching strategies in light of these insights. In doing so, these modifications should result in a much closer partnership of God's education work with each learner, thereby resulting in greater gains in each student's achievement. Given Jesus' preferential option for those who have and continue to be marginalized, such as ADA-identified students, the organization needs to ensure that these learner-centered modifications are indeed personally tailored and effective following current ADA recommendations and accommodations.

Examples of this might include:

- The organization provides a workshop to instructors on how to use ADA checklists or guidelines to help them develop their courses.

---

8. Goggin and Newell, *Digital Disability*.

- As a result of a consultation with a staff member, learners can state what they believe their learning style is and how they have adjusted their study strategies to better fit with this style.

- The organization hosts an event that helps learners reflect on how they have performed in previous classes and then modify their study strategies in light of this.

- The organization provides access to specific resources that instructors can use to help them better understand how their students learn and then works with them to use these resources to develop one or more of their classes.

Level 2

The organization supports learners and instructors in using learners' relevant prior knowledge, interests, skills, and capabilities to plan multiple learning experiences, strategies, and assessments that allow for learner choice in pursuing and demonstrating their achievement of learning goals. The organization helps learners and instructors adapt teaching/learning strategies and use modified ADA resources to address all current learners' needs, interests, capabilities, etc.

Organizations at Level 2 differ from Level 1 by supporting learners and instructors in the development of multiple pathways engaging with core KSAs. These multiple pathways, however, should match current learners' prior knowledge, current interests, capabilities, and skills. For ADA-related resources, the organization should provide the training and support needed for learners and instructors to modify these resources in order to better fit with all learners' needs, interests, and capabilities. Studies on ADA resources/accommodations are revealing that non-ADA as well as ADA-identified students benefit from well-designed ADA compliant resources. The organization at this level should therefore show evidence of helping students, staff, and faculty adapt their programs/strategies to align with ADA best practices for all students.

At Level 1, an instructor will be laboring with God to better understand the students in their course and then modify their course elements (e.g., objectives, assessments, etc.) for the class as a whole. Similarly, a Level 1 learner will seek to develop one set of study strategies that better fits with their unique backgrounds. At this level, however, organizational staff will help faculty and students discern the multiple pathways that God is seeking to work through. In a classroom, such multiple paths will allow learners to choose the path(s) that better fits with their current interests and skills. For individual learners, these multiple paths will empower them with the flexibility to continually adapt to their changing circumstances and interests.

Theologically, it is an assertion that God empowers resilience and ongoing progress by always having multiple options and pathways available at any given moment. As interests change, as knowledge and skills evolve, or as obstacles are encountered,

God is able to have individuals and groups easily shift to other avenues that are already prepared. As a result, the organization is called to help provide the training, resources, and support that learners and instructors need in order to develop these multiple possibilities and then discern when, where, and how to engage with them. For ADA resources and accommodations, this will likely mean developing multiple and modified versions that can be engaged by all students, not just ADA-identified ones.

Examples of this might include:

- After attending a workshop, instructors are observed working with students in one or more of their classes to choose from a number of assessment options, which are better suited to current learners' capabilities, to demonstrate their competencies for specific course concepts or skills.

- Staff are observed working with students to use the closed captioning feature for a video in an effort to help them better understand the concepts/skills in the video.

- There is evidence of staff working with instructors to develop multiple pathways (e.g., two or more: modules, sets of course materials, videos, etc.) to help students achieve learning outcomes in one or more of their courses.

- The organization hosts an event that helps students identify their specific learning style and then select two or more learning activities that align with this style to help them learn a key concept in one of their classes.

Level 3

The organization fosters a culture where learners and instructors collaborate in adapting multiple teaching/learning goals, strategies, activities, resources, and/or assessments to build upon learners' relevant prior knowledge, interests, skills, and capabilities. The organization helps learners and instructors collaborate in expanding the range of ADA resources to enable all learners to exceed high standards.

Level 3 organizations are much more participatory than the previous two levels in that they proactively empower learners and instructors to collaboratively construct multiple pathways to the objectives that are more in line with current learners' backgrounds. Here, the primary focus is on creating an institutional culture that helps students become more self-directed in their own learning. It is also a culture where learners and instructors are better able to cooperatively adapt their teaching/learning approaches to meet current learners' prior knowledge, skills, interests, and capabilities. The organization should also work towards the incorporation and adaptation of ADA resources/support for the purpose of helping all students in the school be more successful.

At first glance, this guideline might seem like it is best embodied at an individual level. However, based on the claim that a significant part of self-understanding comes from the reflections, observations, and insights of others, this level is intended to encourage more communal conversations and adaptations of learning/teaching processes. This is especially important for instructors who will be able to most effectively adapt their courses for learners' backgrounds when they directly involve students in these adaptation processes. Spiritually speaking, it is a work of God within and through the school to continually and cooperatively modify the educational system to be more in line with God's ongoing work with each and every students' interests, and capabilities. By empowering faculty, students, and staff to be involved in these efforts, the organization will be partnering with God to ensure higher levels of achievement for all students.

Examples of this might include:

- The organization provides funding for instructors and staff to attend a conference on developing learner-generated civic engagement projects that are more meaningful to and relevant for current learners at the school.

- A staff member is observed meeting with students one-on-one to develop individualized learning plans for one or more of their courses.

- The organization provides a training session to a class on how to collaboratively engage in Universal Design for Learning (UDL) processes to develop an upcoming unit for the course.

- As a result of attending a workshop, instructors can state how they will work with their students to adapt ADA-compliant resources to better support all students in one or more of their classes.

Guideline #2—Cultural Considerations

The organization supports learners and instructors in being able to appropriately modify teaching/learning strategies in light of learners' diverse cultural locations (e.g., SES, ethnicity, gender, age, etc.).

Somewhat similar to the previous guideline, this one is more directly centered on the cultural considerations of each learner whereas the previous guideline was more related to their unique and individual prior knowledge, interests, capabilities and capabilities. Recognizing that one's culture deeply influences learning and development, this guideline focuses on the organization identifying how learners and instructors are adapting their teaching/learning strategies in light of cultural considerations. A student's cultural location can include one or more of the following: ethnicity, gender, age, SES, educational level, sexual orientation, religious tradition, geographic location, political affiliations, etc. These and other cultural factors influence many of the considerations named in the previous guideline. As a result, when an organization helps ensure that its educational systems are developed to be more aware of these factors and intentionally engage with them, the result will be greater gains in student achievement. Trends for the levels of this guideline range from the organization supporting learners and instructors to simply work to be more aware of how learners' cultural location might influence learning to the organization intentionally fostering a collaborative culture where students, staff, and faculty, as well as community members, work together to modify teaching/learning strategies to be more culturally responsive.

As was discussed for this guideline in previous chapters, God is asserted to work with and through entire cultural groups as well as individuals. The social, political, and economic factors within and among such cultural groups will be manifesting of God's life to varying degrees, just as individuals can freely choose (within limits) to more or less participate in God's work internally as well as externally to them. Since each person is born into experiences throughout their life and can choose to influence and be influenced by God's work via different cultural groupings, educational systems can greatly benefit by better understanding and working with these sociological dynamics. As research studies continue to verify these benefits, this guideline is intended to encourage organizational leaders to help instructors and students continually adapt their learning/teaching practices in light of these cultural influences. Theologically, it is a work of spiritually discerning what God has and continues to do with and through these cultures so that the school might more closely partner with God's educational life in real-time.

Level 1

The organization supports learners and instructors in accessing resources to expand their understanding of the various differences among learners and their communities and to then modify teaching/learning strategies in light of this.

At this beginning level, there should be evidence of the organization working with learners and instructors to identify some of the various cultural locations of students based on ethnicity, age, gender, SES, and so on. The organization should also be found helping learners and instructors identify resources that they might use to better understand these cultural factors and how these factors might influence learning and development. With support from the organization, faculty and students should be able to then use this knowledge to modify their teaching/learning strategies. At this level, then, the organization will provide the necessary training, resources, and support that learners and instructors need to be able to: 1) identify the cultural locations of students and their communities, 2) state which resources they are relying on to inform their understandings of these cultural locations and how these locations might influence learning and development, and 3) articulate/demonstrate how they have adapted their teaching/learning strategies based on these understandings. The primary aim at this level is the organization working directly with learners and instructors in developing a beginning understanding of students' cultural locations and then aiding them in making changes to teaching/learning approaches to be more aligned with these locations.

At this foundational level, organizational staff will essentially be helping students and faculty become more aware of how God works in different ways through different cultures to nurture learning and development. Depending on the cultural grouping that is selected (e.g., age, ethnicity, gender, etc.) as well as the specific course KSAs, some of these educational differences may be very significant and some may be less so. The organization, however, should therefore provide the support that learners and instructors need to not only be aware of these potential cultural differences but also how God seems to work most effectively for each cultural grouping. In essence, organizational staff will be empowering them with the needed awareness, spiritual discernment methods, and concrete strategies that faculty and students need to culturally adapt and thereby more closely partner with God's education life within these cultural influences.

Examples of this might include:

- The organization provides funding for instructors to attend conferences/trainings on culturally responsive teaching practices.
- After attending an organizationally sponsored workshop, learners and/or instructors are able to accurately identify one or more cultural locations (e.g., SES, ethnicity, gender, age, etc.) and can state how they can adapt their teaching/learning strategies in light of this awareness.
- The organization provides faculty and students with resources (e.g., articles, books, mentors, websites, etc.) that they can use to help them better understand various cultural locations.
- The organization assesses classes to help ensure that they contain resources that accurately represent the cultural diversity of students and their communities.

Level 2

The organization provides training that helps learners and instructors plan multiple culturally appropriate pathways of teaching/learning experiences and assessments that allow for learner choice in pursuing and demonstrating their achievement of learning objectives in light of learners' relevant cultural locations (e.g., SES, ethnicity, gender, age, etc.).

Similar to the previous guideline, an organization at Level 2 will differ from Level 1 by empowering learners and instructors to utilize multiple and culturally appropriate pathways to engage with teaching/learning. The organization should also help to ensure that these multiple pathways match the cultural diversity of current students and the wider community. Finally, the organization should be found working with students, staff, and faculty so that these diverse pathways lead students to achieving learning outcomes.

With multiple culturally appropriate pathways in place, God is able to not only help each learner pursue the combination of pathways that will be most effective for them personally, but to also have the potential to help each student become more culturally proficient themselves. One of the great travesties hindering the social justice and intercultural work of God in our school systems is the "one-size-fits-all" approach to lesson planning and curriculum development that has and continues to dominate Western education from pre-kindergarten through graduate school. In order for God to foster more culturally responsive teaching/learning, and to help this planet's populations to become more aware of and skilled at working cross-culturally, people must have access to multiple learning paths that are both relevant for their cultures personally and that expose them to culturally diverse ways of thinking, behaving, and so forth. At this level, then, organizational leaders are called to help empower and support faculty, students, and staff to develop and pursue these multiple culturally responsive pathways to learning and teaching. In doing so, the organization will become an ever more intimate part of God's world-wide work for higher student achievement, equitable educational systems, and interculturally competent global citizens.

Examples of this might include:

- Faculty development staff work with instructors to develop a class activity where students can choose a topic that is relevant to their ethnic heritage.

- A department/program provides students with access to multiple e-learning modules that can help them better understand core concepts/skills in relation to one or more of their own cultural locations.

- The organization provides training to faculty and staff on how to develop multiple service-learning projects with culturally diverse communities.

- Staff are observed working with learners to identify multiple resources that can help them better know how course concepts/skills will need to be adapted for their own community's cultural location.

Level 3

The organization supports learners and instructors in collaborating to develop different culturally appropriate pathways to pursue learning objectives. The organization supports collaboration with a broad range of specialists and/or community members to address learners' cultural needs and to integrate diverse cultural resources, practices, and perspectives into teaching/learning.

Similar to many other guidelines, a Level 3 organization will show evidence of empowering collaboration among students, staff, and faculty, as well as community members, to adapt teaching/learning approaches to better meet diverse cultural locations. The organization should therefore show evidence of supporting the collaborative development of multiple pathways to engage with core concepts/skills. Also, an organization at this level will work with learners and instructors to integrate diverse cultural perspectives via learning materials and activities. Overall, this level is very similar to the previous guideline but has a more specific emphasis on the cultural locations of students as well as collaborative cultural engagement with key KSAs.

It is very difficult for an individual from one cultural grouping to develop a teaching/learning resource or strategy for someone from another grouping. As a result, this guideline really requires a collaborative approach where diverse people join together to continually adapt the school's practices, beliefs, and policies. Theologically, it could be asserted that such required collaboration is by design as God works to achieve the local and global aims articulated at the previous level. The organization is therefore invited to empower such collaboration among its immediate constituency (i.e., students, staff, and faculty) as well as with external community members and experts who can help the school better achieve these aims. In doing so, the organization will be responding to God's culturally responsive educational work according to this evidence-based guideline.

Examples of this might include:

- Staff are observed helping instructors work with students and culturally diverse community members to develop a project that is relevant for the community.

- Students are provided with the support they need to form study groups that seek to create learning strategies that are culturally appropriate for everyone in the group.

- Administration forms a committee of staff, students, and faculty that identifies culturally diverse resources that may be used in various courses and programs.

- Funding is provided to send a team of students and faculty to a training on culturally responsive schools.

Guideline #3—Preferential Option for Vulnerable Populations

Mission-Centered Focus: *Organization aids learners and instructors in engaging in diverse cultural experiences with underrepresented and marginalized communities that proactively reduce biases and increase justice for these populations* (Core Guideline).

Educational studies in the U.S. continue to document a significant gap in achievements between at least two sets of groups: 1) middle/upper and lower SES students, and 2) Euro-American and Non-Euro-American students. In response, nationwide PK-16 initiatives have been launched in an attempt to close these gaps. This guideline is reflective of these initiatives and is intended to help ensure that every part of the organization is adequately addressing the needs of marginalized, under-resourced, and lower performing students. Furthermore, following this guideline, the organization should help prepare students and instructors to proactively engage with marginalized and under-resourced communities in positively transforming ways. Overall, the trends from Level 1 to 3 are from the organization providing necessary training, resources, and support to help staff, students, and faculty be more aware of diverse perspectives towards helping them actively engage with diverse people and communities. It also entails the organization supporting them in not only addressing their own personal biases but also helping one another to do likewise.

A central part of Western Christianity's views of the kin-dom of God entail love and vitality for all of creation. As noted in previous chapters, many scholars and Christian communities have highlighted Jesus' preferential option for the poor and outcasted members of society. As this relates to our educational systems, we can therefore expect that God will especially be working to help under-resourced and marginalized students be successful in their educational endeavors.

In addition, with the challenges of continued and systematic oppression being so great, we might also assert that God is ever-inviting each school to be an agent of positive transformation in their local community and beyond. As a result, organizational leaders are encouraged by this guideline to respond to these God-manifesting movements in the work that they do with underserved students and their communities. In doing so, the school will not only become more profound expressions of God's equitable kin-dom, but also a more powerful force for transformation in the world.

Level 1

The organization provides support for learners and instructors to engage multiple cultural perspectives and experiences of underrepresented and marginalized communities in the pursuit of learning objectives. The organization helps learners and instructors explore how their own personal biases can affect perceptions and actions, particularly as these biases relate to underrepresented and marginalized communities.

Level 1 for this guideline is primarily focused on exposing learners and instructors to diverse perspectives within the class as well as in the community (locally, regionally, nationally, and/or globally). In line with the aims of this guideline, a specific emphasis is given to the lived experiences and perspectives of under-resourced and marginalized communities. As a result, there should be clear evidence of the organization providing support and opportunities for this.

The second part of this level involves the organization working with students, staff, and faculty to become more aware of their own biases and how these might be affecting their actions personally, civically, and/or professionally. Of particular importance for this guideline are biases that are related to lower performing students as well as learners from marginalized and under-resourced communities. The organization should therefore help its constituency be able to: a) articulate/demonstrate awareness some of their own potential biases; b) state/demonstrate how these biases might be affecting their work; and c) take concrete steps to prevent these biases from adversely affecting their actions. The organization might also conduct self-analyses on courses, programs and departments to identify social, political, and/or economic gaps among various groups at the institution (i.e., based on SES, ethnicity, gender, age, job position, etc.).

Foundationally, the organization will be helping lay the necessary groundwork for God to act in a more transformative way in the community. These solid spiritual foundations primarily involve awareness and consciousness raising. By better understanding the lived experiences and ongoing challenges that various marginalized populations endure on a regular basis, students, faculty, and staff will be better enabled to work in solidarity with these communities for positive change. At this level, then, we can assert that God works through the organization to help its constituents build these solid foundations of understanding these lived experiences, as well as their personal biases and how these can and do play themselves out on a daily basis. As these foundations grow, staff, instructors, and students will be able to respond more fully to God's work at higher levels of this guideline.

Examples of this might include:

- There is evidence of the organization helping instructors access course materials (e.g., readings, videos, etc.) that embody diverse perspectives of under-resourced communities.

- The organization is observed working with courses, programs, and departments to identify social, political, and/or economic gaps among various groups at the institution (i.e., based on SES, ethnicity, gender, age, job position, etc.).

- After attending an organizationally hosted workshop, students, instructors, and staff are able to: a) articulate awareness of some of their own potential biases that are related to age, gender, ethnicity, etc.; b) state how these biases might be affecting their interactions with others; and c) identify concrete steps that they are taking to transform and continually minimize these biases.

Level 2

The organization provides training to learners and instructors on developing teaching/learning strategies that facilitate learners' direct engagement with diverse people from underrepresented and marginalized populations. The organization intentionally fosters a culture where learners and instructors assist one another in exploring how their own biases can affect their perceptions and actions, particularly as these biases relate to underrepresented and marginalized communities.

At this level, there are two primary considerations. The first extends Level 1 when the organization supports learners and instructors in developing activities that more directly engage with marginalized and under-resourced communities. Here, the organization should help to ensure that these activities are more immersive and direct rather than simple exposure as it is with Level 1. For the second consideration, the work on identifying and transforming biases also expands at this level when the organization now helps learners and instructors work together on these areas. While it might at first appear that multicultural engagement from the previous guideline includes transformative reflections on biases, this is not always the case. An organization at this level therefore provides training and support staff, students, and faculty to more explicitly and directly address these kinds of personal reflections in collaborative ways. Such support should help to scaffold them in working together towards a deeper awareness of their own biases and how these might be affecting their perceptions of and engagement with diverse people and communities. The organization should therefore have clear evidence of these kinds of collaborative activities across courses and programs, particularly as they relate to under-resourced and marginalized populations.

As God is able to raise awareness of the oppressive systems and structures that marginalized populations are subjected to in the previous level, the hope is that students, faculty, and staff will then become more responsive to God's continual invitations to engage more directly with these communities at this level. Such engagement needs to be more immersive as God works with the organization to develop the necessary social and emotional connections that will be needed for Level 3. In addition, real-world contact with diverse others can often bring more awareness of one's own deep-seated biases, fears, and stereotypes. As a result, the organization should provide the necessary resources and support systems for its constituents to help one another work through these issues in transformative ways. While a collaborative environment is normally a Level 3 attribute, for this guideline it is a necessary foundation for the work that God will be laboring to enact at the next highest level.

Examples of this might include:

- The organization supports student organizations that help to facilitate events and discussions on sexism, racism, etc.
- As a result of organizational support, instructors and students are observed completing a service-learning project together that requires them to connect with local and global peers from marginalized backgrounds.

- Staff are observed supporting study groups that regularly discuss how course content relates to under-resourced and marginalized communities.
- The organization hosts workshops that help staff, students, and faculty to learn how to help others become more aware of their own biases, particularly as these relate to marginalized and under-resourced populations.

Level 3

The organization assists learners and instructors in pursuing learning objectives by engaging with activities that facilitate their development of advanced intercultural and civic engagement competencies, particularly with underrepresented and marginalized communities. The organization provides opportunities and support for learners and instructors to proactively work for equity and justice in solidarity with underrepresented and marginalized communities.

Level 3 continues with both of the considerations from Level 2. The organization will be found intentionally facilitating interactions among students, faculty, and staff with other people/communities in ways that deepen their ability to work with diverse cultures. Again, a central emphasis is given to marginalized and under-resourced populations as learners, instructors, and staff learn how core concepts/skills directly relate and can be applied to working for change in solidarity with these communities. As they engage in this work, attention should be given to developing their civic engagement and intercultural competency KSAs at higher levels as they relate to under-resourced and marginalized communities. Numerous rubrics are available online that outline these KSAs and the organization should identify and integrate the most appropriate ones for their institution. Overall, one of the primary goals is to help equip and empower faculty, staff, and students to better able to work for positive change with underrepresented and marginalized communities.

Most people would agree that life on this planet is less than ideal. Western Christianity has a strong history of turning to prayer in response to many of the debilitating conditions that people are enslaved by around the world as well as locally in our own communities. This level, however, aligns with a different tradition within Christianity and that is the one that proactively works for tangible change.[9] Here, it can be asserted that God invites students, staff, and instructors to be fully engaged in the work bringing about social, political, and/or economic transformation for marginalized communities. Working in full solidarity with, and not for, these populations, the organization can help its constituents fully leverage the growth experienced at levels 1 and 2 in powerful ways. By reaching these higher levels of civic engagement and intercultural competency, staff, learners, and faculty can work collaboratively with underserved communities towards the kinds of positive and systemic changes that God has long

---

9. For example, see Foster, *Streams of Living Water*, ch. 5.

planned for and unceasingly worked to bring about. As a result, organizational leaders are called to provide the training, resources, and support needed for this work and help ensure that such engagement tightly aligns with institutional missions and learning outcomes and vice versa.

Examples of this might include:

- The organization supports student organizations that work with lower income community members to complete neighborhood improvement projects.
- The organization regularly hosts guest speakers on topics related to working for justice and equity in solidarity with marginalized communities.
- There is evidence of the organization adopting civic engagement and/or intercultural competency standards to help guide the development of the courses/programs.
- The organization works with departments to assess students, faculty, and staff competencies in civic engagement and/or intercultural competency.

PROFESSIONAL DEVELOPMENT, LEADERSHIP, AND EVIDENCE-BASED PRACTICE GUIDELINES

It should be clear throughout these administrative guidelines that staff will be providing a great deal of professional development to teachers and students alike. However, as one might guess based on the limited time and resources that administrative personnel have, it is unlikely that a single school will be able to provide all of these training, resources, and support to both students and faculty. As a result, the administration at every school needs to encourage them to not only engage external trainings and support but to also become a more integral part of these educational improvement initiatives. In addition, administration should also support and demonstrate evidence-based approaches to education. In doing so, they will be actualizing God's latent transformative power that exists within the school. When students, staff, and faculty democratically join together to improve the educational systems of which they are a part, such changes are bound to occur.

Guideline #1—Professional Development

Organization supports learners and instructors in their professional development opportunities related to improving discipline-specific and/or educational competencies (Core Guideline).

The craft of any discipline is a lifelong pursuit, one that can be continually improved upon. Whether one is in education, healthcare, management, sciences, or law, there is always more that can be learned and developed. As a result, what is being taught in courses is only a small foundational fraction of what can be known for each field of study. This is particularly true in education. Educational research meta-analyses have found that professional development for instructors can have a tremendous impact on student achievement as the instructor's teaching competencies improve.[10] In order to help foster ongoing growth, then, instructors and learners need to be involved in professional development opportunities. These opportunities should help them identify and become more competent in the KSAs that are integral to their specific discipline. This guideline is therefore intended to help ensure that organizations provide the support that learners and instructors need in order to engage in professional development (PD) in significant ways. At lower levels, the organization will help them more simply participate in PD sessions, whereas at the higher levels, the organization will empower learners and instructors to develop these sessions. Overall, the organization should be found continually and proactively investing in learners' and instructors' deeper, broader, and more expert levels of proficiency in their discipline-specific crafts.

Up until now, these organizational tier guidelines have primarily focused on efforts to improve student learning. For this guideline, while this work continues, it now includes directly helping instructors to become students in their own ongoing development as an educator. For learners and faculty, we can assert that God is everstriving to help them grow in the vocational craft into which they have been called. As mentioned above, each field of study and practice is as rich and expansive as God's infinite life, ones in which each person can continue to grow and develop in across their entire career. Organizations are therefore invited to discern where and how they can provide opportunities and support for students, faculty, and staff to engage in professional development in their discipline-specific and educational crafts via co-curricular and other opportunities. In doing so, the organization will be responding to God's efforts to foster professional proficiency within the community.

Level 1

The organization provides support for learners and instructors to engage in structured individual and/or group PD opportunities that help them stay current with essential KSAs in their discipline-specific and/or educational role(s).

At this level, the organization will be found helping learners and instructors participate in PD opportunities that are readily available to them. These might include hosting lunch-and-learns and guest speakers, offering funds for students and faculty to attend regional trainings in their discipline, or providing access to online webinars on various discipline-specific topics. These PD offerings should help learners and instructors stay current in their own field of study and/or help them better understand how to more effectively engage with their discipline's KSAs.

---

10. Hattie, *Visible Learning*, 109–13, 19–21.

Foundationally, the organization should spiritually discern what kinds of PD opportunities their constituents might need at the moment to help them continue to grow in their areas. For students, God might be wanting them to learn about new innovations in a given discipline that have been researched and developed, or that are being used by organizations in the field. Here, God can be found to be moving not only within the curriculum, but also beyond it to help students more holistically and comprehensively develop in each area of their studies. For instructors, there may be discipline-specific pedagogies through which God is seeking to move that can genuinely improve the quality of their classes. The organization is therefore called to continually assess and discern how God is laboring to help instructors continue to grow. At this foundational level, these PD opportunities are spiritually discerned by the organization and offered to staff, students, and faculty.

Examples of this might include:

- The organization hosts lunch-and-learns and guest speakers on how to improve teaching/learning in specific disciplines.
- Departments offer funds for students and faculty to attend regional trainings in their discipline.
- The organization provides access to online webinars and databases on various discipline-specific topics.
- Staff offer book studies and discussion groups that are relevant to specific fields of study.

Level 2

The organization aids learners and instructors in using personal reflections and feedback from one another, peers, and mentors to identify areas of ongoing PD and participate in learning experiences that address these identified areas of improvement.

This level continues the previous one with the organization helping learners and instructors to continually engage with PD. However, rather than encouraging them to attend PD events as they become available, the organization works with learners and instructors to be more intentional with assessing their current competencies and identifying areas where they need improvement. To help with this, the organization will ensure that learners and instructors have access to various sources and support systems. Based upon intentional self and peer evaluations, the organization will then empower learners and instructors to seek out PD opportunities that directly address these areas—ones that continue to improve noted strengths and/or help with areas of improvement that they have identified. In essence, the organization is aiding them in developing the self-regulated learning skills that they will need to help them continually improve across the whole of their careers. As a result, increased proficiencies in their disciplines should be a measurable outcome of these efforts over the long-term.

At the foundational level (Level 1), organizational leaders took primary responsibility to spiritually discern PD offerings for the community. While they might have engaged in this discernment with learners and faculty, the primary focus was on general PD for members-at-large. At this level, however, the discernment is now conducted on a more individual basis as each student, staff, and instructor is invited to determine which PD offerings might be most appropriate for themselves. Such discernment should be founded on assessments of what their current strengths as well as areas for improvement are. Overall, the organization will essentially be helping each person discern which PD offerings God is inviting them to engage in that will help them take the next step in their ongoing growth as a professional. For students, these PD offerings should closely align with their courses of study, while for instructors they should address both their chosen field(s) of study/practice as well as their educational competencies in these fields. At this level, the organization therefore begins to blossom into a fuller version of what a learning organization is as God works with and through these PD efforts to improve professional proficiencies for the whole of the organization.

Examples of this might include:

- As part of a workshop hosted by the organization, instructors are observed reviewing student course evaluations and then identifying PD opportunities to help them to address noted areas.
- Staff are observed meeting with learners to help them better understand what is going well and what might be improved in their discipline-specific KSAs and then identify PD events that help them improve in these areas.
- The organization provides funds for students to attend a workshop that helps them to evaluate one or more of their discipline-specific competencies and then improve in these areas.
- The organization provides training to instructors and/or students on how to use evidence-based guidelines to self-assess their discipline-specific KSAs and then identify resources that will help them to address noted areas for improvement.

Level 3

In addition to Level 2, the organization helps learners and instructors collaborate with one another and/or peers to collectively create, reflect upon, analyze, and improve professional development opportunities that address Levels 1 and/or 2.

While this level continues to build upon the previous one, it is also characteristically different. Here, the organization will be found not only helping learners and instructors engage in relevant PD opportunities, they will also help them to develop these. Following Level 3 for many other guidelines, these development efforts should be collaborative in nature as the organization encourages faculty, students, and staff to work together to design, implement, and evaluate PD offerings. These PD efforts might occur at the institution or with outside organizations that they are a part of. The PD events that the organization supports them in creating should aid others in their own ongoing journey to continually improve in discipline-specific competencies.

At this highest level, the realities of God's kin-dom in becoming a fully active learning organism start to emerge. No longer is it only organizational leaders and staff that are driving the PD opportunities, but now students and faculty are intimately involved in God's developmental processes. Following the democratic culture of Level 3 for many other guidelines, at this level God can be asserted to work to help students, staff, and faculty to collaboratively discern the PD offerings and opportunities that are currently needed at the school. As part of this communal discernment, participants may be called to help develop and/or modify these PD offerings. Building upon Level 2, this discernment needs to be based upon clear assessments that have been gathered from the community. Overall, then, educational systems at this level are becoming fuller manifestations of God's collaborative, responsive, and continually developing organisms of professional proficiency.

Examples of this might include:

- The organization supports PD initiatives where students, faculty, and/or staff actively work together to develop PD events for the campus.
- The organization provides the support that instructors and students need in order to be active participants in discipline-specific organizations where they work with peers to deliver workshops and resources that help colleagues improve their proficiencies.
- The organization empowers interdepartmental student retention efforts on campus that identify best practices and help instructors, students, and staff align their courses and programs with these practices.
- The organization helps its constituency collaborate with peers to offer training sessions on discipline-specific KSAs.

Guideline #2—Educational Leadership

Organization empowers learners and instructors to actively participate in leadership roles and responsibilities that improve the institution's education and culture.

As may be seen by these guidelines, the institution's culture greatly influences the quality of education. Level 3 for most guidelines is highly collaborative in nature, and educational research studies are finding that the more positive and interactive a school is, the higher the student achievement.[11] This culture is determined by the roles and responsibilities that students, faculty, and staff have. As a result, it is imperative that each individual play an active part in helping continually shape and guide the organization's actions and attitudes. This means that the organization should be found empowering instructors, learners, and staff to take on leadership roles at their institution.

At lower levels, this empowerment will entail encouraging them to participate in positive and collaborative initiatives. At higher levels, there will be evidence of the organization providing opportunities and support for instructors and learners to lead quality improvement projects, actively mentor others, etc. The basic premise here is that the more committed to quality learning and development an organization's members are as a whole, the better the education will be within its classes/programs.

Building upon the theology of the school becoming a living and spiritual organism, this guideline is intended to encourage each person in the organization to be intentional and active expressions of God's life. By continually discerning where and how each student, instructor, and staff member can be intimately involved in the life of the school, they will essentially be responding to God's invitations to be the active part of the organization that God needs each person to be. Just as a puzzle is not complete until each piece joins with the others, so too does each educational system need every person to fit harmoniously in with the community.

Organizational servant leaders are therefore tasked with working to nurture these kinds of highly engaged cultures. In doing so, they will be working with God to not only empower each person to be a leader, but also to unify and actualize the fuller potentials that God has been laboring to cultivate in everyone. Once these latent potentials are set in motion in well-coordinated and planned ways, the school will continue to flourish as a greater communal manifestation of God's transformative life in our world.

Level 1

The organization actively empowers learners and instructors to participate in schoolwide efforts to implement a shared vision and to actively contribute to a supportive and collaborative institutional culture.

At this level, the organization will take concrete steps to ensure that students, faculty, and staff are aware of initiatives at their school that relate to supporting its vision and mission. The organization will support them in serving on standing committees, being able to attend events related to the organization's mission and helping them

---

11. Hattie, *Visible Learning*, 80.

more intentionally develop collegial friendships with one another. Here, the organization will empower learners, instructors, and staff to take an active part of already existing institutional initiatives. Overall, the organization should be found helping them positively support the institution's culture and working to develop collaborative relationships with one another.

At this foundational level, the organization's members are at the beginning stages of becoming a more proactive and transforming part of the community. In essence, God can be asserted to be prompting each member into more participatory roles in the life of the institution. Organizational leaders must therefore respond by helping its constituents heed and respond to these holy promptings. By working to increase accessibility of committees and events, the organization will be working to remove some of the barriers that hinder people from acting on God's invitations to be more involved in the life of the school. Once initiated, however, the momentum of God's empowering life will begin to increase as students, staff, and faculty participate in the organization.

Examples of this might include:

- Administration provides the necessary support so that learners and instructors can actively serve on and positively contribute to committee work.
- The organization hosts events related to the institution's mission.
- There is evidence of the organization hosting events where students, faculty, and staff can intentionally develop collegial friendships with one another.
- The organization provides workshops that help learners, staff, and instructors articulate the organization's vision and mission and then intentionally work to implement this vision in their work.

Level 2

The organization provides opportunities for learners and instructors to engage in institutional decision-making processes with one another to identify common goals, develop strategies for pursuing these goals, and evaluate progress towards them. The organization supports learners and instructors in actively and consistently contributing to the growth of others through mentoring, feedback, and sharing of practice.

Level 2 builds upon Level 1 when the organization is found empowering staff, students, and instructors to participate in initiatives that work to achieve specific goals at the school. At Level 1, the organization will help staff, faculty, and students simply take part in these as a participant. At this level, however, the organization will provide the training, resources, and support they need to be an integral part of the core planning and implementation teams that are leading these projects. In addition, the organization will also be found at this level developing mentoring opportunities for students, staff, and faculty. Such mentoring can happen formally via structured programs or informally as the organization generally encourages its members to work more closely with one another. Overall, this level is characterized by the organization empowering its constituency to take on roles where they help lead organizational projects as well as more proactively mentor one another.

In helping its members move beyond mere participation to become a more integral part of completing projects, the organization will theologically be enacting God's transforming energies with and through each person. Every individual has unique gifts that God has been striving to nurture across their lifespan, and organizational leaders are tasked at this level with helping each person use these spiritual gifts to complete projects that the organization has identified and assigned. In alignment with the democratic/collaborative theologies articulated thus far in this book, this level represents a significant shift towards these ends as the leadership becomes more distributed throughout the organization. As part of this distributed leadership, the organization will proactively work at this level to encourage and support mutual mentoring as described above. Spiritually speaking, such relationships are essentially "God supporting God's work" as people help one another to complete the projects that have been discerned. Overall, this level is therefore one of God's transformative life growing in reach and in power as more and more people respond to the call to take on leadership roles in the school in mutually supportive ways.

Examples of this might include:

- The organization provides the release time and support that instructors, staff, and learners need in order to take on active roles on a task force that is leading a curriculum rewriting effort.

- The organization empowers learners to proactively work with faculty and staff at their school to support initiatives that are being led by discipline-specific organizations.

- There is clear evidence of the administration successfully recruiting learners, instructors, and staff to actively contribute to a committee that is assessing accreditation-related improvements.

- Organizational staff develop structured peer mentoring programs for students, faculty, and staff.

Level 3

The organization intentionally mentors learners and instructors as leaders in identifying and advocating for continuous evaluation and improvement of the institution's vision, mission, and goals that support quality learning and development. The organization empowers learners and instructors to actively mentor and motivate one another to participate in institutional leadership roles.

Extending the work of the previous level, an organization at Level 3 will be found empowering staff, students, and faculty to take a more proactive role in identifying and initiating institutional change projects. At Level 2, the organization helped to ensure that they were active participants on already existing leadership teams that designed and carried out these kinds of projects. At this level, however, there will be strong evidence of the organization providing the mentoring and support that learners, instructors, and staff need to take the initiative to identify opportunities for institutional improvement that are intended to increase student achievement. An organization at this level will also be found working to equip students, faculty, and staff to be better able to help others become more actively involved in leadership roles at their school. Overall, the organization will work so that its constituency is more committed to continuous improvement of the institution, as evidenced by this kind of mentoring, as well as by the initiatives that the organization helps them take a lead role in launching.

Nelson Mandela is often quoted as saying, "Our deepest fear is not that we are inadequate. Our deepest fear is that we are powerful beyond measure."[12] When the organization provides staff, students, and faculty with the spiritual resources, formation, and support they need to be able to discern where and how God is laboring for change in the school, look out! Imagine each person in the institution being a fully confident and competent change agent that is focused on improving the life of the school in well-coordinated ways. Such a community truly is a living and powerful expression of God's world-changing life as God actualizes and mobilizes the latent spiritual potentials of each member of the community.

Level 3 educational systems are therefore highly engaged and dynamic—not only within the school itself, but also in the surrounding community as its members proactively discern and carry out projects of genuine transformation. These organizations, carefully coordinated by its leaders, also work to continually mentor and empower each person towards these kinds of change agent roles. Just as nuclear fission processes unleash the inherent power with an atom, so too do organizational leaders at this level respond to God's guidance in helping to unleash the implicit passions and gifts of each person, thereby uncapping a holy and communal power that is truly beyond measure.

Examples of this might include:

- Administration is observed supporting an instructor who is working to start quality improvement projects.
- The organization hosts training for staff so that they are able to conduct their own asset-needs or SWOT analyses to identify areas for growth at the school.
- Staff provide mentoring to students on how to bring groups together to identify challenges and brainstorm solutions at the school.

12. As quoted in Williamson, *A Return to Love,* 190.

- The organization provides funding to send faculty, students, and/or staff to a workshop on leadership development.

Guideline #3—Evidence-Based Practice

Organization supports learners and instructors in conducting evidence-based practice and/or scholarly projects that improve discipline-specific competencies and/or quality education (Core Guideline).

In any field of study, improvements often come incrementally via an integrated combination of learning, action, and reflection. In other words, we learn about our discipline, we try what we learn, and then we can reflect on how things are going. This basic cycle is the foundation of evidence-based practice, which should be applied to education just as it should to every field. This guideline is therefore intended to encourage organizations to provide the resources, training, and support that learners and instructors need to apply these kinds of approaches to their discipline-specific and/or educational crafts. The organization should help learners and instructors establish habits of continually learning how to engage in their disciplines better, apply what they are learning, and then gather data that helps them identify areas of strength as well as improvement. Such endeavors can be done informally as they engage in these activities, or more formally via scholarly projects where they follow structured research methods. At lower levels, the organization will be found working with learners and instructors to individually improve their own courses/competencies, whereas at higher levels they will help them to collaborate with others to have a wider impact on the institutions and/or their disciplines more broadly. Overall, the organization should help learners and instructors to intentionally and continually use evidence/data to help improve in their disciplines.

One of the core theological claims of these guidelines has been that evidence-based findings coupled with theological reflections rooted in one's tradition can help uncover where and how God is laboring to act in our educational systems. This guideline therefore encourages instructors to engage in these kinds of evidence-based spiritual discernment processes as they continually strive to partner with God's educational life ever more fully. This guideline also invites the organization to equally work with students to use similar processes in the discipline-specific areas that they are currently focusing on. In doing so, learners, staff, and instructors will be developing the kind of God-centered practices that are at the core of continual quality improvement. The organization is therefore called to provide the support that they need to discern and respond to God in these evidence-based and scholarly pursuits.

Level 1

The organization helps learners and instructors improve their discipline-specific and/or educational practices through evidence-based practice and/or scholarly projects.

At this level, the organization will be found helping learners and instructors establish clear habits of gathering data on their classes, or course-related competencies, and then continually working to improve the quality and effectiveness of these classes/competencies based upon the data that they have gathered. The essential component of this level is that the organization will help learners and instructors intentionally gather data that will help them better assess and subsequently improve their discipline-specific or educational competencies. There should therefore be clear evidence of the organization working with them to identify the appropriate data to gather, as well as how they can use this data to guide incremental improvements.

Without clear data to help inform one's spiritual discernment, it can be difficult to know where and how God has been acting. As a result, the organization at this foundational level is invited to help learners and faculty further develop their habits of data gathering so that their discernment processes can be more evidence-based. Theologically, one of the primary aims is for students and instructors to have the information they need to be able to more clearly identify God's movements within and among them as these relate to their educational and/or discipline-specific craft(s). Using this data in these spiritually discerning ways, the organization then aids faculty and students in determining where and how God is calling them to continue to improve.

Examples of this might include:

- After attending a training session, instructors are found using formal and informal assessments of their students to help evaluate the impact of specific class activities.
- Staff work with learners to conduct formal evidence-based practice (EBP) research projects that provide insights into what they are doing well (or not) in relation to their discipline-specific KSAs.
- The organization provides funding for instructors to attend a conference on how to gather and use data to guide incremental improvements in one or more of their courses.
- The organization hosts events where learners are observed meeting with instructors, mentors, and peers to help them better understand how they are doing and what they might do differently in their discipline.

Level 2

The organization empowers learners and instructors to collaborate with one another, and colleagues to jointly conduct EBP and/or scholarly projects that improve instructional and/or discipline-specific practices for themselves and/or others.

This level builds upon the previous one where the organization empowers learners and instructors to team up with others to work towards evidence-based improvements. As with the previous level, these efforts can be supporting more informal collaborations where they use data to improve one or more of their courses or discipline-specific competencies. Or the organization can provide the necessary support needed to help learners and instructors work together to complete Scholarship of Teaching and Learning (SoTL) projects that provide insights into theory and/or practice. The organization at this level will therefore be found helping learners and instructors to actively partner with one another to complete evidence-based practice and/or scholarly projects that are intended to improve the quality of discipline-specific and/or education practice.

Following the more collaborative/democratic approaches to education, this level encourages organizational leaders to help students, staff, and instructors cooperatively engage in evidence-based spiritual discernment processes. By working together to complete these kinds of scholarly and EBPs, they will be collectively partnering with God's continually efforts to improve educational and/or discipline-specific practices. The organization will therefore embrace these kinds of discernment processes as they identify opportunities, support, and projects that students and instructors can work together on. In doing so, the organization will be helping to cultivate a culture of collaborative evidence-based improvements in their school.

Examples of this might include:

- Faculty development staff help instructors form a community of practice that is focused on continually reflecting on and improving one another's classes.
- Staff support learners as they work with their peers to study discipline-specific practices that are more effective.
- Administration creates an institutional committee that gathers and uses data to improve persistence and completion rates in difficult classes.
- The organization provides resources to form mentoring programs where instructors and/or learners meet regularly with a mentor to observe their abilities and brainstorm possible improvements in their practice.

Level 3

The organization supports learners and instructors in working collaboratively to conduct EBP and/or scholarly projects that have an impact on one's educational and/or discipline-specific theories, practices, and/or policies more broadly. The organization provides the resources and support that learners and instructors need in order to disseminate the results of these projects via presentations and/or publications.

Level 3 further extends the work of the two previous levels. There should still be strong evidence of the organization supporting learners and instructors collaborating with others to engage in EBP and/or scholarly projects that are intended to improve the quality of theory/practice. At this level, however, there will be two significant additions. First, the organization will empower learners and instructors to work on projects that have a broader impact in their field(s) of study. An example of this would be providing the necessary resources that learners and/or instructors need to help develop study strategies that are being used across their discipline in an effort to improve practice. Second, the organization will then help learners and instructors widely disseminate the results of these projects with colleagues/peers at their institution and beyond. At this higher level, the organization will help learners and instructors maximize the impact of their evidence-based and/or scholarly projects.

Throughout these guidelines, there has been a repeated emphasis on the educational system having a broader impact in the world. This level further expands this focus as the organization empowers its students, faculty, and staff to engage with evidence-based and/or scholarly projects that impact educational and/or discipline-specific theories or practices. Due to the more significant impact of these projects, the organization will therefore provide the support that is needed for dissemination purposes so that others benefit from this work. In doing so, the organization will be responding to God's unending efforts to transform our world in wider ways. The organization is therefore invited at this level to help its constituents become a more intimate part of God's broader transforming processes.

Examples of this might include:

- The organization supports a research team that is studying the teaching strategies that are being used across multiple classes in their discipline in an effort to help the field more effectively teach their subject.

- The organization provides the funding that a learner needs to attend a discipline-specific conference and present the results of an EBP that they completed with colleagues.

- There is clear evidence of the organization empowering instructors to be active participants on discipline-specific organizational committees that review and revise educational accreditation policies and standards based on assessment data.

- Organizational staff provide support to faculty and students to collaborate and draw on evidenced-based literature to develop revised theories and/or strategies that they share with others via presentations and/or publications.

CLOSING REFLECTIONS

As theistic educators, these guidelines can help us better partner with a God, as it states in Acts 17:28, in whom "we live and move and have our being." It is an image and experience of God that is not far away and distant from our school systems, but rather at the very heart and soul of them in the training, resources, and support that administration provides to both teachers and students. Not only does God have very clear directions for administrators to head towards, according to these guidelines, but God also is with them every step, providing detailed and constructive guidance all along the way.

These guidelines, upon reflection, thrust us deeply into one of the many wonderfully mysterious aspects of God's essence: an infinite God who is fully present within and to the infinitesimal workings of our educational systems. While God clearly has all of creation to work with, God's infinite essence allows God to be fully present in each infinitesimal part of this creation. For school administrators, this means that God is ever-laboring to work through them to develop the kinds of teaching and learning environments that are depicted in these pages. When they do, then we should expect our educational systems not only to be deeply transformative for students but also for teachers, staff, and the communities of which they are a part.

4

Discerning Direction
Applying the Guidelines

THIS CHAPTER CONTAINS A modified report of an actual site visit that was conducted for a college using the guidelines for each of the three tiers from the previous chapters. The purpose of this visit was to use the guidelines to conduct a full assessment of the educational system and then identify its significant strengths as well as recommendations for possible improvements. The following is the report that was submitted to the organization with two modifications. First, in an effort to maintain confidentiality, all information that might identify this school has been removed or changed. Second, the theological reflections have been added to help demonstrate how theistic views and approaches might be used to guide the discernment of how to improve educational systems. Overall, this real-world example is intended to provide further insights into how the guidelines at all three tiers might be utilized to improve the quality of education in our schools.

EXECUTIVE SUMMARY

The following is an overall summary of the full report below, in regard to teaching and learning at the school. Appendix D through Appendix F contain detailed guidelines that were used to guide the collection and assessment of data during the site visit. There are three tiers and sets of guidelines that were used to assess the school: Administration, Instructors, and Students. Based upon the data that was collected for each tier, and their corresponding assessments, numerous strengths and recommendations were identified. The full lists of these strengths and recommendations are contained in the appendices. From these more extensive lists, a smaller set of significant strengths and primary recommendations were extracted for each tier and are presented in the narrative below. Theologically, the strengths are the areas that God has been identified as working most effectively through. The recommendation areas, on the other hand, may be asserted to be areas where God is wanting work with the school to improve in the near-term.

Given the many noted strengths in the full report below, there are at least three areas that the school can be noted as addressing in outstanding ways:

- *Program Alignment of Objectives, Activities, and Assessments*—Occurring across multiple levels, from the accreditation standards to lesson plans as well as being seen in both what students are learning and how they are learning it.

- *Real-world and Community-Based Projects*—These projects have the potential to provide meaningful, relevant, and active learning experiences for students and they appear to align with one of the school's missions to have a positive impact on the local community.

- *College's Culture*—The school was experienced to be respectful, highly disciplined, and positive, making for an environment that can more effectively support student learning and development.

The following are the primary recommendations that were either consistently found across all three tiers or they are of such significance (e.g., a high impact factor) that they need to be addressed. For more detail on each of these areas, see the full report below.

- *Training on Course Development Methods*—Instructors should be provided with additional training and support on how to develop their lesson plans and on how to develop active teaching strategies in particular.

- *Use of Regular Formative Assessments*—Faculty could be provided with training and support in their theory classes as well as in community-based settings on the development of formative assessments that will help them and their students identify current strengths and gaps in students' KSAs, as well as on how to adjust their lessons based upon this assessment data.

- *Training on Multiple Learning Theories*—It is recommended that instructors receive regular training on a wide array of learning theories as well as support in using these theories to guide the development of their courses.

- *Developing Regular Faculty Training and Small Support Groups*—All faculty could be offered PD opportunities on a regular basis. Furthermore, the school is encouraged to expand support for faculty by creating small support groups on general topics related to teaching and learning as well as to help foster a culture of peer mentoring.

- *Integrate Theory and Community-based Portions of the Curriculum*—We recommend that the theory classes be redistributed through the academic year, intermixed with community-based portions, so that there is a closer integration of theory and practice.

Given these recommendations, the following are limitations that need to be taken into consideration:

- *Review of Community-based Curriculum*—These recommendations are based primarily on observations and data from the theory classes. Knowing that the bulk of the curriculum is centered on community-based involvement, some of these recommendations may not apply to these practical portions of the program, and additional ones might be identified if we had conducted a more extensive review of the community-based curriculum.

- *Limited Interactions with Students*—Our schedule was such that we did not have very many opportunities to interact with students in more in-depth ways. These recommendations should therefore be held as being tentative pending more time with students.

- *Time Limitations*—We note that staff and faculty time are an increasingly scarce resource, given the prep time as well as the growing number of seats and programs at the school. As a result, time for additional training and support may be very limited.

In light of these limitations, we do not recommend any significant changes to the recommendations above. However, these recommendations should be held as very tentative, pending a more extensive review of the practical portions of the curriculum. In addition, administration will need to assess any time limitations that faculty have in participating in and/or implementing these recommendations. This concludes the *Executive Summary* and what follows is the narrative of the full report that was submitted to the college.

SIGNIFICANT STRENGTHS

During our time on campus and in the community with students, faculty, and staff, we repeatedly noted several strengths. These strengths are attributes of strong educational systems as identified by the guidelines for each tier. The following are the strengths that were specifically noted for each tier. Theologically, these strengths are indicative of where the college is more fully responsive to God's educational movements as identified by the guidelines.

Administration

For *Administration*, the following are the significant strengths that were noted:

- Administrative staff ensuring curriculum alignment and their planning of topics is an outstanding asset for the institution. This relieves faculty of these responsibilities and empowers them to focus more directly on their classes.

- Administration's support of real-world simulations and learning experiences is perhaps the greatest strength to be noted here. Staff were observed working very hard to make these opportunities available to students and the impact of them was readily apparent.

- Another tremendous asset of the college is the administration's development of a highly structured, well-disciplined, and deeply respectful culture among staff, faculty, and students. Throughout our stay, this very welcoming and positive environment was palpable.

- Allowing our team the privilege and opportunity to give a workshop on active teaching strategies is a strength that we hope will continue. Faculty appeared to be very receptive of the content that we worked with them on and we were told that some of them are excited to try some of these strategies out in their own classes.

- In our conversations with faculty, staff, and administration, it was very obvious that many knew students in very personal ways, understanding the communities and families that some students come from. This level of interpersonal relationships is a tremendous asset that can be leveraged to further strengthen the quality of education at the college.

- A great strength is the ongoing professional development (PD) that faculty and staff are offered when they are sent to conferences and government-sponsored workshops.

- Administrative oversight of faculty's lesson planning and teaching is another tremendous asset of the institution. It appears that faculty regularly receive detailed and constructive feedback on their teaching practices.

Instructors

For *Instructors*, the following are the significant strengths that were noted:

- Direct alignment from accreditation standards to diploma programs and courses to lesson plans is an outstanding feature of this program.

- Listing detailed objectives for each lesson plan is another significant strength that was repeatedly observed.

- The presentations that students gave to our team, the skit that we watched in a local school, and the student's community report that was provided to us were outstanding examples of assessment methods.

- The real-world projects that students are conducting in groups as well as on their own in community settings is perhaps the most powerful part of this college.

These projects integrate many of the recommendations of these guidelines and the college is encouraged to expand these and other similar strategies.

- The cultural expectations of students being attentive, disciplined, and hardworking is another tremendous strength of the college. Students were observed to be very respectful and kind throughout our visit.
- Alignment among objectives, activities, and assessments is a noted strength of the college's courses. The lesson plans showed clear and direct alignment among these elements.
- Students' engagement with local communities to address real-world issues is another tremendous strength of the college.
- Instructors having the opportunity to attend workshops is a strength of the college's PD opportunities.

Students

For *Students*, the following are the significant strengths that were noted:
- Students stated that they would like more resources and readings to help them with their studies. This intrinsic motivation is a tremendous asset to students' learning journey as well as the institution as a whole.
- Students' active participation in community-based projects is a tremendous asset for students. Throughout our time, students appeared to be fully engaged in the active real-world experiences that we observed.
- One of the great strengths at the college is the highly disciplined, respectful, and hard-working culture that is present.
- Students participating in some active teaching strategies in their theory and community-based courses is an outstanding asset of this program.
- Working directly with lower SES and rural communities is a great strength for students.
- The safe training workshops that were offered are another tremendous asset of the college.
- The women's empowerment club is a wonderful outreach program that the college has, and it could be used to further enhance students' educational opportunities.

Common Themes of Significant Strengths

Given these many noted strengths, overall there are at least three areas that the school can be noted as addressing in outstanding ways. These three categories are the strengths that were identified across all three tiers above and can be viewed as being evidence of God's successful work across the college:

- Program Alignment
- Real-world and Community-Based Projects
- College's Culture

The school's staff have clearly worked very hard to ensure that their curriculum aligns with accreditation standards at many levels. Lesson plans for each theory class clearly stated the objectives for the lesson as well as the activities and assessments that would be used in pursuit of these. A review of samples of final exams revealed that the teaching strategies that were being used in the theory classes align very closely with the types of questions that students will be expected to answer on these exams. The majority of the questions on these exams were focused on assessing students' factual knowledge base and the classes that we attended used strategies that helped students to begin to memorize these facts. The alignment that we observed was therefore not only for the concepts and skills (product) that were being taught, but also with how students were being taught (process). Such alignment was observed at each of the three tiers above and is an outstanding aspect of the college's programs. Theologically, such alignment can be asserted to be reflective of God's efforts to ensure well-coordinated and highly effectively programs. By responding to these holy invitations, the college is therefore providing their students with greater opportunities for success on the standardized exams.

Another great strength that was consistently observed across all three tiers were the real-world and community-based projects that students are required to complete as part of their programs. These projects can help students actively engage with theory class content in ways that are more relevant and meaningful for them as they create and deliver models and presentations. The skits that we observed third-year students present to school youth in a local community was an outstanding demonstration of their abilities to identify current issues in this community and then provide education in a narrative form. The KSAs that are required of students to complete such projects align very well with what they will need as professionals in community-based settings. In addition, projects such as these skits are very much in-line with the college's mission to have a positive impact in the local community. Through them, God is able to expand the impact of God's work with and through the educational system as students continue to work for change in the community. As a result, these community-based real-world projects are a tremendous asset of the school's programs.

A third category that emerged from all three tiers was the college's overall culture. Throughout our stay, we regularly observed behaviors of positive respect and students being well-disciplined and attentive. In theory classes, students followed along with lectures verbally finishing instructors' statements when they knew the information that was being presented. Students, faculty, and staff were also observed regularly greeting one another with "Good day, madam/sir." Throughout our time, we witnessed students, faculty, and staff smiling, laughing, and interacting with one another in positive ways. This combination of positivity, discipline, and respect can be a powerful cultural combination out of which deep learning can emerge more completely. This community's culture was therefore experienced to be manifesting of God's love, respect, and connections. We therefore note this learning environment as being a significant strength of the college.

PRIMARY RECOMMENDATIONS

As these strengths highlight, the school has a strong foundation for effective learning to occur. As with every educational system, however, there are also areas that the organization can continue to improve on as they continually pursue educational excellence. In essence, spiritually speaking, these recommendations are the directions that God is seeking to work with the school on in the near-term.

A review of the appendices will show that there were also many secondary suggestions that were made. The primary recommendations presented below were chosen from among these suggestions and are considered to be a higher priority than the other secondary suggestions. Prioritization of these recommendations was made based on: 1) Hattie's impact factor (or effect size); and 2) the school's current resources and limitations. In other words, those recommendations that had the highest effect sizes and that also had the highest likelihood of being implemented by the school in the near future were chosen to be the primary recommendations. From a spiritual discernment perspective, these are the recommendations through which God will be able to work most effectively.

The following are the primary recommendations that emerged for each tier based upon the guidelines listed in the appendices. Next to each recommendation, the impact factor (Hattie's effect size) is noted (e.g., 0.69) and is a measure of the potential impact that making changes in the noted area could have on improved student achievement. In other words, the higher the impact factor, the greater the likelihood of increasing student learning.

Administrators

For *Administration*, the following are the primary recommendations that were noted:
- Administration could provide support to instructors on course development methods, particularly how to choose, adapt, implement, and evaluate active teaching strategies (0.69).

- It is recommended that ongoing PD opportunities be expanded to include on-site workshops, faculty peer support groups, reading/discussion groups (on topics directly related to education), etc. (0.65).
- Administrative staff could provide training and support to instructors on developing multiple types of formal and informal assessment methods that can be used to guide the development of their theory courses (0.62).
- Administration could provide training to instructors and students on learning processes and how to support these processes (0.57).
- Administration could provide training to instructors on evidence-based practice (EBP) as it relates to the field of education. These practices rely on assessment data to inform and guide continuous course improvements. Instructors can learn how to use these methods to continually improve the quality of classes on their own initiative (0.56).
- Administration could provide training to instructors on how to more accurately assess students' prior knowledge and experiences and then modify their classes to better match students' strengths and knowledge/skill gaps (0.54).
- In addition to the accreditation standards, which were observed to be at lower levels of critical thinking (e.g., remember, understand, etc.), it is recommended that administration find and/or develop higher order thinking standards and assessments for their students (e.g., apply, analyze, evaluate, synthesize, create, etc.) (0.50).
- Administration could provide training to instructors on how to adapt learning outcomes to more closely meet the background and experiences of current students (0.47).
- Administration could provide training to instructors on how to develop theory classes and community-based experiences that further develop students' intercultural competencies and civic engagement skills (0.44).
- Administration could modify how the theory and practical portions of the curriculum are distributed. For instance, students could be in theory classes three days of the week (perhaps Mondays, Wednesdays, and Fridays) and then in community-based settings for the other days. Integrating these two parts of the curriculum and distributing the theory portions throughout the year should lead to deeper learning and greater long-term retention of core concepts and skills (0.40).

Instructors

For *Instructors*, the following are the primary recommendations that were noted:

- It is recommended that instructors receive training on course development methods. While the topics that instructors are expected to teach in their theory classes are determined by accreditation standards, instructors must still know how to develop class activities for each of these topics (0.69).

- It is recommended that instructors create professional development plans (PDPs) where they identify areas that they would like to develop as a professional educator. These identified areas should focus on the theory and practice of education (0.65).

- For theory classes, it is recommended that instructors conduct regular formative assessments to see what students are understanding and then adjust their instruction based on the results of these assessments (0.62).

- It is recommended that instructors receive more extensive training on learning theories. In particular, neuroscientific, educational psychology, and social-cultural theories that are relevant for the school's cultural context are recommended (0.57).

- It is recommended that instructors learn the basics of evidence-based practice (EBP) as it relates to the field of education. These practices rely on assessment data to inform and guide continuous course improvements (0.56).

- It is recommended that instructors, in their lesson plans, assess and note the specific prior knowledge that current students have in relation to each topic. Pre-assessments can be used to gather this information. The lesson plans should then be adjusted based upon this assessment data (0.54).

- Instructors are encouraged to integrate more interactive group work in their theory classes (0.51).

- Instructors, as well as colleges as a whole, are encouraged to integrate more critical thinking activities and skills. In particular, following Bloom's Learning Taxonomy, programs are encouraged to develop learning outcomes, experiences, and assessments that help students learn how to analyze, apply, evaluate, and synthesize what they are learning—particularly in relation to real-world scenarios in theory classes (0.50).

- Objectives for theory classes could be rewritten as learning outcomes that are actually assessed by the instructor (0.47).

- It is recommended that, wherever possible, learning outcomes be created for the community-based portions of the programs—ones that directly align with the learning outcomes of the theory classes (0.47).

- It is recommended that instructors receive more training on active teaching strategies. Such training should not only include an overview of various active strategies, but also close support and coaching to help instructors implement these in their classes (0.47).

Students

For *Students*, the following are the primary recommendations that were noted:

- Students are encouraged to learn how to assess their learning needs, choose appropriate study strategies, and then be able to assess the effectiveness of these strategies based on their performance in theory and practical components of their program (0.69).
- It is recommended that students seek out and attend additional PD opportunities in their field to help continually expand upon their knowledge and skill base as well as to help further establish habits of life-long learning (0.65).
- Students could use self- and peer-assessment study strategies to help them learn course content and skills more deeply (0.56).
- Students should know how to use the results and feedback from assessments to help guide their study strategies (0.54).
- Learners are encouraged to continually relate what they are learning to their own background and experiences (0.54).
- It is recommended that students form study groups to help one another more deeply learn course material (0.51).
- It is recommended that students continually work to understand why they are learning what they are learning and how these concepts, skills, and attitudes relate to their personal, professional, and civic lives (0.47).
- To the extent that is possible, students could seek out technology-enhanced resources (e.g., apps, websites, software, etc.) that will help them to engage with key concepts and skills more extensively (0.33).

Common Themes of Primary Recommendations

Based on these lists, the following are the primary recommendations that were either consistently found across all three tiers or they are of such significance (e.g., a high impact factor) that they need to be addressed. It may be noted, in the narrative that follows, that these recommendations are primarily focused on the Administration and Instructor Tiers rather than the Student Tier. Some of the items recommended in the Student Tier do need to be addressed; however, we believe that starting with the other two tiers first will result in a greater institutional impact on learning. In addition, our time and interactions with students were very limited, so there is potentially less reliability and validity for this data. As a result, we recommend focusing on the other two tiers first before moving on to the Student Tier recommendations. Our primary recommendations to the college are the following and, theologically, they may be asserted to be the areas of improvement that God is seeking to work with the school on:

- Training on Course Development Methods
- Use of Regular Formative Assessments
- Training on Multiple Learning Theories
- Developing Regular Faculty Training and Small Support Groups
- Integrate Theory and Practical Portions of the Curriculum

We will now discuss each of these recommendations. First, instructors could be provided with additional training and support on how to develop their lesson plans as well as on active teaching strategies in particular. As was noted in the strengths section of this report above, alignment among objectives, activities, and assessments is a great asset of these programs. However, the objectives listed in the lesson plans appeared to be teaching objectives (e.g., "This is what will be covered in this class period . . . ") rather than learning outcomes (e.g., "By the end of this class period, students will be able to demonstrate their ability to do the following . . . "). A primary way to distinguish between these two (teaching objectives versus learning outcomes) is to review the assessments that were administered during the class period. Formal assessments were not delivered in either of the theory classes that we attended, and when the instructor asked at the end of class if students had any questions, students responded with "No ma'am." Such lack of formal or informal assessments are more indicative of teaching objectives than learning outcomes and it is therefore recommended that faculty be trained in course development methods (e.g., backward design, ADDIE, EBP, universal design for learning, etc.), so that they can build their lesson plans and learning experiences in community-based settings around learning outcomes (rather than teaching objectives) that are then regularly assessed. In doing so, the instructor will be able to better gauge the educational progress that God has been able to make with each student. Knowing this information should therefore empower the instructor to partner more closely with God's work in the class.

In addition, during and after our session on active teaching strategies with faculty, several instructors stated that they would like more training and support on using some of these strategies. Quality education relies on an instructor's ability to carefully select the most appropriate strategies for their courses, adapt them to the current students in the class, and then continually evaluate the impact of these approaches. In short, faculty need to know how to more effectively use course development methods. In essence, these may be viewed as spiritual discernment processes that have been adapted for use in educational settings. In using them, then, the instructor should be empowered to identify where and how God is acting educationally, and thereby partner more closely with God's educational endeavors with students. Training and support on these methods is therefore one of our primary recommendations, particularly as they relate to active teaching and learning strategies.

Secondly, and relatedly, faculty could be provided with training and support in their theory classes, as well as in community-based settings on the development of assessments that help them and their students to identify current strengths and gaps in students' KSAs. In our observations of the theory classes, instructors regularly asked students if they understood what was being presented and/or if there were any questions. In response, students indicated that there was no need for the instructor to cover the concepts in greater detail beyond what had already transpired.

There are two potential challenges to these self-reporting verbal approaches to assessing student understanding. First, students may state that they understand a certain concept (and may believe that they do), but when they are assessed using more formal approaches (e.g., exams, case studies, skill demonstrations, etc.), misconceptions become obvious. Second, the class as a whole may state that they understand the topic, but there may still be students in the class who do not. As a result, each student needs to be assessed to help ensure that the KSAs they are learning are being formed in a more effective manner.

In addition, these assessments should be used on a regular basis (at least weekly), beginning with pre-assessments, and they should help instructors adapt their lessons to more directly address the gaps that have been identified by these formative assessments. Theologically, the instructor will be more aware of the extent to which God has been able to help each student learn. In doing so, the instructor will be able to more clearly discern adaptations to the course that God might be inviting them towards based upon this assessment data. As a result, it is recommended that faculty be provided with regular training and support on using these kinds of assessments.

Thirdly, in the multiple theory classes that we observed, we noted that lecture was the primary teaching strategy that was being utilized. In addition, students were observed regularly repeating exactly what the instructor stated and/or what was listed on the presentation slides. These strategies are indicative of rote memorization approaches to learning that are founded upon behaviorist learning theories, which can be effective for the retention of factual information when done well. However, students are also expected in their profession to be able to apply, analyze, and evaluate using the knowledge and skills that they have learned. As a result, alternative learning theories are needed to better understand how these types of critical and higher order thinking skills can be developed in students. In addition, different KSAs often require different learning theories to help guide the development of more effective teaching strategies. Spiritually speaking, God works in different ways to help students learn different concepts/skills. It is therefore recommended that instructors receive regular training on a wide array of learning theories as well as support in using these theories to guide the development of their courses.

Fourth, all faculty could be offered PD opportunities on a regular basis. We were told that instructors and staff have the opportunity to attend conferences and workshops offered by the government every few weeks or months. However, only two to four persons attend these offerings. As ongoing PD of faculty is one of the most effective ways to improve student learning (i.e., it has a high impact factor), it is recommended that the school expand these offerings to all faculty. The college, however, does not need to send all faculty to every conference/workshop. Rather, we recommend that faculty and administration work together to identify, develop, and offer their own on-campus training sessions on relevant topics related to educational theory and practice. Just as with students, God may be asserted to continually work with each faculty member to help them grow as professional educators. By spiritually discerning and hosting PD programs, the institution will be partnering with God more directly in this work.

Furthermore, the school is encouraged to expand support for faculty by creating formal, small support groups on general topics related to teaching and learning as well as to foster a culture of peer mentoring. The focus of these small support groups could be for faculty to regularly discuss how things are going in their theory classes, as well as in community-based settings, share educational resources and ideas, brainstorm innovative improvements, and discuss challenges that they are having. Known as professional learning networks (PLNs) in the literature, these small support groups should help strengthen their classes as faculty regularly mentor one another. Through such small groups, God can work to shape not only each individual's educational beliefs and practices but also the institution's culture.

Finally, we recommend that the theory classes be redistributed throughout the entire academic year, being intermixed with the community-based portions of the curriculum, so that there is a closer integration of theory and practice. Currently, during the theory portion of each academic year, students attend class sessions throughout each day for one to three months with the rest of the year being spent in community-based settings. The theory classes that we observed covered multiple concepts in a single session. Assuming that this volume of information is being delivered in most class periods, this represents a tremendous amount of information for students to learn in a relatively short period of time. Educational psychology studies on "massed" versus "distributed" practices have found that it is far better for students to be exposed to smaller amounts of information repeatedly over an extended period of time than for them to be exposed to significant amount of information in a short period of time. Theologically, there are very real limits to the work that God can do educationally with each individual. As a result, the sacred invitation is to work within the confines of these limits, trusting that God's plans account for them.

In addition, lumping all of the theory classes together at the beginning of each academic year seems to create a separation between theory and practice. While we were not able to observe the practical portions of the curriculum, we are concerned that separating theory from practice could inhibit student learning. We believe that it would be more beneficial for students to learn core concepts and skills in their theory classes and then have the opportunity to see and practice these in real-world settings almost immediately. As a result, we recommend that the theory and practical portions of the curriculum be integrated with one another. Possibilities for this might include spending three days each week in theory classes and the other days in community-based settings. Or, students could be in theory classes one week and then in community-based settings the next week. The idea is to partner with God to bring theory and practical elements of the curriculum closer together so that they support each other in more direct and mutually beneficial ways.

RESOURCES, LIMITATIONS, AND CONTEXTUAL CONSIDERATIONS

When identifying any set of recommendations based upon external standards (e.g., the Educational System Guidelines), some thought needs to be given to which of these recommendations are most appropriate for the local context given its existing resources, culture, and limitations. Theologically, noting these contextual considerations is an effort to more clearly identify the parameters within which God is working so that we can more closely partner with God's work in the institution. Before asserting the recommendations above as our final ones, then, a few additional considerations need to be addressed.

First and foremost, these recommendations are based primarily on observations and data from the theory classes. Knowing that the bulk of the curriculum is centered on community-based settings, some of these recommendations may not apply to these practical portions of the program, and additional ones might be identified if we had conducted a more extensive review of the community-based settings. As a result, these recommendations should be considered to primarily apply to the theory portion of the curriculum.

Relatedly, another limitation of these recommendations is the limited time that we had to adequately assess the Student Tier. Our schedule was such that we did not have very many opportunities to interact with students in more in-depth ways. As a result, more time with students would be needed to gather and more accurately assess the data upon which the recommendations are made. However, as was noted above, the recommendations that we have put forth are focused at the Administration and Instructor tiers, so the impact of this additional data might not be significant. Nevertheless, these recommendations should be held as being tentative pending more time with students.

Finally, we note that staff and faculty time are an increasingly scarce resource. Faculty are expected to teach multiple classes each day during the theory portion of the curriculum. Preparing for their lessons is likely a significant portion of their day outside of class, especially for new faculty and when creating new classes. As a result, time for additional training and support may be very limited. In addition, while we were at the college, the institution received the outstanding news that they had been granted additional seats for one of their programs. Working with additional students will also likely require additional time.

Looking at the recommendations from the previous section, there may therefore be challenges to implementing some of these. The training sessions and supportive small groups will require additional time on faculty's part. However, if these sessions are designed to help faculty prepare for the theory courses that they are currently teaching, as well as for practical portions of the curriculum, then their time in these sessions will be more efficiently utilized. Furthermore, using formative assessments to continually adjust their lesson plans will also likely require more planning time than faculty (especially experienced ones) are currently used to. However, creating more adaptive classes should result in improved student learning, which will ideally save time in not having to work with struggling students outside of classes later on. So, while time is a scarce resource, using it in the ways that are recommended should help save time in other areas in the long run.

OVERALL RECOMMENDATIONS

Given these additional considerations, we do not recommend that any significant changes be made to the ones noted above. However, these recommendations should be held as being very tentative pending a more extensive review of the practical portions of the curriculum. In addition, administration will need to assess any time limitations that faculty have in participating in and/or implementing these recommendations.

This concludes the final report as it was submitted to this institution. As we can see, the guidelines have the potential to provide detailed insights into the inner workings of educational systems. They can be used to note significant strengths in the organization through which God has and continues to effectively work. The guidelines can also be used to identify areas where additional and ongoing improvements might be made for each of the three tiers: students, instructors, and administrators. By combining the noted effect sizes of each guideline, along with the contextual limitations and existing resources of the school, we can prioritize these recommendations and ideally discern where God is wanting to focus on with the school in the near future. Overall, this report is one example of how the complete Educational System Guidelines might be used towards these holy ends.

5

Educating in the Spirit for Global Change

THROUGHOUT THIS TEXT, WE have seen how God might be asserted to be present with and through our educational systems. At each tier, God labors to help continually improve the quality of learning, teaching, and support so that God's purposes might be more fully manifest in our schools and the communities of which they are a part. Each level outlines the progressive journey that students, instructors, and administrators might move through towards these ends. While each school system, class, and individual needs to be fully present and responsive to God for the level that they are currently at, following these guidelines, the trend culminates at Level 3, thereby providing a horizon towards which our schools might be headed now and in the future. In these closing pages, then, we take a moment to reflect on Level 3 across all three tiers and highlight some of the common characteristics of this horizon. In doing so, we should have a better understanding of the nature of our roles as theistic educators and the work that God continually labors to do in our communities.

DEMOCRATIC PROCESSES

Throughout these guidelines at Level 3, there is a consistent emphasis on the importance of including multiple people in the discernment and implementation of our educational systems. Theologically, as has been asserted, God works with and through each and every part of creation to realize God's aims. If we truly desire to fully partner with God's work, then holistic discernment necessitates our working together to listen deeply for where and how God has and continues to move in each of our lives. In doing so, we will be harmonizing and more fully integrating God's efforts, thereby increasing the effectiveness and impact of God's work within and to our schools. The Level 3 educational kin-dom that God is inviting us to cultivate, as theistic educators, is one that is thoroughly democratic, fully participatory, and completely collaborative.

PERSONALIZED, RELEVANT, AND MEANINGFUL

With such a democratic emphasis on the community, however, Level 3 does not in any way neglect the nuances of each individual. On the contrary, it can be asserted, God's infinite life is fully and mysteriously present with and to each infinitesimal part of creation. Stated differently, God cares infinitely for each atom, organism, person, community, and planet. Philosophically and theoretically, whole systems may be viewed as emergent phenomena of individual parts. As a result, each part has a significant role in the emergent system and the system will likely change if any of the parts change. For example, small group dynamics will emergently shift as the individuals in the group alter their behaviors. Each person is therefore an important part of the democratically emerging community.

Applied to our schools, educational systems become increasingly personalized, relevant, and meaningful for each student, faculty, and staff as we move from Level 1 to 3. There is, it might therefore be asserted, a twofold movement of God: 1) increasing integration and harmonizing of the school and its communities via democratic processes, and 2) increasing attentiveness and responsiveness to each individual and groups of individuals in the system. We might expect God's infinite life to be complex, and we can see some of this complexity with this twofold movement. It can be argued that many schools, with their top-down administrative hierarchies and their discipline-centered standardized curriculum, are not very responsive to either of these movements of God. As theistic educators, then, we are called by God to develop schools that are not only more democratic, but also more personalized, meaningful, and relevant for each individual and group in the system.

AN ADAPTIVE ORGANISM

With increasing and genuine collaboration that is coupled with more personalized actions, one of the results will be an educational system that is continually adaptive to the emerging assets and needs of the community. As stated many times above, we begin to see how our schools can be conceived of as God's living organism that adjusts to each change and challenge. Such an incarnational view implicitly challenges transcendent theological views of God's educational life as being immovable and unchanging. Instead, the Level 3 guidelines depict God as continually laboring within and to each part and whole of the school system and its surrounding communities. God's life adaptively works to foster wholeness, peace, justice, connection, and organization. God works to meet each need, address each challenge, and reconcile each distortion. This fully incarnational view therefore asserts that as conditions and circumstances change, so too does God adapt within and through the community. As theistic educators, we are therefore invited to help our schools, as living, organic expressions of God's life, continually discern and respond to God's movements.

A MULTIPLICITY OF POSSIBILITIES

Such adaptiveness, however, does not occur along a single "one-size-fits-all" path according to these guidelines. At any given point in time, if we have been following the guidelines up through Level 3, God will have developed a range of options, pathways, and possibilities. Each one of these is a stepping stone that God can utilize to help each person or group journey more effectively towards the horizons that God leading them towards. Because of the range of options that are available, the number of combinations and permutations is expansive, thereby empowering the personalized adaptiveness discussed above. When coupled with democratic and innovative processes, this multiplicity of possibilities increases exponentially, allowing for the sacred educational organism to adapt more fluidly and effectively in each moment in time. While the work to initially develop and continually refine each option is intense, with democratic community support our work as theistic educators becomes more manageable.

INCREASING COMPLEXITY, INNOVATION, AND IMPACT

As we can see, this democratic, personalized, living organism of multiple possibilities is quite complex. In addition, as we look at Level 3 for many of the guidelines, the movement tends towards increasing complexity of knowledge, skills, attitudes, and engagement. Theologically, with an infinitely complex God, it should really come as no surprise that God's educational kin-dom would increasingly manifest this complexity. When embodied well, however, such complexity becomes a fertile garden for innovation and creativity. Through these innovations, God can work to further open up the multiplicity of possibilities that then empower the living educational organism to continually and democratically adapt to changing assets and needs. As these innovative holy adaptations continually emerge in response to ever-changing needs and challenges, the school's impact on its constituents and its community increases. In these ways, God can therefore work to expand God's kin-dom. As a result, theistic educators are called to help nurture this growing complexity in ways that breed innovative insights that lead to systemic impact in our world.

SIGNIFICANT SYSTEMS OF SUPPORT

As complex as this is, theistic educators are not alone in these endeavors. Looking at these guidelines, wherever possible, God does not labor in isolation or secrecy. The Course/Instructor Tier, for instance, was developed using evidence-based educational resources. The theological foundation for this is that these studies have documented God's more significant impact on student achievement. It was further argued that if God has successfully worked in these ways in other contexts, then perhaps God might work in similar ways in our own school systems. As a result, these evidence-based resources become a source of support and guidance for theistic educators in these complex and ever-adapting holy environments.

Beyond these resources, Level 3 of the guidelines also encourages the use of many other support systems. Turning to peers, inviting outside experts, and relying on community members were additional sources that we are invited to rely upon for help. Spiritually speaking, God works through these support systems to help further his educational kin-dom in our schools. We must also remember, however, that we too are called to be support systems for other schools as God labors in our communities and around our globe for the flourishing of life. As theistic educators, then, we are invited to not only rely on these sources of support but to also productively contribute to them. In doing so, we will be actively participating in God's world-wide educational organism of increasing democracy, personalization, adaptiveness, multiplicity, complexity, and impact.

THEISTIC EDUCATIONAL DEVELOPMENT FOR OUR WORLD

In closing, the work of theistic educational development is a unique and exciting vocational calling. As we can see, it is one that is as extensive as it is complex and ever-changing. With this stated, however, it is a calling that emerges from humble origins. Stated simply, our primary role is to *help our educational systems continually respond to God's educational life*. Turning from this aim towards the work that will achieve these ends, however, becomes infinitely complex—theologically as well as literally, as we have seen. Nevertheless, God does not and cannot leave us alone to do this work. With so many systems of support available to us, God can work effectively to gradually transform each tier of our schools. When done democratically, this complex work becomes not only more manageable, but also more adaptive, innovative, and impactful. Following the guidelines outlined in this text, such an impact can expand beyond our schools to transform the communities of which we are a part of in increasingly well-harmonized ways. As this occurs, we will come to be more a part of God's living kin-dom organism that is ever-present and striving to manifest its life, love, peace, justice, and harmony. The "high impact" of these evidence-based and theological foundations is therefore not merely intended for our own educational systems—they are intended for our world. To pursue these holy local and global aims with God is what it truly means for us to be "Educating in the Spirit."

Appendix A
Foundations for Theistic Educational Research

HAVING SEEN A BRIEF overview of the evidence-based guidelines and their potential applications to the three tiers of educational systems in the introduction to this book, we are now in a position to develop the necessary foundations to articulate specific theologies related to each one of these guidelines. In order to do so, we must first understand the nature of scientific research methods and how these methods might be viewed through the lens of theology. Based upon these understandings, we will then be able to assert a theistic view of educational research. Emerging out of this theistic view come the theologies that are asserted for each tier.

This appendix is therefore intended to establish some of these necessary research-based and theological foundations. As we will see, there are numerous authors who have engaged in discussions, debates, and explorations of science and theology in Western Christianity and many of these discussions are quite technical and complex. We will attempt to simplify and clearly articulate the essence of these current conversations so that they are comprehensible to a wider audience whilst still retaining the needed foundations for our purposes in this book. This is one of those writings that are intended to provide a deeper basis for the chapters of this book, but it is also one that might be skipped if one finds themselves lost in the forest of theological deliberations presented herein, which is why it is placed in the appendices.

We will begin by providing a brief overview of the nature of scientific methods and the kinds of information that they are intended to provide. We will then turn to different theological positions that might be used to help one to better understand God's relationship to creation. Integrated in these two sections, this will then be followed by an overview of some of the different theological views of science. One of these widely varying views, panentheism will be asserted to be the most useful for helping us develop a theology of education based upon the evidence-based guidelines. Finally, we will state how panentheism might be used to develop a theistic view of educational research. It is hoped that these scientific and theological foundations will help us better understand how the views of God that are articulated in this book were developed. Overall, these explorations are intended to provide strong theological and evidence-based foundations for theistic education.

APPENDIX A

ENDURING REALITY: SCIENCE'S UNIQUE WAY OF KNOWING

One of the primary purposes of scientific endeavors is to develop theories and models about our world, its enduring patterns, and the ways that it works. The aim of these scientifically derived theories is to provide us with a better understanding into the nature of reality. The notion that science's chief purpose is to produce models about how creation works, is widely accepted. "All sciences," asserts philosopher George F. Kneller, "use concrete models."[1] Some, such as world-renowned physicists Stephen Hawking, even go so far as to assert that the only way to understand the universe is through the use of such models.[2] However, it is noted, we must remember that these theories are not reality; they are instead our attempted constructions of reality: an "interpretative description of a phenomenon that facilitates access to that phenomenon."[3] Nevertheless, it is hoped that these models will provide us with a deeper understanding that enables us to predict and control the situations that they are derived from and applied to.[4]

For instance, the uncovering of "laws" has been and continues to be given a central emphasis in scientific endeavors.[5] The laws that some scientists pursue are intended to be logical, universal, and true.[6] These laws, like all models and theories, must therefore meet certain "scientific criteria" in order to be accepted by the wider scientific community. Some of these criteria include: consistency, unification of data, predictive validity, falsifiability, and causal explanations of phenomena.[7] Science, then, is understood as having a primary aim of creating and testing these theories, models, and laws that give us "an increasingly coherent picture of the universe."[8]

Because of these aims, and the criteria by which models are developed and accepted, we can see that science's views of creation are very specific and its methods are very precise. Scientific views of creation are captured succinctly by famed astronomer Karl Sagan when he wrote, "It is an astonishing fact that there are laws of nature, rules that summarize conveniently—not just qualitatively but quantitatively—how the world works . . . so far as we can tell, this is the way the universe is constructed."[9]

---

1. Hatton and Plouffe, *Science,* 14.

2. Hatton and Plouffe, *Science,* 66–67.

3. Machamer and Silberstein, *Blackwell Guide,* 108, 24; Hatton and Plouffe, *Science,* 59; Eisner, *Learning and Teaching,* 62.

4. Hatton and Plouffe, *Science,* vii-viii; Machamer and Silberstein, *Blackwell Guide,* 65.

5. Machamer and Silberstein, *Blackwell Guide,* 4, 66.

6. Machamer and Silberstein, *Blackwell Guide,* 56; Swinton and Mowat, *Practical Theology,* 40–41.

7. Hatton and Plouffe, *Science,* vii-viii, 25–37, 84; Machamer and Silberstein, *Blackwell Guide,* 20, 22, 50.

8. Best and Kahn, *Research in Education,* 6; Hatton and Plouffe, *Science,* vii, viii, x, xi; Machamer and Silberstein, *Blackwell Guide,* 32.

9. Hatton and Plouffe, *Science,* 6–7.

While genuine spontaneity and novelty in creation are recognized,[10] the basic view of creation that is held by many scientists is that it exhibits enduring patterns, regularity, and order. It is therefore the goal of science to document these empirically regularities (i.e., those that can be observed or measured) in creation with its theories and then verify them via its rigorous scientific methods.[11]

The primary view of creation from the perspective of science, then, is that creation exhibits enduring regularities, patterns, and order that can be uncovered and verified by empirically-based scientific methodologies. Restated differently, to help summarize the purpose of scientific endeavors, we can assert: *Science is primarily focused upon theoretically modeling enduring regularities, structures, and order in creation that are verified by communally agreed upon and empirically-based research methodologies.* Their primary emphasis is on constructing and verifying theories about these enduring regularities that are falsifiable, replicatable, and generalizable via current empirically-based and communally accepted research methods.

THEOLOGIZING SCIENCE: ASSERTING GOD'S RELATIONSHIP TO ENDURING PATTERNS

Given this understanding of science being primarily focused on identifying enduring empirical patterns and structure in creation, we next ask how God might be related to this enduring order. By exploring this question, we will be establishing a theological foundation for educational research methods, which have been used to develop the guidelines in this text. In Western Christianity, Michael Brierley asserts that "classical theism, pantheism, and panentheism are recognized as the basic patterns through which the doctrine of God can be analyzed."[12] Each of these perspectives offers a distinct way of conceiving of the nature and relationship of God to creation, and to enduring patterns in particular. For our purposes here, however, we will only consider the first two: classical theism and panentheism. Both of these positions will provide key insights into how God has been conceived of in relation to creation's enduring dynamics.

Two Schools of Theology

Classical theism, represented in this book by evangelical Christian theologian James Spiegel and others,[13] is described by Spiegel as viewing God as being all-powerful,

---

10. Hatton and Plouffe, *Science*, 107.

11. Allport, *Personality*, 3; Eisner, *Learning and Teaching*, 61; Hatton and Plouffe, *Science*, 3, 5, 119; Machamer and Silberstein, *Blackwell Guide*, 55.

12. Clayton and Peacocke, *In Whom We Live*, 3.

13. Clayton and Peacocke, *In Whom We Live*, 95–108; McGrath, *A Fine-Tuned Universe*; Spiegel, *Benefits of Providence*.

APPENDIX A

immutable, and therefore is in perfect control of all events.[14] As Spiegel writes, "The classical Christian view of providence affirms God's exhaustive foreknowledge and complete control over the cosmos."[15] God is, Spiegel asserts, "immutable and timelessly eternal, on the one hand, and . . . personal and fully relational, on the other."[16] Spiegel's classical view is therefore primarily one that affirms the immanent presence and providence of God throughout all creation in addition to God's transcendence.

Panentheism, similar to classical theism, asserts the presence of God "within and through" every part of creation as well as the transcendence of God.[17] Quoted by a number of authors, the *Oxford Dictionary of the Christian Church* defines panentheism as: "The belief that the Being of God includes and penetrates the whole universe, so that every part of it exists in him, but (as against Pantheism) that His Being is more than, and is not exhausted by, the universe."[18] It is, therefore, one that conceives of God being both fully immanent and transcendent in ways that view the relationship between God and creation as being somewhat independent, going both ways, as well as in ways that reduce some of the problems associated with transcendence.[19] Unlike classical versions, however, God is asserted by panentheists as "needing" creation "for the fulfillment of God's nature of love."[20] For some panentheists, God is asserted as being both "fixed and unchanging" as well as "fully responsive to the world."[21] Panentheism is therefore a school that conceives of God's presence within but also beyond creation in mutually influential ways. As we shall see below, it differs from classical theism in that many panentheism authors do not assert that God is complete and total control of creation, whether this is because of the presence of free-will or because of God limiting his own power.

Diving Deeper: The Three Schools and Three Aspects of God

We now turn to three distinct aspects of God that have been found to be repeatedly addressed throughout the Western Christian tradition: transcendent, immanent, and

---

14. *Benefits of Providence*, 9, 14, 19–20, 32. See also Griffin, *Reenchantment without Supernaturalism*, 131, 48.

15. Spiegel, *Benefits of Providence*, 14.

16. Spiegel, *Benefits of Providence*, 158.

17. Clayton, *Adventures in Spirit*, 106, 18, 51; Clayton and Peacocke, *In Whom We Live*, xxi, 158–59, 69, 229, 39; Peacocke, *Paths from Science*, 57; Smith, *God, Energy and the Field*, 12.

18. As quoted by Smith, *God, Energy and the Field*, 13. See also Clayton and Peacocke, *In Whom We Live*, 145.

19. Clayton, *Adventures in Spirit*, 152–53; Clayton and Peacocke, *In Whom We Live*, 8–9, 20–21, 31, 68, 83, 243, 52; Peacocke, *Paths from Science,* 43, 46, 129–30; Smith, *God, Energy and Field*, 4, 15.

20. Clayton, *Adventures in Spirit*, 128; Clayton and Peacocke, *In Whom We Live*, 9, 23, 69, 252.

21. Clayton, *Adventures in Spirit*, 104, 27, 69; Clayton and Peacocke, *In Whom We Live*, 42–44, 82; Griffin, *Reenchantment Without Supernaturalism*, 150.

personhood/deity aspects of God.[22] Of these three theological aspects of God, immanence has the most relevance for our discussions here. We will therefore provide a brief overview of each of these theological assertions before articulating a theistic view of scientific research, with the most emphasis being given to the immanent aspects of God. While some of these discussions may become theologically and technically complex, they are intended to provide further insights into the views that each school of theology has about God and his relationship to creation. In the next section, these explorations will help us better understand how each school understands God's relationship to science.

God as Transcendent

Most commonly upheld in Christianity is the claim that God is transcendent to creation. The transcendence of God is one that views God in a hierarchical and sustaining position in relation to creation. "From moment to moment," writes evangelical Christian theologian James Spiegel, "the cosmos is dependent upon [God], and were God to suddenly withhold his active sustaining power, the world would immediately disappear."[23] In this view, God is viewed as having his own separate life outside of creation. It is a transcendence that is asserted to sustain and uphold creation.[24] For Spiegel, it is from this transcendence—a divine independence—that God "dreams up" and makes creation possible from moment to moment.[25] For others, God is also viewed as being "infinitely transcendent" to, and even ontologically different from, creation (i.e., God's being is completely separate from creation).[26] It is an aspect of God that is "ineffable" and "inherently inexpressible and beyond words;" one that is completely beyond our control as well as beyond all time and space.[27] This transcendent aspect of God is asserted to be the eternal source and sustainer of all existence. The transcendence of God is therefore asserted to be one that is fully independent of creation, but in a way that providentially upholds all of it.

God as Immanent

Following this sustaining transcendence, God's immanent life is also asserted to be everywhere present: guiding and sustaining creation. For Spiegel, the relationship

---

22. Kyle, *Sacred Systems*, ch. 16.
23. Spiegel, *Benefits of Providence*, 80.
24. Clayton, *Adventures in Spirit*, 128, 32, 49, 67; Clayton and Peacocke, *In Whom We Live*, 160.
25. Spiegel, *Benefits of Providence*, 83.
26. Clayton, *Adventures in Spirit*, 149; Clayton and Peacocke, *In Whom We Live*, 160, 70; Peacocke, *Paths from Science*, 42.
27. Clayton, *Adventures in Spirit*, 150; Peacocke, *Paths from Science*, 165–66; Smith, *God, Energy and Field*, 1, 137.

Appendix A

between God and creation is captured by a mind-body metaphor. "The whole cosmos is mind-dependent," he asserts, "Every physical object, including our own bodies, is upheld in existence from moment to moment by the Mind behind the world who also has decreed secondary causes such as the use of our physical senses to perceive the world."[28] Others assert that God is on the "inside of everything," working via the already existing processes of creation such as evolution, giving life to them and possibly direction.[29] The main idea here is that "the world is in God, and God is in the world."[30] Closely related to such language is the metaphor of creation as "God's body."[31] "So the main import of calling the cosmos the body of God," one author writes, "is to affirm that the universe is a necessary self-expression of the divine being."[32]

Because of such a divine presence, creation is therefore viewed by some theologians in sacramental terms with creation being "signs, symbols, and reminders that any and every thing has the potential to become a full vehicle of the divine," thereby giving creation an "ecclesial nature."[33] Overall, such language and metaphors are therefore intended to capture the idea that the divine life is seeking to express itself within and through creation, whilst still maintaining God's transcendent distinction from it.[34] Though it is beyond the scope of this book, there is disagreement in these immanent views of God as it relates to the presence of or lack of free-will in creation.[35]

Specific examples of these immanent views of God come with catholic priest Adrian Smith's views of God as "energy" as well as with Maximus the Confessor, and other Eastern Orthodox theologians', concept of "logoi." Smith views God as "creative energy," a view that is becoming common in contemporary spirituality.[36] "Energy is," he asserts, "the prime reality . . . [it] is the foundation of everything in the Universe from the minute atom to the mighty galaxy."[37] As there are many different kinds of energy, it—and therefore God, or the "Cosmic Christ"—is present everywhere and on every level, inside and a part of all that is giving life to all.[38] God is therefore depicted as attempting to transform God's "Potential Energy," which is as yet unmanifest, into

---

28. Spiegel, *Benefits of Providence*, 145.

29. Clayton, *Adventures in Spirit*, 107–8; Clayton and Peacocke, *In Whom We Live*, 150, 59, 200, 09; Griffin, *Reenchantment Without Supernaturalism*, 318; Peacocke, *Paths from Science*, 47, 58, 67.

30. Clayton and Peacocke, *In Whom We Live*, 62–63, 83.

31. Clayton and Peacocke, *In Whom We Live*, 6.

32. Clayton and Peacocke, *In Whom We Live*, 64.

33. Clayton and Peacocke, *In Whom We Live*, 8, 154, 83; Knight, *God of Nature*, 32, 69, 77; Peacocke, *Paths from Science*, 148, 51.

34. Clayton and Peacocke, *In Whom We Live*, 71; Peacocke, *Paths from Science*, 109.

35. Clayton and Peacocke, *In Whom We Live*, 72.

36. Smith, *God, Energy and Field*, 15–16, 27, 35–36. For contemporary examples, see Cameron, *Artist's Way*, 3; May, *Will & Spirit*, 3.

37. Smith, *God, Energy and Field*, 17.

38. Smith, *God, Energy and Field*, 17–23, 49, 69, 71.

manifesting "Kinetic Energy," and we are therefore viewed as being imperfect mirrors of the divine.[39]

Similarly, "energies" are also found to be a part of Eastern Orthodox views, particularly those of Maximus the Confessor. In these views, God's "hidden essence" is made manifest in energies, which gives life to all of creation.[40] Maximus is reported to have conceived of "logoi," which are the "underlying principles . . . of all created things" that God intends each part to become.[41] The goal of creation, then, is to manifest more and more of the divine Logos—the full presence of God in creation: i.e., all that God intends it to become.[42] Overall, these immanent views depict God as being intimately connected to creation.

God as Personhood/Deity

Finally, we might understand the personhood/deity aspect to be both the view of how God is conceived of as being personal (i.e., having personal attributes such as God's will, consciousness, feelings, etc.)[43] and/or as a deity that externally acts on creation. In accordance with such understandings, Spiegel's classical and evangelical Protestant stance views God as already being personally present to and active within every occurrence in creation in providentially absolute ways, meaning that God personally controls all that happens with absolute power.[44] Illustrating this point, Spiegel considers it "irrationally redundant" to "interpose such things as 'dispositions,' 'powers,' 'forces,' or any other sort of active agent to explain the laws of nature."[45] Spiegel's views of the personhood of God, as we have seen, are more akin to the mind-body metaphor wherein the mind of God expresses its personhood through all that occurs in creation.

Such a classical view is contrasted with those of other historical deists who understand God merely as an external "designer and creator," one who initially sets creation in motion and is now "no more than an observer of its autonomous workings."[46] Such "natural theology" approaches to God, which view God's providence as being very limited, are asserted by some today, such as physicist Paul Davies and philosopher Alister McGrath.[47] In these contemporary versions, God is asserted to selectively and finely tune constants and "very special laws that guarantee a trend toward greater rich-

---

39. Smith, *God, Energy and Field*, 27, 145.
40. Clayton and Peacocke, *In Whom We Live*, 160, 65; Peacocke, *Paths from Science*, 160.
41. Clayton and Peacocke, *In Whom We Live*, 160, 88, 95; Knight, *God of Nature*, 98.
42. Knight, *God of Nature*, 95, 101, 13.
43. Clayton, *Adventures in Spirit*, 101; Levine, *Pantheism*, 2, 159, 93; Knight, *God of Nature*, 111; Smith, *God, Energy and Field*, 12.
44. Spiegel, *Benefits of Providence*, 90.
45. Spiegel, *Benefits of Providence*, 86–87.
46. Knight, *God of Nature*, 23.
47. Knight, *God of Nature*, 2, 5, 114.

APPENDIX A

ness, diversity, and complexity through spontaneous self-organization."[48] This second classical position therefore views the personal aspect and interventions of God to be very limited in its external interventions into the processes of creation. These classical views of God are therefore very diverse, ranging from absolute providence to very limited, almost non-existent, interventions into the "natural" processes of creation. Nevertheless, both of these positions seem to uphold a personal aspect in which God is seen as having personal attributes and/or acting externally on creation as a subject might on an object.

Panentheist theologians, on the other hand, generally affirm that God is "not less than personal."[49] Adrian Smith, discussed above, goes on to assert that while God does not change, our images of God do, and we often conceive of God with human qualities "such as justice, love, peace, forgiveness, mercy."[50] One of the primary questions that the classical positions above might give rise to is how might the Deity be conceived in relation to creation? Is the Deity absolutely controlling and sustaining every part of creation as Spiegel asserts? Does the Deity remain fully external with limited interventions as Davies and McGrath claim? Or is there an alternative way to conceive of the relationship between this personhood aspect of God and creation?

Panentheistic theologian Philip Clayton offers such a third way. In his book, *Adventures in the Spirit*, Clayton affirms the personalness of God, asserting "a divinity that is not inferior in agency to human agents, but rather one that infinitely transcends all forms of finite agency," though Clayton holds that such an aspect is not one that is inherent in material creation, but rather emergent.[51] Calling it "radically emergent theism," which he claims "offers the closest possible parallel between divine agent and human agents,"[52] "deity" is viewed as a property that the material universe comes to have increasingly over time as greater and greater levels of complexity emerge.[53] "God," Clayton writes, "is simply the universe becoming aware of itself."[54] In this scheme, then, the Deity is therefore viewed as "intervening" in increasingly complex ways as new levels of emergence arise.[55] Clayton's radically emergent theism is therefore a panentheist middle one that affirms the personalness and deity of Spiegel's position, but does so in accordance with evolutionary-based concerns of the fine tuners like Davies and McGrath. As we can see, while the doctrine of God being the Deity is

---

48. Clayton and Peacocke, *In Whom We Live*, 106; McGrath, *A Fine-Tuned Universe*, 85, 118.
49. Clayton, *Adventures in Spirit*, 101, 21–22; Peacocke, *Paths from Science*, 141.
50. Smith, *God, Energy and Field*, 8, 12.
51. Clayton, *Adventures in Spirit*, 95–97, 110–11, 31–32, 45. See also Clayton and Peacocke, *In Whom We Live*, 90.
52. Clayton, *Adventures in Spirit*, 102.
53. Clayton, *Adventures in Spirit*, 114, 31, 252.
54. Clayton, *Adventures in Spirit*, 95.
55. Clayton, *Adventures in Spirit*, 98.

common in Christianity, how this divine person is asserted to relate to creation is not only very diverse, but quite complex.

Merging Theology and Science: God and Enduring Patterns

With a better understanding of these three aspects of God in place, we are now in a position to return to science. We have introduced the views of specific theologians above who have directly addressed the relationship between theology and science. We will now provide a brief overview of some of these various and divergent perspectives. Given the complexity of these conversations and their wide variations, we will choose one of these positions as the basis of our own theology of science for this book. As we will see, a consensus has not yet been reached in Western Christian theology as to how God is asserted to relate to the enduring empirically dynamics of creation that are the subject of scientific investigations. In order to develop a foundational theology for the guidelines, we are forced to choose the one that we currently believe is most useful for our purposes here. If consensus is ever reached on how theology and science are related, then our chosen theological stance may need to be modified.

The differences discussed between Spiegel's classical evangelical Protestant theism position and our fine tuners (Davies and McGrath) continues to play itself out here. Because of his omnipotent doctrine, Spiegel views God as being the sole cause of all enduring empirical dynamics that are documented via scientific methods.[56] For him, these phenomena are not somehow an "intrinsic necessity in the nature world," as many secular scientists assert, but are rather simply the regular actions of God being carried out in creation.[57] As such, according to Spiegel, there really are no causal connections in creation, for God "systematically correlates" every event.[58] "Natural 'laws,'" Spiegel goes on to assert, "are simply summations of God's regular providential governance of the physical order."[59] Spiegel can therefore be seen as applying his doctrine of omnipotence to the enduring regularities of creation that are studied by scientists.

Our fine-tuning deists, on the other hand, differ significantly from Spiegel. These authors, as we have already seen, assert that God has set the "finely tuned" and intrinsic laws by which creation unfolds.[60] "In other words," writes physicist-theologian Paul Davies, "life and consciousness emerge as part of the natural outworking of the laws of physics."[61] However, God is also conceived of by these fine-tuning authors as

---

56. Spiegel, *Benefits of Providence*, 86–87.

57. Spiegel, *Benefits of Providence*, 87.

58. Spiegel, *Benefits of Providence*, 87.

59. Spiegel, *Benefits of Providence*, 119–20.

60. Clayton and Peacocke, *In Whom We Live*, 99–100; Knight, *God of Nature*, ix; McGrath, *A Fine-Tuned Universe*, 118, 20–21, 212.

61. Clayton and Peacocke, *In Whom We Live*, 104.

APPENDIX A

creating through chance and probability, and perhaps even sometimes by breaking "the ordinary flow of physical processes."[62] These authors therefore differ greatly from Spiegel's position in that God is viewed as having more of a "hands-off" approach to creation's enduring patterns and order, whereas for Spiegel, God is the direct cause of them.

Panentheist theologians, on the other hand, have found it helpful to distinguish between two views of intervention on the part of God in relation to creation: interventionist and non-interventionist. In the interventionist view, similar to the fine-tuning deists, God is conceived of as occasionally and providentially altering the natural processes and regularities of creation.[63] In the non-interventionist view, the one more commonly held by panentheists, God does not intervene in such ways, for to do so would be to violate God's own nature and being.[64] As God is asserted to be a divinely immanent part of such natural processes, such interventions would therefore be self-contradictory.[65] Panentheists therefore view God as fully working within and through these enduring processes.[66] Though God can still create through other means,[67] the dominant panentheist view is one that sees God as somehow being an inherent and guiding part of these enduring patterns and order, though it may not always be clear as to how.[68]

From the three aspects of God outlined above, panentheist theologians therefore place a primary emphasis on the immanent aspect of God when it comes to viewing science. Spiegel, Davies, and McGrath, on the other hand, primarily emphasize the Deity aspects of God in relation to science and enduring empirical phenomena. To help further illustrate these panentheist views, which will be chosen as the basis for this text, there are two positions that we will now briefly discuss: that of process theologian David Ray Griffin and the one held by scientist-theologian Arthur Peacocke. These two views should help us better understand the panentheistic view of how God works within and through the enduring patterns of creation that scientific methods document and base their theories on.

Griffin, against the interventionist view which he views as "inconsistent" and "incoherent,"[69] upholds a "naturalistic theism" in which God is fundamentally asserted to be incapable of being able to "occasionally interrupt the world's most fundamental

62. Clayton and Peacocke, *In Whom We Live,* 97, 106; McGrath, *A Fine-Tuned Universe,* 186, 98.

63. Clayton and Peacocke, *In Whom We Live,* 37; Knight, *God of Nature,* 111.

64. Clayton and Peacocke, *In Whom We Live,* 43; Peacocke, *Paths from Science,* 91; Peacocke and Clayton, *All That Is,* 163.

65. Knight, *The God of Nature,* 85; Peacocke, *Paths from Science Towards God,* 57, 138.

66. Clayton, *Adventures in Spirit,* 107–8, 48, 202, 15; Clayton and Peacocke, *In Whom We Live,* 97, 201; Knight, *God of Nature,* xi, 111, 30; Peacocke, *Paths from Science,* 80, 146.

67. Knight, *God of Nature,* 25, 42–43.

68. For instance, see Clayton's discussion on how thee can be "purposiveness without purpose": Clayton, *Adventures in Spirit,* 79.

69. Griffin, *Reenchantment Without Supernaturalism,* 202.

causal processes," which are the "root of our universe."[70] "A truly naturalistic theism," he writes, "understands naturalismns ["naturalism non-supernatural"] to mean that the universe is such that any supernatural interruption of its basic causal nexus is metaphysically impossible."[71] In essence, Griffin is asserting the principle that every part of creation possesses free-will and is therefore capable of self-determination.[72] However, against scientific worldviews of creation as being causally closed, Griffin affirms the ever-present, influential, and guiding role that God has in creation's enduring patterns and order.[73] Griffin's model is therefore one example of the position that panentheists hold in relation to the enduring patterns of creation that scientists study and document.

Peacocke, on the other hand, differs somewhat from Griffin's. Whereas Griffin asserts the presence and influence of God in every part of creation, Peacocke sees God's primary movements to "affect holistically the state of the world System."[74] In alignment with causally closed scientific worldviews, yet ones that are open-ended and flexible,[75] he sees creation as an emergent monistic interaction between the parts and wholes of which they are a part.[76] In this scheme, God can therefore be conceived of as acting in ways that do not violate the enduring patterns and structure of creation but still retain a place for "special divine action."[77] While somewhat similar, we can also see how it differs from Griffin's theology thereby showing some of the diversity that exists within the panentheist camp. As with our discussions of the personhood/deity aspect of God, these varying views of God's relationship to creation's enduring dynamics are as intellectually complex as they are widely diverse.

So, as we can see here, there is as yet no consensus on the relationship between theology and science in Western Christianity. These authors, some of the best theologians and scientists in the Western world, are still widely divergent in their views of how God might be asserted to relate to creation, specifically creation's enduring and empirically observable dynamics. In order to move forward and develop a theology of education based upon the evidence-based guidelines, we will therefore need to choose one of these positions.

---

70. Griffin, *Reenchantment Without Supernaturalism*, 21–22, 178.
71. Griffin, *Reenchantment Without Supernaturalism*, 135.
72. Griffin, *Reenchantment Without Supernaturalism*, 137.
73. Griffin, *Reenchantment Without Supernaturalism*, 146–47, 83, 85, 213, 14–15.
74. Peacocke, *Paths from Science*, 109–10.
75. Peacocke, *Paths from Science*, 104.
76. Clayton and Peacocke, *In Whom We Live*, 147; Peacocke, *Paths from Science*, 111; Peacocke and Clayton, *All That Is*, 169.
77. Peacocke, *Paths from Science*, 109–10; Peacocke and Clayton, *All That Is*, 166.

APPENDIX A

FOUNDATIONS FOR THEISTIC EDUCATIONAL RESEARCH

Clearly, there is a wide variety of theological views on how God might be related to the enduring patterns and order of our world, which scientific methods are used to document. For the purposes of this book, however, we must still decide which one of these views might be most helpful for developing a theology that is based upon the evidence-based guidelines detailed in this text. In the final section of this chapter, we will therefore locate our position amongst these varying views and state how our position relates to educational research. We will then be in a position to better understand how the theological claims contained in this text were derived.

Given the different views of theology outlined above, and their views of God's relationship to enduring patterns and structure, the panentheistic view would seem to be the most helpful for our purposes. As stated in the introduction to this book, one of our primary goals as theistic educators is to better understand how God seeks to work with and through our educational systems to help our students learn and develop. In addition, of the three aspects of God explored above, God as being immanent and deity would seem to be the most relevant for helping us better understand how God acts in our schools.

If we were to adopt Spiegel's classical evangelical Protestant theism position, we would be able to use educational research to help us identify many of the enduring patterns that have and continue to exist in classes. Following Spiegel's assertion that God is an all-powerful and all-controlling part of each and every one of these enduring patterns, then we would conclude that by repeating any of these research-identified patterns in our own classes we would be partnering with God's educational life. However, such a view does not seem to be sufficient enough to help us discern which of the patterns, from the many that have been identified by educational research, we should be replicating. We could assert, based on Spiegel's position, that replicating any of these patterns in our classes is good enough since God is in complete control of all of them. While Spiegel does still hold a place for free-will in his omnipotent ("all powerful") theology, he self-admittedly does so in ways that are inconsistent with his classic theistic assertions.[78]

For instance, let's assume that educational research studies have documented the recurring pattern of teachers using corporeal punishment in their classes.[79] Following Spiegel's position, one could assert that since this is a recurring pattern that has been documented, and since God is in control of and/or the cause of all patterns, we should therefore use such negative disciplinary measures in our classes as well. Doing so, however, would contradict other educational and psychological research that has repeatedly found that these negative approaches actually impede healthy human growth

---

78. Spiegel, *Benefits of Providence*, 73–74.
79. Gershoff, "More Harm Than Good."

and development.[80] One of the challenges of the omnipotent classical theistic position is that it can seem to lack evaluation and discernment as a central part of its views of enduring patterns and structure, especially when it comes to such contradictions. This is a particular challenge for theistic educators because some educational influences and have been repeatedly found to be more effective than others.[81]

The view of the fine-tuners, on the other hand, would also seem to be insufficient for our purposes. Since these authors primarily assert a deity view of God that only acts occasionally in creation, this view would not be helpful for theistic educators who would be looking for ongoing guidance in the day-to-day activities of their classes. If we were to follow the fine-tuning position, we might be led to only look for God in special and "miraculous" occurrences rather than finding God in normal daily activities. This fine-tuning position also seems to violate the classical and panentheistic assertions that God is the ongoing and ever-present sustainer of each and every part of creation.

As a result of these and other challenges with the classical and fine-tuning positions, we are choosing to follow the panentheist position when interpreting educational research findings and using them to develop an evidence-based theology of education. In line with the panentheist authors, such a position fundamentally asserts that God acts not only externally as the Deity in our educational systems, but also non-dualistically within and through the behaviors, thoughts, feelings, relationships, policies, and social norms of these systems. Collectively, these deity and immanent divine actions result in enduring empirical patterns that can then be observed and documented by educational research methods.

Contrary to Spiegel's classical theism, however, many panentheists assert that God's influences are not all-powerful and all-controlling because the presence of free-will in creation inherently limits God's influences.[82] This claim, while it will no doubt be problematic for classical theists and evangelical Christians, is a necessary one when engaging with educational research studies. Why is this? If we assert that God's influences in our educational systems are limited, it therefore follows that not all enduring patterns that have been documented by educational researchers are equally representative of the work that God is attempting to do in our classes. In other words, because of the distortions of God's life that enter into our classes through free-will, some of these documented educational patterns may be more or less aligned with and manifesting of God's deity and immanent actions and desires.

These claims therefore bring us to one of the most significant challenges for the panentheistic perspective: How can we know which educational patterns are more aligned with and manifesting of God's educational life in our school systems? To answer this question, we turn to all of the theologians mentioned above, each of which

---

80. Paolucci and Violato, "A Meta-Analysis."
81. Hattie, *Visible Learning*, ch. 9, 10.
82. Griffin, *Reenchantment Without Supernaturalism*, 137; Knight, *God of Nature*, 86.

APPENDIX A

assert that God is a God of justice, goodness, love, mercy, forgiveness, order, progress, and complexity. Following some of our panentheists, such as Clayton, we can assert that God is therefore continually working to ensure that these attributes emerge as enduring patterns and structures in our world. If this is true, then we can apply this theological filter to any scientifically-derived results. In essence, as theistic scientists, *we are looking for those enduring empirical patterns that either align directly with God's nature and/or foster more and more of God's nature to emerge on our planet.*

As it relates to education, more specifically, we can claim that God labors intensely and unremittingly for each student's knowledge, skills, learning, and development. These outcomes should themselves align with God's nature, as well as empower learners to better partner with God's efforts in improving our world. We are therefore, as theistic educators, looking for those enduring educational patterns that accomplish one or both of these aims. So, for instance, we would not utilize corporeal punishment as a physically violent form of extrinsic motivation and/or social obedience, which is a strategy that is relatively and increasingly ineffective. Such strategies, it can be asserted, are not reflective or manifesting of God's love. Rather, we would look for nonviolent strategies that connect the student to God's intrinsic motivations within them, as well as ones that empower God's socially harmonizing efforts in our classes.

So, how do we identify these more God-centered/manifesting strategies? Enter educational research findings and the resulting evidence-based guidelines that are presented in this book. As Appendix B shows, educational research studies that have collectively included millions of students have documented enduring high impact teaching and learning strategies and influences. These enduring strategies and influences are ones that have been repeatedly shown to help students learn more effectively and efficiently compared to other ones. Theologically, based on the claim that God seeks to help students learn as effectively as possible, we can panentheistically assert that these high impact strategies and influences are more fully manifesting of God's educational life in our school systems.

However, they are aligned with God's efforts only to the extent that they are also reflective of our current understandings of God's nature and values. As a result, when we review educational research findings as theistic educators, we are therefore looking for at least these two traits: 1) high impact teaching and learning strategies and influences, and 2) strategies and influences that are aligned with one's current theological understandings of God's nature (e.g., love, justice, compassion, harmony, organization, etc.). With these assertions in place, we now have at least a beginning theological foundation for a theistic view of and approach to educational research. In essence, we have now developed both evidence-based and theological foundations for theistic education.

CLOSING REFLECTIONS

As we identify and compile evidence-based strategies and influences that meet both of the theistic education criteria above, we can then better understand where and how God acts with and through our schools. In the chapters in this book, then, we will be exploring each of the guidelines in greater detail for each of the three tiers. As we develop our understanding of each guideline, we will also be developing our understanding of how God might be asserted to be educationally acting. In line with our panentheistic position, we will be assuming that each guideline can teach us more about God's educational activities in our school systems because these guidelines meet both theistic education criteria above. We will therefore be developing our theology of education from the bottom-up, using each guideline to more clearly identify how God has worked in other classrooms as documented by educational research studies. While this does not automatically mean that this is how God will be laboring in our own schools, it is a good starting place. By the end of this book, we should therefore have a better idea of how we can partner more fully with God's educational Life in our educational systems.

Appendix B
Guidelines' Statistics Table

Area	Guide-line #	Guideline	Hattie (2009) Effect Size > 0.4 is Desirable			InTASC, CLASS, and Quality Matters
			Avg. Effect Size	# studies	Min. # people	# of Criteria (76 possible)
Objectives	1*	Objectives describe observable and measurable levels of proficiency that are aligned with accreditation, institutional, and/or discipline-specific standards.	0.47	1,855	45,247	16
Assessments	1*	The course utilizes varied assessments (e.g., formative and summative, formal and informal) to establish learners' levels of proficiencies in relation to the stated course objectives as well as to guide the course's development.	0.62	334	46,453	19
	2*	Feedback to learners is: a) positive, b) related to specific objectives and criteria, c) provides suggestions for how learners can continue to progress, and d) are conducted in a "timely" manner, providing learners with feedback that can be implemented in subsequent activities.	0.54	3,584	221,744	15
	3	Assessments are utilized in accordance with evidence-based recommendations and, whenever possible, their reliability and validity are established.	0.34	569	135,925	4
	4	When appropriate, self- and/or peer-assessments and reflections are utilized that are intended to lead to improved learning and development.	0.56	805	3,353	9

Guidelines' Statistics Table

Activities, Organization, and Resources	1*	Activities and resources intentionally foster learner-learner interactions.	0.51	3,246	85,263	15
	2*	Activities and resources help learners to progress in higher order thinking to improve learning and development.	0.50	5,665	456,819	15
	3	Course intentionally integrates relevant and interactive technologies to improve learning and development.	0.33	7,724	8,069,961	16
	4	The course helps learners adapt relevant KSAs** to address real-world issues in authentic contexts.	0.34	1,072	60,762	10
	5*	The course has learners engage in activities in ways that consistently scaffolds their increasing competencies for key KSAs.**	0.40	2,535	152,748	23
	6	*Mission-Centered Focus*: The class environment is one that is experienced by learners to be safe, inclusive, and caring.	0.36	825	130,282	9
Teaching and Learning Theories	1*	Instructor is able to articulate: a) specific and holistic learning theories and teaching strategies that they might utilize, and b) when and how these theories and strategies might apply.	0.57	9,422	1,609,707	10
	2*	Course utilizes active teaching and learning strategies. In particular, the following are highlighted in the literature: peer teaching/tutoring; elaboration and self-reflections; real-world projects and activities; metacognitive and study strategies; problem-based learning; workplace experiences; inquiry-based pedagogies; role-playing; modeling followed by learner practice; class discussions; concept mapping; game-based strategies.	0.47	8,731	6,403,329	14
	3*	Instructor is able to demonstrate the processes/methods by which they develop their course, and there is alignment among course elements.	0.69	1,100	54,307	17
Learner-Background	1*	Course is adapted to learners' relevant prior knowledge, interests, skills, and capabilities and ADA considerations are addressed.	0.54	7,123	1,713,214	19
	2	Instructor is able to appropriately modify the course in light of learners' diverse cultural locations (e.g., SES, ethnicity, gender, age, etc.).	0.37	2,355	10,654,625	10

Appendix B

	3*	*Mission-Centered Focus*: In pursuit of learning objectives, the course engages learners in diverse cultural experiences with underrepresented and marginalized communities that proactively reduce biases and increase justice for these populations. (Data presented is for strategies that work directly with students from these backgrounds to help them be successful.)	0.44	2,844	196,355	12
Professional Development, Leadership, and Scholarship	1*	Instructor engages in and supports professional development opportunities related to improving their educational competencies.	0.65	1,084	47,000	7
	2	Instructor actively participates in leadership roles and responsibilities that improve the institution's education and culture.	0.36	491	1,133,657	11
	3*	Instructor conducts evidence-based practice and/or scholarly projects that improve the quality of education.	0.56	1,142	139,760	24

*—Core Guideline; **—Knowledge, Skills, and/or Attitudes (KSAs)

Appendix C
Broad Overview of the Guidelines

Evidence-Based Pillars of Educational Excellence

Objectives	Assessments	Activities, Organization, & Resources	Teaching/ Learning Theories	Learner-Background	Prof. Dev., Leadership, & Scholarship
1. Objectives are SMART (Specific, Measurable, Achievable, Relevant, & Timely)	1. Draws on multiple & varied assessments 2. Uses effective feedback 3. Follows evidence-based assessment practices 4. Integrates self- and peer-assessments	1. Supports learner-learner interactions 2. Fosters higher-order thinking 3. Integrates relevant & interactive technologies 4. Addresses real-world problems 5. Scaffolds learner progress 6. Nurtures safe, inclusive, and caring environments	1. Employs holistic learning theories 2. Utilizes active teaching/ learning strategies 3. Follows course development methods	1. Adapted to learner knowledge, skills, & interests 2. Follows culturally responsive teaching and learning methods 3. Engages with marginalized & under-resourced communities	1. Engages in ongoing professional development 2. Active in leadership roles 3. Conducts evidence-based & scholarly projects

There are 20 Guidelines in all

Appendix D
Case Study—Organization Tier

FEEDBACK TABLE—OBJECTIVES

Guideline	Levels of Development			N/O
	Level 3	Level 2	Level 1	
1) The organization ensures that instructors and learners adequately utilize objectives to guide learning and development. (Core Guideline)	-The organization works to foster a culture where instructors and learners *collaborate in developing personalized learning objectives* that align with accreditation, institutional, and/or discipline-specific standards, and are relevant for learners' professional, civic, and/or personal life. -The organization provides support to instructors and learners on how to ensure that learners are able to *articulate how the activities in courses relate to these* personalized objectives.	The organization *provides the support* instructors and learners need to better *understand the relevancy of learning objectives* for learners' professional, civic, and/or personal life.	The organization *ensures that learners and instructors are aware of accreditation, institutional, and/ or discipline-specific standards* that can be used to develop measurable learning objectives.	

N/O—Not Observed; KSAs*—Knowledge, Skills, and/or Attitudes

NOTES

The organization follows accreditation standards and stated that they work to ensure that their curriculum aligns with these standards.

An administrator stated that there are curriculum maps that link unit and course objectives to accreditation standards.

GENERAL COMMENTS/RECOMMENDATIONS:

Significant Strengths:

-Administrative staff ensuring curriculum alignment and their planning of topics is an outstanding asset for the institution. This relieves faculty of these responsibilities and empowers them to focus more directly on their classes.

Primary Recommendations:

-Administration could provide training to instructors on how to adapt learning outcomes to more closely meet the background and experiences of current students (0.47).

Secondary Suggestions:

-It is recommended that administration work to adapt the learning outcomes to more closely meet the background and experiences of current students (0.47).

-Administration could provide support to students in helping to better know how learning outcomes relate to their personal and professional lives (0.47).

APPENDIX D

FEEDBACK TABLE—ASSESSMENTS

Guideline	Levels of Development		
	Level 3	Level 2	Level 1
1) The organization supports instructors and learners in utilizing varied assessments to support learning and development. (Core Guideline)	-The organization empowers instructors and learners to *work collaboratively to select and analyze a variety of assessments* that will help them better understand what is influencing learner progress. -The organization supports instructors and learners to then *use this data to help scaffold* individual learner development towards learning objectives.	The organization helps instructors and learners *use assessment information to modify their teaching/study strategies in real-time* as courses unfold to better support learner progress in their courses.	The organization provides training and support to instructors and learners on how to *use multiple types of assessments to draw conclusions* about learner progress towards learning objectives.
2) The organization cultivates a teaching and learning environment where quality feedback is used by instructors and learners to continually improve learner competencies and foster self-regulated learning skills. (Core Guideline)	Extending Level 2, the organization cultivates an environment where instructors and learners work together to *build self-regulated learning skills*, helping learners use feedback to reflect on their own performance and then *develop and apply concrete strategies for how they will continue to improve* their progress towards learning goals.	Building on Level 1, the organization supports learners and instructors in *developing learning experiences* that will help learners *apply this feedback* and thereby improve their competencies.	The organization empowers instructors and learners to *use assessment feedback that identifies strengths and weaknesses in learner performance and offers positive and concrete suggestions* for how learners can improve their achievements *using objective-generated criteria*.
3) The organization intentionally works to ensure that assessments are utilized in accordance with evidence-based recommendations and, whenever possible, their reliability and validity is established.	The organization proactively empowers a culture of *collaboration to help learners and instructors engage in Level 1 and 2 activities*.	The organization works with learners and instructors to *minimize bias* for specific evidence-based assessments and to *establish their validity and reliability* in helping improve learning and development.	The organization *provides ongoing training to instructors and learners on evidence-based practices* in implementing, interpreting, and applying specific assessments to improve learning.
4) The organization supports the use of self- and peer-assessments to improve learning and development.	The organization intentionally fosters a culture where *instructors and learners work collaboratively to generate assessment criteria*. The organization then helps them *apply these criteria to self- and/or peer-assessments* to improve learning and development.	Building on Level 1, the organization *provides support to instructors and learners to help them to apply the results of self- and/or peer-assessments* in order to increase student achievement.	The organization *provides instructors and learners with training to be able to use assessment criteria* as the basis for self- and/or peer-assessments.

N/O—Not Observed; KSAs*—Knowledge, Skills, and/or Attitudes

GENERAL COMMENTS/RECOMMENDATIONS

Primary Recommendations:

-Administrative staff could provide training and support to instructors in developing multiple types of formal and informal assessment methods that can be used to guide the development of their courses (0.62).

Secondary Suggestions:

-Administration could provide training to instructors to learn how to give continual feedback to students that identifies strengths and weaknesses in their performance and offers positive and concrete suggestions for how they can improve their achievements using objective-generated criteria (0.54).

-Staff could provide ongoing training to instructors on evidence-based practices in implementing, interpreting, and applying specific assessments to improve learning (0.34).

-Administration could promote and support the use of self- and peer-assessments in theory classes as well as clinicals and community-based settings (0.56).

APPENDIX D

FEEDBACK TABLE—ACTIVITIES, ORGANIZATION, AND RESOURCES

Guideline	Levels of Development			N/O
	Level 3	Level 2	Level 1	
1) The organization intentionally supports learner-learner interactions to support learning and development. (Core Guideline)	Building on Level 2, the organization provides training to instructors and learners so that *long-term group projects/activities* require groups to collaborate in substantive ways (e.g., *decision-making, exploration, invention, etc.*) in relation to relevant KSAs.*	The organization helps learners and instructors cultivate an environment where students learn about *each other's* diverse *perspectives, critically reflect* on these, and/or *help one another* to engage with relevant KSAs* more extensively.	The organization provides education for learners and instructors to know how to intentionally *develop simple interactions among learners* to support learning and development.	
2) The organization provides support that helps learners and instructors use higher order thinking to improve learning and development. (Core Guideline)	The organization *helps learners and instructors design and implement higher order learning experiences* that are aligned with learning objectives, result in a variety of outcomes and artifacts, and that build on learners' interests and backgrounds.	The organization *provides support for more complex higher order thinking skills* (e.g., synthesizing, creating, innovating, etc.) and/or *encourages learners and instructors to challenge assumptions* in course concepts, materials, activities, etc.	The *organization helps guide* learners and instructors in how to engage with *simpler critical thinking skills* (e.g., apply, analyze, and evaluate) for relevant course KSAs.*	
3) The organization intentionally integrates relevant and interactive technologies to improve learning and development.	The organization supports a culture where *instructors and learners collaborate* in identifying relevant *interactive technologies* that *redefine* learning processes in significant ways. These *technologies are essential* in order to engage in the learning experiences and the organization provides training and support for *advanced technical skills*.	The organization *expands the options* for learners' and instructors' responsible use of relevant *interactive technologies* to support learning. The organization provides training so that *technologies are integral to engagement* with learning as well as to help improve *intermediate technical skills* for both learners and instructors.	The organization *provides opportunities* for learners and instructors to *use relevant technologies in simpler ways* that support but do not fundamentally change the learning processes. The organization *provides training and support for very basic technology skills*.	

4) The organization helps learners and instructors adapt relevant KSAs* to address real-world issues in authentic contexts.	The organization helps learners and instructors to identify real-world problems or issues in authentic contexts/scenarios that require KSA* adaptations and supports them in carrying out plans to directly address these issues.	The organization provides training for learners and instructors on how to adapt relevant KSAs* for authentic contexts/scenarios in order to address a given real-world problem or issue.	The organization supports opportunities that help learners and instructors know how to apply relevant course KSAs* in authentic contexts/scenarios in direct and unmodified ways.	
5) The organization supports learners and instructors in developing activities that consistently scaffolds learners' increasing competencies for key KSAs.* (Core Guideline)	The organization fosters an environment where learners and instructors work collaboratively to identify sustained and varied pathways to the development of key KSAs* using a range of resources, learning experiences, and ways of demonstrating scaffolded progress towards these KSAs.*	The organization provides training to learners and instructors on developing a variety of sequenced resources and learning experiences that scaffolds competency in key KSAs* that are matched to learners' experiences, needs, and interests and allow for choice.	The organization supports learners and instructors in developing activities that repeatedly engage key KSAs* and scaffolds learners' growing competencies in these areas (i.e., ensures achievement before moving on to new KSAs*).	
6) Mission-Centered Focus: The organization works to create and sustain a learning environment that is safe, inclusive, and caring.	The organization intentionally helps instructors and learners collaborate in developing and applying expectations for a learning climate that includes openness, mutual respect, and positive peer relationships.	In addition to Level 1, the organization supports activities that require respectful interaction, mutual support, and individual/group responsibility for the learning environment.	The organization has explicit expectations for a safe and positive learning environment and there is evidence of behavior that includes respect and caring for one another.	

N/O—Not Observed; KSAs*—Knowledge, Skills, and/or Attitudes

NOTES

-An administrator stated that it is up to students to study on their own after classes. Students are in class from approximately 8 a.m. to 3:30 p.m. Students have eight classes a day, six days a week during the theory portions of their curriculum. Students are in clinicals and community-based settings for these hours during the clinical/community-based portions of the curriculum.

-A review of final examinations showed that all questions were at a remember/understand level of Bloom's Taxonomy.

Appendix D

-Students have access to and receive training on basic computer skills.

-Students are restricted from using cell phones while at school.

-No students were observed using technology outside of a computer skills training class.

- The administration recently asked for and received funding to purchase a simulation lab. This lab has been installed at the college.

-Students participate in several clinical experiences throughout their program. The administration provides support for these experiences in the form of scheduling, setting up arrangements with local organizations, etc.

-An administrator stated that there are curriculum maps that link unit and course objectives to government standards.

-An administrator provided us with an annual schedule of theory classes and clinicals. They stated that they were the one who designed this schedule to be the way that it is, and this can be changed. The schedule showed all theory classes lumped together at the beginning of each year (first one to three months), with the rest of the year being filled with community-based experiences. They stated that this schedule is arranged this way because of transportation issues, and that it would be difficult to have theory classes on campus in the mornings and then at clinicals in the afternoons—the clinical sites are too far away to accommodate this.

-The school has a dress code for faculty and students.

-Students, faculty, and staff were observed greeting one another with "ma'am" and "sir."

-Faculty, students, and staff are required to attend specific all college functions.

-Some students are required to complete a training on etiquette and how to behave professionally.

GENERAL COMMENTS/RECOMMENDATIONS

Significant Strengths:

-Administration's support of real-world simulations and learning experiences is perhaps the greatest strength to be noted here. Staff were observed working very hard to make these opportunities available to students and the impact of them was readily apparent.

-Another tremendous asset of the college is administration's development of a highly structure, well-disciplined, and deeply respectful culture among staff, faculty, and students. Throughout our stay, this very welcoming and positive environment was palpable.

Primary Recommendations:

-Administration could modify how the theory and practical portions of the curriculum are distributed. For instance, students could be in theory classes three days of the week and in community-based settings for the other three days. Integrating these two parts of the curriculum and distributing the theory portions throughout the year should lead to deeper learning and greater long-term retention of concepts and skills (0.40).

-It is recommended that administration find and/or develop higher order thinking (e.g., apply, analyze, evaluate, synthesize, create, etc.) standards and assessments in addition to the accreditation standards, which are at lower levels of critical thinking (e.g., remember, understand, etc.) (0.50).

Secondary Suggestions:

-Administration could provide training to instructors on how to use group work in their theory classes (0.51).

-Staff could support the formation of student study groups (0.51).

-Administration could provide training to instructors on how to develop critical thinking skills in students, particularly in the theory classes but also in clinicals and community-based settings (0.50).

Appendix D

-Administration could support a more democratic approach to cultural cultivation and policy-making, wherein students, faculty, and staff have more authority to influence decisions that directly affect their work and studies (0.36).

-Administration could further develop the college's technology infrastructure to better support online classes and programs. In particular, higher speed internet and stable/reliable power are needed (0.33).

-Administration could provide training to instructors on how to integrate technology into their courses and further develop students' technical skills, particularly as these relate to the field of nursing (0.33).

-Administration could change their policy on restricting technology use in the classrooms and provide students with training on the responsible use of technology for professional and educational purposes (0.33).

FEEDBACK TABLE—TEACHING AND LEARNING THEORIES

Guideline	Levels of Development			N/O
	Level 3	Level 2	Level 1	
1) The organization helps learners and instructors articulate: a) specific holistic learning theories and teaching/study strategies that they might utilize, and b) when and how these theories and strategies might apply. (Core Guideline)	Recognizing that students *learn and develop in diverse ways,* and building on Level 2, the organization *fosters a collaborative culture* that helps learners and instructors develop and utilize *multiple evidence-based holistic learning theories* to help guide learning and development, as well as to be *able to articulate when and how* each theory is being utilized.	The organization supports learners and instructors in using *observations as well as evidence-based resources to inform and adjust* their own holistic learning theories.	The organization *provides training* that helps learners and instructors *articulate their own holistic understandings of learning and development* and *how to adjust their teaching and/or learning strategies* in light of these understandings.	
2) The organization helps learners and instructors to utilize active teaching and learning strategies. (Core Guideline)	-The organization helps learners and instructors recognize that students *learn in diverse ways* and therefore *collaboratively develop multiple evidence-based active teaching and learning strategies.* -The organization then *empowers learners and instructors to select* personalized and active ways of engaging with relevant KSAs* and to *ensure that these varied pathways align with learning objectives.*	The organization provides training to learners and instructors on utilizing one or more *evidence-based active teaching and learning strategies* and how to adapt these strategies for their current courses.	The organization helps learners and instructors *draw on specific active teaching and learning strategies and to apply these* to help improve learning and development.	
3) The organization ensures that learners and instructors are able to demonstrate the processes/methods by which they develop their courses or learning strategies. There is alignment among these strategies with course elements. (Core Guideline)	-The *organization* fosters a culture where learners and instructors *collaborate with others in evidence-based design, implementation, and evaluation* of teaching/learning strategies. -The organization helps ensure *alignment* for the following *teaching/learning elements:* objectives, activities, assessments, teaching/learning strategies, learner/instructor backgrounds, and teaching/learning theories.	-The organization *supports learners and instructors in drawing from evidence-based literature and data* to design, implement, and evaluate teaching/learning strategies. -The organization helps to ensure there is direct *alignment among course as well as module/unit/weekly* objectives, activities, and assessments for the teaching/learning strategies being used by learners/instructors.	-The organization provides training for learners and instructors in *following some process* to design, implement, and evaluate teaching/learning strategies. -The organization helps ensure *alignment* among *teaching/learning objectives, activities/strategies, and assessments.*	

N/O—Not Observed; KSAs*—Knowledge, Skills, and/or Attitudes

NOTES

-The administration arranged for our team to provide a workshop on active teaching and learning strategies and theories. Faculty were required to attend this workshop.

-The administration arranged for our team to provide a workshop on active teaching and learning strategies and theories. Faculty were required to attend this workshop.

-The administration arranged for our team to offer a session to students where we also discussed learning theory and strategies. Students were required to attend this session.
-The school follows accreditation standards. At least one administrator discussed how specific classes and clinicals align with these standards.

-An administrator stated that instructors must complete lesson plans for each class. These plans are reviewed by administrators on a regular basis.

GENERAL COMMENTS/RECOMMENDATIONS

Significant Strengths:

-Allowing our team the privilege and opportunity to give a workshop on active teaching strategies is a strength that we hope will continue. Faculty appeared to be very receptive of the content that we worked with them on and we were told that some of them are excited to try some of these strategies out in their own classes.

Primary Recommendations:

-Administration could provide training to instructors and students on learning processes and how to support these processes (0.57).

-Administration could provide support to instructors on course development methods, particularly how to choose, adapt, implement, and evaluate active teaching strategies (0.69).

Secondary Suggestions:

-We recommend that administration continue to support training for instructors on active teaching strategies (0.47).

FEEDBACK TABLE—LEARNER BACKGROUND CONSIDERATIONS

Guideline	Levels of Development			N/O
	Level 3	Level 2	Level 1	
1) The organization helps leaners and instructors adapt teaching/learning to learners' relevant prior knowledge, interests, skills, and capabilities. The organization ensures that ADA considerations are addressed. (Core Guideline)	-The organization fosters a culture *where learners and instructors collaborate in adapting multiple teaching/learning* goals, strategies, activities, resources, and/or assessments to build upon learners' relevant prior knowledge, interests, skills, and capabilities. -The organization helps learners and instructors *collaborate in expanding the range of ADA resources* to enable all learners to exceed high standards.	-The organization supports learners and instructors in using learners' relevant prior knowledge, interests, skills, and capabilities to *plan multiple learning experiences/strategies and assessments* that *allow for learner choice* in pursuing and demonstrating their achievement of learning goals. -The organization helps learners and instructors *adapt teaching/learning strategies* and use *modified ADA resources* to *address all current learners' needs, interests, capabilities, etc.*	-The organization helps learners and instructors to *draw on past experiences and external resources to adjust teaching/learning strategies* to appropriately meet the diverse prior knowledge, interests, skills, and capabilities of learners. -The organization provides training on how to apply *interventions, modifications, and accommodations based on ADA requirements.*	
2) The organization supports learners and instructors in being able to appropriately modify teaching/learning strategies in light of learners' diverse cultural locations (e.g., SES, ethnicity, gender, age, etc.).	-The organization supports learners and instructors in *collaborating to develop* different culturally appropriate pathways to pursue learning objectives. -The organization supports *collaboration with a broad range of specialists and/or community members* to address learners' cultural needs and to *integrate diverse cultural resources, practices, and perspectives* into teaching/learning.	The organization provides training that helps learners and instructors to *plan multiple culturally appropriate pathways of teaching/learning experiences* and assessments that *allow for learner choice* in pursuing and demonstrating their achievement of learning objectives in light of learners' relevant cultural locations (e.g., SES, ethnicity, gender, age, etc.).	The organization supports learners and instructors in accessing resources to *expand their understanding* of the SES, ethnic, gender, age, etc. differences among learners and their communities and to then *modify teaching/learning strategies* in light of this.	

APPENDIX D

3) Mission-Centered Focus: *The organization aids learners and instructors in engaging in diverse cultural experiences with underrepresented and marginalized communities that proactively reduce biases and increase justice for these populations.* (Core Guideline)	-The organization assists learners and instructors in pursuing learning objectives by engaging with activities that *facilitate their development of advanced intercultural and civic engagement competencies*, particularly with underrepresented and marginalized communities. -The organization *provides opportunities and support* for learners and instructors to *proactively work for equity and justice in solidarity* with underrepresented and marginalized communities.	-The organization provides training to learners and instructors on developing teaching/learning strategies that *facilitate learners' direct engagement with diverse people* from *underrepresented and marginalized populations*. -The organization intentionally fosters a culture where learners and instructors assist one another in *exploring how their own biases can affect their perceptions and actions*, particularly as these biases relate to underrepresented and marginalized communities.	-The *organization provides support* for learners and instructors to *engage multiple cultural perspectives and experiences* of underrepresented and marginalized communities in the pursuit of learning objectives. -The organization helps learners and instructors to *explore how their own personal biases can affect perceptions and actions*, particularly as these biases relate to underrepresented and marginalized communities.	

N/O—Not Observed; KSAs*—Knowledge, Skills, and/or Attitudes

NOTES

-An administrator stated that if a student is doing poorly on an exam, this student will be provided extra support and is then allowed to retake the exam.

-Administrators were able to articulate specific customs of their students' families that they need to adapt to.

-An administrator stated that the school hosted a training session for female students on how to stay safe when in the city.

GENERAL COMMENTS/RECOMMENDATIONS

Significant Strengths:

-In our conversations with faculty, staff, and administration, it was very obvious that many knew students in very personal ways, understanding the communities and families that some students come from. This level of interpersonal relationships is a tremendous asset that can be leveraged to further strengthen the quality of education at the college.

Primary Recommendations:

-Administration could provide training to instructors on how to more accurately assess students' prior knowledge and experiences and then modify their classes to better match students' strengths and knowledge/skill gaps (0.54).

-Administration could provide training to instructors on how to develop theory classes and practical experiences that further develop students' intercultural competencies and civic engagement skills (0.44).

Secondary Suggestions:

-Administration could provide training to instructors on how to adopt Universal Design for Learning (UDL) Principles when developing their lesson plans to help accommodate students of diverse capabilities and backgrounds (0.54).

-It is recommended that administration consider adopting or developing validated civic engagement and intercultural competency assessment tools to help further guide the development of the real-world projects that students are completing (0.44).

-Administration could offer anti-bias training to students, faculty, and staff (0.44).

-Administration could offer training to instructors on how to ensure that their own personal biases are not significantly influencing their classes or their interactions with students (0.44).

-Administration could provide training to instructors on how to develop culturally appropriate learning outcomes, activities, and assessments for the current students at the college. This training should help these outcomes, activities, and assessments to more closely align with students' cultural beliefs, values, practices, etc. (0.37).

APPENDIX D

FEEDBACK TABLE—PROFESSIONAL DEVELOPMENT, LEADERSHIP, AND EVIDENCE-BASED PRACTICE

Guideline	Levels of Development			N/O
	Level 3	Level 2	Level 1	
1) The organization supports learners and instructors in their professional development opportunities related to improving discipline-specific and/or educational competencies. (Core Guideline)	-In addition to Level 2, the organization helps *learners and instructors collaborate with one another and/or peers* to collectively create, reflect upon, analyze, and improve *professional development opportunities* that address Levels 1 and/or 2.	-The organization aids learners and instructors in using personal reflections and feedback from one another, peers, and mentors to *identify areas of ongoing professional development* and participate in learning experiences that *address these identified areas of improvement*.	The organization provides support for learners and instructors to engage in structured *individual and/or group professional development opportunities* that help them to stay current *with essential KSAs** in their discipline-specific and/or educational role(s).	
2) Organization empowers learners and instructors to actively participate in leadership roles and responsibilities that improve the institution's education and culture.	-The organization intentionally mentors learners and instructors as leaders in *identifying and advocating for continuous evaluation and improvement* of the institution's vision, mission, and goals that support quality learning and development. -The organization empowers learners and instructors to *actively mentor and motivate one another* to participate in institutional leadership roles.	-The organization provides opportunities for learners and instructors to *engage in institutional decision-making processes* with one another to identify common goals, develop strategies for pursuing these goals, and evaluate progress towards them. -The organization supports learners and instructors in *actively and consistently contributing to the growth of others* through mentoring, feedback, and sharing of practice.	The organization actively empowers learners and instructors to *participate in schoolwide efforts* to implement a shared vision and to actively contribute to a *supportive and collaborative institutional culture*.	

| 3) The organization supports learners and instructors in conducting evidence-based practice and/or scholarly projects that improve discipline-specific competencies and/or quality education.

(Core Guideline) | The organization supports learners and instructors in *working collaboratively* to conduct *evidence-based practice and/or scholarly* projects that have an *impact* on one's educational and/or *discipline-specific theories, practices, and/or policies* more broadly. The organization provides the resources and support that learners and instructors need in order to *disseminate the results* of these projects via presentations and/or publications. | The organization empowers learners and instructors to *collaborate with one another and colleagues* to jointly *conduct evidence-based practice and/or scholarly* projects that *improve instructional* and/or *discipline-specific practices* for themselves and/or others. | The organization helps learners and instructors to *improve* their discipline-specific and/or educational practices *through evidence-based practice and/or scholarly projects*. | |

N/O—Not Observed; KSAs*—Knowledge, Skills, and/or Attitudes

NOTES

-One of the administrators shared that a specific staff person was sent to a conference; the staff person shared what the topic of the conference was.

-An administrator stated that two to four instructors are sent to trainings when they are offered, which is every few weeks or months.

-Throughout our visit, faculty, staff, and students participated in sessions, meetings, and meals with us.

-At one lunch, staff spoke about specific committees that they work on and some of the projects that they had been given to work on.

-An administrator stated that faculty also serve on committees.

-An administrator stated that they conduct random classroom observations and then provide feedback based on these.

-An administrator stated that instructors keep a "micro-teaching journal" that administrators review.

Appendix D

-An administrator stated that they also receive voluntary feedback from students and use this to help instructors.

-An administrator stated that instructors must complete lesson plans for each class. These plans are reviewed by administrators on a regular basis.

GENERAL COMMENTS/RECOMMENDATIONS

Significant Strengths:

-A great strength is the ongoing professional development that faculty and staff are offered when they are sent to conferences and government sponsored workshops.

-Administrative oversight of faculty's lesson planning and teaching is another tremendous asset to the institution. It appears that faculty regularly receive detailed and constructive feedback on their teaching practices.

Primary Recommendations:

-It is recommended that ongoing professional development opportunities be expanded to include on-site workshops, faculty peer support groups, reading/discussion groups (on topics directly related to education), etc. (0.65).

-Administration could provide training to instructors on Evidence-Based Practice (EBP) as it relates to the field of education. These practices rely on assessment data to inform and guide continuous course improvements and instructors can learn how to use these methods to continually improve the quality of classes on their own initiative (0.56).

Secondary Suggestions:

-Administration could support a more democratic approach to cultural cultivation and policy-making, wherein students, faculty, and staff have more authority to influence decisions that directly affect their work and studies (0.36).

Appendix E
Case Study—Instructor Tier

FEEDBACK TABLE—OBJECTIVES

Guideline	Levels of Development			N/O
	Level 3	Level 2	Level 1	
1) Objectives describe observable and measurable levels of proficiency that are aligned with accreditation, institutional, and/or discipline-specific standards. (Core Guideline)	-The instructor *collaborates with learners and external resources in identifying personalized learning objectives* to reach long term goals that align with accreditation, institutional, and/or discipline-specific standards and are relevant for learners' professional, civic, and/or personal life. -Learners are able to *articulate* the learning objectives *in their own words* and can describe *how the activities in the course relate to these* objectives.	-While retaining alignment with accreditation, institutional, and/or discipline-specific standards, the *instructor refines learning objectives based on current students'* professional, civic, and/or personal lives. -The instructor *clearly communicates/presents learning objectives* and effectively supports learners' sustained attention on the objectives.	-The instructor *uses given accreditation, institutional, and/or discipline-specific standards* to develop measurable learning objectives. -The instructor *refers to course/module objectives* in general ways.	

N/O—Not Observed; KSAs*—Knowledge, Skills, and/or Attitudes

Appendix E

NOTES

-The college follows the standards set by licensing/accreditation.

-An observed instructor began class by telling students what they were going to be covering in the class.

-An observed instructor provided our team with specific objectives for the class.

-During a class observation, the instructor repeatedly emphasized specific concepts that students should learn very well.

-An administrator stated that there are curriculum maps that link unit and course objectives to accreditation standards.

GENERAL COMMENTS/RECOMMENDATIONS

Significant Strengths:

-Direct alignment from accreditation standards to programs to courses to lesson plans is an outstanding feature of this program.

-Listing detailed objectives for each lesson plan.

Primary Recommendations:

-Objectives for theory classes could be rewritten as learning outcomes that are actually assessed by the instructor (0.47).

-It is recommended that, wherever possible, learning outcomes be created for clinicals and community-based portions of the programs—ones that directly align with the learning outcomes of the theory classes (0.47).

Secondary Suggestions:

-Instructors could work with students to articulate learning outcomes in their own words as well as to state why these outcomes are important for their future professional roles (0.47).

FEEDBACK TABLE—ASSESSMENTS

Guideline	Levels of Development			N/O
	Level 3	Level 2	Level 1	
1) The course utilizes varied assessments (e.g., formative and summative, formal and informal) to establish learners' levels of proficiencies in relation to the stated course objectives as well as to guide the course's development. (Core Guideline)	-The instructor *works with colleagues and learners to select and analyze a variety of assessments* that will help them to better understand what is influencing learner progress. -The instructor and learners then *use this data to help scaffold* individual learner development towards the learning objectives.	Based on Level 1 data, the instructor *uses this information to adjust instruction in real-time* as the course unfolds to provide additional and/or alternative supports for current learners.	The instructor *uses multiple types of assessments to draw conclusions* about learner progress towards the learning objectives.	
2) Feedback to learners is: a) positive, b) related to specific objectives and criteria, c) provides suggestions for how learners can continue to progress, and d) are conducted in a "timely" manner, providing learners with feedback that can be implemented in subsequent activities. (Core Guideline)	Extending Level 2, the instructor works with learners to *build self-regulated learning skills*, helping them use feedback to reflect on their own performance and to then *develop and apply concrete strategies for how they will continue to improve* in the course.	In addition to meeting Level 1, the instructor then *designs learning experiences* that will help learners *apply this feedback* and thereby improve their competencies.	Using objective-generated criteria, the instructor *points out strengths and weaknesses in performance and offers positive and concrete suggestions* for how learners can improve their work on subsequent assignments.	
3) Assessments are utilized in accordance with evidence-based recommendations and, whenever possible, their reliability and validity are established.	The instructor *collaborates with learners and/or others to engage in Level 1 and 2 activities*.	The instructor works to *minimize bias* for specific evidence-based assessments and to *establish their validity and reliability* based on course data.	The instructor *follows evidence-based recommendations* for implementing, interpreting, and applying specific assessments.	

APPENDIX E

4) When appropriate, self- and/or peer-assessments and reflections are utilized and intended to lead to improved learning and development.	The *instructor and learners work collaboratively to generate assessment criteria.* The course then helps build learners' self-regulated learning skills by *guiding them in analyzing and applying the results of self- and/or peer-assessment data* to improve their performance.	Building on Level 1, the instructor helps *learners apply the results of self- and/or peer-assessments* in order to strengthen their performance.	The instructor *provides learners with criteria* for an assignment to guide performance. The instructor then *assists each learner in examining their own and/or each other's work* in relation to these criteria.	

N/O—Not Observed; KSAs*—Knowledge, Skills, and/or Attitudes

NOTES

-Exams are used by instructors.

-Students presented projects that they had completed.

-Question-and-answer teaching strategies were observed.

-An observed instructor began class by reviewing previous concepts and asking students to provide an overview of what they know about the topic.

-An observed instructor asked students if they had any questions, no students asked any questions.

-We were provided a copy of a student's community class project, which detailed the student's gathered data, community assessment, and resulting plan. This project was conducted in the community with a specific family.

-In one class, the instructor called upon a student to explain a class concept. The instructor corrected misconceptions and elaborated on what the student shared.

-An observed instructor asked the class if they understood a concept, the class responded together, "Yes, ma'am." However, comprehension by specific students was not checked.

-We were provided a copy of a student's community class project, which detailed the student's gathered data, community assessment, and resulting plan. This project was conducted in the community with a specific family. There were no comments on this paper from the instructor, only checkmarks on each page.

GENERAL COMMENTS/RECOMMENDATIONS

Significant Strengths:

-The presentations that students gave to our team, the skit that we watched in a local community, and the student's report that was provided to us were outstanding examples of assessment methods.

Primary Recommendations:

-For theory classes, it is recommended that instructors conduct regular assessments to see what students are understanding and then adjust their instruction based on the results of these assessments (0.62).

Secondary Suggestions:

-For theory classes, it is recommended that instructors conduct regular assessments to see what students are understanding and then adjust their instruction based on the results of these assessments (0.62).
-Self- and peer-assessment practices could be adopted for both theory classes as well as in clinicals and community programs (0.56).
-Instructors could provide more detailed feedback to students on their competencies in relation to the learning outcomes that have been set. During our visit and in reviewing students' work, we found little, if any, evidence of this kind of detailed feedback (0.54).
-Instructors could work to establish the validity, reliability, and anti-bias of the exams that they are giving. Correlations between these assessments and how students are performing as nurses during clinicals and after graduation might also be established (0.34).

APPENDIX E

FEEDBACK TABLE—ACTIVITIES, ORGANIZATION, AND RESOURCES

Guideline	Levels of Development			N/O
	Level 3	Level 2	Level 1	
1) Activities and resources intentionally foster learner-learner interactions. (Core Guideline)	Building on Level 2, the course facilitates *long-term group projects/activities* where groups are required to collaborate in substantive ways (e.g., *decision-making, problem solving, exploration, invention, etc.*).	The course facilitates students learning about *each other's* diverse *perspectives*, *critically reflecting* on these, and/or *helping one another* to engage with relevant KSAs* in improved ways.	The course intentionally *structures simple interactions among* learners to support learning and development.	
2) Activities and resources help learners progress in higher order thinking to improve learning and development. (Core Guideline)	The course *helps learners design and implement higher order thinking experiences* that are aligned with learning objectives, result in a variety of outcomes and artifacts, and that build on learners' interests and backgrounds.	The course *facilitates more complex higher order thinking skills* (e.g., synthesizing, creating, innovating, etc.) and/or *guides learners in challenging assumptions* inherent in concepts, skills, materials, theories, methods, activities, etc.	The *course guides* learner engagement with *simpler critical thinking skills* (e.g., apply, analyze, and evaluate) for course KSAs.*	
3) Course intentionally integrates relevant and interactive technologies to improve learning and development.	The instructor *collaborates with learners* in identifying relevant *interactive technologies* that *redefine* course activities in significant ways. The *technologies are essential* in order to engage in learning experiences and *advanced technical skills* may also be required.	The course *expands the options* for learners' responsible use of relevant and more *interactive technologies* to improve learning. The technologies are integral to engagement with learning experiences and *intermediate technical skills* may also be required of the learner.	The course *provides opportunities* for learners to use relevant *technologies* in *simpler ways* that support but do not fundamentally change the learning experiences. Only very basic technology skills are needed by learners.	
4) The course helps learners adapt relevant KSAs* to address real-world issues in authentic contexts.	The course *helps learners identify a real-world problem* or issue in an authentic context/scenario that *requires relevant KSA* adaptations* and requires them to *carry out a plan* to directly address this issue.	The course guides learners in *adapting relevant KSAs* for authentic contexts/scenarios* in order to *address a given real-world problem or issue.*	The course engages learners in *applying course KSAs* in authentic contexts/scenarios* in *direct* and *unmodified ways.*	

5) The course has learners engage in activities in ways that consistently scaffolds their increasing competencies for key KSAs.*

(Core Guideline) | The instructor *works with learners to identify sustained and varied pathways in the development* of key course KSAs* using a range of resources, learning experiences, and ways of *demonstrating scaffolded progress* towards these relevant KSAs.* | The instructor plans a *variety of sequenced resources and learning experiences* that scaffolds competency in key course KSAs* and are *matched to the experiences, needs, and interests of learners* and allow for learner choice. | Learners are clearly and intentionally *guided through activities* across the course that has them repeatedly engage key KSAs* and *scaffolds their growing competencies in these areas* (i.e., ensures achievement before moving on to new KSAs*). | |
| 6) Mission-Centered Focus: The class environment is one that is experienced by learners to be safe, inclusive, and caring. | Building on Level 2, the instructor *collaborates with learners in developing and applying expectations* for a learning climate that includes *openness, mutual respect, and positive peer relationships* in the course. | In addition to Level 1, the course has *activities and assessments that require* respectful interaction, mutual support, and individual/group responsibility for the class environment. | The course has *explicit expectations* for a safe and positive learning environment and there is *evidence of behavior* that includes respect and caring for one another. | |

N/O—Not Observed; KSAs*—Knowledge, Skills, and/or Attitudes

NOTES

-Walking through multiple classrooms, all classes were setup up lecture-style with students seated side-by-side in rows facing the front of the classroom.

-Students presented projects and skits that were prepared in groups. Students were observed presenting a skit to a local community that was prepared after meeting with community members and assessing local needs.

-In walking through multiple classes, multiple instructors were observed using a Q&A teaching strategy. Most of the questions were at a remember/understand level.

-During a course observation, as the instructor was covering course concepts, students were observed completing the instructor's sentences. Example: "The neurons are part of THE BRAIN [students said capitalized words together.]" Most of these concepts were mostly at the remember/understand level.

Appendix E

-During a course observation, all of the concepts covered in the presentation slides were at the remember/understand level.

-Students presented projects that they had been working on where they had to create models of birth, anatomy, villages, etc. for demonstration purposes. These projects identified a real-issue in their community and the groups offered suggestions for how to address the issue.

-During an observation, after the lecture, the instructor called on rows of students to answer specific questions over what was just covered. Most of these questions were at the remember/understand level.

-An administrator provided our team with a sample of an exam; the majority of the questions were remember/understand level.

-Students were observed presenting a skit to a local community that was prepared after meeting with community members and assessing local needs.

-We were provided a copy of a student's community class project, which detailed the student's gathered data, community assessment, and resulting plan. This project was conducted in the community with a specific family.

-Students are not allowed to use cell phones while in school. No laptops were observed being used by students.

-Students have access to computer labs.

-During a class observation, students watched a video with digital simulations of the concepts just covered.

-Students participate in simulation labs and clinicals, where they have to apply their knowledge and skills to real-world situations.

-Students presented projects that they had been working on where they had to create models of birth, anatomy, villages, etc. for demonstration purposes. These projects identified a real-issue in their community and the groups offered suggestions for how to address the issue.

-One instructor stated that in one class, students have to visit a local community, identify the needs of this community, and create a skit that addresses these needs.

-During a class observation, no real-world examples were present in the presentation slides to illustration course concepts.

-Students were observed presenting a skit to a local community that was prepared after meeting with community members and assessing local needs.

-We were provided a copy of a student's community class project, which detailed the student's gathered data, community assessment, and resulting educational plan. This project was conducted in the community with a specific family.

-An observed instructor began class by reviewing previous concepts and asking students to provide an overview of what they know about the topic.

-An observed instructor told students that to help them learn a specific concept, they divided it into different parts.

-During an observation, instructor finished the lecture with a summary.

-Students were observed presenting a skit to a local community that was prepared after meeting with community members and assessing local needs.

-Students presented projects that they had been working on where they had to create models of birth, anatomy, villages, etc. for demonstration purposes. These projects identified a real-issue in their community and the groups offered suggestions for how to address the issue.

-In addressing instructors and staff, students used "ma'am" and "sir".

-Students are required to wear school uniforms.

-An observed instructor, after asking students questions and hearing answers, said "Very good," and "You are very intelligent students."

-An observed instructor used humor with students.

-We were provided a copy of a student's community class project, which detailed the student's gathered data, community assessment, and resulting educational plan. This project was conducted in the community with a specific family.

APPENDIX E

GENERAL COMMENTS/RECOMMENDATIONS

Significant Strengths:

-The real-world projects that students are conducting in groups as well as on their own in clinical and community settings is perhaps the most powerful part of this college. These projects integrate many of the recommendations of these guidelines and the college is encouraged to expand these and other similar strategies.

-The cultural expectations of students being attentive, disciplined, and hardworking is another tremendous strength of the college. Students were observed to be very respectful and kind throughout our visit.

Primary Recommendations:

Instructors are encouraged to integrate more interactive group work in their theory classes (0.51).

-Instructors, as well as college as a whole, are encouraged to integrate more critical thinking activities, skills, etc. In particular, following Bloom's Learning Taxonomy, programs are encouraged to develop learning outcomes, experiences, and assessments that help students to learn how to analyze, apply, evaluate, and synthesize what they are learning—particularly to real-world scenarios in theory classes (0.50).

Secondary Suggestions:

-Instructors are encouraged to develop multiple pathways (e.g., readings, activities, etc.) to learning key concepts and skills that align with current students' backgrounds and capabilities and allow for learner choice among these different pathways (0.40).

-Instructors are encouraged to work directly with current students to develop behavioral expectations that are relevant and meaningful for them and their peers (0.36).

-Instructors are encouraged to develop learning activities that utilize more technologies that help students not only to learn key concepts and skills but also to help develop their technical skills (0.33).

FEEDBACK TABLE—TEACHING AND LEARNING THEORIES

Guideline	Levels of Development			N/O
	Level 3	Level 2	Level 1	
1) Instructor is able to articulate: a) specific and holistic teaching and learning theories that they might utilize, and b) when and how these theories might apply. (Core Guideline)	Recognizing that students *learn and develop in diverse ways*, and building on Level 2, the instructor *collaborates with others* to develop and utilize *multiple evidence-based holistic teaching and learning theories* to help guide course development. They are also able to *articulate when and how* each theory is being utilized.	The instructor uses *observations of students as well as evidence-based resources to inform* their own holistic teaching and learning theories. Based upon this information, they *adjust their course*.	The instructor is able to *articulate their own understanding of holistic student learning* and development and *seeks to adjust the course's teaching strategies* in light of these understandings.	
2) Course utilizes active teaching and learning strategies. (Core Guideline)	-Recognizing that students *learn and develop in diverse ways*, the instructor collaborates with learners and others in utilizing *multiple evidence-based active teaching and learning strategies* to help guide course development. -The instructor *empowers learners to choose and/or develop* their own active ways of engaging with course KSAs* and ensures that these *varied pathways align with course objectives*.	The instructor utilizes one or more *evidence-based active teaching and learning strategies* and is able to *articulate how they have adapted these* strategies for the current course.	Drawing on *specific active teaching and learning strategies*, the *instructor seeks to apply these* to the course.	
3) Instructor is able to demonstrate the processes/methods by which they develop their course and there is alignment among course elements. (Core Guideline)	-The instructor *collaborates with learners, colleagues, and external sources* to engage in evidence-based course development. -There is *direct alignment among course as well as module/unit/weekly* objectives, activities, assessments, teaching and learning theories, and learner background considerations.	-The instructor *draws from evidence-based literature and data* to support course development (e.g., design, implementation, and evaluation). -There is direct *alignment among course as well as module/unit/weekly* objectives, activities, and assessments.	-The instructor *follows some process* to design, implement, and evaluate the course. -There is direct *alignment* among the *course's objectives, activities, and assessments*.	

N/O—Not Observed; KSAs*—Knowledge, Skills, and/or Attitudes

APPENDIX E

NOTES

-Students presented projects that they had been working on where they had to create models of birth, anatomy, villages, etc. for demonstration purposes. These projects identified a real-issue in their community and the groups offered suggestions for how to address the issue.

-In one class, the instructor called upon a student to explain a course concept. The instructor corrected misconceptions and elaborated on what the student shared.

-In walking through multiple classes, multiple instructors were observed using a Q&A teaching strategy. Most of the questions were at a remember/understand level.

-One instructor stated that in one class, students have to visit a local community, identify the needs of this community, and create a skit that addresses these needs.

-During a course observation, as the instructor was covering course concepts, students were observed completing the instructor's sentences. Example: "The neurons are part of THE BRAIN" [students said capitalized words together.] Most of these concepts were mostly at the remember/understand level. A majority of students (eleven out of twelve students) were observed verbally and nonverbally participating in this class activity. During this forty-five-minute lecture, the majority of students were observed to participate for the entire duration of the class.

-During a class observation, students were observed verbally and nonverbally participating, but no students were observed taking notes.

-During an observation, after the lecture, the instructor called on rows of students to answer specific questions over what was just covered. Most of these questions were at the remember/understand level.

-We were provided a copy of a student's community class project, which detailed the student's gathered data, community assessment, and resulting educational plan. This project was conducted in the community with a specific family.

-An observed instructor provided our team with specific objectives for the class. The team was also provided with the lesson plan for the class, which listed objectives, activities, and assessments for each part of the lesson. No assessments were conducted during the class. The objectives were therefore teaching objectives more than they were learning outcomes. This plan did have a section for learner prior knowledge, though the information that was filled in for this only stated something like, "Students have little prior knowledge of the subject." A similar statement was observed on at least two other lesson plans. Reference to supporting teaching/learning theories was not seen.

-During a class observation, the electricity went out and the class had to wait for it to come back on.

-An instructor stated that instructors are required to keep a "micro-teaching" journal and provided a copy of part of one. This sample showed that this journal was lecture notes for a class.

GENERAL COMMENTS/RECOMMENDATIONS

Significant Strengths:

-Alignment among objectives, activities, and assessments is a noted strength of the college's courses. The lesson plans showed clear and direct alignment among these elements.

Primary Recommendations:

-It is recommended that instructors receive more extensive training on learning theories. In particular, neuroscientific, educational psychology, and social-cultural theories that are relevant for their context are recommended (0.57).

-It is recommended that instructors receive more training on active teaching strategies. Such training should not only include an overview of various active strategies but also close support and coaching to help instructors implement these in their classes (0.47).

-It is recommended that instructors receive training on course development methods. While the topics that instructors are to teach in their theory classes are determined by government standards and administration, instructors must still know how to develop class activities for each of these topics and their respective concepts and skills (0.69).

APPENDIX E

FEEDBACK TABLE—LEARNER BACKGROUND CONSIDERATIONS

Guideline	Levels of Development			N/O
	Level 3	Level 2	Level 1	
1) Course is adapted to learners' relevant prior knowledge, interests, skills, and capabilities and ADA considerations are addressed. (Core Guideline)	-The instructor *collaborates with learners in adapting multiple course objectives, activities, resources, and/or assessments to build upon* learners' relevant prior knowledge, interests, skills, and capabilities. -The *instructor collaborates* with learners and colleagues *to expand the range of ADA resources* that *enables all learners to exceed high standards.*	-In light of learners' relevant prior knowledge, interests, skills, and capabilities, the instructor *plans multiple learning experiences and assessments* that *allow for learner choice* in pursuing and demonstrating their achievement of course objectives. -The instructor *adapts instruction* and *uses modified ADA resources to address the learning needs* of all current learners in the course.	-*Drawing on past experiences and/or external resources*, the *instructor seeks to adjust the course* appropriately to meet the diverse prior knowledge, interests, skills, and capabilities of learners. -The instructor applies *interventions, modifications, and accommodations based on ADA requirements.*	
2) Instructor is able to appropriately modify the course in light of learners' diverse cultural locations (e.g., SES, ethnicity, gender, age, etc.).	-The instructor *collaborates with learners to develop course elements* and provide different culturally appropriate pathways to engage with the course. -The instructor *collaborates with a broad range of colleagues, specialists, and/or community members* to understand and address learners' cultural needs and to *integrate diverse cultural resources, practices, and perspectives* into the class.	In light of learners' relevant cultural locations (e.g., SES, ethnicity, gender, age, etc.), the instructor *plans multiple culturally appropriate pathways of learning experiences* and assessments that *allow for learner choice* in pursuing and demonstrating their achievement of course objectives.	The instructor accesses resources to *expand their understanding* of the SES, ethnic, gender, age, etc. differences among learners and their communities and then *modifies the course* in light of this.	

3) Mission-Centered Focus: *In pursuit of learning objectives, the course engages learners in diverse cultural experiences with underrepresented and marginalized communities that proactively reduce biases and increase justice for these populations.* (Core Guideline)	-In alignment with learning objectives, the course has activities that *facilitate learners' development of advanced intercultural and civic engagement competencies*, particularly with underrepresented and marginalized communities. -The course *provides opportunities* for learners to *proactively work for equity and justice in solidarity* with underrepresented and marginalized communities.	-In pursuit of learning objectives, the course has learning experiences that *facilitate learners' direct engagement with diverse people* from underrepresented and marginalized populations. -The instructor assists learners in *exploring how their own biases can affect perceptions and actions*, particularly as these biases relate to underrepresented and marginalized communities.	-The *course includes multiple cultural perspectives and experiences* of underrepresented and marginalized communities that align with course objectives. -The instructor *explores how their own personal biases can affect perceptions and actions*, particularly as these biases relate to underrepresented and marginalized communities.	

N/O—Not Observed; KSAs*—Knowledge, Skills, and/or Attitudes

NOTES

-For a class observation, the team was provided with the lesson plan for the class. This plan included a section listing the "Previous Knowledge of Students."

-A student group was observed presenting a session on disability rights to a local community. However, no discussions or evidence of ADA accommodations was observed during the visit.

-One instructor stated that in one class, students have to visit a local community, identify the needs of this community, and create a skit that addresses these needs.

-A student group was observed presenting a session on disability rights to a local community.

-We were provided a copy of a student's community class project, which detailed the student's gathered data, community assessment, and resulting educational plan. This project was conducted in the community with a specific family.

Appendix E

GENERAL COMMENTS/RECOMMENDATIONS

Significant Strengths:

-Students engagement with rural communities to address real-world issues is another tremendous strength of the college.

Primary Recommendations:

-It is recommended that instructors, in their lesson plans, assess and note the specific prior knowledge that current students have in relation to each topic. Pre-assessments can be used to gather this information. The lesson plans should then be adjusted based upon this assessment data (0.54).

Secondary Suggestions:

-It is recommended that instructors begin to adopt Universal Design for Learning Principles when developing their lesson plans to help accommodate students of diverse capabilities and backgrounds (0.54).

-It is recommended that instructors adopt or develop civic engagement and intercultural competency rubrics to help further guide the development of the real-world projects that students are completing (0.44).

-It is recommended that instructors note the diverse and specific cultural backgrounds of students. In particular, the socioeconomic status, gender, and religious backgrounds of current students might be noted. This information should then be used to help adopt learning outcomes, activities, and assessments to better meet the diverse learning styles, communication patterns, experiences, and values of these cultural communities (0.37).

FEEDBACK TABLE—PROFESSIONAL DEVELOPMENT, LEADERSHIP, AND EVIDENCE-BASED PRACTICE

Guideline	Levels of Development			N/O
	Level 3	Level 2	Level 1	
1) Instructor engages in and supports professional development opportunities related to improving their educational competencies. (Core Guideline)	In addition to Level 2, the *instructor collaborates with colleagues* to collectively create, reflect upon, analyze, and improve *professional development opportunities* that address Levels 1 and/or 2.	Based on personal reflections and feedback from students, peers, and mentors, the instructor *identifies areas of ongoing professional development* and participates in learning experiences that *address these identified areas of educational improvement*.	The instructor engages in structured *individual and/or group professional learning opportunities* that help them to stay current *with essential KSAs** in their discipline as well as *to provide all learners with effective curriculum and learning experiences*.	
2) Instructor actively participates in leadership roles and responsibilities that improve the institution's education and culture.	-The instructor is a leader in *identifying and advocating for continuous evaluation and improvement* of institutional-wide vision, mission, and goals that support student learning and development. -The instructor *actively mentors and motivates colleagues* to participate in institutional leadership roles.	-The instructor *engages in institutional-wide decision-making processes* with colleagues to identify common goals, develop strategies for pursuing these goals, and evaluate progress towards them. -The instructor *actively and consistently contributes to the growth of others* through mentoring, feedback, and sharing of practices.	The instructor *participates in schoolwide efforts* to implement a shared vision and they actively contribute to a *supportive and collaborative institutional culture*.	
3) Instructor conducts evidence-based practice and/or scholarly projects that improve the quality of education. (Core Guideline)	The instructor *works collaboratively* to conduct *evidence-based practice and/or scholarly* projects that have an *impact* on one's educational *discipline* and/or *educational theories, practices, and/or policies* more broadly. The instructor works to *disseminate the results* of these projects via presentations and/or publications.	The instructor *collaborates with colleagues* at their institution to jointly *conduct evidence-based practice and/or scholarly* projects that *improve teaching/learning* for their *own classes* and/or the *institution as a whole*.	The instructor works to *improve* their *instructional practices through evidence-based practice and/or scholarship* projects.	

N/O—Not Observed; KSAs*—Knowledge, Skills, and/or Attitudes

NOTES

-The majority of faculty actively participated in the workshop on active teaching strategies that we offered.

-One instructor stated that they have taken a class on education.

-During our visit, most/all faculty actively participated in events and sessions (e.g., training, session with students, lunches, etc.)

-Faculty have a dress code and they were observed to be compliant with this.

GENERAL COMMENTS/RECOMMENDATIONS

Significant Strengths:

-Instructors having the opportunity to attend government workshops is a strength of the college's professional development opportunities.

Primary Recommendations:

-It is recommended that instructors create Professional Development Plans (PDPs) where they identify areas that they would to develop more in as a professional educator. These identified areas should focus on the theory and practice of education (0.65).

-It is recommended that instructors learn the basics of Evidence-Based Practice (EBP) as it relates to the field of education. These practices rely on assessment data to inform and guide continuous course improvements (0.56).

Secondary Suggestions:

-It is recommended that instructors take a more active role helping to develop the curriculum. Since instructors are the ones tasked with implementing the curriculum, their input is essential to ensuring ongoing improvements (0.36).

Appendix F
Case Study—Learner Tier

FEEDBACK TABLE—OBJECTIVES

Guideline	Levels of Development			N/O
	Level 3	Level 2	Level 1	
1) Learner is able to integrate learning objectives into their professional, civic, and/or personal life. (Core Guideline)	-The learner *collaborates with others in adapting learning objectives* in ways that will help them reach long term goals for their professional, civic, and/or personal life. -The learner is able to *articulate* learning objectives *in their own words* and can describe *how the activities in their course(s)/program(s) relate to these objectives.*	Learner is able to *articulate the relevancy of learning objectives* for their professional, civic, and/or personal life.	-The learner is *able to state general learning goals* for their own educational journey. The learner is also *aware of course/program objectives* and knows where to find them.	

N/O—Not Observed; KSAs*—Knowledge, Skills, and/or Attitudes

GENERAL COMMENTS/RECOMMENDATIONS

-It is recommended that students continually work to understand why they are learning what they are learning and how these concepts, skills, and attitudes relate to their personal, professional, and civic lives (0.47).

Appendix F

FEEDBACK TABLE—ASSESSMENTS

Guideline	Levels of Development			N/O
	Level 3	Level 2	Level 1	
1) The learner utilizes assessment information to support their own development towards their learning goals. (Core Guideline)	-The learner *collaborates with others to analyze* their performance on a variety of *formative and summative assessments* to help them better understand what is influencing their learning. -The learner then *uses this information to help scaffold* their own development towards their learning goals.	The learner *uses assessment information to modify their study strategies* to better support their own learning progress.	The learner *uses assessments to draw conclusions* about their own progress towards their learning goals.	
2) The learner uses feedback from assessments to continually improve their competencies in their courses as well as build their own self-regulated learning capabilities. (Core Guideline)	In addition to Level 2, the learner *takes initiative* and collaborates with others to use feedback to *reflect on their own performance* and to then *develop and apply their own concrete strategies for how they will continue to improve* their progress towards learning goals.	In addition to meeting Level 1, the learner engages in *additional/supplemental learning experiences* that will help them *apply feedback from assessments* and thereby improve their competencies in their courses.	The learner uses feedback from assessments *to identify their own strengths and weaknesses in performance as well as strategies* for how they might improve their progress towards learning goals.	
3) Assessments are utilized by the learner to improve their learning in ways that are in accordance with best practices.	The learner *collaborates* with instructors, staff, and/or peers *to engage in Level 1 and 2 activities.*	The learner *works* to help ensure that *their use of specific assessments is valid and reliable* in helping them improve in their learning and development.	The learner *follows best practices* in engaging, interpreting, and applying insights from specific assessments to help improve their learning.	
4) Learner utilizes self- and/or peer-assessments and reflections to improve their own and/or their peers' learning and development.	The *learner works with instructors and/or peers to collaboratively generate assessment criteria.* The learner then utilizes self-regulated learning skills by *analyzing and applying the results of self- and/or peer-assessment data* to improve their own and/or their peers' competencies.	Building on Level 1, the *learner works with instructors, staff, and/or peers to apply the results of self- and/or peer-assessments* in order to strengthen their own and/or their peers' competencies.	The *learner uses criteria provided* for an assignment to guide their performance. Using these criteria, the *learner examines her/his and/or classmate's work* in relation to the criteria.	

N/O—Not Observed; KSAs*—Knowledge, Skills, and/or Attitudes

NOTES

-Students stated that they would like more resources, readings, etc. to help them with their studies.

GENERAL COMMENTS/RECOMMENDATIONS

Significant Strengths:

-Students stated that they would like more resources, readings, etc. to help them with their studies. This intrinsic motivation is a tremendous asset to students' learning journey as well as the institution as a whole.

Primary Recommendations:

-Students could use self- and peer-assessment study strategies to help them learn course content and skills more deeply (0.56).

-Students should know how to use the results and feedback from assessments to help guide their study strategies (0.54).

Secondary Suggestions:

-Students should draw from multiple types of assessments to draw conclusions about their learning progress and make plans for how to learn better (0.62).

-It is recommended that students learn best practices for interpreting and using assessment data to improve their study strategies (0.34).

APPENDIX F

FEEDBACK TABLE—ACTIVITIES, ORGANIZATION, AND RESOURCES

Guideline	Levels of Development			N/O
	Level 3	Level 2	Level 1	
1) The learner intentionally seeks to engage in learner-learner interactions to support learning and development. (Core Guideline)	Building on Level 2, the learner participates in *long-term group activities* where they are required to collaborate in substantive ways (e.g., *decision-making, problem solving, exploration, invention, etc.*) in relation to relevant KSAs.*	The student proactively learns about *other students'* diverse *perspectives, critically reflects* on these, and/or *helps others* engage with relevant KSAs* in improved ways.	The learner intentionally *engages in simple interactions with other learners* to support their learning and development.	
2) The learner strives to engage in higher order thinking in order to support their learning and development. (Core Guideline)	The *learner seeks to design and implement higher order thinking experiences* that will help them better learn course KSAs,* are aligned with course objectives, and that build on their own interests and background.	The learner uses *more complex higher order thinking skills* (e.g., synthesizing, creating, innovating, etc.) for course KSAs* and/or *challenges assumptions* inherent in course concepts, materials, theories, methods, activities, etc.	The learner intentionally engages with *simpler critical thinking skills* (e.g., apply, analyze, and evaluate) for course KSAs*.	
3) Learner intentionally uses relevant and interactive technologies to improve their learning and development.	The learner *collaborates with others* to identify relevant *interactive technologies* that *redefine* their learning strategies in significant ways. The *technologies are essential* to engage in the learning experience and *advanced technical skills* may also be required.	The learner *expands the options* for their own responsible use of relevant and more *interactive technologies* to improve their learning. The *technologies are integral to their engagement* with learning experiences and *intermediate technical skills* may be required.	The learner *makes use* of relevant *technologies* in *simpler ways* to support their learning. Their technology engagement might support but does not *fundamentally alter* their learning strategies and only *very basic technology skills* are used by the learner.	
4) The learner seeks to adapt relevant KSAs* to address real-world issues in authentic contexts.	Working with others, the learner identifies *real-world problems* or issues in authentic contexts/scenarios that *require KSA* adaptations* and they *develop and implement plans* to directly address these issues.	The learner works to *adapt relevant KSAs* for authentic contexts/scenarios* in order to *address a given real-world problem* or issue.	The learner seeks to *apply course KSAs* in authentic contexts/scenarios* in *direct* and *unmodified* ways.	

5) The learner engages in activities in ways that consistently scaffolds their increasing competencies for key KSAs.* (Core Guideline)	The learner *collaborates with others to identify sustained and varied pathways to the development* of key KSAs* using a range of resources, learning experiences, and ways of *demonstrating scaffolded progress towards these relevant KSAs.*	The learner engages with *a variety of sequenced resources and learning experiences* that scaffolds their competencies for key KSAs* and are *matched to their own experiences, needs, and interests.*	The learner seeks out *activities* that repeatedly engage key KSAs* and *scaffolds their growing competencies in these areas* (i.e., ensures achievement before moving on to new KSAs*).	
6) Mission-Centered Focus: *The learner helps nurture a learning environment that is safe, inclusive, and caring.*	The learner *collaborates with others to develop and apply expectations* for a learning climate that includes *openness, mutual respect, and positive peer relationships.*	In addition to Level 1, the learner proactively engages in *activities that help foster a learning environment* of respectful interactions, mutual support, and individual/group responsibility for the learning environment.	The learner *adheres to explicit expectations* for a safe and positive learning environment and *their behavior demonstrates respect and caring* for others.	

N/O—Not Observed; KSAs*—Knowledge, Skills, and/or Attitudes

NOTES

-An administrator stated that some students will study together in the library.
-Students are not allowed to use cell phones while at school. No students were observed using technology during our visit.

-Students participate in several clinical experiences throughout their program.

-Throughout our visit, many students greeted us with formal greetings. Students would often wave, smile, and nod at us. Students gave hugs to members of our team.

GENERAL COMMENTS/RECOMMENDATIONS

Significant Strengths:

-Students' active participation in community-based settings is a tremendous asset for students. Throughout our time, students appeared to be fully engaged in the active real-world experiences that we observed.

-One of the great strengths at the college is the highly disciplined, respectful, and hardworking culture that is present.

Appendix F

Primary Recommendations:

-It is recommended that students form study groups to help one another more deeply learn course material (0.51).

-To the extent that is possible, students could seek out technology-enhanced resources (e.g., apps, websites, software, etc.) that will help them to engage with key concepts and skills (0.33).

Secondary Suggestions:

-Students should be working to use higher order thinking skills (e.g., applying, analyzing, evaluating, synthesizing, etc.) when they are learning key concepts and skills and not just seeking to memorize what they are being taught (0.50).

-Students should be working to identify their own knowledge/skill gaps and then develop learning strategies that will help them to continue to progress in these areas (0.40).

-Students are encouraged to expand their proactive support of the positive and respectful environment (0.36).

-Students are encouraged to seek out additional real-world and relevant activities (e.g., volunteering, participating in professional organizations, etc.) to further extend and supplement their learning experiences (0.34).

FEEDBACK TABLE—TEACHING AND LEARNING THEORIES

Guideline	Levels of Development			N/O
	Level 3	Level 2	Level 1	
1) Learner is able to articulate: a) specific holistic learning theories that they might utilize, and b) when and how these theories might apply to their own learning. (Core Guideline)	Recognizing that they might learn and develop in diverse ways for different situations, and building on Level 2, the learner *collaborates with others* to develop and utilize *multiple evidence-based holistic learning theories* to help guide their learning. They are also *able to articulate when and how* each theory is being utilized.	The learner uses *observations of their own and others' progress* as well as *evidence-based resources to inform* their own holistic learning theories. Based upon this information, they *adjust their study strategies*.	The learner is able to *articulate their own holistic understanding of learning and development* and *seeks to adjust their study strategies* in light of these understandings.	
2) Learner utilizes active learning strategies to support their learning and development. (Core Guideline)	Recognizing that they *learn and develop in diverse ways*, the learner collaborates with others in utilizing *multiple evidence-based active learning strategies* to help support their learning and development and they can *articulate how they have adapted these* strategies to fit with the classes that they are currently taking.	The learner utilizes one or more *evidence-based active learning strategies* and is able to *articulate how they have adapted these* strategies to fit with the classes that they are currently taking.	Drawing on *specific active learning strategies*, the *learner seeks to apply these* to help improve their learning and development.	
3) Learner is able to demonstrate the processes/methods by which they develop their learning strategies, and there is alignment among their courses and their own learning goals, study strategies, and how they assess these goals and strategies. (Core Guideline)	-The learner *collaborates with others* in evidence-based design, implementation, and evaluation of their learning strategies. -There is direct *alignment* between the modules/units of their courses and the following: *learning goals, study strategies, how they assess these, their understanding of learning processes, and their own unique background, interests, etc.*	-The learner *draws from evidence-based literature and data* to develop (e.g., design, implement, and evaluate) their learning strategies. -There is direct *alignment* between the modules/units of their courses and their own *learning goals, study strategies, and how they assess these goals and strategies.*	-The learner *follows some process* to design, implement, and evaluate their learning strategies. -There is direct *alignment* between their courses and their own *learning goals, study strategies, and how they assess these goals and strategies.*	

N/O—Not Observed; KSAs*—Knowledge, Skills, and/or Attitudes

Appendix F

NOTES

-Students presented projects that they had been working on where they had to create models of birth, anatomy, villages, etc. for demonstration purposes. Some of these projects identified a real-issue in their community and the groups offered suggestions for how to address the issue.

GENERAL COMMENTS/RECOMMENDATIONS

Significant Strengths:

-Students participating in numerous active teaching strategies in their theory and practical courses is an outstanding asset of this program.

Primary Recommendations:

-Students are encouraged to learn how to assess their learning needs, choose appropriate strategies, and then be able to assess the effectiveness of these strategies based on their performance in theory and practical components of their program (0.69).

Secondary Suggestions:

-Students should learn more about learning processes in an effort to improve their study strategies (0.57).

-Students are encouraged to learn and utilize active study strategies to support their learning journey (0.47).

CASE STUDY—LEARNER TIER

FEEDBACK TABLE—LEARNER BACKGROUND CONSIDERATIONS

Guideline	Levels of Development			N/O
	Level 3	Level 2	Level 1	
1) The learner adapts study strategies to their own relevant prior knowledge, interests, skills, and capabilities; ADA considerations are addressed if needed. (Core Guideline)	-The learner *collaborates with others in adapting their multiple learning goals, strategies, activities, resources, and/or assessments to build upon their relevant prior knowledge, interests, skills, and capabilities.* -The learner *collaborates with others to expand the range of ADA resources* that address their own and/or others' learning needs and *enables themselves and/or other students to exceed high standards.*	-In light of their own relevant prior knowledge, interests, skills, and capabilities, the learner *uses multiple learning strategies* to pursue and demonstrate their achievement of learning goals. -The *learner adapts and uses modified ADA resources to address* their own *learning needs.*	-*Drawing on past experiences and external resources, the learner seeks to adjust their learning strategies* to better meet their own prior knowledge, interests, skills, and capabilities. -If appropriate, the learner utilizes *ADA interventions, modifications, and accommodations.*	
2) Learner is able to appropriately modify their learning strategies in light of their own cultural locations (e.g., SES, ethnicity, gender, age, etc.).	The learner *collaborates with a broad range of peers, specialists, and/or community members in developing culturally appropriate* learning strategies, resources, practices, and perspectives in their pursuit of learning goals.	In light of their own cultural locations (e.g., SES, ethnicity, gender, age, etc.), the learner *utilizes multiple culturally appropriate learning strategies* in pursuing and demonstrating their achievement of learning goals.	The learner accesses resources to *expand their understanding* of their own and their communities' cultural locations (e.g., SES, ethnic, gender, age, etc.) and then *modifies their learning strategies* in light of this.	
3) Mission-Centered Focus: *In pursuit of learning goals, the learner engages in diverse cultural experiences with underrepresented and marginalized communities and proactively works to reduce biases and increase justice for these populations.* (Core Guideline)	-In alignment with their learning goals, the learner engages in activities that *help them to develop advanced intercultural and civic engagement competencies,* particularly with underrepresented and marginalized communities. -The learner engages in *opportunities* to *proactively work for equity and justice in solidarity* with underrepresented and marginalized communities.	-In pursuit of learning goals, the learner engages in experiences that *help them to directly work with diverse people* from *underrepresented and marginalized populations.* -The learner proactively assists others in *exploring how their own biases can affect perceptions and actions,* particularly as these biases relate to underrepresented and marginalized communities.	-The *learner seeks out multiple cultural perspectives and experiences of underrepresented and marginalized communities* as part of their pursuit of learning goals. -The learner *explores how their own personal biases can affect perceptions and actions,* particularly as these biases relate to underrepresented and marginalized communities.	

N/O—Not Observed; KSAs*—Knowledge, Skills, and/or Attitudes

Appendix F

NOTES

-One of the projects that students presented was about rural communities and addressing their community's needs.

GENERAL COMMENTS/RECOMMENDATIONS

Significant Strengths:

-Working directly with lower socioeconomic status and rural communities is a great strength for students.

Primary Recommendations:

-Learners are encouraged to continually relate what they are learning to their own background and experience (0.54).

Secondary Suggestions:

-Students are encouraged to expand their work with lower socio-economic status and rural communities in ways that further support their learning (0.44).

-Learners should be seeking to find, adapt, and utilize learning strategies that are integrative of their cultural backgrounds (0.37).

FEEDBACK TABLE—PROFESSIONAL DEVELOPMENT, LEADERSHIP, AND EVIDENCE-BASED PRACTICE

Guideline	Levels of Development			N/O
	Level 3	Level 2	Level 1	
1) Learner engages in and supports professional development opportunities related to improving their discipline-specific competencies. (Core Guideline)	In addition to Level 2, the learner *collaborates with others* to collectively create, reflect upon, analyze, and improve co- and/or non-curriculum *professional development opportunities* that address Levels 1 and/or 2.	Based on personal reflections and feedback from peers and mentors, the learner *identifies needed areas of ongoing discipline-specific professional development* and participates in co- and/or non-curriculum learning experiences that *address these identified areas of improvement*.	The learner engages in structured *individual and/or group professional learning opportunities* (co- and/or non-curriculum) that help them to stay current *with essential KSAs** in their discipline.	
2) Learner actively participates in leadership roles and responsibilities that improve the school's education and culture.	-The learner is a leader in *identifying and advocating for continuous evaluation and improvement* of schoolwide vision, mission, and goals that support quality teaching and learning. -The learner *actively mentors and motivates others* to participate in institutional leadership roles.	-The learner *engages in schoolwide decision-making processes* with others to identify common goals, develop strategies for pursuing these goals, and evaluate progress towards them. -The learner *actively and consistently contributes to the growth of others* through mentoring and feedback.	The learner *participates in schoolwide efforts* to implement a shared vision and they actively contribute to a *supportive and collaborative school culture*.	
3) Learner conducts evidence-based practice and/or scholarly projects that improve their discipline-specific competencies. (Core Guideline)	The learner *works collaboratively* with others to conduct *evidence-based practice and/or scholarly* projects that have an *impact* on one's *discipline-specific theories, practices, and/or policies* more broadly. The learner works to *disseminate the results* of these projects via presentations and/or publications.	The learner *collaborates with others* to jointly conduct evidence-based practice and/or scholarly projects that *improve discipline-specific practices* for themselves and/or others.	The learner works to *improve* their discipline-specific practices *through evidence-based practice and/or scholarly projects*.	

N/O—Not Observed; KSAs*—Knowledge, Skills, and/or Attitudes

APPENDIX F

NOTES

-An administrator stated that the school hosted a training session for female students on how to stay safe when in the city. They also stated that many of the students participated in this event.

-The college hosts a women's empowerment club that works with local women. One of the administrators stated that there are students who also participate in this club.
-text

GENERAL COMMENTS/RECOMMENDATIONS

Significant Strengths:

-The safe training workshops that were offered are another tremendous asset of the college.

-The women's club is a wonderful outreach and empowerment program that the college has and could be used to further enhance students' educational opportunities.

Primary Recommendations:

-It is recommended that students seek out and attend additional professional development opportunities in their field to help continually expand upon their knowledge and skill base as well as to help further establish habits of life-long learning (0.65).

Secondary Suggestions:

-Students should continue to cultivate an evidence-based practice (EBP) approach to their own professional development, wherein they seek to continually improve as professionals based on how well they are working in their professional roles in practicals as well as how they are doing in their theory classes (0.56).

-Students should seek and lobby for more opportunities to be directly involved in the college's decision-making processes (0.36).

Bibliography

Al-Eraky, Mohamed Mostafa. "Twelve Tips for Teaching Medical Professionalism at All Levels of Medical Education." *Medical Teacher* 37 (November 2015) 1018–25.

Albanese, Mark, and Susan M. Case. "Progress Testing: Critical Analysis and Suggested Practices." *Advances in Health Sciences Education* 21 (March 2016) 221–34.

Allport, G. W. Personality: *A Psychological Interpretation*. New York: Holt, 1937.

Alnassar, Sami et al. "Clinical Psychomotor Skills among Left and Right Handed Medical Students: Are the Left-Handed Medical Students Left Out?" *BMC Medical Education* 16 (March 2016) 97.

Alqahtani, Nasser D. et al. "Live Demonstration Versus Procedural Video: A Comparison of Two Methods for Teaching an Orthodontic Laboratory Procedure." *BMC Medical Education* 15 (November 2015) 199.

Amalba, Anthony et al. "The Effect of Community Based Education and Service (COBES) on Medical Graduates' Choice of Specialty and Willingness to Work in Rural Communities in Ghana." *BMC Medical Education* 16 (March 2016) 79.

Ambrose, Susan A. *How Learning Works: Seven Research-Based Principles for Smart Teaching*. The Jossey-Bass Higher and Adult Education Series. 1st ed. San Francisco: Jossey-Bass, 2010.

Amoako-Sakyi, Daniel, and Harold Amonoo-Kuofi. "Problem-Based Learning in Resource-Poor Settings: Lessons from a Medical School in Ghana." *BMC Medical Education* 15 (December 2015) 221.

Andrews, Ben et al. "How We Implemented an Analytical Support Clinic to Strengthen Student Research Capacity in Zambia." *Medical Teacher* 37 (July 2015) 635–40.

Aponte, Judith et al. "Mentoring Hispanic Undergraduate and Graduate Research Assistants: Building Research Capacity in Nursing." *Journal of Nursing Education* 54 (2015) 328–34.

Aquinas, Thomas. *Summa Theologica*. Translated by Fathers of the English Dominicans Province. 1st Complete American ed. 3 vols. New York: Benziger Bros., 1947.

Aronsson, Patrik et al. "The Understanding of Core Pharmacological Concepts among Health Care Students in Their Final Semester." *BMC Medical Education* 15 (December 2015) 235.

Au, Wilkie, and Noreen Cannon Au. *The Discerning Heart: Exploring the Christian Path*. New York: Paulist, 2006.

Augustine. *The Trinity*. Translated by Edmund Hill. Brooklyn: New City Press, 1991.

Avants, S. Kelley, and Arthur Margolin. *The Spiritual Self Schema (3-S) Development Program*. New Haven: Yale University School of Medicine, 2003.

Balmer, Dorene F., Boyd F. Richards, and Lara Varpio. "How Students Experience and Navigate Transitions in Undergraduate Medical Education: An Application of Bourdieu's Theoretical Model." *Advances in Health Sciences Education* 20 (October 2015) 1073–85.

Barnes, Margaret. "Impact of Service-Learning on Leadership and an Interest in Social Justice." *Journal of Nursing Education* 55 (2016) 24–30.

Barry, William A. *Letting God Come Close: An Approach to the Ignatian Spiritual Exercises.* Chicago: Loyola Press, 2001.

Bartlett-Ellis, Rebecca J., Lisa Carter-Harris, and Pam MacLaughlin. "Preparing Students for Success on Examinations: Readiness Assurance Tests in a Graduate-Level Statistics Course." *Journal of Nursing Education* 55 (2016) 41–44.

Barzansky, Barbara et al. "Continuous Quality Improvement in an Accreditation System for Undergraduate Medical Education: Benefits and Challenges." *Medical Teacher* 37 (November 2015) 1032–38.

Batley, Nicholas J. et al. "Cynicism and Other Attitudes Towards Patients in an Emergency Department in a Middle Eastern Tertiary Care Center." *BMC Medical Education* 16 (January 2016) 36.

Beaird, Genevieve. "Care on a Continuum: Interactive Role-Playing Scenarios for Undergraduate Women's Health Students." *Journal of Nursing Education* 54 (2015) 416.

Bellack, Janis P., and George E. Thibault. "Creating a Continuously Learning Health System through Technology: A Call to Action." *Journal of Nursing Education* 55 (2016) 3–5.

Best, John W., and James V. Kahn. *Research in Education.* 8th ed. Boston: Allyn and Bacon, 1998.

Black, Kathy. *A Healing Homiletic: Preaching and Disability.* Nashville: Abingdon, 1996.

Blanchet-Garneau, Amélie. "Critical Reflection in Cultural Competence Development: A Framework for Undergraduate Nursing Education." *Journal of Nursing Education* 55 (2016) 125–32.

Blissett, Sarah, Rodrigo Cavalcanti, and Matthew Sibbald. "ECG Rhythm Analysis with Expert and Learner-Generated Schemas in Novice Learners." *Advances in Health Sciences Education* 20 (October 2015) 915–33.

Blow, Charles M. "A Future Segregated by Science?" *Opinion* (blog), *The New York Times*, Feb. 2, 2015, https://www.nytimes.com/2015/02/02/opinion/charles-=blow-a-future-segregated-by-science.html.

Bok, Harold G. J. et al. "Feedback-Giving Behaviour in Performance Evaluations During Clinical Clerkships." *Medical Teacher* 38 (January 2016) 88–95.

Bonaventure. "Major Life." Translated by Raphael Brown et al. In *St. Francis of Assisi: Writings and Early Biographies*, edited by Marion Alphonse Habig, 627–788. Chicago: Franciscan Herald Press, 1991.

Booker, Staja Q., and Nicole Peterson. "Use of the Knowledge Tree as a Mind Map in a Gerontological Course for Undergraduate Nursing Students." *Journal of Nursing Education* 55 (2016) 182–84.

Boyd, Mary R., Beverly Baliko, and Vera Polyakova-Norwood. "Using Debates to Teach Evidence-Based Practice in Large Online Course." *Journal of Nursing Education* 54 (2015) 578–82.

Boyer, Louise, Jacques Tardif, and Hélène Lefebvre. "From a Medical Problem to a Health Experience: How Nursing Students Think in Clinical Situations." *Journal of Nursing Education* 54 (2015) 625–32.

Bracken, Joseph A. *The Divine Matrix: Creativity as Link Between East and West. Faith Meets Faith.* Maryknoll, NY: Orbis, 1995.

Bradshaw, Martha J., and Arlene J. Lowenstein, eds. *Innovative Teaching Strategies in Nursing and Related Health Professions.* 6th ed. Burlington, MA: Jones and Bartlett Learning, 2014.

Braniff, Conor et al. "Assistantship Improves Medical Students' Perception of Their Preparedness for Starting Work." *Medical Teacher* 38 (January 2016) 51–58.

Brown, Peter C., Henry L. Roediger III, and Mark A. McDaniel. *Make It Stick: The Science of Successful Learning.* N.P.: Author Published, 2014.

Brown, Robert McAfee. *Spirituality and Liberation: Overcoming the Great Fallacy.* 1st ed. Philadelphia: Westminster, 1988.

Bruning, Roger H., Gregory J. Schraw, and Monica M. Norby. *Cognitive Psychology and Instruction.* 5th ed. Boston: Pearson Education, 2011.

Burgess, Annette et al. "Peer Tutoring in a Medical School: Perceptions of Tutors and Tutees." *BMC Medical Education* 16 (March 2016) 85.

Burkhardt, Melanie Sue, Shelley Gower, Helen Flavell, and John Taplin. "Engagement and Creation of Professional Identity in Undergraduate Nursing Students: A Convention-Style Orientation Event." *Journal of Nursing Education* 54 (2015) 712–15.

Bussard, Michelle. "The Nature of Clinical Judgment Development in Reflective Journals." *Journal of Nursing Education* 54 (2015) 451–54.

Cameron, Julia. *The Artist's Way: A Spiritual Path to Higher Creativity.* 10th anniversary ed. New York: J.P. Tarcher/Putnam, 2002.

Cassian, John. *John Cassian: The Conferences.* Translated by Boniface Ramsey. Ancient Christian Writers. Mahwah, NJ: Paulist, 1997.

Castanelli, Damian J., Natalie A. Smith, and Craig L. F. Noonan. "Do Anaesthetists Believe Their Teaching Is Evidence-Based?" *Medical Teacher* 37 (December 2015) 1098–105.

CCSSO. *Intasc Model Core Teaching Standards: A Resource for Ongoing Teacher Development.* Washington, DC: Council of Chief State School Officers (CCSSO), 2013.

Chamberland, Martine et al. "Does Medical Students' Diagnostic Performance Improve by Observing Examples of Self-Explanation Provided by Peers or Experts?" *Advances in Health Sciences Education* 20 (October 2015) 981–93.

Chan, Angela et al. "Part Versus Whole: A Randomized Trial of Central Venous Catheterization Education." *Advances in Health Sciences Education* 20 (October 2015) 1061–71.

Chen, Chen et al. "How We Used a Patient Visit Tracker Tool to Advance Experiential Learning in Systems-Based Practice and Quality Improvement in a Medical Student Clinic." *Medical Teacher* 38 (January 2016) 36–40.

Chen, H. Carrie et al. "Sequencing Learning Experiences to Engage Different Level Learners in the Workplace: An Interview Study with Excellent Clinical Teachers." *Medical Teacher* 37 (December 2015) 1090–97.

Chen, Ken-Zen et al. "Resolving Bottlenecks: Converting Three High-Enrollment Nursing Courses to an Online Format." *Journal of Nursing Education* 54 (2015) 404–8.

Chepulis, Lynne M., and Gael J. Mearns. "Evaluation of the Nutritional Knowledge of Undergraduate Nursing Student." *Journal of Nursing Education* 54 (2015) S103–S6.

Chua, Amelia Z. E. et al. "The Effectiveness of a Shared Conference Experience in Improving Undergraduate Medical and Nursing Students' Attitudes Towards Inter-Professional Education in an Asian Country: A before and after Study." *BMC Medical Education* 15 (December 2015) 233.

Chuang, Chih et al. "Medical and Pharmacy Student Concerns About Participating on International Service-Learning Trips." *BMC Medical Education* 15 (December 2015) 232.

Clark, Ruth Colvin, and Richard E. Mayer. *E-Learning and the Science of Instruction: Proven Guidelines for Consumers and Designers of Multimedia Learning*. 3rd ed. San Francisco: Pfeiffer, 2011.

Clayton, Philip. *Adventures in the Spirit: God, World, Divine Action*. Minneapolis: Fortress, 2008.

Clayton, Philip, and Arthur Peacocke, eds. *In Whom We Live and Move and Have Our Being: Panentheistic Reflections on God's Presence in a Scientific World*. Grand Rapids: Eerdmans, 2004.

Close, Liz, Mary Sue Gorski, Maureen Sroczynski, Pat Farmer, and Jean Wortock. "Shared Curriculum Model: A Promising Practice for Education Transformation." *Journal of Nursing Education* 54 (2015) 677–82.

Cobb, John B., Jr., and David Ray Griffin. *Process Theology: An Introductory Exposition*. Louisville: Westminster John Knox, 1976.

Cowan, Patricia A., Y'Esha Weeks, and Mona Newsome-Wicks. "Promoting Success of Ethnic Minority and Male Students in an Accelerated, Entry-Level Master of Nursing Program: The Sustain Program." *Journal of Nursing Education* 54 (2015) S112–S15.

Curtin, Alicia J. et al. "Exploring the Use of Critical Reflective Inquiry with Nursing Students Participating in an International Service-Learning Experience." *Journal of Nursing Education* 54 (2015) S95–S98.

Darabi, Aubteen et al. "Learning How the Electron Transport Chain Works: Independent and Interactive Effects of Instructional Strategies and Learners' Characteristics." *Advances in Health Sciences Education* 20 (December 2015) 1135– 48.

DeBonis, Ruselle. "Effects of Service-Learning on Graduate Nursing Students: Care and Advocacy for the Impoverished." *Journal of Nursing Education* 55 (2016) 36–40.

Delany, C. et al. "Replacing Stressful Challenges with Positive Coping Strategies: A Resilience Program for Clinical Placement Learning." *Advances in Health Sciences Education* 20 (December 2015) 1303–24.

Dewey, John. *Democracy and Education: An Introduction to the Philosophy of Education*. Text-Book Series in Education. New York: Free Press, 1916; 1944.

Diamond, Robert M. *Designing and Assessing Courses and Curricula: A Practical Guide*. Jossey-Bass Higher and Adult Education Series. 3rd ed. San Francisco: Jossey-Bass, 2008.

Donovan, Mary Lou, and Sara McCumber. "Interprofessional Collaborative Practice: Dementia Case Studies Engage Nurse Practitioner and Occupational Therapy Students." *Journal of Nursing Education* 54 (2015) 536.

Douglas, Kelly Brown. *The Black Christ*. The Bishop Henry McNeal Turner Studies in North American Black Religion. Maryknoll, NY: Orbis, 2005.

Duke, Pamela, Suely Grosseman, Dennis H. Novack, and Steven Rosenzweig. "Preserving Third Year Medical Students' Empathy and Enhancing Self-Reflection Using Small Group 'Virtual Hangout' Technology." *Medical Teacher* 37 (June 2015) 566–71.

Dumas, Bonnie P., Ann D. Hollerbach, Gail W. Stuart, and Nancy D. Duffy. "Expanding Simulation Capacity: Senior-Level Students as Teachers." *Journal of Nursing Education* 54 (2015) 516–19.

Eggenberger, Sandra K., Norma K. Krumwiede, and Patricia K. Young. "Using Simulation Pedagogy in the Formation of Family-Focused Generalist Nurses." *Journal of Nursing Education* 54 (2015) 588–93.

Eisner, Elliot, ed. *Learning and Teaching the Ways of Knowing: Eighty-Fourth Yearbook of the National Society for the Study of Education.* Chicago: National Society for the Study of Education, 1985.

El Hussein, Mohamed Toufic, Sonya L. Jakubec, and Joseph Osuji. "The Facts: A Mnemonic for the Rapid Assessment of Rigor in Qualitative Research Studies." *Journal of Nursing Education* 55 (2016) 60.

Elander, Kelly, and Johannes C. Cronje. "Paradigms Revisited: A Quantitative Investigation into a Model to Integrate Objectivism and Constructivism in Instructional Design." *Educational Technology Research and Development* 64 (June 2016) 389–405.

Elias, Beth, Shea Polancich, Carolynn Jones, and Sean Convoy. "Evolving the Picot Method for the Digital Age: The Picot-D." *Journal of Nursing Education* 54 (2015) 594–99.

Elias, John L. *The Foundations and Practice of Adult Religious Education.* Rev. ed. Malabar, FL: Krieger Pub. Co., 1993.

Eychmüller, S., M. Forster, H. Gudat, U. M. Lütolf, and G. D. Borasio. "Undergraduate Palliative Care Teaching in Swiss Medical Faculties: A Nationwide Survey and Improved Learning Objectives." *BMC Medical Education* 15 (November 2015) 213.

Fitzwater, Julie S., and Vivian Tong. "Clinical Policy Evaluation Activity: Reinforcing Evidence-Based Practice." *Journal of Nursing Education* 54 (2015) 719–20.

Fluit, Cornelia R. M. G. et al. "Understanding Resident Ratings of Teaching in the Workplace: A Multi-Centre Study." *Advances in Health Sciences Education* 20 (August 2015) 691–707.

Ford, Yvonne. "Development of Nurse Self-Concept in Nursing Students: The Effects of a Peer-Mentoring Experience." *Journal of Nursing Education* 54 (2015) S107–S11.

Fossen, Peggy, and Pamella Rae Stoeckel. "Nursing Students' Perceptions of a Hearing Voices Simulation and Role-Play: Preparation for Mental Health Clinical Practice." *Journal of Nursing Education* 55 (2016) 203–8.

Foster, Richard J. *Streams of Living Water: Celebrating the Great Traditions of Christian Faith.* San Francisco: HarperSanFrancisco, 1998.

Fowler, James W. *Stages of Faith: The Psychology of Human Development and the Quest for Meaning.* San Francisco: HarperSanFrancisco, 1981.

Friedman, Myles I., and Steven P. Fisher. *Handbook on Effective Instructional Strategies: Evidence for Decision-Making.* Columbia, SC: The Institute for Evidence-Based Decision-Making in Education, 1998.

Gagnon, Marilou, and Stephany Cator. "Mapping HIV Nursing Core Competencies in Entry-Level Education: A Pilot Project." *Journal of Nursing Education* 54 (2015) 409–15.

Gannon-Tagher, Catherine, and Erin M. Robinson. "Critical Aspects of Stress in a High-Stakes Testing Environment: A Phenomenographical Approach." *Journal of Nursing Education* 55 (2016) 160–63.

García de Leonardo, Cristina et al. "A Latin American, Portuguese and Spanish Consensus on a Core Communication Curriculum for Undergraduate Medical Education." *BMC Medical Education* 16 (March 2016) 99.

Garnett, Susan, Josie A. Weiss, and Jill E. Winland-Brown. "Simulation Design: Engaging Large Groups of Nurse Practitioner Students." *Journal of Nursing Education* 54 (2015) 525–31.

Gauthier, Stephen, Rodrigo Cavalcanti, Jeannette Goguen, and Matthew Sibbald. "Deliberate Practice as a Framework for Evaluating Feedback in Residency Training." *Medical Teacher* 37 (June 2015) 551–57.

Gavin-Knecht, Janet, and Beth Fischer. "Undergraduate Nursing Students' Experience of Service-Learning: A Phenomenological Study." *Journal of Nursing Education* 54 (2015) 378–84.

Gershoff, Elizabeth T. "More Harm Than Good: A Summary of Scientific Research on the Intended and Unintended Effects of Corporal Punishment on Children." *Law and Contemporary Problems* 73 (2010) 31–56.

Gibbs, Jennifer C., and Jim D. Taylor. "Comparing Student Self-Assessment to Individualized Instructor Feedback." *Active Learning in Higher Education* 17 (July 2016) 111–23.

Gilliland, Irene. "Effects of a Community-Based Hospice Experience on Attitudes and Self-Perceived Competencies of Baccalaureate Senior Nursing Students." *Journal of Nursing Education* 54 (2015) 335–38.

Goggin, Gerard, and Christopher Newell. *Digital Disability: The Social Construction of Disability in New Media.* Critical Media Studies. Lanham, MD: Rowman & Littlefield, 2003.

Gonsalvez, David G., Matthew Ovens, and Jason Ivanusic. "Does Attendance at Anatomy Practical Classes Correlate with Assessment Outcome? A Retrospective Study of a Large Cohort of Undergraduate Anatomy Students." *BMC Medical Education* 15 (December 2015) 231.

Goodwin, Dawn, and Laura Machin. "How We Tackled the Problem of Assessing Humanities, Social and Behavioural Sciences in Medical Education." *Medical Teacher* 38 (February 2016) 137–40.

Gooi, Adrian C. C., and Connor S. Sommerfeld. "Medical School 2.0: How We Developed a Student-Generated Question Bank Using Small Group Learning." *Medical Teacher* 37 (October 2015) 892–96.

Gorski, Mary Sue et al. "Nursing Education Transformation: Promising Practices in Academic Progression." *Journal of Nursing Education* 54 (2015) 509–15.

Green, Clifford J. "History in the Service of the Future: Studying Urban Ministry." In *Churches, Cities, and Human Community: Urban Ministry in the United States, 1945–1985*, edited by Clifford J. Green, 1–22. Grand Rapids: Eerdmans, 1996.

Green, Joel B. *Body, Soul, and Human Life: The Nature of Humanity in the Bible.* Studies in Theological Interpretation. Grand Rapids: Baker Academic, 2008.

Griffin, David Ray. *Reenchantment Without Supernaturalism: A Process Philosophy of Religion.* Ithaca, NY: Cornell University Press, 2001.

Grilo Diogo, Pedro, Joselina Barbosa, and Maria Amélia Ferreira. "A Pilot Tuning Project-Based National Study on Recently Graduated Medical Students' Self-Assessment of Competences—the Test Study." *BMC Medical Education* 15 (December 2015) 226.

Gude, T. et al. "Can We Rely on Simulated Patients' Satisfaction with Their Consultation for Assessing Medical Students' Communication Skills? A Cross-Sectional Study." *BMC Medical Education* 15 (December 2015) 225.

Haji, Faizal A. et al. "Measuring Cognitive Load During Simulation-Based Psychomotor Skills Training: Sensitivity of Secondary-Task Performance and Subjective Ratings." *Advances in Health Sciences Education* 20 (December 2015) 1237–53.

Hallam, Karen T. et al. "Do Commencing Nursing and Paramedicine Students Differ in Interprofessional Learning and Practice Attitudes: Evaluating Course, Socio-

Demographic and Individual Personality Effects." *BMC Medical Education* 16 (March 2016) 80.
Hamrin, Vanya et al. "Teaching a Systems Approach: An Innovative Quality Improvement Project." *Journal of Nursing Education* 55 (2016) 209–14.
Harley, Jason M. et al. "Comparing Virtual and Location-Based Augmented Reality Mobile Learning: Emotions and Learning Outcomes." *Educational Technology Research and Development* 64 (June 2016) 359–88.
Hart, Julie A., and Deborah R. Chilcote. "'Won't You Be My Patient?': Preparing Theater Students as Standardized Patients." *Journal of Nursing Education* 55 (2016) 168–71.
Harvey, Giuliana. "Connecting Theory to Practice: Using Guided Questions to Standardize Clinical Postconference." *Journal of Nursing Education* 54 (2015) 655–58.
Hattie, John A. C. *Visible Learning: A Synthesis of over 800 Meta-Analyses Relating to Achievement.* New York: Routledge, 2009.
Hatton, John, and Paul B. Plouffe, eds. *Science and Its Ways of Knowing.* Upper Saddle River, NJ: Prentice Hall, 1997.
Hendrix, Cristina C. et al. "Integrating Mental Health Concepts in the Care of Adults with Chronic Illnesses: A Curricular Enhancement." *Journal of Nursing Education* 55 (2015) 645–49.
Hendry, Graham D., Peter White, and Catherine Herbert. "Providing Exemplar-Based 'Feedforward' Before an Assessment: The Role of Teacher Explanation." *Active Learning in Higher Education* 17 (July 2016) 99–109.
Herr, Keela et al. "An Interprofessional Consensus of Core Competencies for Prelicensure Education in Pain Management: Curriculum Application for Nursing." *Journal of Nursing Education* 54 (2015) 317–27.
Holden, Carol A. et al. "'Men's Health – a Little in the Shadow': A Formative Evaluation of Medical Curriculum Enhancement with Men's Health Teaching and Learning." *BMC Medical Education* 15 (November 2015) 210.
Hole, Grete Oline et al. "Educating Change Agents: A Qualitative Descriptive Study of Graduates of a Master's Program in Evidence-Based Practice." *BMC Medical Education* 16 (February 2016) 71.
Holmes, Cheryl L., Ilene B. Harris, Alan J. Schwartz, and Glenn Regehr. "Harnessing the Hidden Curriculum: A Four-Step Approach to Developing and Reinforcing Reflective Competencies in Medical Clinical Clerkship." *Advances in Health Sciences Education* 20 (December 2015) 1355–70.
Hortsch, Michael. "'How We Learn May Not Always Be Good for Us' – Do New Electronic Teaching Approaches Always Result in Better Learning Outcomes?" *Medical Teacher* 37 (June 2015) 507–9.
Hsih, Katie W. et al. "The Student Curriculum Review Team: How We Catalyze Curricular Changes through a Student-Centered Approach." *Medical Teacher* 37 (November 2015) 1008–12.
Hubach, Stephanie O. *Same Lake, Different Boat: Coming Alongside People Touched by Disability.* Phillipsburg, NJ: P&R Pub., 2006.
Hung, Chia-Hui, and Chen-Yung Lin. "Using Concept Mapping to Evaluate Knowledge Structure in Problem-Based Learning." *BMC Medical Education* 15 (November 2015) 212.

Ingham, Gerard, Jennifer Fry, Simon Morgan, and Bernadette Ward. "ARCADO—Adding Random Case Analysis to Direct Observation in Workplace-Based Formative Assessment of General Practice Registrars." *BMC Medical Education* 15 (December 2015) 218.

Irwin, Pauletta, and Rosanne Coutts. "A Systematic Review of the Experience of Using Second Life in the Education of Undergraduate Nurses." *Journal of Nursing Education* 54 (2015) 572–77.

Isasi-Díaz, Ada María. *Mujerista Theology: A Theology for the Twenty-First Century.* Maryknoll, NY: Orbis, 1996.

Isenhower, Valerie K., and Judith A. Todd. *Living into the Answers: A Workbook for Personal Spiritual Discernment.* Nashville: Upper Room Books, 2008.

Jacobs, Ivo F., Auguste von Bayern, and Mathias Osvath. "A Novel Tool-Use Mode in Animals: New Caledonian Crows Insert Tools to Transport Objects." *Animal Cognition* 19 (November 2016) 1249–52.

Jacobs, Johanna C. G. et al. "Impact of Institute and Person Variables on Teachers' Conceptions of Learning and Teaching." *Medical Teacher* 37 (August 2015) 738–46.

Jagt – van Kampen, Charissa Thari, Leontien C. M. Kremer, A. A. Eduard Verhagen, and Antoinette Y. N. Schouten – van Meeteren. "Impact of a Multifaceted Education Program on Implementing a Pediatric Palliative Care Guideline: A Pilot Study." *BMC Medical Education* 15 (November 2015) 194.

Jeffries, Pamela. "The Good News—Simulations Work, So Now What?" *Journal of Nursing Education* 54 (2015) 603–4.

Johnson, Christina E. et al. "Identifying Educator Behaviours for High Quality Verbal Feedback in Health Professions Education: Literature Review and Expert Refinement." *BMC Medical Education* 16 (March 2016) 96.

Jorm, Christine et al. "A Large-Scale Mass Casualty Simulation to Develop the Non-Technical Skills Medical Students Require for Collaborative Teamwork." *BMC Medical Education* 16 (March 2016) 83.

Joseph, M. Lindell, Ann Rhodes, and Carol A. Watson. "Preparing Nurse Leaders to Innovate: Iowa's Innovation Seminar." *Journal of Nursing Education* 55 (2016) 113–17.

Kan, Carol et al. "How We Developed a Trainee-Led Book Group as a Supplementary Education Tool for Psychiatric Training in the 21st Century." *Medical Teacher* 37 (September 2015) 803–6.

Kant, Immanuel. *Religion Within the Limits of Reason Alone.* Translated by Theodore M. Greene and Hoyt H. Hudson. Chicago: Open Court Publishing, 1793; 1934.

Katz, Jennifer. "The Three Block Model of Universal Design for Learning (UDL): Engaging Students in Inclusive Education." *Canadian Journal of Education* 36 (2013) 153–94.

Kaylor, Sara K. "Fishing for Pharmacology Success: Gaming as an Active Learning Strategy." *Journal of Nursing Education* 55 (2016) 119.

Keegan, Robert D. et al. "Use of a Mobile Device Simulation as a Preclass Active Learning Exercise." *Journal of Nursing Education* 55 (2016) 56–59.

Kelly, Martina et al. "Can Less Be More? Comparison of an 8-Item Placement Quality Measure with the 50-Item Dundee Ready Educational Environment Measure (DREEM)." *Advances in Health Sciences Education* 20 (October 2015) 1027–32.

Khandelwal, Aditi et al. "How We Made Professionalism Relevant to Twenty-First Century Residents." *Medical Teacher* 37 (June 2015) 538–42.

Kharraz, Razan et al. "Perceived Barriers Towards Participation in Undergraduate Research Activities among Medical Students at Alfaisal University—College of Medicine: A Saudi Arabian Perspective." *Medical Teacher* 38 (March 2016) S12–S18.

Kiernan, Jason, and April Hazard-Vallerand. "Cancer as a Platform for Genetics Education in the Undergraduate Nursing Curriculum." *Journal of Nursing Education* 55 (2016) 236–39.

Knight, Christopher C. *The God of Nature: Incarnation and Contemporary Science.* Theology and the Sciences. Minneapolis: Fortress, 2007.

Knowlton, Mary C., and Anne-Marie Jones. "Student-Led Clinical Orientation." *Journal of Nursing Education* 54 (2015) 472.

Kok, Ellen M. et al. "Systematic Viewing in Radiology: Seeing More, Missing Less?" *Advances in Health Sciences Education* 21 (March 2016) 189–205.

Kool, Ada et al. "Goal Orientations of Health Profession Students Throughout the Undergraduate Program: A Multilevel Study." *BMC Medical Education* 16 (March 2016) 100.

Kostiuk, Sarah. "Can Learning the ISBARR Framework Help to Address Nursing Students' Perceived Anxiety and Confidence Levels Associated with Handover Reports?" *Journal of Nursing Education* 54 (2015) 583–87.

Krathwohl, David R. "A Revision of Bloom's Taxonomy: An Overview." *Theory Into Practice* 41 (Autumn 2002) 212–18.

Kretzmann, John P., and John L. McKnight. *Building Communities from the Inside Out: A Path Toward Finding and Mobilizing a Community's Assets.* Evanston, IL: Institute for Policy Research, Northwestern University, 1993.

Kruse, Adam J. "Cultural Bias in Testing: A Review of Literature and Implications for Music Education." *Applications of Research in Music Education* 35 (October 2015) 23–31.

Kulasegaram, Kulamakan et al. "The Mediating Effect of Context Variation in Mixed Practice for Transfer of Basic Science." *Advances in Health Sciences Education* 20 (October 2015) 953–68.

Kunina-Habenicht, Olga et al. "Assessing Clinical Reasoning (ASCLIRE): Instrument Development and Validation." *Advances in Health Sciences Education* 20 (December 2015) 1205–24.

Kyle, Eric. *Living Spiritual Praxis: Foundations for Spiritual Formation Program Development.* Eugene, OR: Pickwick, 2013.

———. *Sacred Systems: Exploring Personal Transformation in the Western Christian Tradition.* Eugene, OR: Pickwick, 2014.

———. *Spiritual Being & Becoming: Western Christian and Modern Scientific Views of Human Nature for Spiritual Formation.* Eugene, OR: Pickwick, 2015.

Laine, Teemu H., Eeva Nygren, Amir Dirin, and Hae-Jung Suk. "Science Spots AR: A Platform for Science Learning Games with Augmented Reality." *Educational Technology Research and Development* 64 (June 2016) 507–31.

Landeen, Janet et al. "Exploring Student and Faculty Perceptions of Clinical Simulation: A Q-Sort Study." *Journal of Nursing Education* 54 (2015) 485–91.

Landheer-Zandee, Gail et al. "Impact of Integrating Community-Based Participatory Research into a Baccalaureate Nursing Curriculum." *Journal of Nursing Education* 54 (2015) 394–98.

Lawrenz, Mel. *The Dynamics of Spiritual Formation.* Ministry Dynamics for a New Century Series. Grand Rapids: Baker, 2000.

LeDuc, Karen. "An Instructional Strategy in Discovery Learning." *Journal of Nursing Education* 54 (2015) S120.

Lee, Ming, and Paul F. Wimmers. "Validation of a Performance Assessment Instrument in Problem-Based Learning Tutorials Using Two Cohorts of Medical Students." *Advances in Health Sciences Education* 21 (May 2016) 341–57.

Leslie, Jamie Lynn. "Expanding the Moral Imagination: The Social Class Dinner." *Journal of Nursing Education* 55 (2016) 240.

———. "Improving Class Discussion for an Evidence-Based Practice Course." *Journal of Nursing Education* 55 (2016) 182.

Levine, Michael P. *Pantheism: A Non-Theistic Concept of Deity.* London; New York: Routledge, 1994.

Lin, Shu-Hui, and Yun-Chen Huang. "Examining Charisma in Relation to Students' Interest in Learning." *Active Learning in Higher Education* 17 (July 2016) 139–51.

Lorio, Anne K. et al. "Power of Peer-Assisted Learning: An Interdisciplinary Mobility Laboratory Experience." *Journal of Nursing Education* 55 (2016) 83–86.

Lucieer, Susanna M. et al. "The Development of Self-Regulated Learning During the Pre-Clinical Stage of Medical School: A Comparison between a Lecture-Based and a Problem-Based Curriculum." *Advances in Health Sciences Education* 21 (March 2016) 93–104.

Lypson, Monica L. et al. "Optimizing the Post-Graduate Institutional Program Evaluation Process." *BMC Medical Education* 16 (February 2016) 65.

Maas, Marjo J. M. et al. "Critical Features of Peer Assessment of Clinical Performance to Enhance Adherence to a Low Back Pain Guideline for Physical Therapists: A Mixed Methods Design." *BMC Medical Education* 15 (November 2015) 203.

Mach, Jeanne R., and Rebecca Lash-Rabick. *Effective Study Strategies for Every Classroom Grades 7–12: 29 Lesson Plans for Teaching Note-Taking, Summarizing, Researching and Test-Taking Skills.* Omaha, NE: Boys Town Press, 2008.

Machamer, Peter, and Michael Silberstein, eds. *Blackwell Guide to the Philosophy of Science.* Malden, MA: Blackwell, 2002.

Mahmoud, Mahmoud Abdulrahman, Abdulmohsen H. Al-Zalabani, and Khalid A. Bin Abdulrahman. "Public Health Education in Saudi Arabia: Needs and Challenges." *Medical Teacher* 38 (March 2016): S5–S8.

Makransky, Guido et al. "Simulation Based Virtual Learning Environment in Medical Genetics Counseling: An Example of Bridging the Gap between Theory and Practice in Medical Education." *BMC Medical Education* 16 (March 2016) 98.

Manyama, Mange et al. "Improving Gross Anatomy Learning Using Reciprocal Peer Teaching." *BMC Medical Education* 16 (March 2016) 95.

Martins, Antonio Camargo et al. "How We Enhanced Medical Academics Skills and Reduced Social Inequities Using an Academic Teaching Program." *Medical Teacher* 37 (November 2015) 1003–7.

MarylandOnline. "Quality Matters Rubric Standards: Fifth Edition 2014 with Assigned Point Values." https://studylib.net/doc/10855797/quality-matters-rubric-standards-fifth-edition--2014--wit.

Matlin, Margaret W. *Cognition.* 6th ed. New York: J. Wiley & Sons, 2005.

May, Gerald. *Will & Spirit: A Contemplative Psychology.* San Francisco: Harper & Row, 1982.

McGettigan, Patricia, and Jean McKendree. "Interprofessional Training for Final Year Healthcare Students: A Mixed Methods Evaluation of the Impact on Ward Staff and

Students of a Two-Week Placement and of Factors Affecting Sustainability." *BMC Medical Education* 15 (October 2015) 185.
McGill, D. A., C. P. M. van der Vleuten, and M. J. Clarke. "Construct Validation of Judgement-Based Assessments of Medical Trainees' Competency in the Workplace Using a 'Kanesian' Approach to Validation." *BMC Medical Education* 15 (December 2015) 237.
McGrath, Alister E. *A Fine-Tuned Universe: The Quest for God in Science and Theology (Gifford Lectures)*. 1st ed. Louisville: Westminster John Knox, 2009.
McGuire, Saundra Yancy. *Teach Students How to Learn: Strategies You Can Incorporate into Any Course to Improve Student Metacognition, Study Skills, and Motivation*. Sterling, VA: Stylus, 2015.
McLellan, Lucy et al. "Preparing to Prescribe: How Do Clerkship Students Learn in the Midst of Complexity?" *Advances in Health Sciences Education* 20 (December 2015) 1339–54.
Mikkonen, Kristina, Helvi Kyngäs, and Maria Kääriäinen. "Nursing Students' Experiences of the Empathy of Their Teachers: A Qualitative Study." *Advances in Health Sciences Education* 20 (August 2015) 669–82.
Milavec, Aaron. *The Didache: Faith, Hope, & Life of the Earliest Christian Communities, 50–70 C.E.* New York: Newman Press, 2003.
Moore, Catherine, Sarah Westwater-Wood, and Roger Kerry. "Academic Performance and Perception of Learning Following a Peer Coaching Teaching and Assessment Strategy." *Advances in Health Sciences Education* 21 (March 2016) 121–30.
Moreau, Katherine A., and Kaylee Eady. "Connecting Medical Education to Patient Outcomes: The Promise of Contribution Analysis." *Medical Teacher* 37 (November 2015) 1060–62.
Morgan, Simon et al. "How We Use Patient Encounter Data for Reflective Learning in Family Medicine Training." *Medical Teacher* 37 (October 2015) 897–900.
Morra, Sergio, Camilla Gobbo, Zopito Marini, and Ronald Sheese. *Cognitive Development: Neo-Piagetian Perspectives*. New York: Lawrence Erlbaum Associates, 2008.
Morris, Cecile, and Gladson Chikwa. "Audio Versus Written Feedback: Exploring Learners' Preference and the Impact of Feedback Format on Students' Academic Performance." *Active Learning in Higher Education* 17 (July 2016) 125–37.
Morrison, Gary R., Steven M. Ross, Howard K. Kalman, and Jerrold E. Kemp. *Designing Effective Instruction*. 7th ed. Hoboken, NJ: Wiley, 2013.
Murray, Teri A. "Culture and Climate: Factors That Influence the Academic Success of African American Students in Prelicensure Nursing Education." *Journal of Nursing Education* 54 (2015) 704–7.
———. "Factors That Promote and Impede the Academic Success of African American Students in Prelicensure Nursing Education: An Integrative Review." *Journal of Nursing Education* 54 (2015) S74–S81.
Myers, Lynnea H. et al. "Building a Community of Scholars: One Cohort's Experience in an Online and Distance Education Doctor of Philosophy Program." *Journal of Nursing Education* 54 (2015) 650–54.
Nasser, Soumana C., Aline Hanna Saad, and Lamis R. Karaoui. "Mapping of the Biomedical Literature Evaluation Competencies Based on Pharmacy Students' Feedback." *BMC Medical Education* 16 (February 2016) 59.
Nicola, Pantelis et al. "How We Did the Question Time Forum (QTF)." *Medical Teacher* 37 (July 2015) 631–34.
Nie, Min et al. "Evaluation of Oral Microbiology Lab Curriculum Reform." *BMC Medical Education* 15 (December 2015) 217.

Norgaard, Birgitte, Eva Draborg, and Jan Sørensen. "Adaptation and Reliability of the Readiness for Inter Professional Learning Scale in a Danish Student and Health Professional Setting." *BMC Medical Education* 16 (February 2016) 60.

O'Rourke, Jennifer, and Julie Zerwic. "Measure of Clinical Decision-Making Abilities of Nurse Practitioner Students." *Journal of Nursing Education* 55 (2016) 18–23.

Orique, Sabrina B., and Mary Ann McCarthy. "Critical Thinking and the Use of Nontraditional Instructional Methodologies." *Journal of Nursing Education* 54 (2015) 455–59.

Paek, Seungoh, Daniel L. Hoffman, and John B. Black. "Perceptual Factors and Learning in Digital Environments." *Educational Technology Research and Development* 64 (June 2016) 435–57.

Paolucci, Elizabeth Oddone, and Claudio Violato. "A Meta-Analysis of the Published Research on the Affective, Cognitive, and Behavioral Effects of Corporal Punishment." *The Journal of Psychology* 138 (January 2004) 197–222.

Park, Eun-Jun, and Mihyun Park. "Effectiveness of a Case-Based Computer Program on Students' Ethical Decision Making." *Journal of Nursing Education* 54 (2015) 633–40.

Park, Sophie et al. "A BEME Systematic Review of UK Undergraduate Medical Education in the General Practice Setting: BEME Guide No. 32." *Medical Teacher* 37 (July 2015) 611–30.

Parker, Stephen E. *Led by the Spirit: Toward a Practical Theology of Pentecostal Discernment and Decision Making.* Journal of Pentecostal Theology Supplement Series. Sheffield, England: Sheffield Academic Press, 1996.

Peacock, Justin G., and Joseph P. Grande. "An Online App Platform Enhances Collaborative Medical Student Group Learning and Classroom Management." *Medical Teacher* 38 (February 2016) 174–80.

Peacocke, Arthur. *Paths from Science Towards God: The End of All Our Exploring.* Oxford: Oneworld, 2001.

Peacocke, Arthur, and Philip Clayton, eds. *All That Is: A Naturalistic Faith for the Twenty-First Century: A Theological Proposal with Responses from Leading Thinkers in the Science-Religion Dialogue.* Minneapolis: Fortress, 2007.

Pears, Angie. *Doing Contextual Theology.* London: Routledge, 2010.

Peltzer, Jill N., Cynthia S. Teel, Elaine Frank-Ragan, and Heather V. Nelson-Brantley. "Strategies for Building Advocacy Skills among Undergraduate and Graduate Nursing Students." *Journal of Nursing Education* 55 (2016) 177–81.

Pianta, Robert C., Karen M. La Paro, and Bridget K. Hamre. *Classroom Assessment Scoring System Manual: Secondary.* Baltimore: Paul H. Brookes, 2008.

Pickover, Clifford A. *The Physics Book: From the Big Bang to Quantum Resurrection, 250 Milestones in the History of Physics.* New York: Sterling Pub., 2011.

Piquette, Dominique, Carol-Anne Moulton, and Vicki R. LeBlanc. "Creating Learning Momentum through Overt Teaching Interactions During Real Acute Care Episodes." *Advances in Health Sciences Education* 20 (October 2015) 903–14.

Pitt, Michael B., Emily C. Borman-Shoap, and Walter J. Eppich. "Twelve Tips for Maximizing the Effectiveness of Game-Based Learning." *Medical Teacher* 37 (November 2015) 1013–17.

Placher, William C. *A History of Christian Theology: An Introduction.* 1st ed. Philadelphia: Westminster, 1983.

Preusche, Ingrid, and Claus Lamm. "Reflections on Empathy in Medical Education: What Can We Learn from Social Neurosciences?" *Advances in Health Sciences Education* 21 (March 2016) 235–49.

Rahner, Karl. *Foundations of Christian Faith: An Introduction to the Idea of Christianity.* Translated by William V. Dych. New York: Crossroad Publishing, 1982.

Raterink, Ginger. "Reflective Journaling for Critical Thinking Development in Advanced Practice Registered Nurse Students." *Journal of Nursing Education* 55 (2016) 101–4.

Read, Catherine Y., Debra Pino-Betancourt, and Chenille Morrison. "Social Change: A Framework for Inclusive Leadership Development in Nursing Education." *Journal of Nursing Education* 55 (2016) 164–67.

Reed-Bouley, Jennifer, and Eric Kyle. "Challenging Racism and White Privilege in Undergraduate Theology Contexts: Teaching and Learning Strategies for Maximizing the Promise of Community Service-Learning." *Teaching Theology and Religion* 18 (2015) 20–36.

Reiser, Robert A. "What Field Did You Say You Were In?: Defining and Naming Our Field." In *Trends and Issues in Instructional Design and Technology*, edited by Robert A. Reiser and John V. Dempsey, 1–7. Boston: Pearson, 2012.

Reiser, Robert A., and John V. Dempsey. *Trends and Issues in Instructional Design and Technology.* 3rd Kindle ed. Boston: Pearson, 2012.

Reynolds, Thomas E. *Vulnerable Communion: A Theology of Disability and Hospitality.* Grand Rapids: Brazos, 2008.

Ritten, Angela, Julee Waldrop, and Diane Wink. "Nurse Practitioner Students Learning from the Medically Underserved: Impact on Attitude toward Poverty." *Journal of Nursing Education* 54 (2015) 389–93.

Roberts, Chris, and Koshila Kumar. "Student Learning in Interprofessional Practice-Based Environments: What Does Theory Say?" *BMC Medical Education* 15 (November 2015) 211.

Rodolfo, Mendoza-Denton. "A Social Psychological Perspective on the Achievement Gap in Standardized Test Performance between White and Minority Students: Implications for Assessment." *The Journal of Negro Education* 83 (2014) 465–84.

Romrell, Danae, Lisa C. Kidder, and Emma Wood. "The SAMR Model as a Framework for Evaluating mLearning." *Journal of Asynchronous Learning Networks* 18 (2014) 1–15.

Rougas, Steven, Bethany Gentilesco, Emily Green, and Libertad Flores. "Twelve Tips for Addressing Medical Student and Resident Physician Lapses in Professionalism." *Medical Teacher* 37 (October 2015) 901–7.

Rue, Shona M., and Jessica Doolen. "Pseudostandardized Patients in Undergraduate Nursing Health Assessment." *Journal of Nursing Education* 54 (2015) 663–64.

Sagasser, Margaretha H., Anneke W. M. Kramer, Chris van Weel, and Cees P. M. van der Vleuten. "GP Supervisors' Experience in Supporting Self-Regulated Learning: A Balancing Act." *Advances in Health Sciences Education* 20 (August 2015) 727–44.

Saint Nicodemus of the Holy Mountain, and Saint Metropolitan of Corinth. *The Philokalia: The Complete Text,* vol. 1. Translated by G. E. H. Palmer, Philip Sherrard, and Kallistos Ware. Four vols. London: Faber and Faber, 1983.

Sandars, John et al. "The Importance of Educational Theories for Facilitating Learning When Using Technology in Medical Education." *Medical Teacher* 37 (November 2015) 1039–42.

Sawyer, R. Keith, ed. *The Cambridge Handbook of the Learning Sciences*. Kindle ed. Cambridge, NY: Cambridge University Press, 2006.

Schlegel, Claudia, Raphael Bonvin, Jan Joost Rethans, and Cees van der Vleuten. "The Use of Video in Standardized Patient Training to Improve Portrayal Accuracy: A Randomized Post-Test Control Group Study." *Medical Teacher* 37 (August 2015) 730–37.

Schoo, M. A., S. Lawn, E. Rudnik, and C. J. Litt. "Teaching Health Science Students Foundation Motivational Interviewing Skills: Use of Motivational Interviewing Treatment Integrity and Self-Reflection to Approach Transformative Learning." *BMC Medical Education* 15 (December 2015) 228.

Searing, Lisabeth Meade, and Wendy Carter Kooken. "The Relationship between the California Critical Thinking Disposition Inventory and Student Learning Outcomes in Baccalaureate Nursing Students." *Journal of Nursing Education* 55 (2016) 224–26.

Shapiro, Johanna, Diane Ortiz, You Ye Ree, and Minha Sarwar. "Medical Students' Creative Projects on a Third Year Pediatrics Clerkship: A Qualitative Analysis of Patient-Centeredness and Emotional Connection." *BMC Medical Education* 16 (March 2016) 93.

Shuttleworth-Edwards, A. B. "Generally Representative Is Representative of None: Commentary on the Pitfalls of IQ Test Standardization in Multicultural Settings." *The Clinical Neuropsychologist* 30 (October 2016) 975–98.

Sittikariyakul, Pat, Darin Jaturapatporn, and A. J. Kirshen. "Acting as Standardized Patients Enhances Family Medicine Residents' Self-Reported Skills in Palliative Care." *Advances in Health Sciences Education* 20 (August 2015) 645–54.

Slavin, Robert E. *Educational Psychology: Theory and Practice*. 9th ed. Boston: Pearson, 2009.

Smith, Adrian B. *God, Energy and the Field*. Ropely, Hants, UK: John Hunt, 2008.

Smith, Carolyn R. et al. "Stimulating Research Interest and Ambitions in Undergraduate Nursing Students: The Research-Doctorate Pipeline Initiative." *Journal of Nursing Education* 55 (2016) 133–40.

Smith, Luther E. Jr. "To Be Untrammeled and Free: The Urban Ministry Work of the CME Church: 1944–90." In *Churches, Cities, and Human Community: Urban Ministry in the United States, 1945–1985*, edited by Clifford J. Green, 52–76. Grand Rapids: Eerdmans, 1996.

Soelle, Dorothee. *The Silent Cry: Mysticism and Resistance*. Minneapolis: Fortress, 2001.

Spiegel, James S. *The Benefits of Providence: A New Look at Divine Sovereignty*. Wheaton, IL: Crossway Books, 2005.

St Clair-Thompson, Helen et al. "Mental Toughness and Transitions to High School and to Undergraduate Study." *Educational Psychology* 37 (August 2017) 792–809.

Stringfellow, Thomas D. et al. "Defining the Structure of Undergraduate Medical Leadership and Management Teaching and Assessment in the UK." *Medical Teacher* 37 (August 2015) 747–54.

Stroup, Linda M., and Linda Kuk. "Nursing as a Career Choice by Hispanic/Latino College Students: A Multi-Institutional Study." *Journal of Nursing Education* 54 (2015) S83–S88.

Sukhato, Kanokporn et al. "To Be or Not to Be a Facilitator of Reflective Learning for Medical Students? A Case Study of Medical Teachers' Perceptions of Introducing a Reflective Writing Exercise to an Undergraduate Curriculum." *BMC Medical Education* 16 (April 2016) 102.

Swinton, John. "Restoring the Image: Spirituality, Faith, and Cognitive Disability." *Journal of Religion and Health* 36 (1997) 21–27.

Swinton, John, and Harriet Mowat. *Practical Theology and Qualitative Research*. London: SCM, 2006.

Taylor, Charles G., Anique Atherley, Colette George, and Clare Morris. "How We Implemented a Classroom-Based Educational Intervention for Ward-Based Diabetes Care." *Medical Teacher* 37 (August 2015) 718–22.

Teilhard de Chardin, Pierre. *Hymn of the Universe*. New York: Harper & Row, 1965.

Teunissen, Pim W. "Experience, Trajectories, and Reifications: An Emerging Framework of Practice-Based Learning in Healthcare Workplaces." *Advances in Health Sciences Education* 20 (October 2015) 843–56.

Thunberg, Lars. *Microcosm and Mediator: The Theological Anthropology of Maximus the Confessor*. Chicago: Open Court Publishing, 1995.

Tiruneh, Dawit Tibebu et al. "Systematic Design of a Learning Environment for Domain-Specific and Domain-General Critical Thinking Skills." *Educational Technology Research and Development* 64 (June 2016) 481–505.

Torrell, Jean-Pierre. *Saint Thomas Aquinas: Volume 2, Spiritual Master*. Translated by Robert Royal. 2 vols. Washington, DC: Catholic University of America Press, 1996.

Vaccani, Jean-Philippe, Hedyeh Javidnia, and Susan Humphrey-Murto. "The Effectiveness of Webcast Compared to Live Lectures as a Teaching Tool in Medical School." *Medical Teacher* 38 (January 2016) 59–63.

Valente-Ferreira, Diogo Antonio, Renata Nunes Aranha, and Maria Helena Faria Ornellas de Souza. "Academic Leagues: A Brazilian Way to Teach About Cancer in Medical Universities." *BMC Medical Education* 15 (December 2015) 236.

van de Ridder, J. M. Monica et al. "Framing of Feedback Impacts Student's Satisfaction, Self-Efficacy and Performance." *Advances in Health Sciences Education* 20 (August 2015) 803–16.

Van Schalkwyk, Susan C., Juanita Bezuidenhout, and Marietjie R. De Villiers. "Understanding Rural Clinical Learning Spaces: Being and Becoming a Doctor." *Medical Teacher* 37 (June 2015) 589–94.

von Pressentin, Klaus B., Firdouza Waggie, and Hoffie Conradie. "Towards Tailored Teaching: Using Participatory Action Research to Enhance the Learning Experience of Longitudinal Integrated Clerkship Students in a South African Rural District Hospital." *BMC Medical Education* 16 (March 2016) 82.

Wheeler, Pamela L. et al. "Storytelling: A Guided Reflection Activity." *Journal of Nursing Education* 55 (2016) 172–76.

Wijma, Barbro, Anke Zbikowski, and A. Jelmer Brüggemann. "Silence, Shame and Abuse in Health Care: Theoretical Development on Basis of an Intervention Project among Staff." *BMC Medical Education* 16 (February 2016) 75.

Wijnen-Meijer, Marjo et al. "Vertically Integrated Medical Education and the Readiness for Practice of Graduates." *BMC Medical Education* 15 (December 2015) 229.

Wilder, Michael S., and Shane W. Parker. *Transformission: Making Disciples through Short-Term Missions*. Nashville: B&H Publishing, 2010.

Williamson, Marianne. *A Return to Love: Reflections on the Principles of a Course in Miracles*. New York: HarperCollins, 1992.

Wong, Carissa et al. "An Integrative Review of Peer Mentorship Programs for Undergraduate Nursing Students." *Journal of Nursing Education* 55 (2016) 141–49.

Wood, Sarah J. et al. "Twelve Tips to Revitalise Problem-Based Learning." *Medical Teacher* 37 (August 2015) 723–29.

Woods, Andrew. "Exploring Unplanned Curriculum Drift." *Journal of Nursing Education* 54 (2015) 641–44.

Woolfolk, Anita. *Educational Psychology.* 11th ed. Upper Saddle River, NJ: Merrill, 2010.

Young, J. E., M. I. Williamson, and T. G. Egan. "Students' Reflections on the Relationships between Safe Learning Environments, Learning Challenge and Positive Experiences of Learning in a Simulated GP Clinic." *Advances in Health Sciences Education* 21 (March 2016) 63–77.

Zaidi, Zareen et al. "Gender, Religion, and Sociopolitical Issues in Cross-Cultural Online Education." *Advances in Health Sciences Education* 21 (May 2016) 287–301.

Zhao, Li et al. "Identifying the Competencies of Doctors in China." *BMC Medical Education* 15 (November 2015) 207.

Zimmermann, Katja et al. "Inter-Professional in-Situ Simulated Team and Resuscitation Training for Patient Safety: Description and Impact of a Programmatic Approach." *BMC Medical Education* 15 (October 2015) 189.

Zitzelsberger, Hilde, Karen A. Campbell, Dorothea Service, and Otto Sanchez. "Using Wikis to Stimulate Collaborative Learning in Two Online Health Sciences Courses." *Journal of Nursing Education* 54 (2015) 352–55.

Zupanc, Christine M. et al. "A Competency Framework for Colonoscopy Training Derived from Cognitive Task Analysis Techniques and Expert Review." *BMC Medical Education* 15 (December 2015) 216.

www.ingramcontent.com/pod-product-compliance
Lightning Source LLC
Chambersburg PA
CBHW080406300426
44113CB00015B/2417